Careers
Encyclopedia

Careers Encyclopedia

CRAIG NORBACK

DOW JONES-IRWIN
Homewood, Illinois 60430

This publication is designed to provide accurate and authoritative information in regard to the subject matter covered. It is sold with the understanding that the publisher is not engaged in rendering legal, accounting, or other professional service. If legal advice or other expert assistance is required, the services of a competent professional person should be sought.

From a Declaration of Principles jointly adopted by a Committee of the American Bar Association and a Committee of Publishers.

ISBN 0-87094-203-4
Library of Congress Catalog Card No. 80-69487
Printed in the United States of America

2 3 4 5 6 7 8 9 0 K 7 6 5 4 3 2 1

Preface

This book exists because now, as never before, up-to-date and accurate information about career opportunities is so badly needed.

The *Careers Encyclopedia* is designed and written with not only the student or job-seeker in mind, but parents, teachers, guidance counselors, and personnel managers as well. An attempt was made to give as much information about 180 careers as possible. Special emphasis is placed not only on a description of each career, but also on qualifications, education, or training required for placement in a particular field.

An added feature of this book is the inclusion of opinions of many qualified people as to the places of employment, working conditions, potential for advancement, as well as salary, for each career.

Providing salary information for each career is a particularly vexing problem. Because of wide geographic differences and double digit inflation, the salary ranges given for each career may vary greatly with time. Care must be taken that these figures are not to be interpreted as absolutes. It would be reasonable to add 7 to 10 percent for example, for each year after 1980.

Finally, I would like to offer special thanks to Dr. Martha Lightwood, head librarian, Lippincott Library, University of Pennsylvania; L. R. Brice, Executive Vice President, American Society for Personnel Administration, Berea, Ohio; Marion S. Kellogg, Vice President, General Electric Company, Fairfield, Connecticut; C. R. Blundell, Vice President, General Foods Corp., White Plains, New York; and, Newell Brown, former head, University Counseling Service, Princeton University, Princeton, New Jersey.

Contents

ACCOUNTANT

The job

Accountants prepare and analyze the financial reports that furnish up-to-date information for businesses, government agencies, and other organizations. The data they provide influence just about every business and government decision, since the financial condition of an organization is an ever-present ingredient of any decision. There are also many opportunities for part-time work, especially with small businesses.

There are three major accounting fields: public, management, and government. About 25 percent of all accountants are *public accountants* who work for a number of clients; they work for themselves or for an accounting firm. Public accountants often specialize in one phase of accounting, such as auditing or taxes. Many also function as management consultants, advising clients on accounting systems and equipment.

Certified public accountants (CPAs) must hold a certificate issued by the state board of accountancy. To obtain certification they usually must have at least two years of public accounting experience and pass the CPA examination prepared by the American Institute of Certified Public Accountants. Most successful CPA candidates also have a college degree.

About 60 percent of all accountants are *management accountants,* employed by a single company to handle the company's financial records. Some management accountants function as internal *auditors.* Auditing entails reviewing financial records and reports to judge their reliability. The internal auditor's evaluation of the financial systems and management control procedures of a company enable the company to function efficiently and economically.

In some companies a management accountant may function as a credit manager, handling the company's accounts receivable and making decisions on extending credit to customers. (See the separate job description for Credit Manager.)

Government accountants maintain and examine the financial records of government agencies and audit the records of businesses and individuals whose financial activities are subject to government regulations.

Beginners in accounting usually start as ledger accountants, junior internal auditors, or as trainees for technical accounting positions.

Junior public accountants usually assist with auditing work for several clients.

About 27 percent of all accountants are women, including 4 percent of all CPAs. Since this is one of the few fields with many jobs available, more women can be expected to move into this traditionally male career area.

Related jobs are: Credit Manager, FBI Special Agent, and Internal Revenue Agent.

Places of employment and working conditions

All business, industrial, and government organizations use the services of accountants. Accountants work for the corner deli operator as well as for AT&T; for the smallest municipal government as well as for the government of the United States. They work throughout the country with the heaviest concentration of job opportunities in large urban areas, where many public accounting firms and central offices of large businesses are located. Over 20 percent of all accountants are employed in Chicago, Los Angeles, New York City, and Washington, D.C.

Accountants have desk jobs and generally work between 35 and 40 hours a week. Those employed by accounting firms carry heavy work loads during tax season. Accountants employed by national firms may travel extensively to conduct audits and perform other services for their clients or employers.

Qualifications, education, and training

If you want to be an accountant, you need an aptitude for mathematics. In addition, you must be neat, accurate, able to work with little super-vision, and able to handle responsibility.

Training in accounting is available at business schools and cor-respondence schools, as well as at colleges and universities. However, most large public accounting and business firms require beginning ac-countants and internal auditors to have at least a bachelor's degree in accounting or in a closely related field. Many employers prefer a master's degree. Many companies also require familiarity with com-puter technology. The federal government requires a bachelor's degree with at least 24 semester hours of accounting or an equivalent com-bination of college and work experience.

Work experience is important and can help an applicant get a job after graduation. Therefore, many colleges provide students with an opportunity to gain experience through internship programs while still in school.

Accountants who wish to advance professionally must continue studying accounting throughout their careers. Seminars and courses are offered by many employers and professional associations. More and more accountants are studying computer operation and programming in addition to accounting subjects.

In the field of internal auditing, the designation Certified Internal Auditor (CIA) is awarded by The Institude of Internal Auditors to those who have three years experience and complete a four-part examination. Candidates for this designation must also have a bachelor's degree from an accredited college or university.

Over half of the states require that public accountants be licensed or registered; some states require only a high school diploma, while others require two or more years of college.

More and more states are requiring both CPAs and licensed public accountants to complete continuing education courses for license renewal.

Potential and advancement

There are about 865,000 accountants in the United States; 20 percent are Certified Public Accountants and 12 percent are Certified Internal Auditors. The demand for skilled accountants is expected to increase over the next decade as business and government agencies continue to grow in size and complexity. Internal auditing is a specialty field that is growing rapidly.

There will be ample job opportunities for accountants without college degrees especially in small businesses and public accounting firms. However, in large companies, when it comes to promotions, accountants who lack academic credentials may find themselves lagging behind those with advanced degrees.

Accountants may advance to such jobs as chief plant accountant, chief cost accountant, budget director, or manager of internal auditing. Some achieve corporate-level positions such as controller, treasurer, financial vice president, or president.

Public accountants can advance from beginner through intermediate-level positions to senior positions in about five years, as they gain experience and handle more complex accounts. In large accounting firms, they often become supervisors, managers, or partners. Some transfer to executive positions in private firms or open their own public accounting offices.

Income

Salaries for beginning accountants and auditors in private industry average $12,800. Salaries of experienced accountants range from $15,700 to $27,000 depending on the level or responsibility and the size and complexity of the accounting system. Experienced auditors earn between $15,700 and $23,000 annually.

Chief accountants who direct the accounting program of a company earn between $23,700 and $40,000 depending on the size of the accounting staff and the scope of authority.

In the Federal Civil Service, salaries for all accountants average about $24,300 a year. Junior accountants and auditors begin at about $10,500; those with superior academic records can begin as high as $13,014. A beginner with a master's degree or two years of professional experience starts at about $16,000 a year.

Additional sources of information

American Institute of Certified Public Accountants
1211 Avenue of the Americas
New York, NY 10036

National Association of Accountants
919 Third Avenue
New York, NY 10022

National Society of Public Accountants
1717 Pennsylvania Avenue, NW
Washington, DC 20006

Institute of Internal Auditors
249 Maitland Avenue
Altamonte Springs, FL 32701

American Society of Women Accountants
327 La Salle Street
Chicago, IL 60604

ACTUARY

The job

Actuaries are, for the most part, mathematicians. They assemble and analyze statistics on probabilities of death, illness, injury, disability, unemployment, retirement, and property losses to design insurance and pension plans and set up the premium structure for the policies.

For example, statistics on auto accidents are gathered and analyzed by actuaries employed by a company selling auto insurance. The actuaries then base the premiums for their company's policies on the accident statistics for different groups of policyholders. They consider age, miles driven annually, and geographic location, among other things.

Since the insurance company is assuming a risk, the premium rates developed by company actuaries must enable the company to pay all claims and expenses and must be adequate to provide the company with a reasonable profit for assuming that risk. To function effectively, actuaries must keep up-to-date on general economic and social trends and on any legislative developments that might affect insurance practices.

Actuaries provide information to executives in their company's investments, group underwriting, and pension planning departments; they prepare material for policyholders and government requirements; and they may be called on to testify before public agencies on proposed legislation on insurance practices.

Actuaries employed by the federal government usually work on a specific insurance or pension program such as Social Security. Those in state government positions regulate insurance companies, supervise state pension programs, and work in the unemployment insurance and workers' compensation programs.

Consulting actuaries set up pension and welfare plans for private companies, unions, and government agencies. Some consulting actuaries evaluate pension plans and certify their solvency in compliance with the Employee Retirement Income Security Act of 1974 (ERISA).

Private insurance companies employ about two thirds of all actuaries, with life insurance companies employing the most—about 90 percent. Large companies may employ as many as 100 actuaries; many smaller companies use the services of consulting firms or rating bureaus, which employ about one fifth of all actuaries. Other actuaries work for private organizations that administer independent pension or welfare plans or for federal and state agencies.

Beginning actuaries often rotate among various jobs within a company's actuarial operation to become familiar with its different phases. In the process, they gain a broad knowledge of insurance and related fields.

Only about 3 percent of all actuaries are women. This is due to women having traditionally avoided mathematics majors in college and will probably change as more female high school and college students are encouraged to study math.

Related jobs are: Mathematician, Statistician, Underwriter.

Places of employment and working conditions

Almost one half of all actuaries work in Boston, Chicago, Hartford, New York, and Philadelphia.

Actuaries have desk jobs and usually work a 37- to 40-hour week. Occasional overtime is necessary.

Qualifications, education, and training

A strong background in mathematics is necessary for anyone interested in a career as an actuary.

Only 25 colleges and universities offer a degree in actuarial science. However, a bachelor's degree with a major in mathematics, statistics, or business administration is also a good educational background for an actuary. Courses in insurance law, economics, and accounting are valuable.

Some companies will also accept an applicant who has a degree in engineering, economics, or business administration if courses in calculus, probability, and statistics have been included.

Of equal importance to a strong mathematics background are the examination programs offered by professional actuarial societies to prospective actuaries. Examinations are given twice a year, and extensive home study, 20 to 25 hours a week, is required to pass the more advanced ones. Completion of one or more of these examinations while still in school helps students to evaluate their potential as actuaries; those who pass one or more examinations usually have better employment opportunities and receive higher starting salaries. Actuaries are encouraged to complete an entire series of examinations as soon as possible in their careers to achieve full professional status. This usually takes from five to ten years.

Associate membership in their respective professional societies is awarded to actuaries after successful completion of five examinations in the life insurance or pension series, or seven examinations in the casualty series. Full membership is awarded, along with the title "fellow," upon completion of an entire series.

Consulting pension actuaries who service private pension plans and certify the plans' solvency must be enrolled by the Joint Board for the Enrollment of Actuaries, which stipulates the experience and education required.

Potential and advancement

There are approximately 9,000 persons employed as actuaries in the United States. Employment in this field is expected to grow rapidly through the 1980s with job opportunities best for college graduates who have passed at least two actuarial examinations while still in school. Even though the field is expected to have substantial growth, the large number of new graduates with degrees in actuarial science, mathematics, and statistics will mean increased competition for available job openings.

Advancement within the field depends on job performance, experience, and the number of actuarial examinations completed successfully. Actuaries can be promoted to assistant, associate, and chief actuary within their company. Because they have a broad knowledge of insurance and its related fields, actuaries are often selected for administrative positions in other company departments such as underwriting, accounting, or data processing. Many actuaries advance to top executive positions, where they help determine company policy.

Income

Recent college graduates just beginning their careers earn about $10,933 a year if they have not passed any actuarial examinations. Those who have completed the first examination earn about $12,754; if they have successfully completed two examinations, they earn about $13,584. Earnings increase with experience and advancement in the examination program with many companies giving merit increases averaging $566 to $966 for each examination successfully completed.

Once membership in a professional society is achieved, associate members average about $18,325; those awarded full fellowships average about $27,163. Top actuarial executives average about $47,600.

Beginning actuaries with a bachelor's degree who work for the federal government earn about $10,500 a year. With either one year of graduate study or relevant work experience, a beginner earns $13,000; with a master's degree or two years' experience, $15,900. The average salary for all actuaries employed by the federal government is $28,350 a year.

Additional sources of information

American Society of Pension Actuaries
1700 K Street, NW
Washington, DC 20006

Casualty Actuarial Society
200 East 42nd Street
New York, NY 10017

Society of Actuaries
208 South La Salle Street
Chicago, IL 60604

National Association of Insurance Women
Room 330-E
823 South Detroit Avenue
Tulsa, OK 74120

ADVERTISING ACCOUNT EXECUTIVE

The job

Each of an advertising agency's clients is assigned to an account executive who is responsible for handling everything concerning the client's advertising campaign. The account executive must know the client's product and marketing plans and the agency's resources for successfully carrying out the client's requirements. Together they plan the advertising campaign and create its components.

The account executive studies a client's company and its sales, its present public image, and its advertising requirements and budget. In developing an advertising campaign to suit the client's needs, the account executive calls upon all the resources of the agency artists and designers, copywriters, media buyers, production staff, and market researchers.

The account executive then has the job of selling the client on the planned advertising campaign. Considerable time may be spent changing and reworking the plan before the client grants approval. As the advertising campaign progresses, the account executive keeps track of sales figures and may further alter the campaign to achieve the results the client wants.

The job of an account executive can sometimes be glamorous—they get to wine and dine the clients and sometimes go on location to oversee the production of commercials or other material for a client—but it also carries with it a great deal of responsibility. The account executive must ensure that artists, copywriters, and production people meet schedules and must act as liaison between the agency and the client, keeping costs within the client's budget.

In some large agencies, account executives report to an *account supervisor*, but in most agencies they are supervised by top management or owners of the agency. In small agencies, the owners of the firm often function as account executives and may even do some of the creative work, such as copywriting.

Places of employment and working conditions

Advertising agencies exist in many cities, but the heaviest concentrations are in New York City, Los Angeles, and Chicago. "Madison Avenue" is, of course, the term applied to the many large and prestigious agencies in New York City.

Pressures are extreme and working hours are long and unpredictable. Advertising is a very competitive field and there is very little job security. The loss of a large account can mean the firing or the laying off of everyone who worked on the account, including the account executive.

Qualifications, education, and training

Job experience in sales, advertising, or market research is valuable, but you also need at least a bachelor's degree to become an advertising account executive. A major in advertising, marketing, business administration, or liberal arts is preferred, and some large agencies prefer a master's degree in business administration.

Training programs for account executives are offered by some agencies.

Potential and advancement

The employment outlook for the advertising field is good, and job opportunities should continue to grow in the 1980s. The advertising field is strongly affected by general business conditions, however, since most firms expand or contract their advertising budgets according to how their own sales are affected by economic conditions. Entry-level jobs and trainee positions usually have an overabundance of applicants, but experienced account executives with a proven track record will continue to be in demand.

Skilled and experienced account executives can advance to the highest positions in an agency. In a large agency, they can become account supervisors of one or more accounts, advance to the executive suite, become partners in the firm, or open their own agencies. Some leave their agency jobs to become advertising managers for former clients.

Income

Trainees start at $11,000–$14,000, depending on education and the size of the agency. Account supervisors average $30,400. Account executives average from $20,000 in smaller agencies to $27,000 or higher in large agencies.

ADVERTISING MANAGER

The job

In many companies the amount of advertising done to place the company's product or service before the public requires the time and talents of a full-time advertising manager. Working in close cooperation with the marketing department, or as part of the marketing department, the advertising manager develops advertising appropriate to the consumers the company wants to attract.

In some companies the advertising manager is the only one on the staff, creating the art and written copy and placing it in newspapers, magazines, and radio or television as well. Other advertising managers supervise a staff that may include artists, copywriters, production and research workers, and media buyers. The department may turn out display ads, point-of-sale and direct mail advertising, a company product catalogue, and trade show displays. In such advertising departments, the advertising manager is responsible for the administration of a large budget, coordinates the activities of the department to meet deadlines and schedules, places the company's advertising in the appropriate media vehicles, and handles the day-to-day administration of the department.

In a company that uses the services of an advertising agency for all or part of its advertising, the advertising manager represents the company in its dealings with the agency. Depending on the extent of the manager's authority, he or she might select the advertising agency, supervise the handling of the account by the agency, supply market research information, apportion the advertising budget, and approve the final advertising campaign. In some companies, top management has the final approval of the advertising campaign and budget.

Regardless of whether the advertising manager works with an advertising agency or supervises an in-house advertising department, and regardless of the size of the company or the budget it allows for advertising, the advertising manager is expected to produce visible results in the form of increased sales volume of the company's product or service.

Places of employment and working conditions

Advertising managers work in all areas of the country, with the most job opportunities in large metropolitan areas.

Advertising managers work under considerable pressure. They generally work long hours, and are required to successfully coordinate the ideas, personalities, and talents of a variety of people—from top management to the creative staff of the advertising department.

Qualifications, education, and training

Success in advertising depends on imagination, creativity, a knowledge of what motivates consumers, and the ability to function as part of a team. An advertising manager must also have supervisory ability, budgeting experience, and a solid grounding in all areas of advertising.

The first step is a must—a college degree. The most useful degrees are liberal arts, business administration, or marketing.

After graduation, beginners in this field usually start in one of the specialty areas of advertising such as art, copywriting, research, production, or media buying in either an advertising department or advertising agency to gain as much experience as possible. Experience in several different specialties provides the best training for a prospective advertising manager.

Potential and advancement

As with all top management positions, there is competition for the top spot in an advertising department. The job outlook is good for the future because a slight growth is expected in the number of company advertising departments. The best jobs will go to those with education, experience, and proven abilities in advertising.

Advertising managers are already in top positions. They advance by moving to larger companies or to advertising agencies where they will have greater responsibilities and more challenging work. Some open their own advertising agencies.

Income

Salaries vary depending on location, sales volume, and size of company. Most are in the $20,000 to $37,000 range. In general, salaries for advertising managers are higher in consumer product firms than in industrial firms.

Many advertising managers also receive bonuses or company stock for effective advertising campaigns and participate in profit-sharing plans.

Additional sources of information

American Advertising Federation
1225 Connecticut Avenue, NW
Washington, DC 20036

Association of National Advertisers
155 East 44th Street
New York, NY 10017

Business/Professional Advertising Association
205 East 42nd Street
New York, NY 10017

ADVERTISING SALES PERSON

The job

The money necessary to finance the activities of radio and television stations and most of the publication costs of newspapers and magazines comes from the sale of time or space to clients who wish to advertise a product or service.

Advertising sales people sell directly to clients or to advertising agencies that represent the clients. Technically, the sales worker is selling broadcasting time segments on the stations or space in the publications, but actually what is being sold is the station's programming or a publication's content and the amount and type of audience that each attracts.

Newspapers get the largest portion of the dollars spent on advertising—almost 30 percent. Advertising sales people in this field work both locally and as *national sales representatives*. There are three principal categories of newspaper advertising: general, retail, and classified. General, also known as national, advertising is the advertising of products and services marketed nationally or regionally through local retail outlets. This type of newspaper advertising is usually handled by independent national sales representatives who deal with national advertisers and their advertising agencies. They usually represent a number of local newspapers.

Retail advertising is local advertising. Sales people handling this type of newspaper advertising may also provide some of the copywriting and layout required or provide advice on an ad content and design. Classified advertising is sold by outside sales persons who call on auto dealers, real estate brokers, and other regular advertisers and by inside sales people who handle walk-in or telephone classified advertising. *Retail* and *classified advertising sales people* keep close track of clients and often provide pick-up service for advertising copy, handle changes in ads, and suggest advertising approaches.

On small newspapers, advertising may be sold by all members of the staff, or the paper may employ a part-time advertising sales person.

Magazines use national sales representatives even more than newspapers since most magazines have a wider, often national distribution. Local and regional magazines employ more local sales people.

Radio stations employ *radio advertising sales people* to sell air time to local businesses and use national sales representatives on a commission basis to sell local time to national and regional advertisers. The radio advertising sales person sells radio time in the form of entire programs or portions of programs or spot announcements. He or she must know not only the type of audience that listens to a particular station but also the time of day that a very specific segment of the audience is most likely to be listening. Radio advertising sales people must be well versed in the latest market research analysis of their local marketing areas and must be prepared to advise a client on the best advertising approach for the money.

At small radio stations, everyone may sell advertising, or the station manager may handle all advertising. Larger stations employ several sales people, and those in large marketing areas may have large sales staffs.

The typical television station in a major city employs six to eight *television advertising sales people* to call on local businesses. A great deal of television advertising time is also sold by national sales representatives who have branch offices in major cities. These "sales reps" sell 53 percent of all television advertising and act as the go-between for local stations and the national advertisers.

Network sales people work for the national television and radio networks and sell network time to national advertisers. They handle accounts worth hundreds of thousands of dollars.

Places of employment and working conditions

Advertising sales jobs can be found in all communities, with the most opportunities in large metropolitan areas. National sales representatives are concentrated in cities such as Chicago, Los Angeles, and New York.

Advertising sales is a combination of office, telephone, and leg work. The sales people work long hours. It is often necessary to spend a great deal of time on a particular account, including the preparation of sales presentations and cost estimates.

Qualifications, education, and training

The personal qualities of a good sales person include aggressiveness, enthusiasm, perseverance, and the ability to get along with people.

Sales experience of any kind is valuable, and experience in selling advertising is especially helpful.

Although a college degree is not required by all employers, large metropolitan newspapers, mass-circulation and trade magazines, major radio and television stations, networks, and national sales representative firms require a bachelor's degree in marketing or journalism. Some require a major in advertising.

Potential and advancement

The future for magazine, newspaper, radio, and television advertising is very good. A survey of the radio industry shows a projected rate of growth in advertising sales positions of about 28 percent by the mid 1980s; national television spot sales are expected to increase about 8 percent to 10 percent through the 1980s. Newspaper growth will be concentrated in medium-sized and suburban newspapers.

Beginners will find the best opportunities with small local newspapers and magazines and small radio and television stations where they can gain valuable experience. There will continue to be opportunities for part-time work with small newspapers and small or local radio and television stations.

Newspaper advertising sales people can advance to positions as general advertising manager, retail advertising manager, classified advertising manager, or advertising director.

Radio advertising sales people can advance to sales manager positions where they would be involved developing sales plans as well as policies and programming.

In television, advertising sales people can advance to regional, national, and general sales manager positions. The top-level positions in television station management are very often filled by former general sales managers.

Income

Advertising sales people work on a commission basis, and the amount of their earnings is governed by their own ability and ambition. Some employers provide a base salary plus a commission. Commission rates vary but are usually between 10 percent and 15 percent.

Sales managers on large magazines earn $27,000 to $42,000 a year. Newspaper space sales people earn from $17,000 to $42,000.

Radio advertising sales people average about $15,000 a year with much higher earnings for network sales people.

Earnings of television national sales representatives are better than sales earnings in just about any other industry. Beginners can earn $22,000 to $32,000 in their first year, and earnings of experienced national sales people often approach six figures. They also take part in company stock or profit-sharing plans.

On a local level, television advertising sales people earn between $12,000 and $42,000 a year. Beginners can earn $12,000 to $17,000 a year; more experienced sales people earn between $20,000 and $27,000. Top local television sales people earn between $32,000 and $42,000. In the largest cities, these figures are even higher.

Additional sources of information

Radio Advertising Bureau
485 Lexington Avenue
New York, NY 10017

National Association of Broadcasters
1771 N Street, NW
Washington, DC 20036

American Newspaper Publishers Association
P. O. Box 17407
Dulles International Airport
Washington, DC 20041

International Newspaper Advertising Executives, Inc.
P. O. Box 147
Danville, IL 61832

Television Bureau of Advertising
1345 Avenue of the Americas
New York, NY 10019

ADVERTISING WORKER

The job

For the thousands of people working in advertising, job satisfaction may come from having their work appear in print or on television or radio.

The work of a number of people with special talents goes into every advertising campaign, and the end result, when the campaign is successful, can make a great difference in the sales figures of a product or service.

Artists, designers, and layout artists create the visual aspects of advertising in magazine and newspaper ads, television commercials, and product packaging. They select photographs, draw illustrations, and decide on the colors and style of type to be used. They also prepare samples of art work for account executives who are planning advertising campaigns with clients and prospective clients.

Copywriters provide the words. A copywriter usually works closely with the account executive to produce just what the client wants to say about his or her product or service. The work of the copywriter is an integral part of almost all advertising but is especially important in radio where words are the *only* vehicle for the advertiser's message.

Production managers arrange for the actual filming, recording, or printing of the completed advertisement. They must be able to produce the finished product on time and within the budget allocated by the client. They normally deal with models, actors, and photographers.

Media buyers are specialists who are well informed on costs and audiences of the various media. They work with account executives to decide on how to reach the largest and most appropriate consumer audience for a client's product or service. Working within the client's budget, they buy advertising time on radio or television and advertising space in newspapers and magazines. In some agencies, the functions are separated into *time buyers* and *space buyers.*

About one third of all advertising workers are employed in advertising agencies, but many job opportunities also exist in the advertising departments of commercial and industrial firms, retail stores, and newspapers and magazines. Printing companies, package design firms, sign companies, and mail order catalogues also employ persons with advertising skills.

Beginners in advertising usually start as assistants in research, production, or media buying. Those with writing ability usually start as *junior copywriters.*

Many women are employed in advertising. Promotions, titles, and salaries for women in advertising still do not equal those for men. The best opportunities for women are in department stores and independent advertising agencies in smaller cities. When women do achieve top positions in larger agencies, they usually work in food, fashion, cosmetics, textiles, and home furnishings.

Related jobs are: Advertising Account Executive, Advertising Manager, Advertising Sales Person, and Marketing Researcher.

Places of employment and working conditions

About half of all advertising workers are employed in the New York and Chicago areas but opportunities exist in most cities.

All advertising workers function under a great deal of pressure. The usual 35- to 40-hour workweek often includes overtime because of deadlines, the demands of clients, and production schedules.

Although advertising agencies are considered the most glamorous places to work, there may be little job security in an agency. If an agency loses a big account, all the people who worked on the account, including the account executive, may lose their jobs.

Qualifications, education, and training

Creativity and a knowledge of what motivates consumers are the keys to success in advertising.

Successful advertising workers also have imagination, a flair for language, and the ability to sell "ideas." They must get along well with people, be able to function as part of a team, enjoy challenge and variety, and thrive on excitement and competition.

High school courses in art and writing are valuable as are experience in selling advertising for a school newspaper or a summer job at a radio station or newspaper office. Any educational or professional experience in marketing, art, writing, journalism, or business and marketing research is valuable.

There are no specific educational requirements in the advertising field, but most employers prefer college graduates; they will accept a degree in almost any field. Some have a preference for a liberal arts background with majors in art, literature, and social sciences; others want applicants with degrees in marketing, business, or journalism.

When seeking a position in advertising, certain job applicants are expected to provide samples of their work. A beginning artist should supply a portfolio of drawings; a writer should supply samples of written work. Experienced advertising workers include samples of the work they have handled for previous employers.

Potential and advancement

About 180,000 persons work in the advertising field, one third of them in advertising agencies. This is a popular field with stiff competition for entry-level jobs and for jobs with the best companies. Job opportunities should increase steadily but, since the amount of money spent on advertising is strongly affected by general business conditions, they may be better in some years than in others. Local television, radio, and newspapers are expected to increase their share of total advertising, while magazines, direct mail, and national newspapers are declining and will provide fewer job opportunities.

Opportunities for advancement usually exist within each specialty area. An artist or designer can become an art director; a copywriter can be promoted to copy chief. Advancement to management is possible from any of the specialties, and experienced advertising workers sometimes open their own advertising agencies.

Income

Entry-level jobs pay $10,000 to $12,000 a year, with top starting salaries going to outstanding liberal arts graduates. Junior layout artists earn about $11,500; junior copywriters about $12,500.

Average salaries for experienced advertising workers include: senior layout artists, $14,900; art directors, $19,000; executive art directors, $26,500; production managers, $16,400; senior copywriters, $18,600. Media space or time buyers average from $11,500 to $14,000; media directors, $18,800. Highly experienced buyers earn more.

Top executive officers in advertising earn about $47,000 annually.

Additional sources of information

American Association of Advertising Agencies
200 Park Avenue
New York, NY 10017

American Advertising Federation
1225 Connecticut Avenue, NW
Washington, DC 20036

AEROSPACE ENGINEER

The job

The design, development, testing, and production of commercial and military aircraft, missiles, and spacecraft are the duties of aerospace engineers. Their work is important to commercial aviation, national defense, and the space program.

Aerospace engineers often specialize in one area such as structural design, instrumentation and communications, or production methods. They may also specialize in one type of product such as helicopters, satellites, or rockets.

Most aerospace engineers are employed by aircraft and aircraft parts manufacturers. The National Aeronautics and Space Administration (NASA) and the Department of Defense employ some aerospace engineers, and a few work for commercial airlines and consulting firms.

Places of employment and working conditions

The aerospace industry is concentrated in Florida and on the West Coast.

Qualifications, education, and training

The ability to think analytically, a capacity for details, and the ability to work as part of a team are all necessary. Good communication skills are important.

Mathematics and the sciences must be emphasized in high school.

A bachelor's degree in engineering is the minimum requirement in this field. In a typical curriculum, the first two years are spent in the study of basic sciences such as physics and chemistry and mathematics, introductory engineering, and some liberal arts courses. The remaining years are usually devoted to specialized engineering courses.

Engineering programs can last from four to six years. Those that require five or six years to complete may award a master's degree or may provide a cooperative plan of study plus practical work experience with a nearby industry.

Because of rapid changes in technology, many aerospace engineers continue their education throughout their careers. A graduate degree is necessary for most teaching and research positions and for many management jobs. Some persons obtain graduate degrees in business administration.

All states require licensing of engineers whose work may affect life, health, or property or who offer their services to the public. Those who are licensed, about one third of all engineers, are called Registered Engineers. Requirements for licensing include graduation from an accredited engineering school, four years of experience, and an examination.

Potential and advancement

There are about 50,000 aerospace engineers. New employment opportunities in this field are not expected in the near future unless the federal government increases its spending on defense and space exploration. Most job openings will occur to replace those who retire or leave the field.

Income

Starting salaries in private industry average $14,800 with a master's degree, and $21,000 or more with a Ph.D.

The federal government pays beginners $9,300 to $20,500 depending on degree and experience. Average salary for experienced aerospace engineers federally employed is about $26,000.

Experienced aerospace engineers average $26,000 in private industry; $15,000 to $21,000 for nine-month faculty positions in colleges and universities.

Additional sources of information

American Institute of Aeronautics and Astronautics, Inc.
1290 Avenue of the Americas
New York, NY 10019

Engineers' Council for Professional Development
345 East 47th Street
New York, NY 10017

National Society of Professional Engineers
2029 K Street, NW
Washington, DC 20006

American Society for Engineering Education
One Dupont Circle, Suite 400
Washington, DC 20036

Society of Women Engineers
United Engineering Center
345 East 47th Street
New York, NY 10017

AGRICULTURAL COOPERATIVE EXTENSION SERVICE WORKER

The job

Extension agents, as they are usually called, are employed jointly by state land-grant universities and the U.S. Department of Agriculture. They conduct educational programs for rural residents in agriculture, home economics, youth activities, and community resource development. Agents usually specialize in one of these areas, and most of them are employed at the county level.

Extension agents usually work with groups of people. An agent for youth activities conducts 4-H meetings and organizes recreational activities such as camping. One whose specialty is home economics would present programs and information on nutrition, food preparation and preservation, child care, and home furnishings. In community resource development, an extension agent would help local community leaders to plan public projects such as water supply and sewage systems, recreational programs, libraries, and schools. Agricultural science extension agents conduct seminars for local farmers and provide advice to individual farmers who have specific problems.

Extension agents use every available communication method to reach as large an audience as possible. They write for local newspapers, appear on local radio and television stations, and sometimes produce films covering specialized subjects.

Some extension agents are employed at the state level at land-grant universities where they coordinate the work of the county agents. State extension agents often conduct research and may spend part of their time teaching classes at the university. About 200 agricultural extension specialists are employed at the federal level by the Extension Service of the U.S. Department of Agriculture in Washington, D.C.

Many women are employed as county extension service workers, especially in home economics, child care, and health services.

Places of employment and working conditions

Extension agents work in rural areas throughout the United States.

Most extension service offices are located in small communities, a fact that appeals to people who do not wish to work in the city. Extension agents lead a very busy, active life and, depending on specialty area, may spend a great deal of time outdoors. Many meetings and seminars are presented in the evening for the convenience of the participants.

Qualifications, education, and training

Extension workers must have the ability to work with people and an interest in farm life.

A bachelor's degree in an appropriate specialty is the basic requirement for extension service agents. Some training in communication skills and teaching techniques is extremely valuable also. Agents usually receive specific training in extension work in a preinduction training program, and may improve their skills through regular in-service training programs.

In most states, specialists and state-level or multicounty agents must have a graduate degree, sometimes a Ph.D.

Potential and advancement

There are about 16,000 cooperative extension workers most of them employed on about 3,000 county extension staffs of varying sizes. Job opportunities should be good through the mid-1980s, especially for those willing to work in depressed rural areas.

Agents at the county level can advance to multicounty or state-level positions, provided they obtain the necessary advanced degrees.

Income

Salaries vary by locality but are usually comparable to salaries of municipal and county professional employees in the area.

Additional sources of information

Extension Service
U.S. Department of Agriculture
Washington, DC 20250

AGRICULTURAL ENGINEER

The job

Agricultural engineers design and develop a variety of products and services for farmers, ranchers, and the agricultural industry.

Agricultural engineers may design the most effective layout for a farm including placement of barns and irrigation systems; others design specific buildings such as dairy barns. Utility companies employ agricultural engineers to develop electrical power systems for farms and food processing companies. Manufacturers of farm equipment and machinery employ them in design and development as well as in sales.

The federal government employs agricultural engineers in soil and water management projects and as cooperative extension service agents, most of them in the Department of Agriculture.

Places of employment and working conditions

Agricultural engineers work mainly in rural areas and their work is often done out of doors.

Qualifications, education, and training

The ability to think analytically, a capacity for details, and the ability to work as part of a team are all necessary. Good communication skills are important.

Mathematics and the sciences must be emphasized in high school.

A bachelor's degree in engineering is the minimum requirement in this field. In a typical curriculum, the first two years are spent in the study of basic sciences such as physics and chemistry and mathematics, introductory engineering, and some liberal arts courses. The remaining years are usually devoted to specialized engineering courses.

Engineering programs can last from four to six years. Those requiring five or six years to complete may award a master's degree or may provide a cooperative plan of study plus practical work experience with a nearby industry.

Because of rapid changes in technology, many agricultural engineers continue their education throughout their careers. A graduate degree is necessary for most teaching and research positions and for many management jobs. Some persons obtain graduate degrees in business administration or in an agricultural field such as soil science or forestry.

All states require licensing of engineers whose work may affect life, health, or property or who offer their services to the public. Those who are licensed, about one third of all engineers, are called Registered Engineers. Requirements for licensing include graduation from an accredited engineering school, four years of experience, and an examination.

Potential and advancement

There are about 12,000 agricultural engineers and the field is expected to show substantial growth. Increasing population means a growing demand for agricultural products and an increasing demand for conservation of resources such as soil and water.

Income

Starting salaries in private industry average $18,700 with a master's degree, and $24,000 or more with a Ph.D.

The federal government pays beginners $13,657 to $20,500 depending on degree and experience. Average salary for experienced engineers federally employed is about $27,700.

Experienced agricultural engineers average $30,500 in private industry; $15,000 to $21,000 for nine-month faculty positions in colleges and universities.

Additional sources of information

American Society for Agricultural Engineers
2950 Niles Road
St. Joseph, MI 49085

Engineers' Council for Professional Development
345 East 47th Street
New York, NY 10017

National Society for Professional Engineers
2029 K Street, NW
Washington, DC 20006

American Society for Engineering Education
One Dupont Circle, Suite 400
Washington, DC 20036

Society for Women Engineers
United Engineering Center
345 East 47th Street
New York, NY 10017

AIR CONDITIONING, REFRIGERATION, AND HEATING MECHANIC

The job

These skilled workers install, maintain, and repair a large variety of complicated equipment and machinery. They usually specialize in one area of the field but often work in several. About one out of seven is self-employed.

Air conditioning and refrigeration mechanics install and repair equipment that ranges in size from small (a window air conditioner) to very large (a central air conditioning system for a large building or the refrigeration system for a frozen food processor). Following blueprints and design specifications, they put the components of a system into place—connecting duct work, refrigerant lines, piping, and electrical power. They are busiest in the spring and summer months.

Furnace installers install oil, gas, and electrical heating units. They install fuel supply lines, air ducts, pumps, and other components and connect electrical wiring and controls. Most furnace installers, as well as air conditioning and refrigeration mechanics, are employed by cooling and heating equipment dealers and contractors.

Oil burner mechanics keep oil-fueled heating systems in good operating condition. They are busiest in the fall and winter months. Most of them are employed by fuel oil dealers.

Gas burner mechanics have duties similar to oil burner mechanics. In addition, they also repair stoves, clothes dryers, and hot water heaters that use gas as their fuel. Their busiest seasons are also fall and winter, and most of them are employed by gas utility companies.

Employers try to provide a full workweek all year around, usually by servicing both air-conditioning and heating equipment or by providing inspection and repair services during off-season months. Reduced hours or layoffs may occur during slow periods, however.

Related jobs are: Appliance Repairer, Electrician, Plumber, and Pipefitter.

Places of employment and working conditions

Air-conditioning and refrigeration mechanics and furnace installers work in all parts of the country. Oil burner mechanics are concentrated in areas that use oil as the major heating fuel, which means that more than half of them work in Illinois, Massachusetts, Michigan, New Jersey, New York, and Pennsylvania. About half of all gas burner mechanics work in California, Illinois, Michigan, Ohio, and Texas, where gas is the major heating fuel.

Most air-conditioning, refrigeration, and heating mechanics work a 40-hour week, with overtime and/or irregular hours during peak seasons. Layoffs or shortened work weeks may occur during slow months.

When installing new equipment, mechanics often work at great heights; much of their work is also done in awkward or cramped positions. They are subject to hazards such as electrical shock, burns, and muscle strain from handling heavy equipment.

Qualifications, education, and training

Good physical condition is an absolute necessity in this field since agility and strength are often required for installation and repair work. Mechanical aptitude is also important.

A high school background that includes shop classes and courses in mechanical drawing or blueprint reading, mathematics, physics, or electronics is helpful.

Most air-conditioning, refrigeration, and heating mechanics acquire their skills through on-the-job training; some enter a formal apprenticeship. In either method, training lasts four or five years. Apprentices must also have related classroom instruction in mathematics, blueprint-reading, and basic construction and engineering concepts.

Courses lasting two or three years are offered by vocational and technical schools and are often taught by personnel from local firms and organizations such as the Air Conditioning and Refrigeration Institute or the Petroleum Marketing Education Foundation.

Potential and advancement

There are about 175,000 qualified mechanics in this field at the present time. Employment will probably increase rapidly, especially for air conditioning and refrigeration mechanics. Employment of furnace installers and gas burner mechanics will also grow but will be more closely tied to trends in the construction industry. Although there may be a trend away from installation of new oil heating equipment, job opportunities for oil burner mechanics should increase as customers demand more frequent maintenance and inspection as a fuel conservation measure.

Income

Mechanics in this field earn between $8 and $13 an hour. Those who work on more than one type of equipment earn more than those who specialize in just one.

Helpers and apprentices earn 40 to 80 percent of the rate for experienced mechanics.

Additional sources of information

Air Conditioning and Refrigeration Institute
1815 North Fort Myer Drive
Arlington, VA 22209

Petroleum Marketing Education Foundation
P.O. Box 11187
Columbia, SC 29211

American Gas Association, Inc.
1515 Wilson Blvd.
Arlington, VA 22209

AIRPLANE MECHANIC

The job

Airplane mechanics perform scheduled maintenance, make repairs, and complete inspections required by the Federal Aviation Administration (FAA).

Many airplane mechanics specialize in either repair work or scheduled maintenance. They specialize further, and are licensed as, *powerplant mechanics,* who work on the engine; *airframe mechanics,* who work on the wings, landing gear, and structural parts of the plane; or *aircraft inspectors.* Some mechanics specialize in one type of plane or in one section of a plane such as the electrical system.

In the course of their work, airplane mechanics take engines apart; replace worn parts; use X-ray and magnetic inspection equipment; repair sheet metal surfaces; check for rust, distortion, or cracks in wings and fuselages; check electrical connections; repair and replace gauges; and then test all work after completion.

Over one half of all airplane mechanics work for airlines; about one third work for the federal government as civilian mechanics at military air bases. The remainder are employed in general aviation including those who work for airports in small repair shops and for companies that own and operate their own planes.

Mechanics employed by most major airlines belong to either the International Association of Machinists and Aerospace Workers or the Transport Workers Union of America. Some belong to the International Brotherhood of Teamsters, Chauffeurs, Warehousemen and Helpers of America.

Places of employment and working conditions

Airplane mechanics in general aviation work in every part of the country, as do civilians employed by the federal government at military bases. Most airline mechanics work near large cities at airports where the airlines have installations.

Mechanics usually work in hangars or other indoor areas; where repairs must be made quickly, however, they may work outdoors. Work areas are often noisy and mechanics do a lot of standing, bending, stooping, and climbing.

Qualifications, education, and training

Physical strength, ability, good eyesight and eye-hand coordination, and mechanical aptitude are necessary.

High school courses in mathematics, physics, chemistry, and mechanical drawing are good preparation for this field. Automotive repair or other mechanical work is helpful.

A few airplane mechanics learn through on-the-job training, but most acquire their skills in two-year training programs at FAA-approved trade schools. Those who receive their training in the armed forces attend a shorter trade-school program to familiarize themselves with material specific to civilian aircrafts. These schools do not, however, guarantee either a job or an FAA license.

Most mechanics who work on civilian aircraft are licensed by the FAA. Applicants for all licenses must pass written and oral tests, give a practical demonstration of their ability to do the work authorized by the particular license, and fulfill the experience requirements.

At least 18 months of work experience is required for an airframe or powerplant license; 30 months for a combination airframe/powerplant license. To obtain an inspector's license, a mechanic must first hold a combination license for at least three years. Unlicensed mechanics must work under the supervision of licensed mechanics.

Potential and advancement

There are about 110,000 airplane mechanics; another 30,000 work for aircraft manufacturers in the assembling of planes. On the whole, this job field is expected to grow steadily. In general aviation, job opportunities should be good. Although pay is often lower, many openings occur as more experienced mechanics move up to the top jobs with private companies or airlines. Competition is keen for airline jobs since the pay scale is high. Federal job opportunities will remain stable, affected primarily only by changes in defense spending.

Advancement to supervisory positions depends on experience and licenses held. Some airplane mechanics advance to executive positions or open their own repair shops.

Income

Airline mechanics average about $23,000 a year. They usually receive the added benefit of reduced airfares for themselves and their family.

Earnings of general aviation mechanics vary greatly depending on the employer and the size of the airport.

Additional sources of information

Aviation Maintenance Foundation
P.O. Box 739
Basin, WY 82410

Air Transport Association of America
1709 New York Avenue, NW
Washington, DC 20006

AIRPLANE PILOT

The job

Pilots work in facilities from tiny country airfields to the huge international complexes located near our largest cities. They work as crop dusters, power line inspectors, aerial photographers, charter pilots, or flight instructors. Many work for federal, state, and local governments, and a rapidly growing number work for businesses that own and operate their own company aircraft.

Except on the smallest aircraft, two pilots are usually needed. The more experienced pilot (called "captain" by the airlines) is in command and supervises all other crew members on board. A copilot assists in communicating with air traffic controllers and monitoring instruments in addition to assisting with flying the plane. Most larger airliners carry a third pilot in the cockpit, a flight engineer, who aids the pilots by monitoring and operating instruments, making minor in-flight repairs, and monitoring other traffic.

Before takeoff, the pilot plans the flight carefully, using information on weather enroute and at destination. Once decisions are made on route, altitude, and speed, the pilot files the flight plan and notifies air traffic control so that the flight can be coordinated with other air traffic. Pilots also check the plane thoroughly before each flight—testing engines, controls, and instruments.

Takeoff and landing are the most difficult parts of a flight and require close cooperation between pilot and copilot. Once in the air, the flight is relatively easy unless the weather is bad. Pilots steer the plane along the planned route, maintain radio contact with air traffic control stations along route, and keep close watch on instruments and fuel gauges. In bad weather, pilots can request information on changes in route or altitude from air traffic controllers as they search for better flying conditions. If visibility is poor, pilots must depend on instruments to fly safely over mountains or other obstacles and to land completely "blind" at their destination.

When a flight is over, pilots must file a complete record of the flight with the airline or other employer and with the Federal Aviation Administration.

Most airline pilots are members of the Airline Pilots Association International; at one major airline they are members of the Allied Pilots Association.

Places of employment and working conditions

Most pilots work out of the larger airports located in major population centers such as Los Angeles, San Francisco, New York, Dallas-Fort Worth, Chicago, Miami, and Atlanta.

The mental stress of flying can be tiring, especially for a pilot who is responsible for the safety of passengers and crew.

By law, airline pilots cannot fly more than 85 hours a month; they actually fly less than 70 hours. Even with additional nonflying hours of duty, they usually work only about 16 days a month. Since most flights involve layovers away from their assigned base, much of the pilots' free time is spent away from home. While pilots are on layover, airlines provide pilots with hotel accommodations and living expense allowances. Pilots with little seniority get the less desirable night and early morning flights.

Pilots employed by other than major airlines often work odd hours and have irregular schedules, perhaps flying 30 hours one month and 90 hours the next. Other nonflying duties add to their work schedule in many instances. Airline pilots have the advantage of large support staffs that handle almost all nonflying duties, but business pilots often make minor plane repairs, schedule and supervise aircraft maintenance, oversee refueling, and load passengers and baggage for proper balance and safety.

Qualifications, education, and training

The FAA regulates the licensing of pilots at all levels of competence and experience. Many FAA-approved flying schools are located at small local airfields. Training consists of about 12 weeks of instruction, including at least 35 hours of air time.

Flying can be learned in either military or civilian flying schools, but service in the armed forces provides an additional opportunity to gain substantial experience on jet aircraft. Airlines and many businesses prefer to hire applicants with this experience.

All pilots who are paid to transport passengers or cargo must have a commercial pilot's license in addition to a pilot's license. The license is issued by the FAA and, to qualify, pilots must be at least 18 years old and have at least 250 hours of flight experience. In addition, they must pass a strict physical examination and have 20/20 vision with or without glasses, good hearing, and no physical handicaps that would prevent quick reactions. Applicants for a commercial license must also pass a written examination covering principles of safe flight, navigation, and FAA regulations and demonstrate their flying ability to FAA examiners.

Pilots who want to fly in all types of weather must be licensed by the FAA for instrument flying. To qualify for this license, pilots must have 40 hours' experience flying by instruments, pass a written examination, and demonstrate their ability to fly by instruments.

There are additional FAA requirements for airline pilots. They must pass written and flight examinations to earn a flight engineer's license. Airline captains must also have an airline transport pilot's license. Applicants for this license must be at least 23 years old and have a minimum of 1,500 hours of flying experience during the previous eight years including night and instrument flying.

All licenses are valid so long as a pilot can pass the required physical examinations and the periodic tests of flying skills required by government regulations.

Pilots who apply for airline jobs must be high school graduates. Most airlines also require at least two years of college and prefer to hire those who are college graduates. Airlines give all applicants psychological tests to assess their ability to make the quick decisions and accurate judgments that are part of an airline pilot's job. All new airline pilots receive several weeks of intensive training including classroom instruction and simulator experience before assignment to a flight, usually as flight engineer. Airlines prefer to hire applicants who already have a flight engineer's license but will sometimes train those who have only a commercial license.

Companies other than airlines usually do not require as much experience or formal education, but a commercial license is necessary. Most companies prefer to hire pilots who have experience in the type of plane they will by flying for the company and will generally start them as copilots.

Potential and advancement

There are about 83,000 civilian pilots; about one half of them work for major airlines. Growth in airline passenger and cargo capacity, as well as the increase in businesses that operate their own aircraft, is expected to increase the demand for pilots. The short-term outlook, however, is not as good. The introduction of larger aircraft has caused a temporary reduction in the job openings for airline pilots. Many job openings in the near future will therefore be taken by experienced airline pilots now on furlough. Even as the need for pilots increases, competition for jobs will remain keen as the number of qualified pilots will continue to exceed the job openings. Recent college graduates who have civilian or military experience flying large multiengine aircraft and who hold both a commercial and flight engineer's license will have the best chance for job openings with major airlines.

Advancement for pilots is generally limited to other flying jobs. As they gain experience and accumulate flying time, they may become flying instructors, fly charter planes, or work for small air transportation firms such as air taxi companies. Some pilots advance to jobs with large companies where they can progress from copilot to pilot and occasionally to chief pilot in charge of aircraft scheduling, maintenance, and flight procedures.

For airline pilots, advancement depends on seniority as established by union contract provisions. It takes 5 to 10 years for a flight engineer to advance to copilot, 10 to 20 years to advance from copilot to captain. Choice of the more desirable routes also depends on seniority.

A few specially trained pilots become evaluators or "check pilots" who test pilots and copilots at least twice a year by flying with them and evaluating their proficiency.

Income

Flight instructors earn $9,000 to $18,000 a year; air taxi pilots $14,000 to $19,000. Salaries for business pilots range from $12,000 for copilots on small planes to $60,000 for chief pilots of companies with large jets. Business pilots flying single-engine planes earn $16,200 to $21,000; while those flying jets earn $18,000 to $34,000.

Airline pilots are among the highest paid professionals in the United States, averaging about $57,000 a year. Flight engineers start around $14,400 a year while some senior captains on the largest aircraft earn over $110,000 annually. Earnings depend on type, size, and speed of planes and number of hours and miles flown with extra pay for night and international flights. In addition, pilots and their families usually are entitled to reduced air fares on their own and other airlines.

Additional sources of information

For information about job opportunities in companies other than airlines, consult the classified sections of aviation trade magazines or apply to companies that operate aircraft at local airports.

For information on requirements for airline pilots, contact:

Public Relations Department
Air Transport Association of America
1709 New York Avenue, NW
Washington, DC 20006

Air Line Pilots Association, International
1625 Massachusetts Avenue, NW
Washington, DC 20036

AIRPORT MANAGER

The job

Whether it is a small local airport or an elaborate complex handling international flights, there has to be an airport manager in charge. An airport manager is responsible for the efficient day-to-day operation of the airport including provisions for aircraft maintenance and fuel, condition and safety of runways and other facilities, budget and personnel, negotiation of leases with airport tenants such as airlines and terminal concessionaires, enforcement of airport and government regulations, record keeping, and public relations.

An airport manager must be familiar with state and federal regulations pertaining to airports and must strive to maintain good relations with local communities. An important part of the job is making local businesses and industries aware of the services available at the airport. In an airport operated by a local government agency, the airport manager may be responsible for reporting to a variety of boards or committees.

At a small installation, the owner-operator may handle all duties, while at a large airport the manager, or director, is assisted by a number of specialists, each of whom is responsible for specific areas of airport operation.

An *assistant airport director* assists the director or manager with administrative responsibilities and may be in charge of public relations, maintenance, personnel, or tenant relations. An *engineer* handles maintenance of runways, terminal buildings, hangars, and grounds. The engineer oversees new construction, handles real estate and zoning matters, and administers Federal Aid to Airports programs.

An important position at all but the smallest airports is that of *fixed based operator* (FBO). At owner-operated airports, the manager may fulfill this function personally, but at other airports it is handled by a retail firm employing from one or two people to several hundred. The FBO provides (sells) general aviation products and/or services at an airport. This can include aircraft repair services, flight training, aircraft sales, fuel and spare parts, air taxi service, and charter flights.

Places of employment and working conditions

Airport managers are employed throughout the United States in airports of all sizes. The most job opportunities are in California, Florida, Illinois, Indiana, Michigan, Missouri, New York, Ohio, Pennsylvania, and Texas.

In a small airport, the manager usually works long hours, many of the hours outdoors. At large facilities, the manager usually works regular hours, in an office, but is on call for emergency situations. Managers do some traveling in the course of their work as they negotiate with airport tenants, such as airlines, or when they appear before state and federal regulatory agencies. Community activities and meetings usually require some evening hours.

Qualifications, education, and training

Leadership qualities, tact, initiative, good judgment, and the ability to get along with people are important qualities. Managers of airports with airline service usually need a college degree in airport management, business or public administration, or aeronautical or civil engineering. Colleges and universities that offer these degrees sometimes offer flight training as well.

At smaller airports, experience as a fixed base operator or superintendent of maintenance plus a pilot's license are often sufficient for the position of airport manager.

Potential and advancement

There are approximately 13,000 airports of various sizes in the United States. Substantial growth is expected in this field as existing airports are enlarged and new ones built to handle increased passenger travel, air cargo tonnage, and general aviation activity.

The present heavy air traffic at major airports, which creates takeoff and landing delays, is expected to lead to the construction of a network of smaller satellite airports to service general aviation aircraft and helicopters that will ferry passengers to and from the major airports. Both airport managers and fixed based operators will be in demand for these new facilities.

Advancement in this field usually takes the form of moving to a larger airport with more complex responsibilities. Some airport managers move up to state or federal positions in regulatory agencies.

Income

Earnings range from about $11,000 at a small general aviation airport to over $42,000 at a major international airport.

Additional sources of information

Airport Operators Council International
1700 K Street, NW
Washington, DC

Office of General Aviation
Federal Aviation Administration
Washington, DC 20591

AIR TRAFFIC CONTROLLER

The job

The safe and efficient operation of the nation's airways and airports is the responsibility of air traffic controllers. They coordinate all flight activities to prevent accidents. Some regulate airport traffic; others regulate planes in flight between airports.

Airport traffic controllers monitor all planes in and around an airport. Planes that are not visible from the control tower are monitored on a radar screen. When the airport is busy, controllers fit the planes into a holding pattern with other planes waiting to land. The controller must keep track of all planes in the holding pattern while guiding them in for landings and instructing other planes for takeoffs.

After a plane departs the airport, the airport traffic controller notifies the appropriate *enroute controller*. There are 25 enroute control centers in the United States where enroute controllers work in teams of two or three. Each team is assigned a specific amount of airspace along one of the designated routes generally flown by all airplanes.

Before taking off, each pilot files a flight plan that is sent by teletype to the appropriate control center. When a plane enters a team's airspace, one member of the team will communicate with the pilot by radio and monitor the flight path on radar. This controller will provide information on weather, nearby planes, and other hazards and can approve and monitor such things as altitude changes.

All civilian air traffic controllers work for the Federal Aviation Administration (FAA), most of them at major airports and air traffic control centers located near large cities. Military and naval air installations use their own personnel as air traffic controllers, and many civilian controllers acquire their skills during military service.

There are very few women air traffic controllers. Aviation has always been a male-dominated field, and many air traffic controllers come from the ranks of civilian and military pilots, navigators, and controllers. As more women become pilots, they will have the required experience and background to move into jobs as air traffic controllers.

Places of employment and working conditions

Air traffic controllers work at civilian and military installations throughout the country, but most of them work at main airports and air traffic control centers near large cities.

Because control towers and centers operate around the clock, seven days a week, controllers work night and weekend shifts on a rotating basis. They work under great stress because they usually have several planes under their control at one time. They must make quick decisions that affect the safety of many people.

Qualifications, education, and training

Potential controllers need a decisive personality, since they must make quick decisions; and they should be articulate, since instruction to pilots must be given quickly and clearly. A quick and retentive memory is a must as is the ability to work under pressure and to function calmly in an emergency.

Air traffic controller trainees are selected through the Federal Civil Service System. Applicants must be under 31 years of age, in excellent health, and have vision correctable to 20/20. They must pass a written examination that measures their ability to learn and their aptitude for the work. In addition, applicants must have three years of general work experience or four years of college or a combination of both. Applicants with experience as military controllers, pilots, or navigators may be hired without the written test.

Trainees receive approximately 16 weeks of intensive on-the-job training combined with formal training. They learn the fundamentals of the airway system, federal aviation regulations, aircraft performance characteristics, and the use of controller equipment. Their training also includes practice on simulators at the FAA Academy in Oklahoma City.

After training, it usually takes two to three years of progressively more responsible work experience to become a fully qualified controller.

A yearly physical examination is required of all controllers, and they must pass a job performance examination twice a year.

Potential and advancement

There are about 21,000 air traffic controllers.

Job opportunities will increase considerably during the 1980s. Competition for jobs will be stiff, however, since the number of qualified applicants is expected to exceed the number of openings. College graduates with civilian or military experience as controllers, pilots, or navigators will have the best chance of being hired.

Controllers can advance by transferring to different locations and larger airports. In installations with a number of air traffic controllers, experienced controllers can advance to supervisory positions. Some advance to management jobs in air traffic control or to administrative jobs in the FAA.

Income

The average salary for controllers is about $25,400 a year, over twice the average for all nonsupervisory workers in private industry. Trainees earn about $12,500 a year. Air traffic controllers receive overtime pay or equal time off for any hours worked over 40 hours per week.

Depending on length of service, controllers receive 13 to 26 days of paid vacation and 13 days of paid sick leave each year; they also receive life insurance, health benefits, and a retirement program. Because of the stress of this occupation, the retirement program is more liberal than for other federal employees.

Additional sources of information

A pamphlet on air traffic controllers is available from the U.S. Civil Service Commission Job Information Center in your area. Ask for Announcement #418.

APPLIANCE REPAIRER

The job

Appliance repairers service the many laborsaving appliances in use in just about every home today. These include stoves and ovens, washing machines and dryers, dishwashers, refrigerators and freezers, and small appliances. Appliance repairers usually specialize in one or two of these items.

Large appliances are usually serviced in the customers' homes, while small appliances or parts from large appliances may be taken back to a repair shop by the appliance repairer.

Most appliance repairers work in independent appliance stores and repair shops. Others work for service centers operated by appliance manufacturers, department stores, and utility companies. Every community also has its share of appliance repairers who conduct their own small independent businesses.

In addition to servicing appliances, the repairer sometimes gives instruction in the correct use and care of an appliance; prepares estimates of repair costs; keeps records of service, parts, and working time on each job; and may be responsible for collecting payment for completed work.

Related jobs are: Air Conditioning, Refrigeration, and Heating Mechanic; Television and Radio Service Technician; Business Machine Service Technician.

Places of employment and working conditions

Appliance repairers work in just about every community with the highest concentrations in highly populated areas.

Those who work in repair shops usually work in quiet, well-lighted areas. Repairers who work on the customers' premises must sometimes work in cramped or dusty areas and often spend several hours a day in travel. Repairers are subject to electrical hazards and muscle strain from moving large appliances.

Independent appliance repairers must supply their own tools, equipment, truck, and parts inventory.

Qualifications, education, and training

Anyone interested in this field should have mechanical aptitude and manual dexterity. The ability to work independently is important, and a pleasant personality is an asset when dealing with customers.

High school shop classes in electricity are helpful as are mechanical drawing and mathematics.

Most appliance repairers acquire their skills through on-the-job training, which takes between two and three years. Although formal training in appliance repair is available from some vocational and technical schools and community colleges, additional on-the-job training is also necessary to become fully qualified.

In companies that repair major appliances, trainees start as helpers and accompany experienced repairers as they make house calls. Those who work in repair shops learn basic skills by repairing and rebuilding increasingly more complicated appliances or parts. Trainees receive supplementary training by attending one- and two-week courses conducted by appliance manufacturers. Some large companies, such as department store chains, have formal training programs that include shop classes and home study courses.

Experienced appliance repairers attend manufacturers' training courses periodically to keep up with the changes in the field.

Potential and advancement

There are about 144,000 appliance repairers. Job opportunities are expected to grow steadily because the ever-increasing number and types of home appliances will require a constant and expanding supply of qualified people to service them.

Workers who prefer to work on their own find this a good field, since even a one-man operation can provide a good living wage in many communities.

Appliance repairers who work in large shops or for service centers may be promoted to supervisor or service manager. A few may advance to management positions such as regional service manager or parts manager for appliance manufacturers.

Income

Inexperienced trainees start at the minimum wage rate or slightly above and receive periodic increases as they gain experience.

Experienced appliance repairers earn from $5 to $10 an hour, depending on experience and type of appliance serviced. Income is steady all year in this field without any seasonal peaks or slow months.

Additional sources of information

Local appliance repair shops, appliance dealers, chain stores, and utility companies can provide information about job opportunities. Local technical and vocational schools can provide information on courses available.

Association of Home Appliance Manufacturers
20 North Wacker Drive
Chicago, IL 60606

ARCHITECT

The job

An architect designs buildings and other structures—anything from a private home to a large office building or an entire city's redevelopment.

The architect must oversee all phases of the project from initial idea to completed structure. He or she must solve complex technical problems while retaining artistic design and must be able to function in a highly competitive atmosphere.

After discussing ideas, needs, and concepts with the client, the architect prepares preliminary drawings and then detailed plans for the project including the plumbing, electrical, and heating systems. He or she must specify materials that comply with local building regulations and must stay within the client's budget.

All through this process, the architect may have to make changes at the request of the client. Once plans are ready and approved, the architect may help the client select a contractor and will continue to check the work while it is in progress to ensure that all design specifications are being carried out. The architect's responsibility does not end until the structure is completed and has successfully passed all required inspections.

Architects can work in salaried positions for architectural firms or they can go into private practice. Those who decide to open their own businesses usually begin their careers with a few years in salaried positions to accumulate experience.

Most architects are employed by architectural firms, building contractors, and community planning and redevelopment authorities. About 1,300 architects work for government agencies such as the Department of Defense, Housing and Urban Development (HUD), and the General Services Administration.

Only about 3 percent of all architects are women, but about 18 percent of the new degrees being awarded in architecture now go to women. Because this is a field where part-time practice is possible and since architects often work from their homes, the field has advantages for people with family responsibilities. There is, however, a wide salary inequality between men and women in architecture.

Related fields are: Building Contractor, Urban Planner.

Places of employment and working conditions

Architects are employed throughout the country, in towns and cities of all sizes. A large proportion of all architectural work, however, is concentrated in Boston, Chicago, Los Angeles, New York, Philadelphia, San Francisco, and Washington, D.C.

Architects spend many hours drawing plans and sometimes must put in overtime to meet deadlines. Once building is under way, they spend a great deal of time outdoors inspecting the progress of construction.

Qualifications, education, and training

Architecture requires a wide variety of technical, artistic, and social skills. Anyone planning a career in this field should be able to work independently, have a capacity for solving technical problems, and be artistic. Good business skills are also helpful.

High school students interested in architecture should take courses in mathematics, physics, and art. Summer jobs with architects or building contractors can provide useful experience.

College preparation can be either a five-year program leading to a bachelor of architecture degree or a six-year program leading to a master of architecture degree. Courses typically include architectural theory, design, graphics, engineering, urban planning, English, mathematics, chemistry, sociology, economics, and a foreign language.

Although many architects work without a license, all states require that a licensed architect take the final legal responsibility for a completed project. To qualify for the licensing examination, the applicant must have a bachelor's degree plus three years of experience in an architect's office or a master's degree plus two years of experience. Long experience (usually 12 years) may be substituted in some states, if the person can pass a preliminary qualifying test.

Potential and advancement

There are approximately 50,000 architects in the country at present, most of them in large cities. Prospects for employment in architecture depend upon the number of degrees being granted and the rise and fall of the building market. With an increase in schools that grant architectural degrees and a growing interest in more efficient housing and public construction, jobs will be available, but competition is expected to be keen. Most openings will occur in architectural firms, but some jobs will also be available in government agencies and in colleges and universities.

New graduates usually begin as junior drafters and work their way up to increased responsibility. They may be promoted to chief or senior drafter or put in charge of one phase of a large project such as design, specification writing, or construction supervision.

Income

Salaries for experienced architects average well over $25,000 a year. Those who are associates in their firms may also receive a share of the profits in addition to their salary.

Architects in private practice usually go through a period with high expenses and low income. Once a practice is established, salaries average $40,000 a year or more, well above the earnings of architects in salaried positions.

The average income for architects is $25,000.

Additional sources of information

The American Institute of Architecture
1735 New York Avenue, NW
Washington, DC 20006

The Association of Collegiate Schools of Architecture, Inc.
1735 New York Avenue, NW
Washington, DC 20006

The National Council of Architectural Registration Boards
1735 New York Avenue, NW, Suite 700
Washington, DC 20006

ATHLETIC COACH

The job

A coach must be a leader who can draw out the talent of each individual player and, at the same time, mold the players into an effective team. A good coach uses sports as a means of developing the personal qualities as well as the physical abilities of the athletes he or she coaches.

Most athletic coaches are employed in secondary schools where they are regular members of the faculty. They usually teach physical education classes and some classroom subjects and may coach several different sports.

Athletic coaches are also employed by colleges, professional teams, and, in a few instances, by elementary schools. Colleges, professional teams, and large high schools employ one or more assistant coaches as well as a head coach.

A coach is usually an experienced player in the sport he or she coaches. The coach must be able to teach the finer points of the sport, direct the physical training of the team members, judge abilities and personalities, plan game strategy and playing schedules, and, in some instances, function as a substitute parent. In addition, a coach should be able to administer first aid in emergency situations.

New laws that require equality for women in school sports programs have resulted in a substantial increase in athletic programs and scholarships for women athletes. Because high school sports for girls has grown especially fast in the past few years, the need for qualified women coaches should remain high for some time.

Places of employment and working conditions

Athletic coaches work throughout the country with the most job opportunities in metropolitan areas large enough to support a number of secondary schools.

Working conditions vary depending on the employer. In a sports-minded community, a coach will usually have modern equipment and a liberal budget; in other areas, a tight budget and poor facilities. During the sports season, a coach's life can be hectic, but this is offset by the fact that coaches have the summer months free.

Qualifications, education, and training

Coaches need physical stamina and good health and, of course, must possess athletic ability. They should like to work with young people and possess qualities of honesty and fair play.

High school courses should include English, public speaking, biology, and sports. Volunteer work or a part-time job at a summer camp or community center can provide valuable experience.

In college, a physical education major plus experience in competitive sports at the varsity level are considered the minimum requirements. A graduate of a small college who has varsity experience will find it easier to get a job than the physical education major from a big university who lacks varsity experience.

Most states require high school coaches to be certified teachers and some require them to be certified coaches. Coaches who wish to maximize their job opportunities usually have at least one additional area besides coaching in which they can receive certification, since budget restrictions in some schools require that the athletic coach be able to fill a teaching position as well.

Potential and advancement

Over 100,000 athletic coaches are employed in the United States. The demand for qualified coaches should increase in the next decade because of population growth and the increase in athletic opportunities for girls and women.

Coaches usually advance by moving to larger schools or colleges as they build a reputation for turning out winning teams. In large schools, a coach can be promoted to athletic director or move into educational administration as a school principal or superintendent. As they reach the end of their peak physical years, some coaches prefer to move into related fields such as sportswriting, physical rehabilitation, or sporting goods sales. Some become managers or owners of health centers or summer camps.

Income

High school coaches usually earn slightly higher salaries than regular classroom teachers. Salaries range from $15,000 to $27,000 a year.

College athletic coaches earn up to $37,000 a year, while coaches of top professional teams can earn $100,000 or more.

Additional sources of information

National High School Athletic Coaches Association
3423 East Silver Springs Blvd.
Ocala, FL 32670

American Alliance for Health, Physical Education, and Recreation
1201 16th Street, NW
Washington, DC 20036

Association for Intercollegiate Athletics for Women (AIAW)
1201 16th Street, NW
Washington, DC 20036

AUCTIONEER

The job

The sale of various kinds of property at public sale is the work of auctioneers. Such public sales, or auctions, may be held for individuals or businesses and can take the form of country auctions, industrial auctions, produce auctions, or gallery sales.

Country auctions are held on the customer's premises and usually include a wide variety of merchandise. In this type of sale, the auctioneer must be able to appraise the worth of the merchandise.

Industrial auctions are a highly specialized field, and the auctioneer is usually an expert in machinery and industrial equipment.

At produce auctions, the auctioneer sells such items as fruits, vegetables, tobacco, livestock, and grains to food brokers, retailers, and wholesalers. Some produce auctions are conducted by telephone with the auctioneer relaying the sellers' descriptions of their goods and the buyers' bids back and forth by phone.

Gallery sales take place in a showroom and are usually advertised and accompanied by a catalog containing photographs and descriptions of the items to be sold. Almost all gallery sales involve art works or antiques.

Most auctioneers specialize in one type of merchandise such as antiques, livestock, or industrial equipment. Auctioneers usually are self-employed and are hired on a job-by-job basis. Art and antique galleries sometimes employ their own auctioneers on a full-time basis.

The auctioneer is responsible for advertising an auction. He or she usually advertises in magazines and publications aimed at special audiences in addition to local newspapers, radio, and television. During an auction, the auctioneer describes each item to the audience and calls for an opening bid. By means of his personality and selling ability, the auctioneer can often persuade an audience to bid up the price. If an item does not draw an acceptable bid, the auctioneer may withdraw it from the sale.

Places of employment and working conditions

Auctioneers are employed throughout the country with those who work in a specialty field, such as tobacco or industrial equipment, traveling throughout the United States or a specific agricultural area in the course of their work.

Auctioneers have highly irregular working hours and often work weekends and evenings.

Qualifications, education, and training

To be successful in this field, a person should have physical stamina, a talent for organizing and promoting, and a knack for public speaking and entertaining.

A high school education is recommended since auctioneers need a broad general knowledge to make intelligent appraisals. Business courses are helpful as well as any courses or experience in public speaking.

Auctioneers who specialize in art or antiques usually have a college background in fine arts. Many auctioneers find college work in economics, business administration, accounting, and advertising to be very helpful in their work.

There are some auction schools that offer two- and four-week training programs in auctioneering techniques. Those who complete these courses sometimes serve an apprenticeship with an experienced auctioneer for an agreed-upon length of time. Other aspiring auctioneers secure jobs as assistants to experienced auctioneers or at auction houses until they feel qualified to work on their own.

Potential and advancement

There are no employment figures available for this job field, but the increasing popularity of the auction method of selling undoubtedly means more jobs for auctioneers. Job openings will also occur to replace those who retire or leave the field.

Auctioneers receive more lucrative assignments and larger commissions as they build their reputations.

Income

Auctioneers receive a commission on the price of each item they sell; rates range from less than 1 percent up to 30 percent depending on the experience and reputation of the auctioneer and the value of the property being sold.

Additional sources of information

National Auctioneers Association
135 Lakewood Drive
Lincoln, NB 68510

BANK OFFICER

The job

Bank officers are responsible for carrying out the policy set by the board of directors of the bank and for overseeing the day-to-day operations of all the banking departments. A thorough knowledge of business and economics is necessary plus expertise in the specialized banking area for which each officer is responsible.

Bank officers and their responsibilities include: *loan officer,* who evaluates the credit and collateral of individuals and businesses applying for loans; *trust officer,* who administers estates and trusts, manages property, invests funds for customers, and provides financial counseling; *operations officer,* who plans and coordinates procedures and systems; *branch manager,* who is responsible for all functions of a branch office; *international officer,* who handles financial dealings abroad or for foreign customers; and *cashier,* who is responsible for all bank property. Other officers handle auditing, personnel administration, public relations, and operations research. In small banks there may be only a few officers, each of whom handles several functions or departments.

About 24 percent of all bank officers are women, but they are usually locked into middle, rather than top, management positions. Women officers are usually found in the trust, personnel, and public relations departments of a bank.

Places of employment and working conditions

Bank officers are employed in towns and cities of all sizes, throughout the country.

Bank officers are usually involved in the civic and business affairs of their communities and are often called upon to serve as directors of local companies and community organizations. This can entail evenings spent away from home attending meetings and functions related to these positions.

Qualifications, education, and training

The ability to inspire confidence in others is a necessary characteristic of a successful bank officer. Officers should also display tact and good judgment in dealing with customers and employees. The ability to work independently and to analyze information is also important.

High school students interested in banking should study mathematics and take any available courses in economics.

Potential bank officers usually start their careers at a bank by entering the bank's management training program after graduation from college. Occasionally, outstanding clerks and tellers work their way up the ladder through promotions and are also accepted into these training programs, but the usual background is a college degree.

The ideal preparation for a banking officer has been described as a bachelor's degree in social science along with a master of business administration degree. A business administration degree with a major in finance, or a liberal arts degree with courses in accounting, economics, commercial law, political science and statistics, are also good college backgrounds.

Potential and advancement

There are about 300,000 bank officers and managers at present, with employment expected to increase substantially. Banking is one of the fastest-growing industries in our economy; expanding bank services and the increased use of computers will continue to require trained personnel in all areas of banking.

It usually takes many years of experience to advance to senior officer and management positions. Experience in several banking departments, as well as continuing education in management-sponsored courses, can aid and accelerate promotion.

Income

Income varies, with banks in large cities paying more than those in small towns.

Management trainees usually earn between $900 and $1,000 a month. Those with an M.B.A. degree can command starting salaries of $1,400 to $1,600 a month.

Additional sources of information

American Bankers Association
Bank Personnel Division
1120 Connecticut Avenue, NW
Washington, DC 20036

National Association of Bank Women, Inc.
National Office
111 East Wacker Drive
Chicago, IL 60601

National Bankers Association
4310 Georgia Avenue, NW
Washington, DC 20011

Federal Deposit Insurance Corporation
Director of Personnel
550 17th Street, NW
Washington, DC 20429

Board of Governors
The Federal Reserve System
Personnel Department
Washington, DC 20551

BANK WORKER

The job

Banks employ the same clerical workers as other businesses and industries—file clerks, stenographers, secretaries, typists, and receptionists. But there are two groups of clerical employees that perform duties unique to the banking industry—clerks and tellers.

Bank clerks are responsible for all the records of the monetary activities of the bank and its customers. They have specialized duties and often use office machines that are designed especially for banking functions. Some of their titles are: sorter, proof machine operator, bookkeeping machine operator, bookkeeping and accounting clerk, transit clerk, interest clerk, and mortgage clerk. With the wide use of electronic data processing equipment in the banking industry, bank clerk occupations also now include such jobs as electronic reader-sorter operator, check inscriber or encoder, control clerk, coding clerk, tape librarian, and teletype operator.

Tellers are the most visible employees of a bank and should project an efficient, pleasant, and dependable image, both for themselves and for their employer. Tellers cash checks, handle deposits and withdrawals, sell savings bonds and travelers' checks, keep records, and handle paperwork. In the course of this work, they must be thorough and accurate in checking identification, verifying accounts and money amounts, and counting out money to customers. At the end of their working day, all transactions must balance.

Some opportunities for part-time teller work exist in larger banks. These extra tellers are used during peak banking hours and on peak banking days.

Places of employment and working conditions

Bank clerks and tellers work in all areas of the country, in communities of all sizes.

In small banks, clerks and tellers usually perform a variety of duties, while in large banks they work in one specialty area. Boredom can be a problem in some of the clerical functions, and some bank workers object to the close supervision that is part of their working atmosphere.

Tellers stand on their feet during much of their workday; anyone who does not like to be confined to a small space might find the teller cages of some banks unpleasant.

Qualifications, education, and training

Personal qualities of honesty and integrity are necessary for a job in banking. A fondness for working with numbers, attention to detail, and the ability to work as part of a closely supervised team are essential. Tellers should have a pleasant personality and like to work with people.

A high school diploma is adequate preparation for entry-level jobs, especially if the applicant has had courses in typing, bookkeeping, office machine operation, and business arithmetic.

Banks usually train beginning clerks to operate various office machines. Tellers receive anywhere from a few days to three weeks or more of training and spend some time observing an experienced teller before handling any work on their own.

Bank training courses are available to all bank employees throughout their working years. Employees who avail themselves of these courses can advance by gaining new skills. The successful completion of specific banking courses can lead to promotion.

Potential and advancement

There are about 182,500 persons in banking who could be classed as bank clerks, and about 310,000 tellers. Employment in banking will grow steadily in spite of the increasing use of automated equipment and electronic data processing. This employment picture is due not only to the growth of the banking industry but also to the fact that this is an industry that traditionally has a large turnover.

Bank clerks may be promoted to supervisory positions within their own specialty area, to teller or credit analyst, and eventually to senior supervisory positions. Tellers can advance to head teller. Additional education, in the form of courses offered by the American Institute of Banking, can aid advancement, and outstanding clerks and tellers who have college training in addition to banking courses can sometimes advance to bank officers.

Income

The banking industry has traditionally paid lower clerical salaries than many other industries, and it has not changed this policy in recent years.

Bank clerks, depending on specialty and experience, earn from $110 to $160 a week, with senior clerks earning up to $170.

Beginning tellers earn $110 to $135 a week; experienced tellers between $135 and $180.

Additional sources of information

American Bankers Association
1120 Connecticut Avenue, NW
Washington, DC 20036

American Savings and Loan League
1435 G Street, NW
Suite 1019
Washington, DC 20005

BIOCHEMIST

The job

Biochemists study the chemical composition and behavior of living things and the effects of food, drugs, hormones, and other chemicals on various organisms. Their work is essential to a better understanding of health, growth, reproduction and heredity in human beings and to progress in the fields of medicine, nutrition, and agriculture.

Most biochemists are involved in basic research; those engaged in applied research use the results of basic research to solve practical problems. For example, basic research into how an organism forms a hormone has been used to synthesize and produce hormones on a mass scale.

Laboratory research can involve weighing, filtering, distilling, and culturing specimens or the operation of electron microscopes and centrifuges. Biochemists sometimes design new laboratory apparatus or develop new techniques to carry out specific research projects.

About half of all biochemists are employed in colleges and universities, where they combine their research work with teaching positions. Other job opportunity fields for biochemists are the drug, insecticide, and cosmetic industries, where about one fourth work, and nonprofit research foundations and government agencies in the areas of health and agriculture.

Places of employment and working conditions

Biochemists are employed in all regions of the country, mainly in areas where chemical, food, and drug industries and colleges and universities are located.

Laboratory work can involve the handling of dangerous or unpleasant substances. Biochemists involved in research projects may work irregular or extended hours during certain phases of a project.

Qualifications, education, and training

Keen powers of observation, a curious mind, patience and perseverence, mechanical aptitude, and good communication skills are among the abilities necessary for the biochemist. Anyone planning a career in this field should be able to work either independently or as part of a team.

An advanced degree is the minimum required, even for many beginning jobs in this field. The prospective biochemist should begin with an undergraduate degree in chemistry, biology, or biochemistry, which will also involve courses in mathematics and physics.

About 150 colleges and universities offer graduate degrees in biochemistry. These programs require research as well as advanced science courses, usually in some specialized area. The student should choose a graduate school carefully because certain types of research facilities exist only at certain schools.

A Ph.D. degree is almost mandatory for anyone who hopes to do significant biochemical research or advance to management and administrative levels. This degree requires extensive original research and the writing of a thesis.

Potential and advancement

There are presently about 12,700 biochemists in the United States. Job prospects in the next ten years are expected to be very good, as a result of efforts to cure major diseases, concern for the safety of food and drug products, and public awareness of environmental and pollution problems. Biochemists will also be needed in the drug manufacturing industry, in hospitals and health centers, in colleges and universities, and in federal regulatory agencies.

Beginners in biochemistry jobs usually start work as technicians or assistants doing testing and analysis. They may advance, through increased experience and education, to positions that involve planning and supervising research. Positions in administration and management can be achieved by those with experience and advanced degree, but many prefer to remain in the laboratory—doing basic biochemical research.

Income

Salaries for experienced biochemists in industry are generally high, averaging $18,000 for those with a bachelor's degree, $21,000 with a master's degree, and $28,000 with a Ph.D.

Biochemists employed by colleges and universities receive salaries comparable to other faculty members, with average salaries much lower than in industry.

Additional sources of information

American Society of Biological Chemists
9650 Rockville Pike
Bethesda, MD 20014

BIOMEDICAL ENGINEER

The job

Biomedical engineers apply engineering principles to medical and health-related problems.

Most engineers in this field are involved in research. They work with life scientists, chemists, and members of the medical profession to design and develop medical devices such as artificial hearts, pacemakers, dialysis machines, and lasers for surgery. Others work for private industry in the development, design, and sales of medical instruments and devices.

Biomedical engineers with computer expertise adapt computers to medical needs and design and build systems to modernize laboratory and clinical procedures. Some work for the National Aeronautics and Space Administration (NASA) developing life support and medical monitoring systems for astronauts.

Places of employment and working conditions

Some phases of this work may be unpleasant when one is working with certain illnesses or medical conditions.

Qualifications, education, and training

The ability to think analytically, a capacity for details, and the ability to work as part of a team are all necessary. Good communication skills are important.

Mathematics and the sciences must be emphasized in high school .

A bachelor's degree in engineering is the minimum requirement in this field. In a typical curriculum, the first two years are spent in the study of basic sciences such as physics and chemistry and mathematics, introductory engineering, and some liberal arts courses. The remaining years are usually devoted to specialized engineering courses. For this field that means a sound background in mechanical, electrical, industrial, or chemical engineering plus additional specialized biomedical training.

Engineering programs can last from four to six years. Those that require five or six years to complete may award a master's degree or may provide a cooperative plan of study plus practical work experience with a nearby industry.

All states require licensing of engineers whose work may affect life, health, or property or who offer their services to the public. Those who are licensed, about one third of all engineers, are called Registered Engineers. Requirements for licensing include graduation from an accredited engineering school, four years of experience, and an examination.

Potential and advancement

There are only about 3,000 biomedical engineers. Substantial growth is expected, but, since the field is relatively small, few actual job openings will occur. Those with advance degrees will have the best job opportunities.

Income

Starting salaries in private industry average $18,700 with a master's degree, and $24,000 or more with a Ph.D.

The federal government pays beginners $13,657 to $20,500, depending on degree and experience. Average salary for experienced engineers, federally employed, is about $27,700.

Experienced biomedical engineers average $30,500 in private industry; $15,000 to $21,000 for nine-month faculty positions in colleges and universities.

Additional sources of information

Alliance for Engineering in Medicine and Biology
Suite 404
4405 East-West Highway
Bethesda, MD 20014

Biomedical Engineering Society
P.O. Box 2399
Culver City, CA 90230

Engineers' Council for Professional Development
345 East 47th Street
New York, NY 10017

National Society of Professional Engineers
2029 K Street, NW
Washington, DC 20006

American Society for Engineering Education
One Dupont Circle, Suite 400
Washington, DC 20036

Society of Women Engineers
United Engineering Center
345 East 47th Street
New York, NY 10017

BROADCASTING TECHNICIAN

The job

The operation and maintenance of the electronic equipment used to record and transmit radio and television programs is the responsibility of broadcasting technicians, also called broadcasting engineers.

In small stations, broadcasting technicians perform a variety of duties. In large stations and in networks, technicians are more specialized. They may perform any or all of the following functions.

Transmitter technicians monitor and log (keep records of) outgoing signals and are responsible for transmitter operation. *Maintenance technicians* set up, maintain, and repair the broadcasting equipment. *Audio control technicians* regulate sound; *video control technicians* regulate the quality of television pictures; and *lighting technicians* direct the lighting. *Recording technicians* operate and maintain sound recording equipment, while *video recording technicians* operate and maintain video tape recording equipment. When programs originate outside of a radio or television station, *field technicians* set up and operate the broadcasting equipment.

Radio stations usually employ only a few broadcasting technicians, three to ten, depending on the size and broadcasting schedule of the station. Television broadcasting is more complex, and television stations usually employ between 10 and 30 technicians in addition to supervisory personnel.

Related jobs are: Communications Technicians, Television and Radio Service Technician.

Places of employment and working conditions

Broadcasting technicians are employed in all areas of the United States, especially in large metropolitan areas. The highest paid and most specialized jobs are in Los Angeles, New York, and Washington, D.C., where most network programs originate.

In large stations, broadcasting technicians work a 37- to 40-hour week. In smaller stations, the workweek is usually longer. In stations that broadcast 24 hours a day, seven days a week, some weekend, evening, and holiday work is necessary. Network technicians covering an important event often have to work continuously and under great pressure until the event is over.

Qualifications, education, and training

Manual dexterity, good eyesight and hearing, reliability, and the ability to work as part of a team are all requisites for anyone interested in this field.

High school should include algebra, trigonometry, physics, and electrical shop. Electronics courses can also provide valuable background.

Many technical schools and colleges offer special courses for broadcasting technicians. These courses are designed to prepare the student to take the Federal Communications Commission (FCC) licensing examinations.

The FCC issues a Third Class Operator License and a First Class Radiotelephone Operator License. Applicants for either license must pass a series of examinations. Anyone who operates a transmitter in a television station must have a First Class license; the chief engineer at any broadcasting station must have one as well. Some radio and television stations require all technicians to have at least a Third Class license.

A college degree in engineering is becoming necessary for many supervisory and executive positions in broadcasting.

Potential and advancement

There are about 22,500 broadcasting technicians. Any job openings that are likely to occur will be to replace technicians who retire or transfer to other occupations. Although the growth of cable television will provide some new jobs, this could be offset by the increasing use of automated equipment for some jobs normally handled by broadcasting technicians.

Beginners will face the most competition for available jobs, and for them the best opportunities will be in smaller cities.

Broadcasting technicians can advance to supervisory positions such as chief engineer. Top-level technical positions such as director of engineering usually require a college degree.

Income

Beginning salaries in commercial radio and television stations range from $155 to $215 a week. Experienced broadcasting technicians earn $200 to $450. Educational stations pay less.

In general, television stations pay more than radio stations.

Additional sources of information

National Association of Broadcasters
1771 N Street, NW
Washington, DC 20036

Corporation for Public Broadcasting
1111 16th Street
Washington, DC 20036

Federal Communications Commission
Washington, DC 20554

BUILDING CONTRACTOR

The job

A building contractor, or *builder*, is responsible for the actual erection of a structure. The contractor is hired at an agreed-upon fee to handle all phases of building. Working within the client's budget, the contractor orders all materials, schedules work, and hires all necessary labor. The contractor usually assigns specific parts of the construction to subcontractors such as electricians and plumbers.

Places of employment and working conditions

Building contractors work in all areas of the country, in communities of all sizes and in urban areas.

The building contractor has all the headaches—bad weather that delays construction, materials that don't arrive on time, security at the building site, subcontractors that don't complete their work on schedule and hold up subsequent construction steps, labor problems, cost overruns. For small contractors, a few of these problems on a single job can put them out of business.

For further information

Building contractors usually start out in one of the building trades. See the job descriptions for Carpenter; Electrician; Air Conditioning, Heating, and Refrigeration Mechanic; Plumber and Pipefitter for specific information on training, potential, and income.

BUILDING OR PROPERTY MANAGER

The job

A building or property manager is responsible for overseeing the day-to-day happenings of a building with multiple tenants such as office buildings, apartment houses, or shopping centers.

A building or property manager is a combination administrator, rental agent, accountant, public relations expert, purchasing agent, and maintenance person. The manager may simply have an office on the premises, or he or she may live there in an apartment supplied by the owners of the building.

In a single building with only a handful of tenants, the manager handles everything with the help of a small clerical and maintenance staff. In large units, the manager supervises a large staff that handles the details of maintenance, security, leases and rent collection, accounting, and other matters.

One of the most important duties of a building manager is securing tenants for the facility. That involves showing available units to prospective tenants, arranging leases, and providing renovations to suit commercial tenants. Each of these activities is of prime importance to the profitable operation of the building. The reputation of the building manager and staff for competence and service may influence the prospective tenant's decision to move into a building.

Most building managers are employed by real estate and development firms, banks or trust companies, or insurance companies that own investment property. Government agencies employ building managers in subsidized public housing projects. Some building managers are self-employed.

A beginner in this field usually works under the supervision of an experienced manager. To gain experience, the beginner might be given responsibility for a small building or hired as a resident supervisor or maintenance manager.

A related job is: Real Estate Agent/Broker.

Places of employment and working conditions

Building managers must recognize that tenants can sometimes be demanding, troublesome, and unreasonable, and the building manager is on call at all times for emergencies and problems.

Qualifications, education, and training

Reliability, good judgment, tact, and diplomacy are all necessary. A building manager must also have initiative and a well-developed sales ability.

High school preparation should include business courses and the development of communication skills.

A college education is becoming more and more important in this field. A background in accounting, law, finance, management, government, or economics is helpful; a business degree with a major in real estate is ideal. Junior and community colleges offer two-year programs leading to an associate degree, which is also acceptable to many employers.

As in all real estate jobs, continuing education is important. The Institute of Real Estate Management of the National Association of Realtors offers courses in all parts of the country at frequent intervals. Those who have adequate education and experience can receive the designation Certified Property Manager upon completion of certain courses and examinations.

The Institute of Real Estate Management also offers courses and certification as an Accredited Management Organization (AMO) to management firms that meet its standards.

Potential

Experienced building managers are always in demand. Large metropolitan areas, retirement and resort communities, and industrial areas all provide numerous job opportunities.

Advancement usually takes the form of increased responsibility in larger buildings or management firms. Some experienced managers go into business for themselves and many of them eventually go into real estate investing.

Income

Earnings vary greatly depending on geographic area, size of buildings, and level of responsibility. Beginners earn about $170 a week, sometimes with living facilities provided.

Experienced managers earn from $12,000 to $32,000 a year or more. Owners of management firms earn as much as $80,000 to $100,000.

Additional sources of information

Building Owners and Managers Association International
1221 Massachusetts Avenue, NW
Washington, DC 20005

American Industrial Real Estate Association
5670 Wilshire Boulevard, Suite 1250
Los Angeles, CA 90036

Institute of Real Estate Management
430 North Michigan Avenue
Chicago, IL 60611

BUSINESS MACHINE SERVICE TECHNICIAN

The job

Maintenance and repair of business and office machines is the work of business machine service technicians. About 80 percent of these technicians work for business machine manufacturers and dealers or repair shops; the remainder work for large organizations that have enough machines to employ an in-house, full-time technician.

The majority of business machine service technicians work on typewriters, calculators and adding machines, and copiers and duplicating equipment. A few repair and service dictating machines; the remainder service accounting-bookkeeping machines, cash registers, and postage and mailing equipment.

Technicians usually specialize in one type of business machine, such as typewriters or copiers. Those who work for a manufacturer or dealer probably service only the brand produced or sold by their employer.

Related jobs are: Appliance Repairer, Computer Service Technicians, Communications Technicians, Television and Radio Service Technician.

Places of employment and working conditions

Business machine service technicians work in communities of all sizes throughout the country. Even small communities have at least one repair shop or self-employed technician.

Servicing business machines is cleaner work than most mechanical jobs, and business machine service technicians usually wear business clothes. There are no slow periods since business machines must be serviced regardless of slack economic periods.

Qualifications, education, and training

Mechanical ability, manual dexterity, good eyesight and hearing, and the ability to work without supervision are required for this work. Since these technicians work directly with the customer, they must also be pleasant and tactful.

High school classes in electrical shop, mechanical drawing, mathematics, and physics are helpful.

There are no specific educational requirements for this field, but many employers prefer some technical training in electricity or electronics. Courses are available at trade and technical schools and junior and community colleges. Training received in the armed forces is also valuable.

Trainees who are hired by a manufacturer or dealer attend a training program sponsored by the manufacturer. Such programs last from several weeks to several months and are followed by one to three years of on-the-job training. Training offered by independent repair shops is less formal but basically the same.

All business machine service technicians keep up with technological changes by attending frequent training seminars sponsored by manufacturers when new machines are developed. Many companies also provide tuition assistance for technicians who take additional work-related courses in colleges or technical schools.

Potential and advancement

There are about 58,000 business machine service technicians, and the field is expanding rapidly. Job opportunities will be especially good for those with some training in electronics. Since electronic business machines are becoming more and more popular, in a few years, an electronics background will be essential for all business machine service technicians.

Advancement to positions such as service manager or supervisor is possible for experienced technicians. Some open their own repair business or go into business machine sales.

Income

Trainees earn from $150 to $200 a week. Those with technical school or armed forces training may start higher.

Experienced technicians earn from $200 to over $300 a week. Those who work on more than one type of equipment earn $240 to $340.

Technicians who service electronic business machines and complex copiers earn the highest wages.

Additional sources of information

Local offices of firms that sell and service business machines can provide information on job opportunities and training.

CARPENTER

The job

Carpenters are the largest group of building trades workers in the United States and are employed in almost every type of construction activity. Carpentry is divided into "rough" and "finish" work, and a skilled carpenter is able to do both.

Rough work includes erecting the wood framework in buildings, including subfloors, partitions, and floor joists; installing the heavy timbers used in the building of docks and railroad trestles; erecting scaffolds and temporary buildings at construction sites; and making the chutes for pouring concrete and the forms to enclose the concrete while it hardens. Rough work must be completed before finish work can begin.

Installing molding, wood paneling, cabinets, windows and doors, and hardware, as well as building stairs and laying floors, is finish work. In some construction jobs, finish work may also include installing wallboard and floor coverings such as linoleum or asphalt tile.

In small communities and rural areas, carpenters often install glass and insulation and do the painting; in large metropolitan areas, carpenters tend to specialize in just one phase of carpentry.

Carpenters work from blueprints or from instructions given by supervisors and must use materials and building techniques that conform to local building codes. They use hand tools such as hammers, saws, chisels, and planes (which each carpenter usually provides for him- or herself), as well as portable power saws, drills, and rivet guns (which are usually supplied by the builder or contractor).

Most carpenters work for contractors and builders who construct new buildings or renovate and remodel older structures; many are self-employed or combine wage employment with a part-time business of their own. Some are employed by government agencies, manufacturing firms, and other large organizations.

A large proportion of carpenters belong to the United Brotherhood of Carpenters and Joiners of America.

Slowly but surely, women are beginning to enter this field—currently less than 1 percent of all carpenters are women. One major attraction is the high hourly wage, which is more than twice that paid in the clerical and health fields where so many women work. Women carpenters often face resentment and sometimes discrimination in this traditionally male field, but affirmative action programs and equal employment opportunity regulations are helping smooth the way. A woman interested in carpentry as a career should make sure she acquires the best technical skills possible in high school if she expects to be considered for acceptance into an apprenticeship program.

Places of employment and working conditions

Carpenters work throughout the country in communities of all sizes and in rural areas.

A carpenter's work is always active and sometimes strenuous, depending on whether it is rough or finish work. Prolonged standing, climbing, and squatting are necessary, and there is danger of injury from falls, sharp or rough materials, and the use of sharp tools and power equipment.

Qualifications, education, and training

Manual dexterity is an extremely important qualification as is the ability to solve mathematical problems quickly and accurately. Anyone interested in carpentry as a career should also be in good physical condition, have a good sense of balance, and be unafraid of working on high structures.

Although a large number of workers in this field have acquired their skills by working as carpenters' helpers or for contractors who provide some training, the best training is obtained in a formal apprenticeship program. Carpenters with such training are in greater demand, command better pay, and have greater opportunities for advancement.

Apprenticeship applicants generally must be at least 17 years old; a high school or vocational school education is usually, but not always, required. Courses in carpentry shop, mechanical drawing, and general mathematics are helpful. Applicants are usually given an aptitude test to assess their suitability for carpentry work.

An apprenticeship consists of four years of on-the-job training supplemented by 144 hours per year of related classroom instruction. The classroom instruction includes drafting, blueprint reading, mathematics for layout work, and the use of woodworking machines to familiarize the apprentice with the materials, tools, and principles of carpentry.

Most apprenticeship programs are sponsored and supervised by a joint committee of local contractors and builders and representatives of the local chapter of the carpenters' union. The committee determines the number of carpenters the local job market can support and establishes the minimum standards of education, training, and experience. If specialization by local contractors is extensive, the committee sometimes rotates apprentices among several employers to provide training in all areas of carpentry.

Potential and advancement

There are about one million carpenters in the United States, one fifth of whom are self-employed. Job opportunities should be plentiful over the next decade as population growth adds to the demand for housing and other structures. The construction industry is very sensitive to the national economy, however, and the number of job openings can fluctuate greatly from year to year.

Carpenters have greater opportunity for advancement to general supervisory positions than other construction workers because they are involved in the entire construction process. For this same reason, carpenters often become building contractors.

For women in this field, the best areas for job opportunities are in the building trade groups and in companies being formed by women to create jobs for women in the building trades.

Income

Carpenters in large metropolitan areas average about $10.00 an hour. Annual earnings, however, do not always reflect this high hourly rate, since many carpenters have periods of lost work time due to poor weather and occasional unemployment between jobs.

Apprentices usually start at about 50 percent of the hourly rate paid to experienced carpenters. They receive 5 percent increases every six months during their training.

Additional sources of information

Associated General Contractors of America, Inc.
1957 E Street, NW
Washington, DC 20006

United Brotherhood of Carpenters and Joiners of America
101 Constitution Avenue, NW
Washington, DC 20005

National Association of Women in Construction
2800 West Lancaster Avenue
Fort Worth, TX 76107

CARTOONIST

The job

Cartoonists are specialized artists who use small drawings to illustrate ideas, concepts, text, customers' products, or humorous situations. Many cartoonists are free-lancers and may work for a number of clients. Often, their work is syndicated and appears in a number of publications. A cartoonist may specialize in one of a number of areas.

A *political or editorial cartoonist* uses his/her skill to focus attention on political issues and personalities of the day, local issues, or other community activities and personalities. Political cartoons are not always humorous—many are sad and some almost brutal. The political cartoonists, the fewest in number of all cartoonists, usually have a broad background in history, politics, literature, and human behavior as well as artistic talent.

Sports cartoonists use their talents to depict sports figures and situations. They usually work for newspapers and must have an eye for physical action and a knowledge of the fine points of various sports.

Commercial, or advertising cartoonists work in the field of advertising. This is a rapidly growing field and one that offers many opportunities to beginners. Most cities have at least one art studio that supplies drawings for local businesses and industries to use in their ads; larger cities have a number of such studios. Experienced commercial cartoonists are also employed by advertising agencies, advertising departments of large industries and businesses, educational publishers, and many federal and state agencies.

Comic strip cartoonists combine writing and drawing techniques to produce a small story in cartoon form. In longer, continuous comic strips or comic books, where a more complex story line is used, the cartoonist often works in conjunction with a writer.

Magazine cartoonists usually work on a free-lance basis by submitting humorous cartoons to magazines. Some specialize in a particular topic such as industrial safety or sales and submit their work to trade magazines.

Caricaturists are basically very talented portrait artists who exaggerate and distort to portray the qualities of a personality in terms of physical characteristics. Caricature is more subtle, and usually less kind, than political cartooning.

Motion picture cartoonists draw a series of pictures, or frames, each one differing only slightly from the preceding one. When reproduced on film and projected, the cartoon characters appear to move. More than any other cartoonists, motion picture cartoonists work as part of a team rather than as individual drawings. Some cartoonists draw and paint in the background; others make rough sketches of the main points of the story. *Animators* fill in these sequences by preparing the detailed drawings of every movement.

One of the newest fields is that of *television cartoonist*. These cartonists usually have a solid background in several phases of cartooning—especially advertising and animation—and a working knowledge of television production techniques and requirements.

Places of employment and working conditions

Job opportunities are everywhere, especially for a beginner. Boston, Chicago, Los Angeles, and New York provide many jobs in the newspaper and publishing fields, while most motion picture cartoonists, animators, and television cartoonists work in Los Angeles or New York.

Most cartoonists work regular schedules of 35 to 40 hours a week. Comic strip and editorial cartoonists must meet deadlines. Free-lance cartoonists set their own hours.

Qualifications, education, and training

Artistic talent and a sense of humor are the prime requisites. Creativity, imagination, an understanding of human nature, manual dexterity, good color vision, and perseverance are also necessary.

Sometimes talent alone is enough, but a solid foundation provided by formal art training is the best preparation. This training can begin in high school. An aspiring cartoonist should take any available art courses and should follow an academic program as preparation for college or art school. Any opportunity to draw for school or local publications, or to make posters for community events, can provide valuable experience.

Most art schools provide a few courses in cartooning plus comprehensive training in commercial art; a few offer special programs in cartooning. These are: Chouinard Art Institute (Los Angeles), Corcoran School of Art (Washington, D.C.), Chicago Academy of Fine Arts (Chicago), and Cartoonists and Illustrators School (New York).

Some accredited home study courses provide art training, but these should be checked out thoroughly before a person decides to enroll.

Walt Disney studios offer a limited number of apprenticeships to artists who have completed two or three years of formal art training. Some large art studios also have apprenticeship programs.

The accumulation of a portfolio should start as early as possible. Samples of a cartoonist's work are always the best way to impress an employer or a school with the quality of one's work and imagination.

Potential and advancement

This is a growing field with many job opportunities for those with talent and training. Competition is keen but beginners with persistence will find opportunities, especially for free-lance work or in small art studios. The biggest money is in syndication, but this is the toughest field to break into.

Income

Salaried cartoonists earn from $10,000 to $44,000 a year. Syndicated cartoonists earn from $7,000 to $52,000 or more.

Free-lance cartoonists earn from $5 to $1,000 for a single cartoon, depending on their talent and reputation.

Additional sources of information

National Cartoonists Society
9 Ebony Court
Brooklyn, NY 11229

National Home Study Council
1601 18th Street, NW
Washington, DC 20009

The Newspaper Comics Council
260 Madison Avenue
New York, NY 10016

CERAMIC ENGINEER

The job

Ceramic engineers work not only with ceramics (as in pottery) but with all nonmetallic, inorganic materials that require high temperatures in their processing. Thus these engineers work on such diverse products as glassware, heat-resistant materials for furnaces, electronic components, and nuclear reactors. They also design and supervise construction of plants and equipment used in the manufacture of these products.

Ceramic engineers normally specialize in one or more ceramic products—whiteware (porcelain and china or high-voltage electrical insulators); structural materials such as brick and tile; electronic ceramics, glass, or fuel elements for atomic energy, to name a few. Most are employed in the stone, clay, and glass industries. Others work in industries that use ceramic products including the iron-and-steel, electrical equipment, aerospace, and chemical industries.

Places of employment and working conditions

Ceramic engineers are employed in all areas of the country. Their work locations vary from laboratories to factory production areas, depending on the product and the industry.

Qualifications, education, and training

The ability to think analytically, a capacity for details, and the ability to work as part of a team are all necessary. Good communication skills are important for the ceramic engineer.

Mathematics and the sciences must be emphasized in high school.

A bachelor's degree in engineering is the minimum requirement in this field. In a typical curriculum, the first two years are spent in the study of basic sciences such as physics and chemistry and mathematics, introductory engineering, and some liberal arts courses. The remaining years are usually devoted to specialized engineering courses. Engineering programs can last from four to six years. Those requiring five or six years to complete may award a master's degree or may provide a cooperative plan of study plus practical work experience with a nearby industry.

Because of rapid changes in technology, many ceramic engineers continue their education throughout their careers. A graduate degree is necessary for most teaching and research positions and for many management jobs. Some persons obtain graduate degrees in business administration.

Engineering graduates usually work under the supervision of an experienced engineer or in a company training program until they become acquainted with the requirements of a particular company.

All states require licensing of engineers whose work may affect life, health, or property or who offer their services to the public. Those who are licensed, about one third of all engineers, are called Registered Engineers. Requirements include graduation from an accredited engineering school, four years of experience, and an examination.

Potential and advancement

There are about 12,000 ceramic engineers, and job opportunities in this field are expected to increase substantially into the 1980s. Nuclear energy, electronics, defense, medical science, pollution control, energy, and conservation will all offer increasing job opportunities for ceramics engineers.

Income

Starting salaries in private industry average $18,700 with a master's degree; and $24,000 or more with a Ph.D.

The federal government pays beginners $13,657 to $20,500, depending on degree and experience. Average salary for experienced engineers federally employed is about $27,700.

Experienced ceramic engineers average $30,500 in private industry; $15,000 to $21,000 for nine-month faculty positions in colleges and universities.

Additional sources of information

American Ceramic Society
65 Ceramic Drive
Columbus, OH 43214

Engineers' Council for Professional Development
345 East 47th Street
New York, NY 10017

National Society of Professional Engineers
2029 K Street, NW
Washington, DC 20006

American Society for Engineering Education
One Dupont Circle, Suite 400
Washington, DC 20036

Society of Women Engineers
United Engineering Center
345 East 47th Street
New York, NY 10017

CHEF

The job

The preparation of food for public consumption in restaurants, schools, hospitals, hotels, and numerous other establishments is the work of chefs and cooks.

Cooks vary from the short-order cook in a small restaurant serving only a few easily prepared dishes to a highly trained specialist in a large institution or expensive restaurant. These large facilities employ a number of cooks and assistant cooks who specialize in one type of food such as pastry or sauces.

In a kitchen that employs a number of cooks, a head cook—or *chef*—coordinates the activities of the entire staff and may him- or herself cook certain foods. The chef is also responsible for planning menus and ordering food supplies.

Places of employment and working conditions

Cooks and chefs are employed throughout the country in communities of all sizes.

Many kitchens are spacious and pleasant, with air conditioning and the latest appliances. In older buildings or in small restaurants, conditions are not always as pleasant. All cooks and chefs must stand most of the time, lift heavy pots and kettles, and work near hot ovens and stoves. They are also subject to burns and cuts from sharp implements.

Qualifications, education, and training

Cleanliness, a keen sense of taste and smell, and physical stamina are important qualities for a cook or chef. They must also work well as part of the team.

High school or vocational school courses in business arithmetic and food preparation are helpful; part-time or summer work in a fast-food restaurant can be valuable.

Although many cooks acquire their skills through on-the-job training, larger institutions and the better hotels and restaurants prefer to hire those with more formal training.

Some professional associations and trade unions offer apprenticeship programs in cooperation with local employers and junior colleges, and a few large hotels and restaurants have their own training programs. Colleges and universities offer courses in commercial food preparation as part of their hotel management curriculum; the armed forces are also a good source of training in this field. Courses and training programs vary in length from a few months to several years. Students study basic food preparation, care of kitchen equipment, food storage, menu planning, and food purchasing.

Most states require cooks and chefs to have health certificates indicating that they are free from contagious diseases.

Potential and advancement

Employment opportunities for cooks and chefs are expected to grow steadily. Small restaurants, school cafeterias, and other places serving simple foods will offer the best opportunities for beginners.

Advancement in this field usually takes the form of moving to larger food-service facilities or restaurants. Some chefs gradually advance to supervisory or management positions in hotels, clubs, or the more elegant restaurants. Others open their own restaurants or catering businesses.

Income

Assistant cooks earn from $3.68 to $7.15 an hour; cooks earn from about $2.81 to $6.36 an hour.

Chefs earn about $125 to $250 a week, with those in the best restaurants earning much more. Several chefs with national reputations earn over $40,000 a year.

Additional sources of information

American Culinary Federation
Educational Institute
1407 South Harrison Road
East Lansing, MI 48823

Culinary Institute of America
P.O. Box 53
Hyde Park, NY 12538

Education Director
National Institute for the Foodservice Industry
120 South Riverside Plaza
Chicago, IL 60606

The Educational Institute
American Hotel and Motel Association
1407 South Harrison Road
Michigan State University
East Lansing, MI 48823

CHEMICAL ENGINEER

The job

The duties of chemical engineers entail a working knowledge of chemistry, physics, and mechanical and electrical engineering.

Chemical engineers design chemical plants, manufacturing equipment, and production methods; they develop processes for such things as removing chemical contaminants from waste materials.

This is one of the most complex and diverse areas of engineering. Chemical engineers often specialize in a particular operation such as oxidation or polymerization. Others specialize in plastics or rubber or in a field such as pollution control.

Most chemical engineers work in manufacturing firms primarily in chemicals, petroleum, and related industries. A number of them work in the nuclear energy field.

Places of employment and working conditions

Chemical engineers may be subject to hazards that occur when working with dangerous chemicals.

Qualifications, education, and training

The ability to think analytically, a capacity for details, and the ability to work as part of a team are all necessary. Good communication skills are important for anyone who holds chemical engineering as a career goal.

Mathematics and the sciences should be emphasized as much as possible in high school.

A bachelor's degree in engineering is the minimum requirement in this field. In a typical curriculum, the first two years are spent in the study of basic sciences such as physics and chemistry and mathematics, introductory engineering, and some liberal arts courses. The remaining years are usually devoted to specialized engineering courses. Engineering programs can last from four to six years. Those requiring five or six years to complete may award a master's degree or may provide a plan of study plus a work experience with a nearby industry.

Because of rapid changes in technology, many engineers continue their education throughout their careers. A graduate degree is necessary for most teaching and research positions and for many management jobs. Some chemical engineers obtain graduate degrees in business administration.

Graduates usually work under the supervision of an experienced chemical engineer or in a company training program until they become acquainted with the requirements of a particular company.

73

All states require licensing of engineers whose work may affect life, health, or property or who offer their services to the public. Those who are licensed, about one third of all engineers, are called Registered Engineers. Requirements for licensing include graduation from an accredited engineering school, four years of experience, and an examination.

Potential and advancement

There are about 50,000 chemical engineers. Job opportunities should be good through the 1980s, especially in the fields of pollution control and environmental protection, development of synthetic fuels, and nuclear energy.

Income

Starting salaries for all engineers in private industry average $18,700 with a master's degree; and $24,000 or more with a Ph.D. Chemical engineers earn slightly more.

The federal government pays beginners $13,657 to $20,500, depending on degree and experience. Average salary for experienced engineers federally employed is about $27,700.

Experienced engineers average $30,500 in private industry; $15,000 to $21,000 for nine-month faculty positions in colleges and universities.

Additional sources of information

American Institute of Chemical Engineers
345 East 47th Street
New York, NY 10017

Engineers' Council for Professional Development
345 East 47th Street
New York, NY 10017

National Society of Professional Engineers
2029 K Street, NW
Washington, DC 20006

American Society for Engineering Education
One Dupont Circle, Suite 400
Washington, DC 20036

Society of Women Engineers
United Engineering Center
345 East 47th Street
New York, NY 10017

CHEMIST

The job

Chemists perform laboratory research to gain new knowledge about the substances that make up our world. Knowledge gained in basic research is then put to practical use and applied to the development of new products. For example, basic research on the uniting of small molecules to form larger ones (polymerization) led to the development of products made from synthetic rubber and plastic.

Many chemists work in industrial production and inspection, where they must coordinate their efforts with a manufacturing operation. They give directions for the carrying out of a manufacturing process and then take periodic samples to check that process. Others work as marketing sales representatives because of the technical knowledge needed to market certain products. Chemists also work as college teachers and researchers and as consultants.

Chemists often specialize in one of the subfields of chemistry. *Analytical chemists* study the structure, composition, and natures of substances. *Organic chemists* study all elements made from carbon compounds, which include vast areas of modern industry. The development of plastics and many other synthetics is the result of the work of organic chemists. *Inorganic chemists* study compounds other than carbon and are involved in the development of such things as solid-state electronic components. *Physical chemists* study energy transformation and are engaged in finding new and better energy sources.

More than half of all chemists work in the chemical, food, petroleum, paper, electrical, and scientific instrument industries. About 25,000 work in colleges and universities and another 25,000 for government agencies, primarily in health and agriculture.

About 12 percent of all chemists are women.

Related jobs are: Biochemist, Food Scientist, and Life Scientist.

Places of employment and working conditions

Although chemists work in all parts of the country, the largest concentrations are in New York, New Jersey, California, Pennsylvania, Ohio, and Illinois.

Chemists usually work in modern facilities in laboratories, classrooms, and offices. In certain industries, hazards are present in the handling of explosive or otherwise dangerous materials, but safety regulations in these industries are very strict.

Qualifications, education, and training

The student who plans a career as a chemist should enjoy performing experiments and building things and should have a genuine liking for math and science. A wide range of abilities is necessary including perserverance, concentration on detail, good eye-hand coordination, and the ability to work independently.

High school students looking forward to a career in chemistry should take as many math and science courses as possible and should develop good laboratory skills. Foreign language courses can also prove valuable.

Over 1,000 colleges and universities offer a bachelor's degree in chemistry. Courses include analytical, organic, and inorganic and physical chemistry as well as mathematics and physics.

A master's degree in chemistry, usually requiring extensive, independent research, is offered by about 350 colleges and universities. Original research is required for a Ph.D. degree.

Potential and advancement

About 150,000 people are presently employed as chemists. The outlook for employment is good primarily because of the development of new products by private industry. In addition, problems of pollution, energy, and health care must be addressed by chemists in both government agencies and private industry. Employment of chemists in crime detection work is also expected to increase on local, state, and federal levels.

Little growth is expected in college and university positions, and competition for existing teaching jobs is expected to be very strong. Candidates for advanced degrees may secure teaching or research positions while completing their studies, but these positions are usually at the assistant or instructor level.

In all areas, advanced degrees will continue to be the key to administrative and managerial positions. College professors, chemists doing basic research, and those employed in the top administrative positions in both industry and teaching will need a Ph.D. degree to achieve these levels.

Income

Salaries for chemists vary according to experience, education, and place of employment. Entry-level starting salaries in private industry average $13,000 with a bachelor's degree, $15,600 with a master's degree and $21,500 with a Ph.D.

Experienced chemists with comparable degrees average $23,900, $25,400, and $29,200, respectively.

Federal government salaries range from $10,507 with a bachelor's degree to $23,087 with a Ph.D.

In colleges and universities, salaries average from $18,100 with a master's degree to $23,400 with a Ph.D. In addition, many experienced chemists supplement their incomes by consulting, lecturing, and writing.

Additional sources of information

American Chemical Society
1155 16th Street, NW
Washington, DC 20036

Manufacturing Chemists Association
1825 Connecticut Avenue, NW
Washington, DC 20009

Interagency Board of U.S. Civil Service
  Examiners for Washington, DC
1900 E Street, NW
Washington, DC 20415

CHIROPRACTOR

The job

Chiropractors treat patients by manual manipulations (called adjustments) of parts of the body, especially the spinal column. This system of treatment is based on the theory that pressure on nerves that pass from the spinal cord to different parts of the body interfere with nerve impulses and their functioning causing disorders in parts of the body. By means of certain manipulations of the vertebrae, the chiropractor seeks to relieve the pressure on specific nerves and thus remove the cause of a specific ailment.

Most chiropractors also employ X rays to aid in locating the source of an ailment. They use supplementary treatment with water, light, or heat therapy and may prescribe diet, exercise, and rest. Drugs and surgery are not used in this system of treatment.

Newly licensed chiropractors often start their careers by working in salaried positions—as assistants to established practitioners or in chiropractic clinics.

About 6 percent of all chiropractors are women. Most of them are in private practice and specialize in the treatment of women and children. Since a chiropractic practice can be conducted on a part-time basis, it is a good field for people with family responsibilities.

Places of employment and working conditions

Chiropractors often locate in small communities, with about half of all chiropractors practicing in cities of 50,000 or less. California, Michigan, Missouri, New York, Pennsylvania, and Texas have the most chiropractors.

Most chiropractors are in private practice, which allows them to schedule their own working hours. Evening and weekend hours are sometimes necessary to accommodate their patients.

Qualifications, education, and training

Manual dexterity rather than strength is necessary for a chiropractor. A keen sense of observation, an ability to deal with people, and a sympathetic manner with the sick are also important.

High school courses in science are important, and the two years of college required before entrance into chiropractic school must include chemistry, biology, and physics.

There are 12 chiropractic colleges that are accredited by the American Chiropractic Association. The four-year course of study emphasizes courses in manipulation and spinal adjustment, but most schools also offer a broad curriculum that includes English, social sciences, physiotherapy, and nutrition.

The first two years of study include classroom and laboratory work in anatomy, physiology, and chemistry. The last two years are devoted to practical experience in college clinics. The degree of Doctor of Chiropractic (D.C.) is awarded upon completion of the course.

All chiropractors must be licensed to practice. In addition to a state board examination, licensing requirements usually include two years of college and the successful completion of an accredited four-year chiropractic course, as described above. Some states also require a basic science examination.

Potential and advancement

There are about 18,000 practicing chiropractors. This number will increase because the profession is gaining greater public acceptance.

Enrollment in chiropractic colleges has increased in recent years. New chiropractors may find it increasingly difficult to establish a practice in areas where other practitioners are located; the best opportunities will be in areas with few established chiropractors.

Income

As in any type of independent practice, earnings are relatively low in the beginning. Experienced chiropractors earn about $25,000 a year, with many earning considerably more.

Newly licensed chiropractors who start out in salaried positions earn between $12,000 and $15,000 a year.

Additional sources of information

American Chiropractic Association
2200 Grand Avenue
Des Moines, IA 50312

Council on Chiropractic Education
3209 Ingersoll Street
Suite 206
Des Moines, IA 50312

American Council of Women Chiropractors
c/o Elizabeth C. Gerit, D.C.
3169 South Grand Blvd.
St. Louis, MO 63118

CIA WORKER

The job

The Central Intelligence Agency (CIA) gathers and analyzes information from all over the world that might affect the interests of the United States. This information is used by the government's senior policy makers as they make decisions on United States policy concerning many issues and areas.

In addition to employing those who gather information, the CIA employs intelligence analysts, economists, geographers, and other specialists in science and technology to provide additional information on foreign countries and governments. Career fields within the CIA include computer sciences, economics, engineering (especially mechanical, electrical/electronic, aerospace, nuclear, and civil engineering), foreign area studies, languages, mathematics, photographic interpretation, the physical sciences, psychology, and library science.

The CIA career development program provides orientation, training, opportunities for growth, and advancement in specialty fields as well as in general intelligence work.

A full range of clerical positions are also available with the Central Intelligence Agency, including some overseas assignments.

Places of employment and working conditions

Most CIA employees work in the Washington, D.C. area, but some positions require foreign travel or assignment for varying lengths of time. Overseas tours of duty are optional for clerical personnel and usually last for a two-year period.

The usual workweek is 40 hours, but this may vary depending on specialty field and area of assignment.

Qualifications, education, and training

General qualifications for anyone interested in working for the Central Intelligence Agency include good character, intelligence and resourcefulness, willingness to accept responsibility, and a strong motivation for public service. Applicants should be willing to serve overseas if necessary and be aware that their work must often remain anonymous. United States citizenship is required.

An undergraduate or graduate degree in an appropriate field is necessary; related work experience is a plus. Some colleges and universities take part in a cooperative education program with the CIA. Interested undergraduates who are majoring in engineering, physics, mathematics, computer science, business administration, or accounting may spend part of their time in a cooperative work program.

The CIA also has a summer intern program available to a limited number of graduate students. Students in economics, geography, political science, history, linguistics, international relations, or the specific areas of China, Southeast Asia, Latin America, Africa, the Middle East, and Russia may participate. Foreign language ability is useful, but not essential, for this program.

Applicants for clerical positions must meet the basic requirements for specific jobs and must complete an aptitude test.

A background security investigation will be completed on all accepted applicants before assignment to duty. Because this investigation takes time, applicants should apply well in advance of the time they wish to start working.

Potential and advancement

Although the Central Intelligence Agency employs a wide variety of people in many fields, active recruitment of specific specialties varies from year to year. For example, current needs for foreign language specialists are Russian, Eastern European, Middle Eastern, and Oriental. Information on current job opportunities in other fields is available from the CIA; see listings at the end of this article.

The CIA offers advancement opportunities to all employees. Formal and on-the-job training is available during early and midcareer stages, and professional level training is given not only within the CIA but also at other government training establishments and at local colleges and universities. The CIA has its own highly regarded Language Learning Center for employees who wish to study a foreign language.

For clerical employees, the CIA's Office of Training offers courses in administrative procedures, writing, employee development, and supervision and management. Off-campus courses are offered by some local universities and specialized schools at the CIA Headquarters Building; tuition costs for approved job-related courses are paid by the CIA. Foreign language training is provided for those who are to serve overseas.

Income

Employees of the Central Intelligence Agency are paid according to the federal General Schedule (GS) pay scale.

Starting salaries are GS-7 to GS-9—approximately $13,000 to $16,000—depending on qualifications. Starting salaries for clerical workers are GS-3 or GS-4 ($7,400 or $8,300) for clerk-typists; GS-4 or GS-5 ($8,300 or $9,300) for clerk-stenographers and secretaries.

Those on overseas assignments receive regular government allowances including transportation and housing.

Benefits include 13 to 26 vacation days per year, depending on years of service; 13 paid sick-leave days; and nine paid holidays.

Additional sources of information

If you are in college, see your placement officer and request an interview with the CIA representative who visits your campus from time to time, or whose regional office may be situated nearby.

Write to the Director of Personnel, Central Intelligence Agency, Washington, DC 20505. Enclose a résumé of your education and experience and ask for preliminary application forms.

Visit the CIA Recruitment Office, Ames Center Building, 1820 North Fort Myer Drive, Arlington (Rosslyn), Virginia. No appointment is necessary for an interview during weekday business hours. Employment inquiries may be made by telephoning (703)351-2028.

CITY MANAGER

The job

A city manager, usually appointed by the elected officials of a community, administers and coordinates the day-to-day activities of the community. The city manager oversees such functions as tax collection and disbursement, law enforcement, public works, budget preparation, studies of current problems, and planning for future needs. In a small city, the manager handles all functions; in a larger city, the manager usually has a number of assistants, each of whom manages a department.

City managers and their assistants supervise city employees, coordinate city programs, greet visitors, answer correspondence, prepare reports, represent the city at public hearings and meetings, analyze work procedures, and prepare budgets.

Most city managers work for small cities (under 25,000) that have a council-manager type of government. The council, which is elected, hires the manager who is then responsible for running the city as well as for hiring a staff. In cities with a mayor-council type of government, the mayor hires the city manager as his or her top administrative assistant.

A few managers work for counties and for metropolitan and regional planning bodies.

Most city managers begin as management assistants in one of the city departments such as finance, public works, or planning. Experience in several different departments is valuable and can provide a well-rounded background.

There are almost no women in this field, but this is a new and growing profession with room for people with training in a variety of disciplines that relate to the functions and problems of urban life.

Places of employment and working conditions

City managers are employed throughout the country in cities of all sizes, but job opportunities are greatest in the eastern states.

Working conditions for a city manager are usually those of an office position with considerable public contact. Most than 40 hours a week is usually required, and emergency situations and public meetings frequently involve evening and weekend work.

Qualifications, education, and training

Persons planning a career in city management must be dedicated to public service and willing to work as part of a team. They should have self-confidence, be able to analyze problems and suggest solutions, and should function well under stress. Tact and the ability to communicate well are very important.

A graduate degree is presently required even for most entry-level positions in this field. An undergraduate degree in a field such as engineering, recreation, social work, or political science should be followed by a master's degree in public or municipal administration or business administration.

Requirements in some of the 185 colleges and universities that offer advanced degrees in this field include an internship of six months to a year, in which the candidate must work in a city manager's office to gain experience.

Potential and advancement

Approximately 12,000 persons are presently employed as city managers and assistants, and the field is growing rapidly. However, job competition is expected to be very strong over the next few years, due to an increase in the number of graduates in this field.

Recent computerized management techniques for taxes, traffic control, and utility billing will create openings for those trained in finance, while increasing emphasis on broad solutions to urban social problems will result in job opportunities for those with a strong public administration background. In addition, the council-manager system of government is the fastest growing type of government in the country, and the move is toward professional, rather than elected, city management.

Generally, one begins as an assistant to a city manager or department head with promotions leading to greater responsibility. A city manager will probably work in several different types and sizes of cities in his or her career, which will further broaden the person's experience and promotion potential.

Income

Salaries for city managers depend on education, experience, job responsibility, and the size of the employing city. Salaries are generally high, ranging from $22,000 in cities of 5,000 to $50,000 in cities of 100,000 or more. Those who work as assistants earn $12,000 to $20,000 in cities of comparable size.

Benefits usually include travel expenses, and a car is often provided for official business.

Additional sources of information

The International City Management Association
1140 Connecticut Avenue, NW
Washington, DC 20036

CIVIL ENGINEER

The job

This is the oldest branch of the engineering profession. Civil engineers design and supervise construction of buildings, roads, harbors, airports, dams, tunnels and bridges, and water supply and sewage systems.

Specialties within civil engineering include structural, hydraulic, environmental (sanitary), transportation, geotechnical, and soil mechanics. Many civil engineers are in supervisory or administrative positions. They may supervise a construction site or administer a large municipal project such as highway or airport construction.

Most civil engineers work for construction companies or for federal, state, and local government agencies. Others work for public utilities, railroads, architectural firms, and engineering consulting firms. A number of them work in the nuclear energy field.

Places of employment and working conditions

Civil engineers work in all parts of the country, usually in or near major industrial and commercial centers. Some work for American firms in foreign countries.

A great deal of the civil engineer's time is spent outdoors. They sometimes work in remote areas and may have to move from place to place as they work on different projects.

Qualifications, education, and training

The ability to think analytically, a capacity for detail, and the ability to work as part of a team are all necessary. Good communication skills are important.

Mathematics and the sciences must be emphasized in high school.

A bachelor's degree in engineering is the minimum requirement in this field. In a typical curriculum, the first two years are spent in the study of basic sciences such as physics and chemistry and mathematics, introductory engineering, and some liberal arts courses. The remaining years are usually devoted to specialized engineering courses. Engineering programs can last from four to six years. Those requiring five or six years to complete may award a master's degree or may provide a cooperative plan of study plus practical work experience in a nearby industry.

Because of rapid changes in technology, many engineers continue their education throughout their careers. A graduate degree is necessary for most teaching and research positions and for many management jobs. Some persons obtain graduate degrees in business administration.

Engineering graduates usually work under the supervision of an experienced engineer or in a company training program until they become acquainted with the requirements of a particular company or industry.

All states require licensing of engineers whose work may affect life, health, or property or who offer their services to the public. Those who are licensed, about one third of all engineers, are called Registered Engineers. Requirements include graduation from an accredited engineering school, four years of experience, and a written examination.

Potential and advancement

There are about 155,000 civil engineers. Job opportunities in this field will increase somewhat because population growth will create an increasing demand for housing, transportation, power generating plants, and other energy sources.

Income

Starting salaries in private industry average $16,800 with a bachelor's degree; $18,700 with a master's degree; and $24,000 or more with a Ph.D.

The federal government pays beginners $13,657 to $20,000 depending on degree and experience. Average salary for experienced engineers federally employed is about $27,700.

Experienced engineers average $30,500 in private industry; $15,000 to $21,000 for nine-month faculty positions in colleges and universities.

Additional sources of information

American Society of Civil Engineers
345 East 47th Street
New York, NY 10017

Engineers' Council for Professional Development
345 East 47th Street
New York, NY 10017

National Society of Professional Engineers
2029 K Street, NW
Washington, DC 20006

American Society for Engineering Education
One Dupont Circle, Suite 400
Washington, DC 20036

Society of Women Engineers
United Engineering Center
345 East 47th Street
New York, NY 10017

CIVIL SERVICE WORKER, FEDERAL

The job

The federal government is the largest single employer in the United States. Above 2,750,000 civilian workers are employed in a full range of occupational and professional fields plus some that are unique to the federal government such as postal worker, foreign service officer, and internal revenue agent.

There are over 470,000 general clerical workers and 500,000 postal clerks and mail carriers employed by the federal government. About 150,000 civilians are employed in engineering and related fields, about two thirds of them in the U.S. Department of Defense. Over 120,000 accounting workers, including 35,000 professional accountants, are employed throughout the federal government, with the largest concentrations in the Department of Defense, the Treasury Department, and the General Accounting Office.

Nearly 120,000 federal civilian employees work in hospitals or other health care facilities and public health activities. Most are employed by the Veterans Administration, the Department of Defense, the Department of Education, or the Department of Health and Human Services.

The federal government employs almost 60,000 people in the field of law and another 45,000 in investigative and inspection work. Most of these jobs are in the Departments of the Treasury, Justice, and Agriculture.

About 50,000 persons work in jobs in the social sciences; 45,000 in biological and agricultural sciences; 40,000 in the physical sciences; and 15,000 in the field of mathematics.

The federal government employs over half a million blue-collar workers throughout the United States with about three quarters of them employed by the Department of Defense. Skilled craft workers in all fields and mobile equipment operators and mechanics make up a large segment of these jobs.

About 10,000 college graduates obtain federal civil services jobs each year; about one third of them are women. Even in the federal government, women have difficulty getting any higher than middle levels of management—only 1.5 percent of federal employees earning over $20,000 a year are women. Sixty-four percent of the women college graduates who worked in federal civil service jobs from 1970 to 1974 were at grades 1 through 8 (grade 18 being the highest possible); while 65.5 percent of the equally qualified men were in grades 9 and above. It remains to be seen if these statistics will change since federal jobs are not covered by affirmative action programs.

Places of employment and working conditions

Only one out of every eight (about 350,000) federal employees works in the Washington, D.C. area. They work throughout the country with the largest concentrations in California (nearly 300,000) and New York, Pennsylvania, Texas, and Illinois (over 100,000 each). About 50,000 work in the U.S. territories and foreign countries. Most federal employees work a 40-hour, 5-day week; for extra hours worked, they receive overtime pay or compensatory time off.

Working conditions vary depending on the job. Consult this section under individual job titles for working conditions appropriate to each one.

Qualifications, education, and training

The federal government usually has the same educational and experience requirements as private employers. Jobs requiring licensing, however, may have different requirements at the federal level. Check this section under each individual job description for detailed information.

Almost all federal jobs are under a merit system of one kind or another. The U.S. Civil Service Commission covers 60 percent of all federal jobs. Most of those not governed by the Civil Service requirements are covered by separate merit systems within a specific agency such as the Foreign Service of the State Department or the Federal Bureau of Investigation.

An applicant for a federal job must fulfill the minimum age, training, and experience requirements for a particular job and usually must take the appropriate competitive examination. Applicants are notified as to their eligibility or ineligibility and rating, and eligible applicants are listed according to their test scores. Job openings are filled as they occur from the three top positions on a list. Persons not chosen for immediate job openings remain on the list for a period of time and may be selected for subsequent job openings.

Potential and advancement

The federal government employs almost three million people. On the whole, federal employment will rise somewhat but not nearly as much as in state and local governments. Job opportunities in some agencies such as the Postal Service will decline. Other agencies (the Department of Defense, for example) expect to remain at present levels of employment. Agencies that deal with energy and environmental protection will probably expand. Employment opportunities for professional, administrative, and technical workers are expected to increase, while opportunities for clerical and blue-collar jobs will likely decline.

Advancement opportunities for each individual job follow the same patterns as in the private sector. The top positions in many agencies, however, are filled by presidential or congressional appointments.

Income

Information on federal government salaries for individual jobs appears under this section for most job descriptions in the book. An explanation of federal pay systems follows.

About one quarter of all federal civilian workers are paid according to the coordinated Federal Wage System. Under this system, wage rates for craft, service, and manual workers vary by locality since their hourly wage rates are based on prevailing rates paid by local private employers.

The Postal Service Schedule actually consists of several rate schedules that cover different types and levels of postal workers such as production, supervisory, technical or clerical workers, rural carriers, and postal executives. Pay schedules, except for executives, include periodic "step" increases, and most postal workers receive cost-of-living adjustments.

About half of all federal workers are paid under the General Pay Schedule, where jobs are graded according to difficulty of duties, knowledge, education, skills, and experience required; and level of responsibility. Each of the 18 grades has an entrance and maximum pay range, and employees receive within-grade pay increases for acceptable work at stipulated time periods. Within-grade increases may also be given in recognition of superior work.

Some examples of grade levels and pay ranges follow.

Graduates of two-year colleges and technical schools with no related work experience would probably begin at GS-4 level with a starting salary of $8,316 a year. The maximum amount in that grade is $10,809 a year.

Professional and administrative employees enter at GS-5 or GS-7, depending on their academic record. The GS-5 pay range is $11,243 to $14,618; the GS-7 range is $13,925 to $18,101.

Those with a master's degree or equivalent education or experience usually enter the GS-9 or GS-11 level, where pay ranges are $17,035 to $22,147 and $20,611 to $26,794, respectively.

Federal employees receive 13 days of annual leave (vacation) during each year of their first three years of employment, 20 days per year until 15 years of employment, and 26 days per year after that. Other benefits include nine paid holidays, a contributory retirement system, optional participation in group life and health insurance programs which are partly paid by the government, and government-provided training and educational programs.

Additional sources of information

State employment service offices have information on some federal job openings.

The U.S. Civil Service Commission has 62 area offices and over 100 Federal Job Information centers in various cities throughout the country. These offices announce and conduct examinations for federal jobs; they can be located under the "U.S. Government" listing in most telephone books. Job openings and local test and interview schedules are sometimes also listed in the help-wanted sections of local newspapers.

Applicants can also obtain information from the individual agency in which they are interested.

CIVIL SERVICE WORKER, MUNICIPAL AND STATE

The job

Government employees make up a significant portion of every state's work force. The range of job opportunities includes just about every occupational and professional field.

About 6.3 million government employees provide educational services including 3.5 million instructional personnel and 2.7 million administrative and support services personnel. Three fifths of these work in elementary and secondary schools administered by local governments; the remainder work for state governments, usually at college, university, and technical school levels.

About 1.2 million state and local government workers are employed in some phase of health care. This includes a full range of health care professionals such as physicians, nurses, dentists, and technical personnel.

About 750,000 persons work in general governmental control and finance activities including those employed in the administration of justice, tax collection, and general administration. Police and fire protection is supplied by 600,000 law enforcement officers and support personnel and 300,000 firemen. Most of the police and practically all of the firemen are employed by local governments.

Over 600,000 work in street and highway construction and maintenance. This includes civil engineers and surveyors, operators of construction machinery and equipment, truck drivers, carpenters, construction laborers, and highway toll collectors.

Other state and local government workers are employed in utilities (such as water), transportation, conservation and utilization of natural resources, parks and recreation, sanitation, sewage disposal, correctional institutions, public welfare, and housing. Clerical, administrative, maintenance, and custodial jobs are available in just about every agency of state and local governmment. Craft workers and security personnel will also find numerous job opportunities.

Places of employment and working conditions

About three quarters of the workers in this category are employed at the local community level. Those who work for state governments are located throughout the state, with most clerical and administrative facilities located at the state capitol.

Working conditions vary depending on the job. (Consult this section under individual job titles for working conditions appropriate to each one.)

Qualifications, education, and training

State and local governments usually require the same educational and professional backgrounds as private employers. (Check this section under each individual job description for detailed information.)

Just about all state jobs and a majority of local government jobs are filled through some type of formal civil service test or examination. Most jobs are ranked by grade with each grade level having specific educational and experience requirements and pay ranges.

Qualified applicants are notified of testing dates; the test grades (plus a score for relevant circumstances such as area of residence or veteran's preference) then determine an applicant's position on the civil service list for that position. As openings occur, they are filled from the top of the list.

Potential and advancement

Over 12 million persons are employed by state and local governments. Employment opportunities are expected to increase substantially because of population increases and the trend toward providing more social services at taxpayers' expense.

Advancement to jobs at higher grade levels for state and municipal workers is usually through civil service examinations. Promotion to other positions is also possible, but the promoted worker is usually required to pass the appropriate examination at a later date.

Income

Government pay scales are usually comparable to those in the private sector. (Check this section under individual job descriptions for detailed information on average earnings in each field.)

Additional sources of information

Anyone interested in working for a state or local government should contact the appropriate agency or departments for job information and examination dates. The local office of the state employment service can also provide job information and will usually supply a list of current openings including requirements, pay scale, and examination dates.

CLAIM REPRESENTATIVE

The job

Claim representatives, including both claim adjusters and claim examiners, investigate claims for insurance companies, negotiate settlements with policyholders, and authorize payment of claims.

Claim adjusters work for property-liability (casualty) insurance companies and usually specialize in specific types of claims such as fire, marine, or automobile. They determine whether their company is liable (that is, whether the customer's claim is a valid one covered by the customer's policy) and recommend the amount of settlement. In the course of investigating a claim, adjusters consider physical evidence, testimony of witnesses, and any applicable reports. They strive to protect their company from false or inflated claims and at the same time settle valid claims quickly and fairly. In some companies, adjusters submit their findings to *claim examiners* who review them and authorize payment.

In states with "no-fault" auto insurance, adjusters do not have to establish responsibility for a loss but must decide the amount of the loss. Many auto insurance companies employ special inside adjusters who settle smaller claims by mail or telephone or at special drive-in centers where claims are settled immediately.

Most claim adjusters work for insurance companies, but some work for independent firms that contract their services to insurance companies for a fee. These firms vary in size from local firms employing two or three adjusters to large national organizations with hundreds of adjustment specialists.

A few adjusters represent the insured rather than the insurance company. These "public" adjusters are retained by banks, financial organizations, and other businesses to negotiate settlements with insurance companies.

In life insurance companies, claim examiners are the equivalent of claim adjusters. In the course of settling a claim, an examiner might correspond with policyholders or their their families, consult medical specialists, calculate benefit payments, and review claim applicants for completeness. Questionable claims or those exceeding a specified amount would be even more thoroughly investigated by the examiner.

Claim examiners also maintain records of settled claims and prepare reports for company data processing departments. More experienced examiners serve on company committees, survey claim settlement procedures, and work to improve the efficiency of claim handling departments.

Related jobs are: Actuary, Insurance Agent and Broker, and Underwriter.

Places of employment and working conditions

Claim adjusters work in all sections of the United States, in cities and towns of all sizes. Claim examiners, on the other hand, work in the home offices of insurance companies most of which are located in and around Boston, Chicago, Dallas, New York City, Philadelphia, and San Francisco.

Adjusters make their own schedules, doing whatever is necessary to dispose of a claim promptly and fairly. Since most firms provide 24-hour claim service, adjusters are on call all the time and may work some weekends and evenings. They may be called to the site of an accident, fire, or burglary or to the scene of a riot or hurricane. They must be physically fit since they spend much of their day traveling, climbing stairs, and actively investigating claims. Much of their time is spent out-of-doors—this is not a desk job.

Claim examiners, by contrast, do have desk jobs. Their usual work-week is 35 to 40 hours, but they may work longer hours during peak claim loads or when quarterly and annual reports are prepared. They may travel occasionally in the course of their investigations and are sometimes called upon to testify in court regarding contested claims.

Qualifications, education, and training

Claim representatives should be able to communicate tactfully and effectively. They need a good memory and should enjoy working with details. Claim examiners must also be familiar with medical and legal terms, insurance laws and regulations, and have mathematical skills.

Insurance companies prefer to hire college graduates for positions as claim representatives, but will sometimes hire those with specialized experience, for example, automobile repair experience for automobile claims adjuster positions. Because of the complexity of insurance regulations and claim procedures, however, claim representatives without a college degree may advance more slowly than those with two years or more of college.

Many large insurance companies provide on-the-job training combined with home-study courses for newly hired claim adjusters and claim examiners. Throughout their careers, claim representatives continue to take a variety of courses and programs designed to certify them in many different areas of the profession.

Licensing of adjusters is required in about three quarters of the states. Requirements vary, but applicants usually must be 20 or 21 years of age and a resident of the state, complete an approved training course in insurance or loss adjusting, provide character references, pass a written examination, and file a surety bond (a bond guaranteeing performance of a contract or obligation).

Potential and advancement

About 155,000 persons are employed as claim representatives. While all indications point to continued growth of the insurance industry and a continued need for claim representatives, persons trying to enter the field will have an advantage if they have certain specialized skills. The growing trend toward drive-in claim centers and claim handling by telephone will probably reduce the demand for automobile adjusters but increase the demand for inside adjusters. Those who specialize in workers' compensation, product liability, and other types of complex business insurance will be more in demand than ever. Job opportunities for claim examiners are becoming more numerous in property-liability companies than in life insurance companies, where computers are processing more and more of the routine claims and group policy claims.

Claim representatives are promoted as they gain experience and complete courses and training programs. Those who demonstrate unusual ability or administrative skills may become department supervisors or may advance to management jobs. Some qualified adjusters, however, prefer to broaden their knowledge by transferring to other departments such as underwriting or sales.

Income

Claim adjusters working for property-liability companies have average earnings of about $14,700 a year; inside adjusters average about $11,215. Public adjusters are paid a commission usually 10 percent, of the amount of settlement.

Claim examiners in life insurance companies average about $13,870 a year, while those working for property-liability companies average $17,100. Claim supervisors in both types of insurance companies average about $18,650.

Claim representatives working for large insurance companies usually have life and health insurance and retirement plans. Paid holidays are more numerous in the insurance industry than in most other industries, and two-week paid vacations are usual after one year of service. In most large companies, employees receive three weeks of paid vacation after five years.

Additional sources of information

Insurance Information Institute
110 William Street
New York, NY 10038

American Mutual Insurance Alliance
20 North Wacker Drive
Chicago, IL 60606

National Association of Independent Insurers
Public Relations Department
2600 River Road
Des Plaines, IL 60018

National Association of Public Adjusters
1613 Munsey Building
Baltimore, MD 21202

American Council of Life Insurance
1850 K Street, NW
Washington, DC 20006

COMMUNICATIONS TECHNICIAN

The job

The installation, maintenance, and repair of communications equipment are the responsibility of communications technicians. This equipment includes telephone, telegraph, wireless, and cable equipment as well as radio, television, and radar broadcasting equipment. (Broadcasting Technicians, who are equipment operators, are covered in another job description under that title.)

Communications technicians are employed by communications systems, manufacturers of communications equipment, air lines, police and fire departments, government agencies, and radio and television studios.

Communications technicians have various duties and specialties:

Central office equipment installers handle the installation of switchboards, dialing equipment, and other equipment in the central office of a telephone company. *Station installers* and *repairmen* install and service telephone equipment in homes, offices, businesses, and telephone booths and maintain outside facilities. *PBX installers* and *repairmen*

95

work on private switchboard equipment. *Linemen* and *cable splicers* install and maintain aerial and underground wires and cables.

Radio and telephone technical operators set up and adjust overseas radio-telephone communication equipment. They contact foreign terminals and make mutually agreed upon adjustments in transmitting power, frequency, and speech levels.

In radio and television studios, a *construction technician* installs broadcasting equipment, assembles and wires units of technical equipment, and assists in testing the equipment.

Radar technicians install and service radar equipment.

Related jobs are: Broadcasting Technician, Television and Radio Service Technician.

Places of employment and working conditions

Positions for communications technicians are available throughout the United States and in many locations overseas.

Technicians usually work a 40-hour week. Emergency situations caused by bad weather or such incidents as fires or accidents may require periods of long or irregular work hours. Communications technicians are also subject to injury from electrical shocks and falls.

Qualifications, education, and training

Mechanical aptitude, manual dexterity, normal eyesight and hearing, physical stamina, and the ability to work as part of a team are necessary.

High school should include courses in mathematics, physics, and electrical shop. Hobbies that deal with electronics and communication equipment are helpful.

Some companies, especially telephone companies, provide their own training programs and require only a high school diploma. Other employers prefer a year or two of training at a technical or trade school or a junior or community college. Some communications equipment manufacturers also offer training courses.

Training received in communications operation and service in the armed forces is very valuable in civilian jobs. Correspondence courses are also available.

Because of rapid technological changes in communications equipment, technicians usually take frequent company-sponsored courses to keep themselves up-to-date. Many organizations provide tuition assistance for technicians who take work-related courses at technical schools and colleges.

Some technicians in this field are required to have a Federal Communications Commission radio operator's license. Most technical courses prepare the student for the appropriate licensing examination.

Potential and advancement

The rapidly expanding demand for communications systems and equipment of all types makes this an excellent employment field. In many areas of the country, qualified technicians are in short supply, especially in areas experiencing rapid population growth.

Experienced communications technicians can advance to supervisory positions. Advanced technical training is necessary for some positions.

Income

Telephone installers and other telephone technicians earn between $200 and $300 a week, depending on local union wage scales.

Earnings for communications technicians in other fields vary so greatly, depending on size and location of employer, that average figures are not available.

Additional sources of information

Local telephone and telegraph companies and radio and television stations can provide information on job requirements.

COMPUTER PROGRAMMER

The job

Computer programmers write detailed instructions, called programs, that list the orderly steps a computer must follow to solve a problem. Once programming is completed, the programmer runs a sample of the data to make sure the program is correct and will produce the desired information. This is called "debugging." If there are any errors, the program must be changed and rechecked until it produces the correct results. The final step is the preparation of an instruction sheet for the computer operator who will run the program.

A simple program can be written and debugged in a few days. Those that use many data files or complex mathematical formulas may require a year or more of work. On such large projects, several programmers work together under the supervision of an experienced programmer.

Programmers usually work from problem descriptions prepared by *systems analysts* who have examined the problem and determined the next steps necessary to solve it. In organizations that do not employ systems analysts, employees called *programmer-analysts* handle both functions. An *applications programmer* then writes detailed instructions for programming the data. Applications programmers usually specialize in business or scientific work.

A *systems programmer* is a specialist who maintains the general instructions (software) that control the operation of the entire computer system.

Beginners in this field spend several months working under supervision before they begin to handle all aspects of the job.

Most programmers are employed by manufacturing firms, banks, insurance companies, data processing services, utilities, and government agencies. Systems programmers usually work in research organizations, computer manufacturing firms, and large computer centers.

About 22 percent of all computer programmers are women.

Places of employment and working conditions

Programmers are employed in all areas of the country.

Most programmers work a 40-hour week, but their hours are not always 9:00 to 5:00. They may occasionally work on weekends or at other odd hours to have access to the computer when it is not needed for scheduled work.

Qualifications, education, and training

Patience, persistence, and accuracy are necessary characteristics for a programmer. Ingenuity, imagination, and the ability to think logically are also important.

High school experience should include as many mathematics courses as possible.

There are no standard training requirements for programmers. Depending on the work to be done, an employer may require only some special courses in computer programming, or a college education, or a graduate degree in computer science, mathematics, or engineering.

Computer programming courses are offered by vocational and technical schools, colleges and universities, and junior colleges. Home-study courses are also available, and a few high schools offer some training in programming.

Scientific organizations require college training; some require advanced degrees in computer science, mathematics, engineering, or the physical sciences.

Because of rapidly changing technologies, programmers take periodic training courses offered by employers, software vendors, and computer manufacturers. Like physicians, they must keep constantly abreast of the latest developments in their field. These courses also aid in advancement and promotion.

Potential and advancement

There are about 230,000 computer programmers. This is a rapidly growing field because of the expanding use of computers. Simpler programming needs will be increasingly handled by improved software so that programmers with only the most basic training will not find as many job openings as in the recent past. A strong demand will continue, however, for college graduates with a major in computer science or a related field. Graduates of two-year programs should find ample job openings in business applications.

There are many opportunities for advancement in this field. In large organizations, programmers may be promoted to lead programmers with supervisory responsibilities. Both applications programmers and systems programmers can be promoted to systems analyst positions.

Income

Programmer trainees earn about $240 to $250 a week.

Experienced systems programmers earn about $430 a week; applications programmers about $360. Lead programmers earn between $415 and $465 a week.

Programmers who work in the North and West earn more than those who work in the South. Data processing services and utility companies pay higher salaries than banks or educational institutions.

Additional sources of information

Data Processing Management Association
505 Busse Highway
Park Ridge, IL 60068

American Federation of Information Processing Societies
210 Summit Avenue
Montvale, NJ 07645

Association for Computing Machinery
1133 Avenue of the Americas
New York, NY 10036

COMPUTER SERVICE TECHNICIAN

The job

Computer systems perform a wide variety of tasks in business and industry. Keeping the systems in working order is the responsibility of computer service technicians.

Computer service technicians not only do repair work but also provide regular scheduled maintenance checks to prevent emergency breakdowns of equipment. Some computer technicians install new equipment, while others design and develop maintenance and repair schedules and manuals. Some technicians specialize in a particular computer model or system or in a certain type of repair.

Most computer service technicians are employed by the manufacturers of computer equipment or by firms that contract to provide maintenance service to a manufacturer's customers. A few are employed directly by organizations that have large computer installations.

Related jobs are: Appliance Repairer, Business Machine Service Technician, Communications Technician, Television and Radio Service Technician.

Places of employment and working conditions

Computer service technicians work out of regional offices located in major urban areas. About one quarter of all technicians work in Chicago, Los Angeles, New York, Philadelphia, and Washington, D.C.

The normal workweek is 40 hours, but large amounts of overtime are standard. Many service technicians work rotating shifts or are on call 24 hours a day because many businesses run their computers around the clock.

Qualifications, education, and training

Mechanical aptitude, manual dexterity, good eyesight and color vision, normal hearing, patience, and the ability to work without supervision are necessary. Because technicians work directly with customers, they must get along well with people.

A high school student interested in this field should take courses in mathematics, physics, and electrical shop. Hobbies that involve electronics, such as ham radio operation or building stereo equipment, are helpful.

Employers usually prefer to hire trainees with one or two years of technical training in electronics or electrical engineering. Technical and vocational schools, junior colleges, and the armed forces provide this training.

Trainees usually attend a company training center for three to six months and then complete six months to two years of on-the-job training. Because of constant technological changes in the field, all technicians normally take periodic training courses as new equipment is developed.

Experienced technicians may take advanced courses for specialization in particular systems or repairs. Some technicians study computer programming and systems analysis to broaden their general knowledge of computer operation.

Potential and advancement

There are about 50,000 computer service technicians, and the field is expanding rapidly. Since most people in the computer field are relatively young, few job openings will occur because of death or retirement; almost all openings will result from the rising demand for computers.

Experienced technicians may advance to supervisory positions or may become specialists or troubleshooters who diagnose difficult problems. Some transfer into sales.

Income

Trainees average $200 a week. Experienced technicians earn about $240.

Senior technicians with eight to ten years of experience earn $250 to $350 a week; specialists from $310 to $400.

Additional sources of information

Manufacturers of computers can provide information on job opportunities and training programs.

CONTROLLER

The job

The briefest and broadest definition of a controller (or the comptroller) is: the key financial executive who controls, analyzes, and interprets the financial results and records of a company or an organization.

The *treasurer*, on the other hand, is responsible for the receipt, custody, and properly organized disbursement of an organization's or company's funds.

Some organizations also have a *vice president of finance* who has overall financial responsibility and reports to the chief executive officer—president or chairman of the board—of the company.

A company may have one or all of these financial officers or may combine all three into one executive-level position with any of the above titles. This job description will be confined to the usual duties of a controller in an organization that has a separate treasurer position.

The controller is responsible for the design of a company's accounting system(s), the preparation of budgets and financial forecasts, internal auditing of company operations and records, controls of company funds kept by the treasurer, establishment and administration of tax policies and procedures, and preparation of reports to government agencies. Since an organization's financial operations involve the accumulation, interpretation, and storage of vast amounts of detailed information, a controller is very often in charge of the company's computerized data processing operation, too. Few women have reached the level of controller.

Places of employment and working conditions

Controllers are employed throughout the country. They work for government agencies, businesses, industry, nonprofit organizations, hospitals, and other institutions of all sizes.

As with many top-level jobs, controllers often work long hours under great pressure. Peak work loads occur when tax reports and stockholders' reports are prepared.

Qualifications, education, and training

A controller needs more than facility with mathematics and the ability to do accurate work. At this level of responsibility, good judgment, planning ability, administrative and management skills, ability to motivate other people, and communication skills must be combined with expertise in cost accounting, budgeting, taxes, and other specialized areas.

A college background in finance, accounting, economics, mathematics, or business administration is usually the basic education for this field. The majority of people who reach this level have a master's degree in business administration or a CPA (certified public accountant) certificate (see Accountant job description for information on CPA requirements).

Potential and advancement

The career paths to the post of controller are varied. Cost analysis and accounting, budgeting, tax auditing, financial analysis, planning and programming, credit collections, systems and procedures, and data processing are all training grounds for executive-level financial positions.

Once the top management level has been reached, the usual method of advancement for a controller is to transfer to a larger organization where the responsibilities are greater and more complex. Some advance by moving from a top financial position in a large organization to the chief executive post in a smaller one. About 30 percent of all chief executive officers come up through the financial area.

Income

Financial compensation at this level is excellent. Even the smallest companies pay their controllers at least $30,000 a year. In large companies, the controller very often has a six-figure income.

Additional sources of information

Financial Executives Institute
633 Third Avenue
New York, NY 10017

CREDIT INVESTIGATOR

The job

The work of a credit investigator varies greatly, depending on the employer and the size of the organization.

In a local department store extending credit in the form of a charge account or for the purchase of a home appliance, the credit investigator will probably be a clerical employee who calls the applicant's employer to verify employment and earnings and the local credit bureau to ascertain the applicant's credit rating.

In a bank or savings and loan association, the credit department is large and is usually called a loan department. Credit investigators in this setting do more in-depth analysis of a credit applicant's finances and require more information than a retail store credit department because the amounts of bank loans are usually much larger. In the case of business loans, huge sums of money may be involved. The credit investigation would probably include acquisition and analysis of a firm's records including financial statements, inventory records, details of operation, and other information.

Manufacturers, wholesalers, and distributors who extend credit to their customers also employ credit investigators. Because the sums of money involved are often very large, the credit investigation is a thorough one and often as detailed as a bank's investigation.

Additional information relative to this occupational field is contained in the job description for Credit Manager.

CREDIT MANAGER

The job

When either a business or an individual requests credit, the financial background of the requestor is investigated by the lender. Final acceptance or rejection of an application for credit is the responsibility of a credit manager.

In extending credit to a business (commercial credit), the credit manager or an assistant analyzes financial reports submitted by the applicant, checks the firm's credit record, and checks with banks or other institutions that handle the firm's accounts.

In extending credit to individuals (consumer credit), credit managers must rely on personal interviews, credit bureau reports, and the applicant's bank to provide relevant information.

In large companies, credit managers analyze the information gathered by application clerks or credit investigators and that provided in financial reports. In small companies, credit managers do much of the information gathering themselves and may also be involved in collecting delinquent accounts. In some large organizations, executive-level credit managers formulate company credit policies and establish credit department procedures.

About one half of all credit managers are employed in wholesale and retail trade; another one third work for manufacturing firms and financial institutions.

Beginners in this field usually gain experience as management trainees. They learn to deal with credit bureaus, banks, and other businesses and receive a thorough grounding in the company's credit procedures and policies.

About 40 percent of all credit managers are women. Now that new laws have given women equality in credit ratings, some firms are seeking women to work in credit management to encourage other women to seek customer credit.

Related jobs are: Accountant, Bank Officer, Economist.

Places of employment and working conditions

Credit managers work in all areas of the country in communities of all sizes. Most job opportunities are in urban areas having many financial and business firms.

This is an office job and usually consists of a 35- to 40-hour week. In some businesses, there may be seasonal peak work loads that require overtime.

Qualifications, education, and training

The ability to analyze and draw conclusions, a pleasant personality, and communication skills are necessary for this career.

High school courses in business, bookkeeping, and public speaking are helpful. Summer or part-time jobs in business offices or credit agencies provide valuable experience.

Even though some employers will promote high school graduates to the position of credit manager if they have substantial experience in credit collection or processing of credit information, a college degree is becoming inceasingly important, even for entry-level jobs in credit management. A bachelor's degree in business administration, economics, accounting, or liberal arts with a business or accounting major is the preferred educational background.

Some professional organizations in the credit and finance field offer formal training programs that include home-study courses, college courses, or other special instruction. These programs aid beginners who are developing their skills and help experienced credit managers keep abreast of new developments.

Potential and advancement

There are about 53,000 credit managers, and the field is expected to have only slow growth through the 1980s. The use of computers for storing and retrieving information and telecommunications networks that give retail outlets access to centralized credit information will speed up the credit investigation process; the use of bank and credit cards instead of individual charge accounts will mean the reduction or elimination of many credit departments. The best job opportunities will be in the area of commercial, rather than consumer, credit.

Advancement is limited in small and medium-sized companies, but, in large companies, credit managers can advance to top executive positions.

Income

Credit manager trainees with a college degree earn between $11,000 and $12,000 a year. Assistant credit managers earn between $13,000 and $16,000. Credit managers average $20,000. Those in top-level positions often earn $40,000 a year or more.

Additional sources of information

International Consumer Credit Association
375 Jackson Avenue
St. Louis, MO 63130

National Consumer Finance Association
1000 16th Street, NW
Washington, DC 20036

National Association of Credit Management
475 Park Avenue, South
New York, NY 10016

CRIMINOLOGIST

The job

The field of criminology broadly covers all those who work in law enforcement, criminal courts, prisons and other correctional institutions, and counseling and rehabilitation programs for offenders. Many jobs in these categories are covered elsewhere in this book. This job description, however, focuses on the term "criminologist" as it applies to those who are involved in the scientific investigation of crime through analysis of evidence.

The scientific gathering, investigation, and evaluation of evidence is known as criminalistics, and those who work in this field are called *forensic scientists*. These technical experts, including specially trained police officers and detectives, carefully search victims, vehicles, and scenes of crimes. They take photographs, make sketches, lift fingerprints, make casts of footprints and tire tracks, and gather samples of any other relevant materials.

Once the evidence has been gathered, scientists and technicians trained in various natural sciences analyze it along with reports from medical examiners and pathologists. Other specialists interview victims to prepare composite pictures or psychological profiles of the criminal. Those who specialize in firearms and ballistics conduct tests that identify weapons used in specific crimes.

Forensic specialists also include handwriting experts, fingerprint and voiceprint specialists, polygraphy (lie detector) examiners and odontologists (teeth and bite-mark specialists).

Almost all the people in this field work for federal, state, or local law enforcement and investigative agencies. Municipal and state police departments all have investigative responsibilities that include the processing of evidence. Some employ civilian scientists and technicians, but many utilize specially trained police officers in police crime laboratories.

The federal government employs forensic scientists in a number of agencies including the FBI and the Secret Service.

Related jobs are: Chemist, Medical Laboratory Technologist, Biochemist, Police Officer.

Places of employment and working conditions

Forensic scientists may be on call at all hours and may be required to work out-of-doors or in unpleasant conditions when gathering evidence.

Qualifications, education, and training

Personal traits of curiosity, ability to work with detail, patience, and good eyesight and color vision are necessary.

High school should include mathematics and science courses.

College training depends on the specialty field selected. A degree in chemistry, biology, electronics, or whatever related field is appropriate should be obtained. Course work in forensic science is offered by some colleges and by law enforcement training programs and police departments.

Potential and advancement

The increasing sophistication of crime detection and investigative procedures will mean growth of job opportunities for those trained in the scientific methods necessary. Growth in population and the resulting increase in crime will increase the demand for qualified forensic scientists.

Income

Crime lab personnel earn between $10,000 and $17,000 a year. Some specialists, however, have higher earnings.

Additional sources of information

Federal Bureau of Investigation
U.S. Department of Justice
Washington, DC 20535

American Society of Criminology
1314 Kinnear Road
Columbus, OH 43212

DANCER

The job

Professional dancers perform classical ballet, modern dance, and other forms of dance; work in opera, musical comedy, movies, and television; and teach dancing. Some specially trained dance teachers also use dance therapy in working with the mentally ill.

Dancers who perform lead a very demanding life with little job security. Shows can close unexpectedly and movie and television assignments are of short duration. Unemployment rates are high, and even highly qualified dancers find it difficult to obtain year-round work. Dancers who are part of an established dance company or who are in a long-running hit show have the most stable performing life. Many dancers take part-time jobs to support themselves between dancing assignments, and those who are qualified to teach often combine teaching and performing.

Dancers who teach full time have the most stable working life. Those who teach at colleges and universities have the same schedule as other faculty members. Others teach in private studios, professional dancing schools, and dance companies. Those who work for dance companies also travel with the group when it goes on tour.

Dancers who create dance routines or new ballets are called *choreographers*. They usually have experience as performers and can continue their careers as choreographers long after their active performing years. *Dance directors* train dancers in new routines or productions.

Dancers who perform usually are members of one of the unions affiliated with the Associated Actors and Artists of America (AFL—CIO).

Eighty-five percent of all dancers are women. In ballet and modern dance, however, the division is about even, with 50 percent of the dancers being male.

Places of employment and working conditions

New York City is *the* city for performing dancers. Other cities that provide substantial numbers of job opportunities are Boston, Philadelphia, Miami, Cincinnati, Chicago, Minneapolis, Houston, Salt Lake City, Seattle, Los Angeles, and San Francisco.

Just about every town and city has at least one dancing school that employs teachers. Job openings for dancing teachers also exist in colleges and universities and in secondary schools, dance companies, and private studios.

A dancer's life is one of rigorous practice and self-discipline, with strict dieting a constant factor. Performances are scheduled on evenings and weekends, and lessons and practice take up daytime hours, leaving little time for personal life. Heavy travel schedules and the unstable nature of show business can drain a performer's physical and emotional strength. The physical demands of this career mean that a dancer's active performing career is usually over by age 35.

Qualifications, education, and training

Good health and physical stamina are absolutely essential for a dancer. Body build and height should be average with good feet and normal arches. Agility, grace, creativity, and a feeling for music are also necessary. Dancers should also be able to take direction and function as part of a group.

Selection of a good professional dance school is very important. Serious training for a dancer begins before the age of 12. In ballet, training must begin even earlier, at about age 7. Most dancers are ready for professional auditions by age 17 or 18, but training never ends. Ten to 12 lessons a week and many hours of practice make up the life of a dancer, even when performing with a dance company or in a show.

Because of the strenuous training schedule, a dancer's general education may suffer. Some dancers solve this problem by taking correspondence courses. In addition to dancing, professional dancing schools usually teach music, literature, and history to aid students in dramatic interpretation of the dance.

An alternative to professional school training is a college or university degree in dance. Bachelor's and master's degrees are usually offered in the departments of physical education, music, theater, or fine arts. A college degree is usually necessary for teaching at the college or university level but is not required for teaching in a professional school or dance studio where performing experience is preferred. College-trained dancers who wait to begin a performing career until graduation from college may find themselves at a disadvantage when competing with beginners of 17 or 18.

Potential and advancement

There are about 8,000 dancers performing on stage, screen, and television, and many others are involved in teaching. This is a field where qualified applicants always exceed the number of job openings. The best employment opportunities are in teaching.

Income

Basic agreements between unions and producers specify minimum wages, working hours, and other employment conditions, but individual contracts signed by each dancer with a producer may be favorable.

Dancers in opera and other stage productions earn about $300 a week. Ballet dancers are usually paid per performance: about $70 as part of a group, $110 for a solo. Movie and television rates are higher, but the engagements are brief and the work is not steady. Dancers on tour receive about $35 a day for living expenses and the employer provides transportation.

The normal workweek for a dancer under a union contract is 30 hours (6 hours per day maximum) of rehearsals and performances. Extra compensation is paid for any additional hours worked.

Dancers who teach earn salaries that vary with location, prestige of the school or dance company for which they work, and personal reputation of the teacher. At colleges and universities, dance teachers earn the same salaries as other faculty members.

Additional sources of information

National Dance Association
American Alliance for Health, Physical Education and Recreation
1201 16th Street, NW
Washington, DC 20036

American Dance Guild
1619 Broadway, Room 603
New York, NY 10019

Ballet Society
New York State Theater
1865 Broadway
New York, NY 10023

DENTAL ASSISTANT

The job

Dental assistants work with dentists and oral hygienists as they examine and treat patients. They are usually employed in private dental offices and often combine office duties such as making appointments, maintaining patient records, and billing with chair-side assisting.

Dental assistants prepare instruments and materials for treatment procedures, process dental X-ray films, sterilize instruments, prepare plaster casts of teeth from impressions taken by the dentists, and sometimes provide oral health instructions to patients. In some states, they are permitted to apply medications to teeth and gums, remove excess filling materials from surfaces of teeth, and fit rubber isolation dams on individual teeth before treatment by the dentist.

Dental assistants are also employed in dental schools, hospital dental departments, state and local public health departments, and private clinics. The federal government employs them in the Public Health Service, the Veterans Administration, and the armed forces.

Most dental assistants are women. Opportunities for part-time work are numerous making this a good field for people with family responsibilities.

A related job is: Dental Hygienist

Places of employment and working conditions

Dental assistants are employed in communities of all sizes with the most job opportunities in large metropolitan areas.

A 40-hour workweek is usual for full-time dental assistants, but this includes some evening and Saturday hours in most dental offices.

Qualifications, education, and training

Neatness and the ability to help people relax are important personal qualities.

High school courses in biology, chemistry, health, typing, and office practices are helpful.

Most dental assistants acquire their skills on the job. Office skills often provide entry into a dental office where a beginner handles appointments, acts as receptionist, and performs routine clerical and record-keeping chores. Dental assisting skills are then acquired over a period of time.

An increasing number of dental assistants are acquiring their training in formal programs at junior and community colleges, and vocational and technical schools. Most of these programs require one year to complete. Two-year programs include some liberal arts courses and offer an associate degree upon completion. Some private schools offer four- to six-month courses in dental assisting, but these are not accredited by the American Dental Association (ADA). Dental assistants who receive their training in the armed forces usually qualify for civilian jobs.

An ADA-accredited correspondence course is also available. It is equivalent to one year of academic study.

Graduates of accredited programs may receive professional recognition by completing an examination given by the Certifying Board of the American Dental Assistants Association. They are then designated as Certified Dental Assistants.

Potential and advancement

There are about 135,000 people working as dental assistants; 10 percent work part-time. Job opportunities should be excellent for the future, especially for graduates of formal training programs.

Dental assistants in large dental offices or clinics are sometimes promoted to supervisory positions. Some advance by fulfilling the educational requirements necessary to become oral hygienists.

Income

Salaries vary widely from community to community and depend on training and experience, job responsibilities and duties, and size of dental practice.

Dental assistants employed by the federal government average $10,500 a year.

Additional sources of information

American Dental Assistants Association
211 East Chicago Avenue
Chicago, IL 60611

Division of Dentistry
Public Health Service
U.S. Department of Health, Education, and Welfare
9000 Rockville Pike
Bethesda, MD 20014

DENTAL HYGIENIST

The job

Dental hygienists are involved in both clinical dental work and education with specific responsibilities governed by the state in which the hygienist is employed.

Working as part of a dental health team under the supervision of a dentist, a dental hygienist may: clean and polish a patient's teeth, removing deposits and stains at the same time; apply medication for the prevention of tooth decay; take and develop X rays; make model impressions of teeth for study; take medical and dental histories; and provide instruction for patient self-care, diet, and nutrition. In some states, pain control and restorative procedures may also be performed by dental hygienists.

Some dental hygienists work in school systems where they examine students' teeth, assist dentists in determining necessary dental treatment, and report their findings to parents. They give instruction in proper mouth care and develop classroom or assembly programs on oral health.

Most dental hygienists are employed in private dental offices; many are employed part-time.

Other employers are: public health agencies, industrial plants, clinics and hospitals, dental hygienist schools, the federal government, and the U.S. armed forces (those with a bachelor's degree are commissioned officers). A few dental hygienists are involved in research projects.

Places of employment and working conditions

Dental hygienists work in communities of all sizes.

They usually work a 35- to 40-hour workweek; those employed by a dentist in private practice usually have some weekend and evening hours. Dental hygienists are required to stand for a good part of the working day.

Certain health protection procedures are important for anyone working in this field. These include regular medical checkups and strict adherence to established procedures for disinfection and use of X-ray equipment.

Qualifications, education, and training

An enjoyment of people and the ability to put a patient at ease are strong assets. Manual dexterity is necessary. Good health, personal cleanliness and neatness, and stamina are very important.

High school courses recommended for anyone interested in a career in this field include biology, chemistry, health, and mathematics.

Competition for admission to dental hygienist schools is keen. Some hygienist schools that offer a bachelor's degree require two prior years of college. Dental hygienist training obtained in the armed forces may be accepted for partial credit by accredited dental hygienist programs, but armed forces training is not sufficient by itself for passing state licensing examinations. Many schools require an aptitude test given by the American Dental Hygienists' Association.

There are 182 schools of dental hygiene in the United States that are accredited by the American Dental Association. Students in dental hygienist programs study anatomy, physiology, chemistry, pharmacology, nutrition, tissue structure, gum diseases, dental materials, and clinical dental hygiene. Liberal arts courses are also part of the program. Most programs grant an associate's degree with some schools awarding a bachelor's degree. Eighteen schools offer master's degree programs in dental hygiene or related fields.

Licensing is required for all dental hygienists; most states require graduation from an accredited dental hygienist school as well as written and clinical examination. To pass the clinical examination, the applicant for licensing is tested on proficiency in performing dental hygiene procedures. Most states will accept a passing grade on the written examination given by the National Board of Dental Examiners as part of the licensing requirement.

Potential and advancement

About 27,000 persons work as dental hygienists.

This is a field where current job openings outnumber qualified graduates, and the employment outlook for potential dental hygienists is excellent. An expanding population, increased participation in dental insurance plans, more group practice by dentists, and dental care programs for children will all contribute to a still greater demand for trained dental hygienists in the future. There will also be many opportunities for dental hygienists who desire part-time work and for those willing to work in rural areas.

Income

Dental hygienists working in private dental offices are usually salaried. Some are paid on a commission basis for work performed or a combination of commission and salary.

Dental hygienists in private offices average about $13,000 a year. The average for those employed by the federal government is $12,100.

Additional sources of information

Office of Education
American Dental Hygienists' Association
211 East Chicago Avenue
Chicago, IL 60611

Division of Dentistry
Public Health Service
U.S. Department of Health and Human Services
9000 Rockville Pike
Bethesda, MD 20014

DENTIST

The job

Graduates of approved dental schools are entitled to use the designations D.D.S. (Doctor of Dental Surgery) or D.M.D. (Doctor of Dental Medicine).

Most dentists are general practitioners who provide many types of dental care. They examine teeth and mouth tissues to diagnose and treat any diseases or abnormalities of the teeth, gums, supporting bones, and surrounding tissues. They extract teeth, fill cavities, design and insert dentures and inlays, and perform surgery. The dentist, or someone on his or her staff, takes dental and medical histories, cleans teeth, and provides instructions on proper diet and cleanliness to preserve dental health.

About 10 percent of all dentists are specialists. The two largest fields are made up of *orthodontists,* who straighten teeth, and *oral surgeons,* who operate on the mouth and jaws. Other specialties are pedodontics (dentistry for children), periodontics (treatment of the gums), prosthodontics (artificial teeth and dentures), endodontics (root canal therapy), oral pathology (diseases of the mouth), and public health dentistry.

Close to 7,000 dentists are employed by the federal government. These include over 1,500 dentists who work in hospitals and clinics of the Veterans Administration or who serve as commissioned officers in the U.S. Public Health Service. Over 5,000 serve as commissioned officers in the armed forces, where they enter as captains in the army and air force and as lieutenants in the navy.

Qualifications, education, and training

Students interested in dentistry as a career should possess a high degree of manual dexterity and scientific ability and have good visual memory and excellent judgment of space and shape.

High school courses should include biology, chemistry, health, and mathematics.

Dental education is very expensive because of the length of time required to earn a dental degree. From two to four years of pre-dental college work in the sciences and humanities is required by dental schools with most successful applicants having a bachelor's or master's degree. Since competition for admission is stiff, dental schools give considerable weight to the amount of pre-dental education and to college grades. Schools also require personal interviews and recommendations as well as completion of the admission testing program used by all dental schools. In addition, state-supported dental schools usually give preference to residents of the state.

Dental school training lasts four academic years after college or, in some dental colleges, three calendar years. The first two years consist of classroom instruction and laboratory work in anatomy, microbiology, biochemistry, physiology, clinical sciences, and preclinical technique. The remainder of the training period is spent in actual treatment of patients.

Federal assistance in the construction of dental training facilities has resulted in expanding educational facilities that can accommodate the growing number of dental school enrollments. Federal loans and scholarships are also available to dental students who argree to serve a minimum of two years for the federal government upon graduation.

A license to practice is required by all states and the District of Columbia. Requirements include a degree from a dental school approved by the American Dental Association and written and practical examinations. A passing grade on the written examination given by the National Board of Dental Examiners is accepted by most states as fulfilling part of the licensing requirements; 21 states will grant a license without examination to dentists already licensed by another state.

In 14 states, dentists who wish to specialize must have two or three years of graduate training and, in some cases, pass an additional state examination. In the remaining states, a licensed dentist may engage in general or specialized dentistry. In these states, the additional education is also necessary to specialize; however, specialists are regulated by the state dental profession rather than by state licensing.

Potential and advancement

There are about 12,000 active dentists, 90 percent of them in private practice. The demand for dentists is expected to grow because of population growth, increased awareness of the necessity of dental health, and the expansion of prepaid dental insurance benefits to employees in many industries.

Income

Dentists setting up a new practice can look forward to a few lean years in the beginning. As the practice grows, income will rise rapidly with average yearly earnings around $50,000.

A practice can usually be developed most quickly in small towns where there is less competition from established dentists. Over the long run, however, earnings of dentists in urban areas are higher than earnings in small towns. Specialists generally earn much more than general practitioners, whatever the location.

Experienced dentists working for the federal government average about $39,500, with newly graduated dentists starting at about $19,300 a year.

Additional sources of information

American Dental Association
Council on Dental Education
211 East Chicago Avenue
Chicago, IL 60611

American Association of Dental Schools
1625 Massachusetts Avenue, NW
Washington, DC 20036

Division of Dentistry
Public Health Service
U.S. Department of Health and Human Services
9000 Rockville Pike
Bethesda, MD 20014

DIETICIAN

The job

Dieticians plan nutritious and appetizing meals, supervise the preparation and service of food, and manage the purchasing and accounting for their department. Others are involved in research and education.

More than half of all dieticians are employed in hospitals, nursing homes, and other health care facilities. Colleges, universities, and school systems. Restaurants and cafeterias, large companies that provide food service for their employees, and food processors and manufacturers also employ dieticians.

Some serve as commissioned officers in the armed forces. The federal government also employs dieticians in Veterans Administration hospitals and in the U.S. Public Health Service.

Clinical dieticians form the largest group of dieticians. They plan the diets and supervise the service of meals to meet the various nutritional needs of patients in hospitals, nursing homes, and clinics. They confer with doctors and instruct patients and their families on diet requirements and food preparation.

Administrative dieticians manage large-scale meal planning and preparation. They purchase food, equipment, and supplies; enforce safety and sanitary regulations; and train and direct food service and supervisory workers. If they are directors of a dietetic department, they may also have budgeting responsibilities, coordinate dietetic service activities with other departments, and set department policy. In a small institution, the duties of administrative and clinical dieticians are usually combined into one position.

Research dieticians evaluate the dietary requirements of specific groups such as the aged, space travelers, or those with a chronic disease. They also do research in food management and service systems and equipment. *Dietetic educators* teach in medical, dental, and nursing schools.

Nutritionists provide counseling in proper nutrition practices. They work in food industries, educational and health facilities, agricultural agencies, welfare agencies, and community health programs.

Ninety percent of all dieticians are women. The fact that small hospitals, other small institutions, and local school systems offer opportunities for part-time work in this field makes it attractive to people with family responsibilities.

Places of employment and working conditions

Dieticians are employed throughout the country with most job opportunities in large metropolitan areas and in areas with large colleges and universities.

Most universities work a 40-hour week but this usually includes some weekend hours.

Qualifications, education, and training

Anyone interested in this career field should have scientific aptitude, organizational and administrative ability, and the ability to work well with people.

High school courses should include biology, chemistry, home economics, mathematics, and some business courses, if possible.

A bachelor's degree in the home economics department with a major in foods and nutrition or institutional management is the basic requirement for a dietician.

A six- to 12-month internship or a one- to two-year traineeship program should also be completed by any dietician who wants professional recognition. These programs consist primarily of clinical experience under the direction of a qualified dietician. Some colleges and universities have coordinated undergraduate programs that enable students to complete both the clinical and bachelor's degree requirements in four years.

Vocational and technical schools as well as junior colleges also offer training in dietetic services. Students who complete these training courses can work as dietetic assistants or technicians, and usually find ample job opportunities.

The American Dietetic Association (ADA) registers dieticians who meet their established qualifications. The designation Registered Dietician (RD) is an acknowledgement of a dietician's competence and professional status.

Potential and advancement

About 45,000 people work as dieticians. Job opportunities, both full- and part-time, should be plentiful, as job openings in this field exceed the number of qualified dieticians.

Dieticians usually advance by moving to larger institutions. In a large institution, they may advance to director of the dietetic department. Advancement in research and teaching positions usually requires a graduate degree.

Income

Beginners in this field earn about $12,600 a year. Experienced dieticians earn from $15,000 to $30,000 a year.

Additional sources of information

The American Dietetic Association
430 North Michigan Avenue
Chicago, IL 60611

The U.S. Civil Service Commission
Washington, DC 20415

DRAFTER

The job

Drafters prepare detailed drawings from rough sketches, specifications, and calculations made by engineers, architects, designers, and scientists. Work completed by a drafter usually includes a detailed view of the object from all sizes, specifications for materials to be used, and procedures to be followed. Any other information necessary to carry out the job is also included by the drafter.

Drafters usually specialize in a particular field such as mechanical, electronic, structural, architectural, electrical, or aeronautical drafting. They are classified according to the work they do and their level of responsibility. *Senior drafters* translate preliminary drawings and plans into design layouts—scale drawings of the object to be built. *Detailers* draw each part shown on the layout giving dimensions, materials, and other information. *Checkers* examine drawings and specifications for errors. Supervised by experienced drafters, *tracers* make minor corrections and trace drawings for reproduction on paper or plastic film. Beginners usually start as tracers or junior drafters and work their way up through checker and detailer positions.

Ninety percent of all drafters work in private industry. Engineering and architectural firms employ the most; other large employers are fabricated metals, electrical equipment, machinery, and construction firms. About 20,000 drafters work for federal, state, and local government agencies. The U.S. Defense Department is the main federal employer; state and local governments employ drafters mainly in highway and public works departments.

Places of employment and working conditions

Drafters work in all areas of the country with the largest concentrations in industrialized areas.

Working areas are usually pleasant, but drafters do very detailed work and must often sit for long periods of time.

Qualifications, education, and training

Drafters need good eyesight, manual dexterity, and drawing ability and must be able to do accurate, detailed work. They must have the ability to work as part of a team. In some specialized fields, artistic ability is also necessary.

High school courses should include mechanical drawing, science, and mathematics. Shop skills are also helpful.

121

Drafting skills may be acquired in several ways. Vocational and technical high schools provide enough training for entry-level jobs at companies with on-the-job training programs. Technical institutes, junior and community colleges, and extension divisions of universities provide training for full-time and evening students. The armed forces also train drafters.

Potential and advancement

There are about 320,000 drafters and the field is expected to grow substantially. Job opportunities should be good into the mid-1980s with the best job opportunities for those with an associate (two-year) degree or other formal training.

Experienced drafters can advance to senior drafter and supervisory positions. Some drafters become independent designers or continue their education to transfer to engineering positions.

Income

In private industry, experienced drafters average $11,200 to $13,700 a year; senior drafters about $16,900. Average federal government salaries are about $12,200.

Additional sources of information

American Institute for Design and Drafting
3119 Price Road
Bartlesville, OK 74003

International Federation of Professional and
  Technical Engineers
1126 16th Street, NW
Washington, DC 20036

ECONOMIST

The job

Economists study and analyze the relationship between the supply and demand of goods and services and how they are produced, distributed, and consumed.

About three fourths of all economists work in private industry of businesses such as manufacturing firms, banks, insurance companies, securities and investment firms, and management consulting firms. They provide information to management that affects decisions on marketing and pricing of company products, long- and short-term economic forecasts, and the effect of government policies on business.

Ten percent of all economists are employed by colleges and universities where they teach or are engaged in research and writing. These economists are often called upon to act as consultants to business firms and government agencies.

Economists employed in government prepare studies to assess economic conditions and the need for changes in government policies. They usually work in the fields of agriculture, forestry, business, finance, labor, transportation, and international trade and development.

Although there are a few very famous women economists in the United States today, women are not very well represented in this field.

Places of employment and working conditions

Economists work in all large cities and in university towns. The largest concentrations are in the New York City and Washington, D.C. metropolitan areas.

Qualifications, education, and training

Anyone interested in this career field should be able to work accurately and in detail since economics entails careful analysis of data. Good communications skills are also necessary.

High school should include as many mathematics courses as possible.

A college major in economics, mathematics, or a related social science is the basic preparation for a career in economics. Students should also study statistics and computer science. A bachelor's degree is sufficient for many beginning research, administrative, management trainee, and sales jobs.

Graduate training in a specialty area such as advanced economic theory, labor economics, or international economics is necessary for college teaching positions. The larger colleges and universities require a Ph.D.

Potential and advancement

There are about 115,000 economists in the United States. Some growth is expected in this field, but not all areas of economics will experience the same rate of growth. Colleges and universities will provide job openings on a limited basis, usually to replace economists who retire or die. Federal job opportunities should increase slowly; state and local governments will offer more opportunities. Private industry and business will continue to provide the largest number of job openings.

Advancement in this field usually requires advanced degrees.

Income

New graduates with a bachelor's degree earn from $12,200 to $16,200 a year. Those with a Ph.D. degree start at about $13,300 for a nine-month academic year at colleges and universities; from $20,000 to $24,000 in private industry or business; $19,263 in government.

Additional sources of information

American Economic Association
1313 21st Avenue, South
Nashville, TN 37212

National Association of Business Economists
Suite 201
28349 Chagrin Blvd.
Cleveland, OH 44122

EDITOR, BOOK PUBLISHING

The job

An editor has two basic functions: to work with the author in the preparation of the author's work for publication and to prepare the manuscript for the various phases of the production process. Because no one person could handle all the editorial details involved in publication, specific areas of responsibility are usually assigned to individual members of an editorial staff.

The *editor-in-chief,* sometimes called executive editor, manages the editorial department, organizes the editorial staff, sets the budget, and makes key decisions on editorial policy. Editors function within the financial and policy goals of the publisher and editor-in-chief. They work with authors, agents, and other publishers; develop authors and manuscripts; and prepare contracts. Editors have titles in accordance with their seniority. After the editor-in-chief and executive editor, *senior editors* have the most seniority, followed by *full editors, associate editors,* and *assistant editors.*

In some publishing houses, there is an added distinction between *acquisitions editors* and *production editors* or *project editors.* Acquisitions editors scout for manuscripts and read and evaluate submissions. Production or project editors edit the manuscript and work with production and art department personnel to turn the manuscript into a finished book.

A *managing editor* coordinates all editorial functions on each project and acts as a traffic manager, seeing that all production schedules are met. A *copy editor* does a careful reading of the manuscript with attention to grammar, spelling, and punctuation as well as to coherence, arrangement, and accuracy. The copy editor marks all necessary directions for the typesetter and may query (question) the author on any material that is not clear.

Editorial assistants handle incoming manuscripts, give a first reading to unsolicited ones, return rejected manuscripts, and handle clerical duties.

An important job in the editorial and production processes is that of the *proofreader,* who checks material after it has been set into type. The proofreader checks the typeset copy against the copy edited manuscript to make sure that the typesetter has set the material exactly as indicated. The proofreader is expected to catch any mistakes in spelling, design specifications, or other printer's errors, as well as any errors of grammar or discrepancies overlooked by the copy editor. Although proofreading is a specialty in itself, most editors have done their share of it at some point in the careers.

Although, in the past, men have generally held the higher-paid, executive editorial positions, and women have performed the lower-level editorial functions, this situation is changing. Now, women compete with men for top management positions and generally earn equal, or near equal, salaries.

Places of employment and working conditions

Every city has some job opportunities for editors. The biggest publishing center is New York followed by Philadelphia, Boston, Chicago, Los Angeles, San Francisco, and Washington, D.C. Most college communities also provide a number of job openings in this field.

The usual workweek is 40 hours, but production deadlines and large work loads frequently make overtime necessary.

Qualifications, education, and training

The ability to work with people, tact, an ability to recognize not only what is well written but also what will sell, attention to detail, good judgment, and excellent communication skills are necessary.

High school courses in English are very important, but a student interested in this field should also get a well-rounded education to prepare for college. Typing is a must.

Liberal arts with a major in English, or a bachelor's degree in journalism is the usual preparation for this field. Textbook, scientific, and technical publishers usually require a background in specific subject areas as well as proficiency in English.

Potential and advancement

There are about 6,000 book publishers that employ editors. Since there is always an overabundance of English and journalism majors seeking jobs in this field, the best job prospects are with small publishers, especially for beginners.

Promotion up through the various editorial positions occurs as an editor gains experience, but advancement in this field very often takes the form of moving to a larger company.

Income

The publishing field is not a well-paid field on the whole. Salaries are low compared to other fields that require comparable education and experience.

Beginning editorial positions pay $8,000 to $10,000 a year. Assistant editors and junior copy editors earn $10,000 to $12,000.

Full editors earn $17,000 and up; a few earn as much as $30,000 a year.

Additional sources of information

Association of American Publishers, Inc.
One Park Avenue
New York, NY 10016

EDITOR, NEWSPAPER AND MAGAZINE

The job

The editorial positions and responsibilities on a newspaper differ in many respects from those in book publishing; those in magazine publishing cover aspects of both publishing fields. (See the job description for Editor).

The editor or *editor-in-chief* of a magazine or newspaper sets general editorial policy in accordance with the wishes of the publisher, who may also be the editor. The editor may write some or all of the editorials and may be involved to varying degrees in the daily operation of the paper or magazine.

A *managing editor* directs and supervises the day-to-day operation of the publication. On a newspaper, the managing editor usually has the responsibility of selecting the news stories that will receive top play. Some newspapers and magazines also have an *executive editor* whose responsibilities lie between those of the editor and the managing editor, taking some of the work load from each job.

On a newspaper, the *city editor* directs local and area news coverage. He or she schedules reporters and assigns the news stories they are to cover. The city editor also supervises the rewrite staff. The *wire editor* handles the national and foreign news. On some papers, a *news editor* rather than the managing editor decides on the final mix of local, national, and foreign news and on which stories will receive top play. Weekly news magazines also have foreign and news editors.

The *makeup editor* on a newspaper or magazine is responsible for page layout. On a newspaper, the makeup editor must be able to work swiftly to meet deadlines and may have to remake pages at the last minute when late-breaking news bumps previously positioned stories.

Both magazines and newspapers employ *copy editors,* or *copy-readers,* who prepare all material for typesetting. They correct grammar, spelling, and punctuation; check names, dates, and other facts; and write headlines to go with each item or article. Some copy editors also handle page layout and photo editing. On a daily newspaper, all of this must be done quickly to meet production deadlines.

Various special editorial positions may include: women's editor, sports editor, financial editor, food editor, and many others. These editors have responsibility for news and features in their specialty area and sometimes supervise large staffs.

Women are being hired by newspapers and magazines in growing numbers. Once relegated to handling the women's pages and food sections, women now handle politics, economics, sports, and other topics on an equal footing with men.

Places of employment and working conditions

Large metropolitan areas provide the most opportunities for newspaper and magazine editors, but opportunities exist throughout the country in communities of all sizes.

Constant deadline pressure is a fact of life for newspaper editors and, to a lesser extent, magazine editors. For newspaper and news magazine editors, personal plans must often be subordinated to the demands of the job. The pace and pressure can be physically and emotionally wearing.

Although the workweek is supposed to be about 40 hours, very often this is not the case, since important news stories can mean longer hours and irregular schedules. Those who work on morning papers usually work evening hours.

Qualifications, education, and training

A newspaper or magazine editor needs a sense of what is important and interesting to the reader. An excellent command of the English language, management skills, good judgment, and the ability to motivate people are necessary skills.

A broad high school curriculum with emphasis on the development of communication skills is important. Experience on school publications or as a "stringer" (covering local events such as sports for several newspapers) can provide valuable background. Typing is a must.

College is very important for anyone interested in working as an editor. A liberal arts degree or a degree in journalism is the usual preparation with employers about evenly divided on which they prefer.

Potential and advancement

There are about 1,750 daily and 9,000 weekly newspapers as well as 1,200 consumer magazines, 2,500 business publications, and 8,000 house organs (internal publications of a business) that employ editors. Competition for all editorial jobs on large newspapers and magazines is the norm; publications in smaller communities and in areas away from large metropolitan areas offer the best employment opportunities. Beginners will find the best opportunities on small magazines and weekly newspapers where they can accumulate experience in a variety of editorial functions.

Promotion in this field is usually up through the ranks, with many editors starting as reporters, feature writers, and rewriters. Advancement also takes the form of movement to larger publications or larger cities.

Income

Beginners average about $150 to $200 a week, less on small papers and magazines, more on larger ones. After a few years' experience, salaries average $250 a week.

Experienced copy editors earn about $15,000 on larger publications with other editorial positions paying up to $25,000 a year.

Mass-circulation magazines pay slightly higher salaries.

Additional sources of information

American Newspaper Publishers Association
Box 17407
Dulles International Airport
Washington, DC 20041

ELECTED PUBLIC OFFICIAL

The job

The variety of the public offices to which a man or woman may be elected in this country is enormous. These offices range from unpaid minor posts in small towns up to the President of the United States.

At the local level, aspiring officeholders in small communities often run as nonpartisan candidates for such bodies as the school board or town council. In most instances, however, candidates run as members of a particular political party.

Although some candidates for public office run because they have special training or unique qualifications for a particular office, most people begin their political careers by working with local groups or political clubs in their election campaigns. They may start as volunteer workers stuffing envelopes, handing out campaign literature, or answering the phone. As they gain knowledge and experience, they may serve as precinct leaders with the responsibility of getting people in a certain area to register and vote. As they acquire a favorable reputation and experience, they may be asked to run for a public office them- selves. For public offices beyond the local level, affiliation with one of the two major political parties in the United States is usually standard.

Places of employment and working conditions

The only general requirement for elective office is U.S. citizenship and eligibility to vote. At the local level, this usually means the candidate must be of voting age and a resident for a specified length of time.

At the national level, a member of the House of Representatives must be at least 25 years of age, a citizen of the United States for at least seven years, and live in the state that he or she represents. A senator must be at least 30 years old, a citizen for at least nine years, and live in the state that he or she represents.

The President of the United States must be a natural-born citizen, at least 35 years old, and must have lived in the United States at least 14 years.

Campaigning for public office at any level extracts a heavy cost in time and energy. For most offices, it is also very expensive. Since most elected officials only serve for a specific term, a career politician faces a new campaign every few years either for reelection or for a new office.

When a political office is held in addition to a regular job or business responsibilities, the officeholder may have very little time left for a per- sonal life.

Qualifications, education, and training

A strong desire to serve the public is the most basic requirement for an elected public official. Leadership qualities, a pleasant personality, physical energy and stamina, excellent communication skills, a genu- ine liking for people, and the ability to get along with people of all social and economic levels are all very important.

A high school student interested in a political career should get a well-rounded education. A thorough knowledge of history and govern- ment and as much training as possible in writing and speaking skills are recommended. Debating teams, school plays, and musical and sports activities before an audience. Running for class or school elective of- fices is also good training.

Although a college education is not a requirement for public office at any level, it does provide a necessary background for any public servant. The most popular program for those interested in a political career is law, but economics, political science, finance, history, business administration, and urban affairs are also excellent choices. Development of administrative skills through work experience is also important for a prospective public official.

A Government Intern Program for college seniors and graduate students is sponsored by some colleges, public and private organizations, and labor unions. These programs provide summer work in Washington, D.C., in some branch of the federal government. These programs are administered by the participating schools or organizations.

Basic information in politics and government is offered to men and women seeking state and national level offices through a discussion course, "Action Course in Practical Politics," sponsored by the U.S. Chamber of Commerce. The course is given in cities throughout the country and has no academic requirements.

Potential and advancement

Anyone interested in a career—or even a part-time career—in politics and public service can become involved at some level. Opportunities exist in communities of all sizes, and advancement to the top—the presidency—is possible for anyone.

Income

Income varies, from the numerous unpaid positions to those paying six figures plus expenses.

At the state level, governor's salaries range from $10,000 to $50,000 a year plus official expenses. Thirty-five states pay $25,000 or more. All but a few states provide an official residence for the governor.

State legislators usually continue to hold their regular jobs while they serve in the legislature. Their biennial (two-year) salaries range from $200 to $34,000 in the 36 states that pay a salary. The remaining states pay the legislators from $5 to $50 per day while the legislature is in session. All states provide a travel allowance, and a number also provide expense accounts.

At the national level, senators and representatives are paid $60,000 a year plus an allowance for expenses. The Speaker of the House and the President of the Senate (who is also the Vice President of the United States) receive more than $75,000.

Additional sources of information

Public Affairs Department
Chamber of Commerce of the United States
1615 H Stree, NW
Washington, DC

ELECTRICAL/ELECTRONICS ENGINEER

The job

Electrical and electronics engineering is the largest branch of engineering. These engineers design and develop electrical and electronic equipment and products. They may work in power generation and transmission; machinery controls; lighting and wiring for buildings, automobiles, and aircraft; computers; radar; communications equipment; missile guidance systems; or consumer goods such as television sets and appliances.

Engineers in this field usually specialize in a major area such as communications, computers, or power distribution equipment or in a subdivision such as aviation electronic systems. Many are involved in research, development, and design of new products; others in manufacturing and sales.

The main employers of electrical engineers are companies that manufacture electrical and electronic equipment, aircraft and parts, business machines, and professional and scientific equipment. Telephone, telegraph, and electric light and power companies also employ many electrical engineers. Others work for construction firms, engineering consulting firms, and government agencies. A number of them work in the field of nuclear energy.

Places of employment and working conditions

Engineers are employed in all areas of the country, in towns and cities of all sizes as well as rural areas, with some specialties concentrated in certain areas.

Qualifications, education, and training

The ability to think analytically, a capacity for detail, and the ability to work as part of a team are all necessary. Good communications skills are important.

Mathematics and the sciences must be emphasized in high school.

A bachelor's degree in engineering is the minimum requirement in this field. In a typical curriculum, the first two years are spent in the study of basic sciences such as physics and chemistry and mathematics, introductory engineering, and some liberal arts courses. The remaining years are usually devoted to specialized engineering courses. Engineering programs can last from four to six years. Those requiring five or six years to complete may award a master's degree or may provide a cooperative plan of study plus practical work experience with a nearby industry.

Because of rapid changes in technology, many engineers continue their education throughout their careers. A graduate degree is necessary for most teaching and research positions and for many management jobs. Some persons obtain graduate degrees in business administration.

Engineering graduates usually work under the supervision of an experienced engineer or in a company training program until they become acquainted with the requirements of a particular company or industry.

All states require licensing of engineers whose work may affect life, health, or property or who offer their services to the public. Those who are licensed, about one third of all engineers, are called Registered Engineers. Requirements include graduation from an accredited engineering school, four years of experience, and a written examination.

Potential and advancement

There are about 300,000 electrical engineers. Increased demand for computers, communications, and military electronics is expected to provide ample job opportunities for electrical engineers into the 1980s. A sharp rise or fall in government spending for defense could change this picture in either direction.

Income

Starting salaries in private industry average $16,800 with a bachelor's degree; $18,700 with a master's degree; and $24,000 or more with a Ph.D.

The federal government pays beginners $13,657 to $20,500, depending on degree and experience. Average salary for experienced engineers federally employed is about $27,700.

Experienced engineers average $30,500 in private industry; $15,000 to $21,000 for nine-month faculty positions in colleges and universities.

Additional sources of information

Institute of Electrical and Electronics Engineers
United States Activities Board
2029 K Street, NW
Washington, DC 20006

Engineers' Council for Professional Development
345 East 47th Street
New York, NY 10017

National Society of Professional Engineers
2029 K Street, NW
Washington, DC 20006

American Society for Engineering Education
One Dupont Circle, Suite 400
Washington, DC 20036

Society of Women Engineers
United Engineering Center
345 East 47th Street
New York, NY 10017

ELECTRICIAN

The job

The installation and maintenance of electrical systems and equipment is handled by electricians. They follow National Electrical Code specifications and any state and local electrical codes. Observance of safety practices is very important in this field, and electricians often use protective equipment and clothing.

Construction electricians, following blueprints and specifications, install wiring systems in newly constructed or renovated homes, offices and factories. They also install electrical machinery, electronic equipment and controls, and signal and communications systems. Most construction electricians are employed by electrical contractors; some are self-employed.

Maintenance electricians maintain the electrical systems installed by construction electricians and usually work in factories or other large buildings such as office buildings and apartment houses. They also install new electrical equipment and keep lighting systems, generators, and transformers in good working order. Maintenance electricians spend much of their time doing preventive maintenance, inspecting equipment to locate and correct problems before breakdown can occur. More than half of all maintenance electricians are employed in manufacturing industries. Others are employed by public utilities, mines, and railroads and by federal, state, and local governments.

Electricians usually furnish their own hand tools (screwdrivers, pliers, knives, hacksaws), while employers furnish heavier tools (pipe threaders, conduit benders) and most test meters and power tools.

Most construction electricians are members of the International Brotherhood of Electrical Workers.

Places of employment and working conditions

Electricians are employed throughout the country, but the greatest numbers are in industrialized and urban areas. The heavily industrialized states such as California, New York, Pennsylvania, Illinois, and Ohio employ many maintenance electricians.

Electricians do not need great physical strength, but they must be in good physical condition since they must stand for long periods and often work in cramped spaces. Because they usually work indoors, they are not exposed to bad weather as much as other workers in the building trades; however, they do risk injury from falls, electrical shock, and falling objects. Maintenance electricians work near high voltage industrial equipment and are exposed to noise and the grease and oil of machinery.

Qualifications, education, and training

Electricians need at least average physical strength, agility, and dexterity. Good color vision is important since electrical wires are often identified by color.

High school or vocational school courses in electricity, electronics, mechanical drawing, science, and electrical shop are a good background for someone interested in becoming an electrician.

Because completion of a formal apprenticeship program is considered the best way to become an electrician, this trade has a higher percentage of apprenticeship-trained workers than most other construction trades. A local union-management commission sponsors and supervises each program. Those who complete an apprenticeship program can usually qualify as either a construction or maintenance electrician.

Applicants for apprenticeship should be in good health and at least 18 years of age. Most programs require a high school or vocational school diploma and one year of algebra. Most programs last four years and include comprehensive on-the-job training as well as 144 hours per year of classroom instruction. Classroom courses include blueprint reading, electrical theory, electronics, mathematics, and safety and first-aid training.

Some people learn the trade informally, by working as electricians' helpers in construction or maintenance jobs. They can gain additional knowledge through trade schools, correspondence courses, or through special training in the armed forces. This method, however, often takes longer than a formal apprenticeship program.

In many urban areas electricians must be licensed. The examination for licensing requires a thorough knowledge of the craft and of state and local building codes. Electricians who start their own electrical contracting business also are usually required to have an electrician contractor's license.

Potential and advancement

The need for construction electricians is expected to grow faster than the average for all occupations through the mid-1980s; employment of maintenance electricians is expected to increase about as fast as the average for all occupations. In addition, many openings will occur to replace experienced electricians who retire, die, or leave the field.

There are approximately 260,000 construction electricians and 300,000 maintenance electricians. Job opportunities will be more plentiful for construction electricians, but there will be steady growth in this field.

While job openings in the construction field may fluctuate from year to year, construction electricians are able to transfer to electrical work in fields such as shipbuilding and aircraft manufacturing or to maintenance electrician positions in factories. The demand for maintenance electricians is not very sensitive to fluctuations in the economy; in times of depressed activity in the construction industry, however, experienced construction electricians often apply for openings that would normally go to beginning maintenance electricians.

Experienced construction electricians can be promoted to supervisory jobs or become estimators for contractors. Many start their own contracting businesses. Maintenance electricians can become supervisors and occasionally advance to jobs such as plant electrical superintendent or plant maintenance superintendent.

Income

Union construction electricians working in large metropolitan areas average more than $11.25 an hour. Construction electricians are affected less than other workers in the building trades by the seasonal nature of construction work; therefore their annual earnings are usually high. Maintenance electricians average $8.44 an hour.

Apprentices start at 40 to 60 percent of the hourly rate of experienced electricians and receive periodic increases during the course of their training.

Additional sources of information

International Brotherhood of Electrical Workers
1125 15th Street, NW
Washington, DC 20005

National Electrical Contractors Association
7315 Wisconsin Avenue, NW
Washington, DC 20014

National Joint Apprenticeship and Training Committee
 for the Electrical Industry
9700 East George Palmer Highway
Lanham, MD 20801

International Union of Electrical, Radio and
 Machine Workers
1126 16th Street, NW
Washington, DC 20036

International Association of Machinists and Aerospace Workers
1300 Connecticut Avenue
Washington, DC 20036

United Steelworkers of America
Five Gateway Center
Pittsburgh, PA 15222

EMPLOYMENT COUNSELOR

The job

Employment counselors, also called vocational counselors, help jobseekers who have difficulties finding jobs. They provide services to experienced workers who have been displaced by automation or who are unhappy in their present jobs and to returning veterans, school dropouts, handicapped and older workers, ex-prisoners, and those with minimal job skills.

In-depth interviews with jobseekers, aptitude tests, and other background information help the counselor evaluate the capabilities of each person. The counselor then helps the jobseeker develop a vocational plan and a job goal that will be implemented using whatever remedial action is necessary. This could include education or retraining, physical rehabilitation or psychological counseling, specific work experience, or development of appropriate work skills. Once the jobseeker obtains a position, the counselor usually provides follow-up counseling for a period of time.

Counselors must be familiar with the local labor market and with the job-related resources of the community. Some employment counselors contact local employers and keep abreast of job openings within local industries to refer jobseekers to specific jobs.

Most employment counselors work for state employment centers or community agencies. Others work for private agencies, prisons, training schools, and mental hospitals. The federal government employs employment counselors in the Veterans Administration and in the Bureau of Indian Affairs.

Places of employment and working conditions

Employment counselors work throughout the country in communities of all sizes.

Counselors usually work a 40-hour week. Those in community agencies may work overtime or some evening and weekend hours.

Qualifications, education, and training

Anyone interested in this field should have a strong interest in helping others, should be able to work independently and keep detailed records, and should possess patience.

Graduate work beyond a bachelor's degree, or equivalent counseling-related experience, is necessary for even entry-level jobs in employment counseling. Undergraduate work should include courses in psychology and sociology; graduate work includes actual counseling experience under the supervision of an instructor.

Employment counselors working for state and local government agencies must fulfill local civil service requirements, which include specific education and experience requirements and a written examination.

Potential and advancement

There are about 6,500 employment counselors. Growth in this field will depend on the federal funding to state and local agencies which provide counseling services. Some competition for available job openings is expected in the future.

Income

Earnings vary widely from state to state. The average starting salary is about $10,500. Experienced counselors earn up to $21,000, but the average is about $13,800.

In private nonprofit organizations, the average starting salary is about $12,500; experienced workers average $18,000.

Additional sources of information

National Employment Counselors Association
1607 New Hampshire Avenue, NW
Washington, DC 20009

U.S. Department of Labor
Employment and Training Administration, USES
Division of Counseling and Testing
Washington, DC 20210

ENGINEER

The job

Engineers apply the theories and principles of science and mathematics to practical technical problems. This is one of the largest professions in the country, second only to teaching.

Most engineers specialize in one of the 25 major branches of engineering. Within these branches there are over 85 subdivisions, and engineers may further specialize in one industry, such as motor vehicles, or one field of technology, such as propulsion or guidance systems. This job description provides an overall picture of engineering as a career. Information on 12 major branches of this profession appear elsewhere in this book (Aerospace Engineer, Civil Engineer, and so forth).

In general, engineers in a particular field may be involved in research, design, and development; production and operation; maintenance; time and cost estimation; sales and technical assistance; or administration and management. Engineers usually work as part of a team and, regardless of specialty, may apply their knowledge across several fields. For example, an electrical engineer can work in the medical field, in computers, missile guidance systems, or electric power distribution. An agricultural engineer may design farm equipment, manage water resources, or work in soil conservation.

While more than half of all engineers work for manufacturing industries, about 31 percent work in nonmanufacturing industries such as construction, public utilities, engineering and architectural services, and business and consulting services.

Federal, state and local government agencies employ about 14 percent of all engineers. Federally employed engineers work mainly for the Departments of Defense, Interior, Agriculture, Transportation, and NASA. In state and local governments, engineers usually work for highway and public works departments.

About 4 percent of all engineers teach and do research.

Women make up only 2 percent of the total in this profession. Many firms, however, as well as engineering schools, are actively recruiting women to comply with affirmative action programs and other government regulations on equal employment opportunity.

A related job is: Industrial Designer.

Places of employment and working conditions

Engineers are employed in all areas of the country, in towns and cities of all sizes as well as rural areas, with some specialties concentrated in certain areas.

Most engineers work indoors but some, depending on specialty, work outdoors or at remote locations.

Qualifications, education, and training

The ability to think analytically, a capacity for detail, and the ability to work as part of a team are all necessary. Good communication skills are important.

Mathematics and the sciences must be emphasized in high school.

A bachelor's degree in engineering is the minimum requirement in this field. In a typical curriculum, the first two years are spent in the study of basic sciences such as physics and chemistry and mathematics, introductory engineering, and some liberal arts courses. The remaining years are usually devoted to specialized engineering courses. Engineering programs can last from four to six years. Those requiring five or six years to complete may award a master's degree or may provide a cooperative plan of study plus practical work experience with a nearby industry.

Because of rapid changes in technology, many engineers continue their education throughout their careers. A graduate degree is necessary for most teaching and research positions and for many management jobs. Some specialties such as nuclear engineering are taught only at the graduate level. Some persons obtain graduate degrees in business administration or in a field such as law (for patent attorneys).

Engineering graduates usually work under the supervision of an experienced engineer or in a company training program until they become acquainted with the requirements of a particular company or industry.

All states require licensing of engineers whose work may affect life, health, or property or who offer their services to the public. Those who are licensed, about one third of all engineers, are called Registered Engineers. Requirements include graduation from an accredited engineering school, four years of experience, and a written examination.

Potential and advancement

There are approximately 1.1 million engineers. The employment outlook for engineers is good for the foreseeable future with some specialties more in demand than others. In general, qualified engineers and available job openings will be in balance.

Experienced engineers may advance to administrative and management positions. Many of the highest-level executives in private industry started their careers as engineers.

Income

Starting salaries in private industry average $16,800 with a bachelor's degree; $18,700 with a master's degree; and $24,000 or more with a Ph.D. Starting salaries for civil engineers average slightly less, chemical engineers slightly more.

The federal government pays beginners $13,657 to $20,500, depending on degree and experience. Average salary for experienced engineers federally employed is $30,500.

Experienced engineers average $26,000 in private industry; $15,000 to $21,000 for nine-month faculty positions in colleges and universities.

Additional sources of information

Engineers' Council for Professional Development
345 East 47th Street
New York, NY 10017

National Society of Professional Engineers
2029 K Street, NW
Washington, DC 20006

American Society for Engineering Education
One Dupont Circle, Suite 400
Washington, DC 20036

ENGINEER

Society of Women Engineers
United Engineering Center
345 East 47th Street
New York, NY 10017

FARMER

The job

Farmers today are businessmen. They buy seed, fertilizer, and equipment; plant only a few crops, or even one crop; follow scientific production methods; and sell all they grow or raise.

The dwindling supply and high cost of available farmland, plus the cost of the equipment necessary to run a farm using today's agricultural technology, are leading to an increase in some alternative styles of farming. And farmers in areas with long winters often take jobs in nearby cities during the cold months, working their farms through the spring, summer, and fall.

Tenant farmers rent their land from farm owners, usually in return for a percentage of the crop. Some owners also supply machinery, seed, and fertilizer.

Large corporate and partnership farms are usually operated by *farm managers* who handle all the day-to-day responsibilities as well as decisions on what crops to plant.

Firms that supply seed, feed, fertilizer, and farm equipment also attract experienced farmers to work as salespeople and dealers for their products. Some farmers use their accumulated knowledge in other areas related to farming such as farm insurance, banking and credit, real estate sales and appraisals.

Related jobs are: Agricultural Engineer, Soil Scientist, Range Manager.

Places of employment and working conditions

Some farming is done in just about every county in the United States. The eastern and southern states have smaller farms than the midwestern and western states. Many of the larger or corporate farms employ many laborers.

The workweek for a farmer during the planting, growing, and harvesting seasons is often six or seven days and much longer than eight hours a day. Farmers who raise livestock and poultry have a more even work schedule year around, but their work is always seven days a week since animals must be cared for every day.

Farmers face constant financial risk due to the uncertainties of weather, which can ruin a crop and eliminate an entire year's income.

Qualifications, education, and training

To successfully run a modern farm, a farmer needs managerial and business skills, mechanical ability, physical stamina, patience, and a love of working outdoors.

Probably the best background is growing up on a farm or working for a farmer. Organizations such as the 4-H Clubs and Future Farmers of America provide valuable preparation for young people interested in farming.

The complexities of modern scientific farming make formal training in a two- or four-year agricultural college almost a necessity. Most such colleges offer majors in areas such as dairy science, crop science, agricultural economics, horticulture, and animal science, plus special course work in the products produced in the area in which the college is located.

Colleges that offer degrees in agricultural engineering sometimes offer degrees or course work in mechanized agriculture. These programs provide broad basic agricultural training, practical application of farm machinery and equipment to agricultural production, and economics and management courses.

Potential and advancement

There are about five million farmers in the United States. The trend toward fewer but larger farms and the loss of over 1.5 million acres of farmland to urbanization each year means a continued decline in the demand for farmers. There will be job opportunities for farm managers, however.

Young farmers will find opportunities to gain experience as tenant farmers. They may move up to positions as farm managers or may buy their own farms.

Income

No information is available on average earnings for farmers, since farm size and products vary so greatly and earnings fluctuate from year to year.

Salespeople and dealers who supply farm-related products earn from $17,000 to $27,000 a year.

Farm managers earn from $20,000 to $50,000 a year, depending on size or number of farms managed.

Additional sources of information

U.S. Department of Agriculture
Washington, DC 20250

Northwest Farm Managers Association
State University Station
Fargo, ND 58105

American Society of Agricultural Engineers
2950 Niles Road
St. Joseph, MO 49085

FASHION DESIGNER

The job

Fashion and clothing designers create new styles or adjust and change existing styles. They may work in men's, women's or children's clothing design.

Designers work with sketches or directly with fabric in creating a design. They must understand color, fabrics, production processes, and costs as well as the public's tastes and preferences. Many designers work on one type of apparel such as sports clothes or evening wear.

People who want a career in designing often take any job they can in the fashion field to get a start. The field is popular and always has more new talent than it can adequately support.

Places of employment and working conditions

New York City is the *center* of the fashion industry; Los Angeles is an important swimsuit and casual clothes fashion center, and other cities produce limited fashion trends.

Fashion is a hectic and fast-paced field with seasonal peaks that often require long hours.

Qualifications, education, and training

Fashion designers must have a flair for clothes, a sense of style, a keen sense of color, and the ability to turn their ideas into reality.

High school courses in art, merchandising, and business are helpful. Sewing experience is important.

Apparel firms prefer to hire designers with formal training, and they often recruit designers from colleges and schools that provide specialized training in fashion design. A few designers work their way up through the ranks from tailoring or cutting jobs.

Beginners should be prepared to serve as sample makers or assistant designers or even work in clerical jobs for their first few years.

Potential and advancement

Fashion is a crowded, popular, and often cut-throat career field. There are always many more eager jobseekers than there are job openings, and there will be stiff competition for all designer positions.

Income

Salaries vary greatly and many designers put up with low salaries because they like the work and are eager to gain experience.

Additional sources of information

American Apparel Manufacturers Association
1611 North Kent Street
Arlington, VA 22209

The Fashion Group
9 Rockefeller Plaza
New York, NY 10020

Fur Information and Fashion Council
855 Avenue of the Americas
New York, NY 10001

FBI SPECIAL AGENT

The job

Special agents for the Federal Bureau of Investigation (FBI) investigate violations of federal laws in connection with bank robberies, kidnappings, white-collar crime, thefts of government property, organized crime, espionage, and sabotage. The FBI, which is part of the U.S. Department of Justice, has jurisdiction over many different federal investigative matters. Special agents, therefore, may be assigned to any type of case, although those with specialized training usually work on cases related to their background. Agents with an accounting background, for example, may investigate white-collar crimes such as bank embezzlements or fraudulent bankruptcies or land deals.

Because the FBI is a fact-gathering agency, its special agents function strictly as investigators, collecting evidence in cases in which the U.S. Government is, or may be, an interested party. In their casework, special agents conduct interviews, examine records, observe the activities of suspects, and participate in raids. Because the FBI's work is highly confidential, special agents may not disclose any of the information gathered in the course of their official duties to unauthorized persons, including members of their families. Frequently, agents must testify in court about cases that they investigate.

Although they usually work alone on most assignments, two agents or more are assigned to work together when performing potentially dangerous duties such as arrests and raids. Agents communicate with their supervisors by radio or telephone as the circumstances dictate.

There are about 30 women special agents in the FBI.

Places of employment and working conditions

Most agents are assigned to the FBI's 59 field offices located throughout the nation and in Puerto Rico. They work in cities where field office headquarters are located or in resident agencies (suboffices) established under field office supervision to provide prompt and efficient handling of investigative matters arising throughout the field office territory. Some agents are assigned to the Bureau headquarters in Washington, D.C., which supervises all FBI activities.

Special agents are subject to call 24 hours a day and must be available for assignment at all times. Their duties call for some travel, for they are assigned wherever they are needed in the United States or Puerto Rico. They frequently work longer than the customary 40-hour week.

Qualifications, education, and training

To be considered for appointment as an FBI special agent, an applicant usually must be a graduate of a state-accredited law school or a college graduate with a major in accounting. The law school training must have been preceded by at least two years of undergraduate college work.

From time to time, as the need arises, the FBI accepts applications from persons who have a bachelor's degree with a physical science major; who are fluent in a foreign language, or who have three years of professional, executive, complex investigative, or other specialized experience.

Applicants for the position of FBI special agent must be citizens of the United States; be at least 23 years old but not have reached their thirty-fifth birthday before they begin duty; and be willing to serve anywhere in the United States and Puerto Rico. They must be capable of strenuous physical exertion and have excellent hearing and vision, normal color perception, and no physical defects that would prevent their using firearms or participating in dangerous assignments. All applicants must pass a rigid physical examination as well as written and oral examinations testing their aptitude for meeting the public and conducting investigations. All of the tests except the physical examinations are given by the FBI at its facilities. Background and character investigations are made of all applicants. Appointments are made on a probationary basis and become permanent after one year of satisfactory service.

Each newly appointed special agent is given about 15 weeks of training at the FBI Academy at the U.S. Marine Corps Base in Quantico, Virginia, before assignment to a field office. During this period, agents receive intensive training in defensive tactics and the use of firearms. In addition, they are thoroughly schooled in federal criminal law and procedures, FBI rules and regulations, fingerprinting, and investigative work. After assignment to a field office, the new agent usually works closely with an experienced agent for about two weeks before handling any assignments independently.

Potential and advancement

There are about 8,600 special agents.

The jurisdiction of the FBI has expanded greatly over the years. Although it is impossible to forecast personnel requirements, employment may be expected to increase with growing FBI responsibilities.

The FBI provides a career service and its rate of turnover is traditionally low. Nevertheless, the FBI is always interested in applications from qualified persons who would like to be considered for the position of special agent.

All administrative and supervisory jobs are filled from within the ranks by selection of those agents who have demonstrated the ability to assume more responsibility.

Income

The entrance salary for FBI special agents is about $17,532 a year. Under specified conditions, agents may receive overtime pay up to about $4,400 a year. Special agents are not appointed under Federal Civil Service regulations; like other federal employees, however, they receive periodic within-grade salary raises if their work performance is satisfactory. They can advance in grade as they gain experience. Salaries of supervisory agents start at about $32,442 a year.

Agents receive paid vacations, sick leave, and annuities on retirement. They are required to retire at age 55 if they have served for at least 20 years.

Additional sources of information

The Federal Bureau of Investigation
U.S. Department of Justice
Washington, DC 20535

FIREFIGHTER

The job

Firefighters must be prepared to respond to a fire and handle any emergency that arises. This is dangerous work that requires courage and expert training.

Firefighting requires organization and teamwork. Each firefighter at the scene of a fire has specific duties assigned by a company officer; but each must also be ready to perform any of the duties—such as connecting hoses to hydrants, positioning ladders, or operating pumps—at any time, because duties change in the course of a fire. Firefighters may also be called on to rescue people or to administer first aid.

Between fires, firefighters spend their time cleaning and maintaining equipment, carrying out practice drills, and maintaining their living quarters. They also take part in fire prevention activities such as building inspections and educational programs for schools and civic groups.

Ninety percent of all firefighters work for municipal fire departments. The remainder work on federal installations or in large manufacturing plants.

Women have been accepted as firefighters in some communities but usually find it difficult to overcome traditional attitudes about women being involved in dangerous work.

Most firefighters are members of the International Association of Firefighters (AFL-CIO).

Places of employment and working conditions

In some cities, firefighters are on duty for 24 hours and then off for 48 hours. In other cities, they work a 10-hour day shift or a 14-hour night shift, with shifts rotated frequently. The average workweek varies from 42 to 52 hours, but some firefighters work as many as 84 hours a week. These duty hours usually include free time which can be used for personal interests or study.

Firefighters face the risk of injury or death in the course of their work and must work outdoors in all kinds of conditions and weather.

Qualifications, education, and training

A firefighter must have courage, mental alertness, physical stamina, mechanical aptitude, and a sense of public service. Initiative, good judgment, and dependability are essential. Because firefighters live together as well as work together they should be able to get along with others.

Applicants for municipal firefighting jobs must pass a written test and medical examination and tests of strength, physical stamina, and agility. They must meet other local regulations as to height and weight, have a high school education or equivalent, and be at least 18 years old. Experience as a volunteer firefighter or firefighting training received in the armed forces improve an applicant's chances for appointment to a job, and some communities also give extra credit to veterans of the armed forces.

Beginners are usually trained at the city's fire school for several weeks and are then assigned to a fire company for a probationary period.

Fire departments frequently conduct training programs to help firefighters upgrade their skills, and many colleges offer courses such as fire engineering and fire science that are helpful to firefighters. Experienced firefighters also continue to study to prepare for promotional examinations.

Potential and advancement

There are about 210,000 professional firefighters working in cities and towns all over the country; and many volunteer firefighters work in suburban and rural areas. Employment of firefighters will increase as the population grows and as many small communities replace their volunteer firefighters with professionals. There is usually competition for existing job openings in large urban areas and, in financially troubled cities, employment of firefighters will remain about the same or decline slightly.

Opportunities for promotion are good in most fire departments. Promotion to lieutenant, captain, battalion chief, assistant chief, deputy chief, and finally chief depend on written examination, seniority, and rating by supervisors.

Income

Beginning salaries range from about $11,000 to $14,500, depending on city size and location. Experienced firefighters earn from $14,200 to $18,000.

Lieutenants earn from $15,700 to $18,000; captains $17,500 to $21,000.

Generally, firefighters are paid more in suburban districts than in large cities. Earnings are highest in the West and lowest in the South.

Most fire departments provide allowances to pay for protective clothing such as helmets, boots, and rubber coats, and many also provide dress uniforms.

Firefighters are usually covered by liberal pension plans that often provide retirement at half pay at age 50 after 25 years of service or at any age if disabled in the line of duty. Generous sick leave and compensation are usually provided for any firefighter injured in the line of duty.

Additional sources of information

Information is available from local civil service commission offices or fire departments.

International Association of Fire Chiefs
1725 K Street, NW
Washington, DC 10006

National Fire Protection Association
470 Atlantic Avenue
Boston, MA 02210

FLIGHT ATTENDANT

The job

Few jobs appear as glamorous as that of a flight attendant. The lure of travel and the opportunity to meet all kinds of people appeal to those interested in this field.

Formerly called stewardesses and stewards, flight attendants are aboard almost every commercial passenger plane to look after passenger safety and comfort. Airliners usually carry from one to ten flight attendants, depending on the number of seats and the proportion of economy to first-class passengers. (The Boeing 747 carries up to 16 flight attendants.) FAA safety regulations require at least one attendant for every 50 seats.

Before each flight, attendants check supplies such as food, beverages, blankets, reading material, first-aid kits, and emergency equipment. During flight, they instruct passengers in the use of emergency equipment; check seat belts before takeoff or landing; and help care for small children, the elderly, and handicapped. They also distribute reading material and serve food and beverages.

The main reason planes carry flight attendants is to provide assistance to passengers in the event of an emergency. A calm and reassuring manner is very important, whether the emergency is a sick passenger or an emergency landing. Flight attendants are trained to handle many situations including evacuation of the plane.

Most flight attendants are members of either the Transport Workers Union of America or the Association of Flight Attendants.

This has always been a traditionally female career and women still predominate. But the number of male flight attendants is increasing, and the entrance of men into this job has prompted the name change from stewardess (and steward) to flight attendant.

Places of employment and working conditions

Over one half of all flight attendants work out of Chicago, Dallas, Los Angeles, Miami, New York City, and San Francisco. The remainder are assigned to the other cities where airlines maintain facilities.

Since airlines operate around the clock for 365 days a year, flight attendants must be prepared to work nights, weekends, and holidays. They usually fly about 80 hours a month with about 35 additional hours of ground duties. Their workweek is not divided into neat segments, and because of scheduling and limitations on flying time, many have 15 or more days off each month. As much as one third of their time may be spent away from their home base. Airlines provide hotel accommodations and meal allowances for these periods.

Flight attendants are on their feet during most of a flight. Poor weather can cause difficulties as can sick or frightened passengers. Flight attendants are expected to be pleasant and efficient under all circumstances and with even the most difficult passengers.

Qualifications, education, and training

Anyone considering this career field should be poised and tactful, enjoy working with people, and be able to talk comfortably with strangers. Excellent health is a must as is good vision. (Contact lenses and eyeglasses are acceptable on most airlines, however.) Airlines also have height and weight requirements, and all flight attendants must be at least 19 years old, have a high school diploma, and be single at the time they are hired.

Airlines give preference to applicants with two years of college, nurse's training, or experience in dealing with the public. Fluency in a foreign language is required on international airlines.

Large airlines provide about five weeks of training in their own schools. Some also provide transportation to the training center and an allowance while training. Instruction includes emergency procedures, evacuation of a plane, operation of emergency equipment, first aid, flight regulations and duties, and company operations and policies. On international airlines, flight attendants also study passport and customs regulations. Practice flights complete the training. After assignment to a home base, new flight attendants begin their careers by "filling in" on extra flights or replacing attendants who are sick or on vacation.

Potential and advancement

There are about 42,000 flight attendants working for airlines in the United States. Employment of flight attendants is expected to grow as increases in population and income increase the use of air transportation. Air travel, however, is sensitive to the ups and downs of the economy, and job opportunities may vary from year to year.

Opportunities for advancement are limited to choice of flight assignment and home base, which flight attendants are entitled to as they accumulate seniority. A few attendants do advance to positions as flight service instructors, customer service directors, or recruiting representatives.

Income

Salaries for beginners range from $690 to $780 a month for domestic flights; $830 to $980 on international flights. The average monthly earnings of experienced flight attendants is about $1,200.

An attractive fringe benefit is the reduced airfare for flight attendants and their families, on their own and most other airlines.

Additional sources of information

Information about job opportunities and requirements for a particular airline may be obtained by writing to the personnel manager of the company. Addresses are available from:

Air Transport Association of America
1709 New York Avenue, NW
Washington, DC 20006

FLORAL DESIGNER

The job

Floral designers, also called *florists,* combine a knowledge of flowers and plants with design techniques to produce floral and plant gifts and decorations.

Just about all floral designers work in retail flower shops, many of which are small and employ only a few people. Many of the shops are owner-operated.

Floral designers must know the seasonal availability and lasting qualities of many flowers and have a sense of form, color harmony, and depth. They prepare bouquets, corsages, funeral pieces, dried flower arrangements, and decorations for weddings, parties, and other events.

Places of employment and working conditions

Flower shops are located throughout the country with at least one in nearly every city and town.

Floral designers stand during much of their workday. Work areas are kept cool and humid to preserve the flowers, and designers are subject to sudden temperature changes when entering or leaving refrigerated storage areas.

A 40-hour workweek is usual, but this often includes Saturday hours. Floral designers work very long hours around certain holidays such as Valentine's Day and Mother's Day.

Qualifications, education, and training

Good color vision and manual dexterity are necessary for a floral designer. Business and selling skills are important for those who operate their own shops.

High school courses in business arithmetic and bookkeeping are helpful. Part-time or summer jobs in a plant nursery or flower shop can provide valuable experience.

Many floral designers acquire their skills through on-the-job training. They work under the guidance of an experienced floral designer for about two years to become fully qualified.

The trend in recent years, however, is toward more formal training. Adult education programs and flower shops offer courses in flower arranging, while junior colleges and commercial floral design schools offer wider training. The longer programs provide training in basic horticulture, flower marketing, and flower shop management as well as floral design. Such training is especially useful for floral designers who intend to open their own shops.

Potential and advancement

There are about 37,000 floral designers, and the field is expected to grow as the population increases. Ups and downs in the economy may cause temporary slow periods, but over the long run the outlook is good.

Income

In large flower shops, flower designers may advance to shop manager or to design supervisor. Others advance by opening their own shops. A new flower shop in an area with many other florists faces stiff competition and must establish a reputation by efficient operation and outstanding work if the business is to succeed. Floral designers who can provide such work are always in demand.

Experienced floral designers make from $3.50 to $7.00 an hour.

The earnings of shop owners vary greatly depending mainly on locality and the size of the community being served.

Additional sources of information

Society of American Florists
901 North Washington Street
Alexandria, VA 22314

FORESTER

The job

The forest lands of the United States—whether publicly or privately owned—must be carefully and efficiently managed if they are to survive. It is the work of the professional forester to develop, manage, and protect forest lands and their resources of timber, water, wildlife, forage, and recreation areas. If properly protected and managed, these resources can be utilized repeatedly without being destroyed.

Foresters often specialize in one type of work such as timber management, outdoor recreation, or forest economics. In these capacities, they might plan and supervise the planting and cutting of trees or devote themselves to watershed management, wildlife protection, disease and insect control, fire prevention, or the development and supervision of recreation areas.

About two fifths of all foresters work for private industries such as pulp and paper, lumber, logging, and milling companies. The federal government employs about one fourth of all foresters, most of them in the Forest Service of the Department of Agriculture. Others do research, teach at the college and university level, or work as consultants. State and local governments also employ foresters.

Related jobs are: Environmentalist, Soil Scientist, Soil Conservationist.

Places of employment and working conditions

Foresters are employed in just about every state, but the largest numbers are employed in the heavily forested areas of the northwest, northeast, and southern states.

Foresters, especially beginners, spend a great deal of time outdoors in all kinds of weather and often at remote locations. During emergencies such as fires and rescue missions, they may work long hours under difficult and dangerous conditions.

Qualifications, education, and training

Anyone interested in forestry as a career should be physically hardy, enjoy working outdoors, and be willing to work in remote areas.

A bachelor's degree with a major in forestry is the minimum requirement, but employers prefer to hire applicants with advanced degrees. About 50 colleges offer degrees in forestry, most of them accredited by the Society of American Foresters. Scientific and technical forestry subjects, liberal arts, and communication skills are emphasized along with courses in forest economics and business administration. All schools encourage work experience in forestry or conservation, and many of the colleges require at least one summer at a college-operated field camp.

Potential and advancement

About 25,000 persons are employed as foresters. Employment opportunities are expected to grow somewhat, but the number of degrees being awarded in forestry will soon exceed the number of job openings, creating competition among applicants. Those with advanced degrees or several years of experience have the best chance of securing a job. Job opportunities will probably be greatest with private owners of timberland and with state governmental agencies in cooperative federal-state programs of fire prevention, insect and disease control, and recreation.

Advancement in this field depends on experience with federally employed foresters able to advance through supervisory positions to regional forest supervisors or to top administrative positions. In private industry, experienced foresters may advance to top managerial positions within a company.

Income

Starting salaries for federally employed foresters varies: those having a master's degree or equivalent experience receive about $13,014 a year; Ph.D.'s start at $15,920 to $19,263; with a bachelor's degree, the salary is about $9,300. In state and local governments, starting salaries average above $10,000 annually; the median annual salary is $17,000.

College teaching positions in forestry start at about $14,000 annually. Median salary for faculty positions is over $22,000. Many faculty members within this field supplement their regular salaries by consulting, lecturing, and writing.

In private industry, starting salaries average $12,000 a year, with an overall salary average for foresters in private industry of about $21,000.

Additional sources of information

Society of American Foresters
5400 Grosvenor Lane
Washington, DC 20014

American Forest Institute
1619 Massachusetts Avenue, NW
Washington, DC 20036

U.S. Department of Agriculture
Forest Service
Washington, DC 20250

FORESTRY TECHNICIAN

The job

Forestry technicians assist foresters in the care and management of forest lands and their resources. They estimate timber production, inspect for insect damage, supervise surveying and road-building crews, work in flood control and water quality programs, supervise firefighting crews, supervise planting and reforestation programs, and maintain forest areas for hunting, camping, and other recreational uses.

About half of all forestry technicians work for private logging, lumber, paper, mining, and railroad companies. The federal government employs about an equal number. Many of the technicians employed by the federal and state governments work during the summer only or during the spring and fall fire seasons.

There are few women in this field but their number is increasing steadily.

Places of employment and working conditions

Forestry technicians work throughout the country in just about every state.

Outdoor work in all kinds of weather is the norm for this job field. In emergencies such as forest fires and floods, the working hours are very long and the work can be dangerous. In many areas, the work is seasonal.

Qualifications, education, and training

Good physical condition, stamina, love of the outdoors, and ability to work with or without supervision and to work with a variety of people are all necessary for a forestry technician.

High school should include as many science courses as possible.

Some technicians acquire their training through experience on fire-fighting crews, in recreation work, or in tree nurseries. Because this is a very competitive job field, however, those with specialized training in forestry have better opportunities for full-time employment.

One- and two-year courses for forestry technicians are available in technical institutes, junior colleges, and colleges and universities. Subjects studied include mathematics, biology and botany, land surveying, tree identification, aerial photography interpretation, and timber harvesting.

Potential and advancement

There are about 11,000 full-time forestry technicians; an equal number are employed seasonally. This field is expected to grow steadily, but applicants will continue to exceed job openings due to the popularity of the work. Private industry will continue to provide the bulk of the full-time positions.

Income

Beginning salaries range from $8,000 to $10,000. Experienced forestry technicians earn $12,000 or $13,000 a year.

Additional sources of information

American Forestry Association
1319 18th Street, NW
Washington, DC 20036

Forest Service
U.S. Department of Agriculture
Washington, DC 20250

Society of American Foresters
5400 Grosvenor Lane
Washington, DC 20014

FUNERAL DIRECTOR

The job

While this job field does not appeal to everyone, persons involved in funeral directing take great pride in the fact that they provide efficient and appropriate service to their customers. Probably more than in any other job situation, personal qualities of tact, compassion, and the ability to deal with people under difficult circumstances come into play. A funeral director arranges for the transportation of the deceased to the funeral home, obtains information for the death certificate and obituary notices, and arranges all details of the funeral and burial as decided upon by the family of the deceased. The funeral director must be familiar with the funeral and burial customs of many faiths, ethnic groups, and fraternal organizations. Even after the funeral, the funeral director assists the family in handling social security insurance and veteran's claims.

An *embalmer* prepares the body for viewing and burial. Embalming is a sanitary, cosmetic, and preservative process and is required by law in some areas. The body is washed with germicidal soap, blood is replaced with embalming fluid, cosmetics are applied to provide a natural appearance or to restore disfigured features, and the body is placed in the casket.

In small funeral homes, the duties of funeral director and embalmer may be handled by one person; in large funeral homes, an embalming staff of one or more embalmers plus several apprentices may be employed. Embalmers are also employed by hospitals and morgues.

In most funeral homes, one of the funeral directors is also the owner. The staff may consist of from one to twenty or more funeral directors, embalmers, and apprentices. In some communities, it is customary for a prospective embalmer or funeral director to obtain a promise of employment from a local funeral home before starting mortuary training.

About 2 percent of all funeral directors and embalmers are women. Traditionally they are usually employed in family-owned funeral homes working with their husbands or fathers.

Places of employment and working conditions

There are approximately 22,000 funeral homes in the United States, at least one in every community, so job opportunities are everywhere.

In smaller funeral homes, working hours may vary, but in larger homes employees work eight hours a day, five or six days a week. Shift work is sometimes necessary since funeral-home hours include evenings.

Embalmers occasionally come into contact with contagious diseases but are not likely to become ill because of strict observance of sanitary procedures.

Qualifications, education, and training

High school courses in biology, chemistry, and public speaking are helpful, and a part-time or summer job at a funeral home car provide exposure to the profession for anyone considering the field.

There are 34 mortuary science programs that are accredited by the American Board of Funeral Service Education. Some vocational schools offer a one-year program emphasizing basic subjects such as anatomy, physiology, embalming techniques, and restorative art. Community colleges offer two-year programs, and a few colleges and universities offer both two- and four-year programs. The longer programs include liberal arts and management courses in addition to mortuary science. Psychology, accounting, and funeral law are also studied.

A period of apprenticeship must be completed under the guidance of an experienced funeral director or embalmer. Depending on state regulations, this apprenticeship consists of from one to two years and may be served before, during, or after mortuary school.

All states require embalmers to be licensed, and all but six states also require funeral directors to be licensed. Since about one half of the states require at least one or more years of college in addition to mortuary training, a training program should be selected that meets the requirements of the student's state of residence.

State board licensing examinations vary but usually consist of written and oral tests as well as a demonstration of skills. Other state licensing standards usually require the applicant to be 21 years old, have a high school diploma or its equivalent, and complete a mortuary science program and an apprenticeship.

Some states issue a single license to funeral directors and embalmers. In states that have separate licensing and apprenticeship requirements for the two positions, most people in the field obtain both licenses. Some states will accept the credentials of those licensed by another state without further examination.

Potential and advancement

There are about 45,000 licensed funeral directors and embalmers. Employment opportunities in this field should remain constant because the number of mortuary school graduates just about equals the number of job openings each year. Although the demand for funeral services will rise due to population increases, the existing funeral homes should be able to handle the increase without creating additional job openings, since many funeral homes now handle only three or four funerals each week.

Advancement opportunities are best in large funeral homes where higher-paying positions exist such as general manager or personnel manager. Directors and embalmers who accumulate enough money and experience often establish their own businesses.

Income

Apprenticeship wages vary from $135 to $220 a week. Funeral directors and embalmers earn from $11,000 to $17,000; managers earn from $13,000 to $24,500 a year. Owners earn $20,000 a year or more.

Additional sources of information

Information on licensing requirements is available from the appropriate state office of occupational licensing.

American Board of Funeral Service Education
201 Columbia Avenue
Fairmont, WV 26554

National Funeral Directors Association of the United States, Inc.
135 West Wells Street
Milwaukee, WI 52203

G

GEOGRAPHER

The job

Geographers study and analyze the distribution of land forms; climate; soils; vegetation; and mineral, water, and human resources. These studies help to explain the patterns of human settlement.

Over half of all geographers are employed by colleges and universities. The federal government also employs many geographers for mapping, intelligence work, and remote sensing interpretation. State and local governments employ geographers on planning and development commissions.

Textbook and map publishers; travel agencies; manufacturing firms; real estate developers; and insurance, communications, and transportation companies employ geographers. Those with additional training in another discipline such as economics, sociology, or urban planning have a wider range of job opportunities and can work in many other fields.

Cartographers design and construct maps and charts. They also conduct research in surveying and mapping procedures. They work with aerial photographs and analyze data from remote sensing equipment on satellites.

About 15 percent of all geographers in the United States are women.

Places of employment and working conditions

Geographers are employed throughout the country and on foreign assignment as well. The largest single concentration of geographers is in the Washington, D.C. area.

Field work sometimes entails assignment to remote areas and primitive regions of the world. A geographer should be prepared for the physical and social hardships such relocation may require.

Qualifications, education, and training

Anyone interested in this field should enjoy reading, studying, and research and be able to work independently. Good communication skills are also necessary.

High school should include as many mathematics and science courses as possible.

A bachelor's degree with a major in geography is the first step for a would-be geographer. Course work should also include some specialty fields such as cartography, aerial photography, or statistical analysis.

Advanced degrees are required for most teaching positions and for advancement in business and government; a Ph.D. is necessary for the top jobs. Mathematics, statistics, and computer science are of increasing importance in graduate studies; students interested in foreign regional geography are usually required to take a foreign language as well.

Potential and advancement

There are about 10,000 people working as geographers. In general, the field will grow, but some areas will offer more job opportunities than others. College and university teaching positions will remain about the same, and job openings will occur only to replace those who retire, die, or leave the field. The federal government will employ a growing number of geographers and cartographers as will state and local governments. Private industry will provide the largest increase in job openings in this field. Persons with only a bachelor's degree will face competition for jobs.

Advancement in this field depends on experience and additional education.

Income

Geographers with a bachelor's degree start at about $10,700 a year in private industry. The federal government pays between $10,507 and $13,014.

Those with a master's degree begin at about $16,000 in private industry; at $15,920 with the federal government.

A person with a Ph.D. but no experience starts between $12,000 and $14,000 for a nine-month academic year at colleges and universities; the federal government pays $19,263.

Additional sources of information

Association of American Geographers
1710 16th Street, NW
Washington, DC 20009

GEOLOGIST

The job

By examining surface rocks and rock samples drilled from beneath the surface, geologists study the structure, composition, and history of the earth's crust. Their work is important in the search for mineral resources and oil and in the study of predicting earthquakes. Geologists are also employed to advise on the construction of buildings, dams, and highways.

Geologists study plant and animal fossils as well as minerals and rocks. Some specialize in the study of the ocean floor or the composition of other plants. *Vulcanologists* study active and inactive volcanoes and lava flows. *Mineralogists* analyze and classify minerals and precious stones.

Over half of all geologists work in private industry mainly for petroleum and mining companies. The federal government employs over 2,000 geologists in the U.S. Geological Survey, the Bureau of Mines, and the Bureau of Reclamation. State and local governments employ geologists in highway construction and survey work.

Colleges and universities, nonprofit research institutions, and museums also employ geologists.

Only about 4 percent of all geologists are women. Traditionally, this has been a male field, but women with a strong background in mathematics and science are entering the field and liking it.

Related jobs are: Geophysicist, Meteorologist, and Oceanographer.

Places of employment and working conditions

Five states account for most jobs in geology: Texas, California, Louisiana, Colorado, and Oklahoma. Other areas with large oil and mineral deposits also provide job opportunities. American companies often send their geologists to overseas locations for varying periods of time.

Much of the work done by geologists is out-of-doors, often at remote locations. Geologists also cover many miles on foot. Those involved in mining often work underground; geologists in petroleum research often work on offshore oil rigs.

Qualifications, education, and training

Curiosity, analytical thinking, and physical stamina are all necessary for a geologist.

High school work should include as much science and mathematics as possible.

A bachelor's degree in geology or a related field is the basic preparation and is adequate for some entry-level jobs. Teaching and research positions require advanced degrees with specialization in one particular branch of geology.

Potential and advancement

About 34,000 people work as geologists. This is a growing field, and job opportunities will increase steadily as the nation pushes for development of petroleum and other resources.

Those with advanced degrees will have the most job opportunities and the best chances for promotion.

Income

Beginners with a bachelor's degree earn about $15,400 a year in private industry; $19,000 with a master's degree.

The federal government pays beginners from $10,507 to $13,014 with a bachelor's degree; $13,014 to $15,920 with a master's; $19,263 to $23,087 with a Ph.D. Average salary for all geologists employed by the federal government is over $25,000 a year.

Additional sources of information

American Geological Institute
5205 Leesburg Pike
Falls Church, VA 22041

Interagency Board of U.S. Civil Service
 Examiners for Washington, DC
1900 E Street, NW
Washington, DC 20415

GEOPHYSICIST

The job

In general terms, geophysicists study the earth—its composition and physical aspects and its electric, magnetic, and gravitational fields. They usually specialize in one of three general phases of the science—solid earth, fluid earth, or upper atmosphere—and some also study other planets.

Solid earth geophysicists search for oil and mineral deposits, map the earth's surface, and study earthquakes.This field includes *exploration geophysicists,* who use seismic prospecting techniques (sound waves) to locate oil and mineral deposits; *seismologists,* who study the earth's interior and earth vibrations caused by earthquakes and man-made explosions, explore for oil and minerals, and provide information for use in constructing bridges, dams, and large buildings (by determining where bedrock is located in relation to the surface); and *geologists* who study the size, shape, and gravitational field of the earth and other planets and whose principal task is the precise measurement of the earth's surface.

Hydrologists are concerned with the fluid earth. They study the distribution, circulation, and physical properties of underground and surface waters including glaciers, snow, and permafrost. Those who are concerned with water supplies, irrigation, flood control, and soil erosion study rainfall and its rate of infiltration into the soil. *Oceanographers* are also sometimes classified as geophysical scientists.

Geophysicists who study the earth's atmosphere and electric and magnetic fields and compare them with other planets include: *geomagneticians,* who study the earth's magnetic field; *paleomagneticians,* who study rocks and lava flows to learn about past magnetic fields; and *planetologists,* who study the composition and atmosphere of the moon, planets, and other bodies in the solar system. They gather data from geophysical instruments placed on interplanetary space probes or from equipment used by astronauts during the Apollo missions. *Meteorologists* sometimes are also classified as geophysical scientists.

Most geophysicists work in private industry chiefly for petroleum and natural gas companies. Others are in mining, exploration, and consulting firms or in research institutes. A few are independent consultants doing geophysical prospecting on a fee or contract basis.

Approximately 2,300 geophysicists work for the federal government mainly in the U.S. Geological Survey, the National Oceanic and Atmospheric Administration (NOAA), and the Defense Department. Other employers are colleges and universities, state governments, and research institutions. Some geophysicists are also employed by American firms overseas.

New geophysicists usually begin their careers doing field mapping or exploration. Some assist senior geophysicists in research work.

Places of employment and working conditions

In the United States, many geophysicists are employed in southwestern and western states and along the Gulf Coast where large oil and natural gas fields are located.

Many geophysicists work outdoors and must be willing to travel for extended periods. Some work at research stations in remote areas or aboard ships and aircraft. When not in the field, geophysicists work in modern, well-equipped laboratories and offices.

Qualifications, education, and training

Geophysicists should be curious, analytical, and able to communicate effectively and should like to work as part of a team.

High school courses should include as many science courses as possible and mathematics.

A bachelor's degree in geophysics or in a geophysical specialty is acceptable for most beginning jobs. A bachelor's degree in a related field of science or engineering is also adequate, provided courses in geophysics, physics, geology, mathematics, chemistry, and engineering have been included.

About 50 colleges and universities award a bachelor's degree in geophysics. Other training programs offered include geophysical technology, geophysical engineering, engineering geology, petroleum geology, and geodesy.

More than 60 universities grant master's and Ph.D. degrees in geophysics. Geophysicists doing research or supervising exploration should have graduate training in geophysics or a related science, and those planning to do basic research or teach at the college level need a Ph.D. degree.

Potential and advancement

About 12,000 people work as geophysicists; employment opportunities are expected to grow substantially through the 1980s. The number of qualified geophysicists will fall short of requirements if present trends continue. As known deposits of petroleum and other minerals are depleted, petroleum and mining companies will need increasing numbers of geophysicists to find less accessible fuel and mineral deposits. In addition, geophysicists with advanced training will be needed to research alternate energy sources such as geothermal power (use of steam from the earth's interior) and to study solar and cosmic radiation and radioactivity. Federal agencies are also expected to hire more geophysicists for research and development in the earth sciences, energy research, and environmental protection.

Geophysicists with experience can advance to jobs such as project leader or program manager. Some achieve management positions or go into research.

Income

Geophysicists earn relatively high salaries. The average starting salary for graduates with a bachelor's degree is $15,000 a year. Those with a master's degree in geology or related geophysical sciences receive average starting salaries of about $15,600 a year.

The federal government pays geophysicists with a bachelor's degree a starting salary of between $10,507 and $13,014 depending on their college records. Those with a master's degree start at $13,014 to $15,920 a year; with a Ph.D. degree, from $19,263 to $23,087. The average salary for all geophysicists employed by the federal govenment is about $27,600 a year.

Additional sources of information

American Geophysical Union
1909 K Street, NW
Washington, DC

Society of Exploration Geophysicists
P.O. Box 3098
Tulsa, OK 74101

GOLF/TENNIS PROFESSIONAL

The job

Golf professionals provide golf management expertise to all types of golf courses and clubs. Some own and operate their own golf courses, but most are under contract to a course or club.

Most golf professionals are members of the Professional Golfers Association of America (PGA), the largest professional sports organization in the world. Although most people think of professional golfers as those who play on the PGA tour, the majority of PGA members are club professionals. They function as independent businesspeople and teach, plan, and administer a complete golfing facility at private, public, resort, municipal, or military clubs and courses. Their duties cover a large range of activities and responsibilities, and they contribute to the prestige of their course or club by their PGA training and professional status.

Many women are involved in professional golf, and the number is increasing rapidly. Opportunities for women as club professionals should increase throughout the 1980s.

Tennis professionals function in much the same way as golf professionals. They provide tennis instruction at clubs and resorts and may also operate a tennis pro shop or a combination golf and tennis pro shop at the facility.

Places of employment and working conditions

Golf professionals work in all parts of the United States.

They work from daylight to dark, six or seven days a week during most of the year. In some areas, winter weather closes the golf courses for a few months each year.

Qualifications, education, and training

In addition to a complete and fundamental knowledge of golf and tennis along with the ability to play a respectable game, golf and tennis professionals need patience, tact, enthusiasm, and good business skills. The ability to get along with people is also very important.

All PGA golf professionals must complete an apprenticeship program. Applicants must be at least 18 years old. Although a college education is not a requirement, many golf professionals, especially those under 35 years of age, do have some college background.

The PGA apprenticeship program takes at least three years—usually four to seven years—to complete. The program includes active work under a Class A professional golfer, formal study in two business schools, successful completion of the demanding "Playing Ability Test," and an oral examination.

A playing professional who has qualified at a PGA Tour Qualifying School is an Approved Tournament Player and as such is registered in the apprentice program. Players remain active in the program and continue to accumulate the necessary 36 experience credits needed, so long as they maintain an eligible playing position.

Apprentices who complete all requirements are designated as "Class Junior A" if they work in an assistant's position. Once they are employed as a head professional, they are reclassified as "Class A."

A nonmember who already works as a head professional may apply for PGA apprentice status after at least six months of employment at a recognized club or course and successful completion of the Playing Ability Test.

Potential and advancement

There are approximately 8,200 PGA golf professionals and 4,500 apprentices, and there are always more people competing for an opening than there are places for them.

The growing interest in tennis is providing increasing opportunities for tennis pros. Municipal recreation facilities are providing many opportunities.

Income

Golf professionals' earnings vary depending on size and type of club or course and on whether the golf professional is self-employed (owns the course). About one fourth of all professionals earn less than $20,000 a year. Half of them earn between $20,000 and $30,000; the remaining quarter earn over $30,000.

Assistant golf professionals start at very low salaries. The average is about $750 a month plus whatever is earned by giving golf lessons.

Income for tennis professionals varies widely depending on size and type of employer.

Additional sources of information

The Professional Golfers Association of America
Club Relations Department
P.O. Box 12458
Lake Park, FL 33403

GRAPHIC DESIGNER

The job

The field of commercial art includes not only *illustrators* but a variety of other art and graphic specialists who contribute to the final ad or design. For this reason, the title graphic designer has gradually replaced the term "commercial artist."

In a small firm or art department, an *art director*, assisted by a few trainees, might perform all or most of the work. In a large office, however, the art director would develop the artistic theme or idea and supervise the preparation of the material by the various graphic specialists in the department.

The *sketch artist*, also called a *renderer*, prepares a rough drawing of any pictures required. A *layout artist* arranges the illustrations or photographs, plans the typography (typeset material), and selects colors. Once the art director, sketch artist, and layout artist agree on the composition and layout, other graphic artists complete the detail work.

Letterers use a variety of methods and materials to insert headlines and other words. They may hand letter with pen and ink or apply prepared set or photo lettering. *Mechanical artists* prepare mechanicals—illustrations with all of the elements, in exact size, pasted in place as they are to appear. This is a very precise part of the artwork.

Pasteup artists do more routine work; this position is often filled by a beginner.

Many commercial artists work as free-lance illustrators, some in addition to a regular salaried position. They provide sketches and other graphic specialties to advertising agencies, magazines and newspapers, medical or other technical book publishers, and greeting-card manufacturers.

Most people in this field work as salaried staff artists for advertising agencies or departments, commercial art studios, printing and publishing firms, textile companies, photographic studios, television and motion picture studios, and department stores. The federal government employs several thousand commercial artists mainly in the Department of Defense.

Others work for architectural firms and toy manufacturers and in the fashion industry, industrial designing, and theater set and costume designing.

About 35 percent of all commercial artists are women, who work in all phases of this field. Women with exceptional artistic ability find that the best jobs are in the textile industry and in department store fashion illustrating.

Places of employment and working conditions

Opportunities exist in all parts of the country, but the majority are in large cities such as Boston, Chicago, Los Angeles, New York, and Washington, D.C.

The workweek for salaried artists and designers is usually 35 to 40 hours. They sometimes put in additional hours, often under considerable pressure, to meet deadlines.

Qualifications, education, and training

Artistic talent, imagination and style, manual dexterity and the ability to work with great precision, and the ability to transform ideas into visual concepts are all necessary for anyone interested in this field.

Prospective graphic designers should tailor their high school work to the requirements of the art school or college they wish to attend. Any training in art is valuable and students should begin to accumulate a portfolio of their work, since art schools and colleges usually require a sample of the applicant's work as well as an aptitude test.

Art schools, trade schools, junior colleges, and universities offer two- and four-year courses in commercial art or graphic design; some offer fine arts with some course work in commercial art. Art directors especially need a broad background in art plus experience and training in business, photography, topography, and printing production methods.

The continued accumulation of a portfolio representative of the artist's talents and abilities is necessary for employment. Free-lance artists especially must be prepared to display their work for prospective clients.

Potential and advancement

There are about 67,000 people working in this field. Competition for all jobs is normal, and beginners with little specialized training or experience face the stiffest competition. Beginners are usually willing to take any design job they can get just to get into the field and gain some experience.

Some jobs will be more in demand than others. Free-lance illustrators and pasteup and mechanical artists are always needed. Jobs for art directors and layout artists will be fewer and available only to very talented, creative, and experienced artists. This field is also very sensitive to changes in general economic conditions.

Advancement in commercial art usually depends on specialization in either the mechanical elements of graphic design (letterers and mechanical and layout artists) or the pictorial elements (sketch artists, illustrators).

Income

Beginners earn from $110 to $200 a week depending on education. A very talented artist with a strong educational background and good portfolio can start higher.

Experienced artists and designers earn $10,000 to $30,000 a year. Art directors earn $14,000 to $18,000 depending on size of agency or art department. Senior and executive art directors earn up to $45,000.

Free-lance illustrators earn from $10,000 to $38,000 although very talented, well-known illustrators earn above $75,000 a year.

Additional sources of information

National Art Education Association
1916 Association Drive
Reston, VA 22091

National Association of Women Artists
156 Fifth Avenue
New York, NY 10010

The School Art League
131 Livingston Street
Brooklyn, NY 11201

School of Visual Arts
209 East 23rd Street
New York, NY 10010

H

HISTORIAN

The job

The description and analysis of events of the past through writing, teaching, and research is the work of historians. Historians usually specialize in the history of an era—ancient, medieval, or modern—or in a specific country or area. They may also specialize in the history of a field such as economics, the labor movement, architecture, or business.

In the United States, many historians specialize in the social or political history of either the United States or modern Eurpoe. The fields of African, Latin American, Asian, and Near Eastern history are becoming popular as well.

About 70 percent of all historians are employed in colleges and universities where they lecture, write, and do research in addition to teaching. Historians are also employed by libraries, museums, research organizations, historical societies, publishing firms, large corporations, and state and local government agencies.

The federal government employs historians primarily in the National Archives, Smithsonian Institution, and the Departments of Defense, Interior, and State.

Archivists collect historical objects and documents, prepare historical exhibits, and edit and classify historical materials for use in research and other activities. They are employed by museums, special libraries, and historical societies.

About 13 percent of all historians are women.

A related job is: Museum Curator.

Places of employment and working conditions

Historians are employed in just about every college and university, and most cities have at least one museum. Those who work for the federal government work mostly in Washington, D.C.

Qualifications, education, and training

Anyone interested in this field should have an interest in reading, studying, and research and should have the ability and desire to write papers and reports. A historian needs analytical skills and should be able to work both independently or as part of a group.

High school should include as many social science courses as possible. Summer or part-time jobs in museums or libraries are helpful.

Although a bachelor's degree with a major in history is sufficient for a few entry-level jobs, almost all jobs in this field require advanced degrees. A master's degree is the minimum requirement for college instructors with a Ph.D. necessary for a professorship and administrative positions.

History curriculums vary, but all provide training in the basic skills of research methods, writing, and speaking that are needed by historians. Also important are training in archival work and quantitative methods of analysis, including statistical and computer techniques.

Potential and advancement

There are about 22,500 people working as professional historians. Competition will continue to be stiff for all job openings in this field, since there will soon be thousands more Ph.D.'s in the history field than there will be jobs for them to fill. Most openings will occur to replace those who retire or leave the field. Those graduating from prestigious universities and those well-trained in quantitative methods of historical research will have the best job opportunities.

Historians with a master's degree will find teaching positions in community and junior colleges or high schools, but these jobs may also require state teaching certification.

Those with only a bachelor's degree will find very limited opportunities, but their major in history can be an excellent background for a career in journalism, politics, and other fields or for continuing education in law, business administration, or other related disciplines.

Income

Starting salaries in large colleges and universities range from $13,000 to $15,000 a year. Full professors and top administrators earn $25,000 to $30,000.

Salaries for all historians and archivists employed by the federal government average about $24,350.

Additional sources of information

American Historical Association
400 A Street, SE
Washington, DC 20003

National Trust for Historical Preservation
740 Jackson Place, NW
Washington, DC 20006

Organization of American Historians
Indiana University
112 North Bryan Street
Bloomington, IN 47401

HOME ECONOMIST

The job

The comfort and well-being of the family, and the products, services, and practices that affect them are the concern of home economists. Some have a broad knowledge of the whole professional field, while others specialize in consumer affairs, housing, home management, home furnishings and equipment, food and nutrition, clothing and textiles, or child development and family relations.

Over half of all home economists teach. The 50,000 who teach in secondary schools provide instruction in foods and nutrition, child development, clothing selection and care, sewing, consumer education, and other homemaking subjects. About 15,000 teach in adult education programs and present material on improving family relations and homemaking skills; some teach the handicapped and the disadvantaged. College teachers, who number about 7,000, often combine research and teaching duties.

Home economists who are employed by private business firms and trade associations do research, test products, and prepare advertising and instructional materials. Some study consumer needs and advise manufacturers on products to fill those needs.

The federal government employs home economists in the U.S. Department of Agriculture to do research into the buying and spending habits of families in all socioeconomic groups and to develop budget guides for them. Federal, state, and local governments, as well as private agencies, employ home economists in social welfare programs to instruct clients in homemaking skills and family living.

About 5,600 home economists work as cooperative extension service agents and provide adult education programs for rural communities and farmers. They also provide youth programs such as 4-H Clubs and train and supervise volunteer leaders for these programs.

Most home economists are women, although a growing number of men have entered the field in recent years.

Related jobs are: Cooperative Extension Service Worker, Dietician.

Places of employment and working conditions

A 40-hour workweek is the norm in this field, but those in teaching positions usually work some evening hours.

Qualifications, education, and training

Leadership, poise, communication skills, the ability to work with people of many cultures and levels of income, and an interest in the welfare of the family are necessary for this work.

High school courses should include English, home economics, health mathematics, chemistry, and the social sciences. Part-time or summer jobs in children's camps or day nurseries provide valuable experience.

A bachelor's degree in home economics qualifies graduates for most entry-level positions. A master's degree or Ph.D. is required for college teaching, some research and supervisory positions, extension service specialists, and most jobs in nutrition.

Students who intend to teach at the secondary level must complete courses required for teaching certification. Those who intend to specialize in a particular area of home economics need the appropriate advanced courses: chemistry and nutrition for work in foods and nutrition; science and statistics for research work; journalism for advertising and public relations; art and design for clothing and textiles.

Potential and advancement

About 141,000 people work as home economists. Job competition is keen, especially for teaching positions in secondary schools. The best opportunities are for Ph.D.'s in college teaching and in consumer-related jobs in government and business.

Income

Starting salaries for home economists who teach in secondary schools are between $10,000 and $11,000 a year. Average salaries for experienced teachers are about $14,000.

Those who teach at the college level receive average annual salaries that range from $9,300 for instructors to $27,000 for full professors.

The federal government pays from $11,000 to $22,400 depending on education, experience, and level of responsibility.

Cooperative extension workers average $17,000 at the county level, substantially more at the state level.

Sources of information

American Home Economics Association
2010 Massachusetts Avenue, NW
Washington, DC 20036

HOSPITAL ADMINISTRATOR

The job

The exact title may vary from institution to institution—with some calling their chief executive a director, superintendent, executive vice president, or president, but the responsibilities are the same. The administrator must provide the managerial skills necessary to run a hospital or health care facility with all its complex and varied departments and functions. To accomplish this, the administrator must have a working knowledge of all departments and their relationship to each other.

The administrator must: staff the hospital with both medical and nonmedical personnel; provide all aspects of patient care services; purchase supplies and equipment; plan space allocations; and arrange for housekeeping items such as laundry, security, and maintenance. The administrator must also provide and work within a budget; act as liaison between the directors of the hospital and the medical staff; keep up with developments in the health care field including government regulations; handle hospital community relations; and sometimes act as a fund raiser.

In large facilities, the administrator has a staff of assistants with expertise in a variety of fields, but, in small and medium-sized institutions, the administrator is responsible for all of them.

In addition to working in hospitals, health care administrators are employed by nursing homes and extended care facilities, community health centers, mental health centers, outreach clinics, city or county health departments, and health maintenance organizations (HMOs). Others are employed as advisors and specialists by insurance companies, government regulatory agencies, professional standards organizations such as the American Cancer Society and the American Heart Association. Some serve as commissioned officers in the medical service and hospitals of the various armed forces or work for the U.S. Public Health Service or Veterans Administration.

Depending on the size of the institution, a new graduate might start as an administrative assistant, an assistant administrator, a specialist in a specific management area, a department head, or assistant department head. In a small health care facility, the new graduate would start in a position with broad responsibilities, while in a large hospital the position might be narrow in scope with rotating work in several departments necessary to gain broad experience.

There are many women employed in various types and levels of health care administration, and, among the recent recipients of master's degrees in this field, about 14 percent are women. At the present time, however, most of the women who achieve top administrative positions are members of religious orders and are employed in hospitals run by religious organizations.

Places of employment and working conditions

Hospital administrators work throughout the country in hospitals and health care facilities of all sizes.

Administrators put in a full day, usually 60 hours or more a week. They are on call at all times for emergency situations that affect the functioning of the institutions. They have very heavy work loads and are constantly under a great deal of pressure.

Qualifications, education, and training

Administrators should have health and vitality, maturity, sound judgment, tact, patience, the ability to motivate others, good communication skills, and sensitivity for people.

Good grades in high school are important. Courses should include English, science, mathematics, business, public speaking, and social studies. Volunteer work or a part-time job in a hospital is helpful.

Preparation for this career includes four years of college plus two years of special graduate training. Above-average college grades are necessary to gain entry into a graduate program. In general, courses in economics, accounting, statistics, finance, psychology, political science, and as many liberal arts courses as possible are recommended.

Because some graduate programs require a liberal arts background while others require a college background in personnel, business administration, finance, or psychology, students should tailor their college work to the requirements of the specific graduate program they hope to enter.

The administrators of nursing homes must be licensed. Licensing requirements vary from state to state, but all require a specific level of education and experience.

Potential and advancement

There are over 160,000 persons working in some phase of health care administration, but there are only about 17,000 hospital and health care administrators at the upper levels. The field is expanding, but so are the number of colleges and universities offering degrees in the field. The employment picture is especially tight for entry-level jobs. There are between 2,000 and 3,000 graduates in hospital administration every year but only about 750 job openings. Those with a master's degree plus diverse experience have the best chance.

Hospital administrators are already in the top level of their profession and advancement usually takes the form of moving to a larger institution with an increase in responsibility. Advancement is also achieved by a person moving from a single area of responsibility in a large institution to the top post in a small hospital.

Income

Earnings in this field cover a wide range depending on the size of the hospital or health care facility, geographic location, health services provided, and responsibilities of the administrator.

Beginners with a master's degree earn between $14,000 and $22,000. Experienced administrators earn between $20,000 and $55,000, depending on the size of the facility. Those in the top positions in large hospitals earn $50,000 to $70,000 and sometimes more.

Fringe benefits for administrators in hospitals of all sizes are often comparable to those of top executives in industry.

Additional sources of information

American College of Hospital Administrators
840 North Lake Shore Drive
Chicago, IL 60611

American Osteopathic Hospital Association
930 Busse Highway
Park Ridge, IL 61168

Association of University Programs in Health Administration
One Dupont Circle
Suite 420
Washington, DC 20036

American Public Health Association
Division of Program Service
1015 18th Street, NW
Washington, DC 20036

HOTEL/MOTEL AND RESTAURANT MANAGER

The job

The manager of a hotel or motel is responsible for the profitable operation of the facility and for the comfort and satisfaction of the guests.

The manager is responsible for setting room rates and credit policies, the operation of the kitchen and dining rooms, and the housekeeping, accounting, and maintenance departments. In a large hotel or motel, the manager may have several assistants who manage some parts of the operation while, in small facilities, the manager may handle all aspects of the business personally including front-desk clerical work such as taking reservations. This is especially true in owner-operated facilities.

Hotels and motels that have a restaurant and/or cocktail lounge usually employ a *restaurant manager* or *food and beverage manager* to oversee these functions since this is usually an important part of the hotel's business.

More than a third of all hotel and motel managers are self-employed. A significant number work for large hotel and motel chains.

Places of employment and working conditions

Managers and their families very often live in the hotel or motel they manage, and they are on call at all times. Owner-operators often work very long hours.

Qualifications, education, and training

Initiative, self-discipline, and a knack for organization are necessary in this field. Summer or part-time work in a hotel, motel, or restaurant is helpful.

Although small hotels, motels, and restaurants do not have specific educational requirements, they do require experience for manager positions. Some employers, especially in larger facilities, require a bachelor's degree in hotel and restaurant administration.

Training is also available at many junior and community colleges, technical institutes, and through the home study courses of the American Hotel and Motel Association.

Some large hotels have on-the-job management programs in which trainees rotate among various departments to acquire a thorough knowledge of the hotel's operation.

Potential and advancement

There are about 137,000 hotel and motel managers, and the field is expected to have only slow growth in the next decade. Most openings will occur to replace those who retire or leave the field. Those with a college degree in hotel administration will have the best job opportunities.

Assistant managers can advance to manager positions, but they often advance by moving to a larger hotel. Hotel and motel chains usually provide better opportunities for advancement than independent hotels since employees can transfer to another hotel in the chain or to the central office.

Income

Salaries of hotel and motel managers and assistants depend on the size, location, and sales volume of the facility.

Manager trainees with a college degree usually start at about $12,000 a year and receive periodic increases for a year or two.

Experienced managers earn from $22,000 to $55,000 a year. Restaurant managers average from $19,500 to $40,000. Managers may also earn bonuses and are usually provided with lodging, meals, laundry, and other services for themselves and their families.

Additional sources of information

American Hotel and Motel Association
888 Seventh Avenue
New York, NY 10019

Club Managers Association of America
7615 Winterberry Place
P.O. Box 34482
Washington, DC 20034

Council on Hotel, Restaurant, and Institutional Education
1522 K Street, NW
Washington, DC 20005

The Educational Institute of the American
 Hotel and Motel Association
1407 South Harrison Road
East Lansing, MI 48823

National Executive Housekeepers Association, Inc.
Business and Professional Building
414 Second Avenue
Gallipolis, OH 45631

IMPORT/EXPORT WORKER

The job

The buying and selling of raw materials and finished products between U.S. companies and companies in foreign countries are typically handled by import and export workers. Some workers handle both importing and exporting materials; others specialize in one or the other.

Import and export workers may work for firms that do only importing, only exporting, or both. Some work in the foreign trade divisions of large companies.

An *export manager* is responsible for overall management of a company's exporting activities. He or she supervises the activities of sales workers called *foreign representatives* who live and work abroad. These foreign representatives may work in a single country or travel between several countries in the course of servicing the company's customers. They also keep the company informed of any foreign political or economic conditions that might affect business. Orders from foreign customers are processed by *export sales managers*, who draw up contracts and arrange shipping details, and *export credit managers*, who review the customer's financial status and arrange credit terms.

For importing functions, a company usually employs a *support manager* to handle the purchase of foreign goods or raw materials. He supervises the work of *buyers* who live and work abroad.

Companies that do not employ their own import and export workers may utilize the services of *export brokers*, who sell the companies' goods abroad for a commission, or *import merchants* who sell products from foreign countries in this country. A company may also sell its goods to an *export commissionhouse broker*. These brokers are speculators who buy domestic goods outright and then sell them in foreign countries.

Related jobs are: Sales Manager, Wholesaler, Translator, Interpreter.

Places of employment and working conditions

Most import and export workers are employed in the United States. The few overseas positions usually go to those with many years of experience or a special area of expertise.

Workers employed in the United States usually work a 35- to 40-hour week; in foreign countries they are expected to adapt to local working conditions and hours. They may be exposed to extremes in climate and living conditions and may have to spend a great deal of time traveling.

Qualifications, education, and training

Ability to work with detail, administrative talents, diplomacy, and tactfulness are necessary. Those in sales need aggressiveness and the ability to get along with people as well as adaptability for living in foreign cultures. Knowledge of a foreign language is also usually required.

Most employers require a college degree. Some will accept a liberal arts degree but most prefer specific areas such as law, engineering, or accounting. An advanced degree in business administration is necessary for some positions.

Many employers provide training for new employees. This usually includes classroom and on-the-job training that covers U.S. laws governing foreign trade and the practices of foreign countries.

Potential and advancement

Job opportunities in this field are expected to increase through the mid-1980s. Population growth and expanding foreign trade will account for a number of new job openings.

Import and export workers can advance to management and executive positions. Buyers and foreign representatives sometimes advance by going into business for themselves as export brokers or import merchants.

Income

Beginners earn starting salaries of $11,000 to $14,000 a year.

Experienced workers in management-level positions average from $17,000 to $32,000, sometimes much more.

Import and export workers stationed overseas receive overseas incentive allowances.

Additional sources of information

American Importers Association
420 Lexington Avenue
New York, NY 10017

International Group
Chamber of Commerce of the United States
1615 H Street, NW
Washington, DC 20006

National Foreign Trade Council
10 Rockefeller Plaza
New York, NY 10020

INDUSTRIAL DESIGNER

The job

Industrial designers develop new styles and designs for products ranging from pencil sharpeners and dishwashers to automobiles. Some specialize in package design or the creation of trademarks; others plan the
entire layout of commercial buildings such as supermarkets.

Industrial designers combine artistic talent with knowledge of
materials and production methods. Teamwork is necessary in this
field, and input from many people goes into a finished product. Working closely with engineers, production personnel, and sales and marketing experts, industrial designers thoroughly research a product.
They prepare detailed drawings, then a scale model of a new design.
After approval of a design, a full-scale working model is built and tested
before production begins.

Most industrial designers work for large manufacturing firms where
they fill day-to-day design needs and work on long-range planning of
new products; or for design consulting firms that service a number of
industrial companies. Some do free-lance work or work for architectural and interior design firms. A few teach in colleges and universities
or art schools.

There are very few women in this field.

Places of employment and working conditions

Industrial designers work for manufacturing firms in all parts of the
United States. Industrial design consultants work mainly in New York,
Chicago, Los Angeles, and San Francisco.

A five-day, 35- to 40-hour week is usual with occasional overtime
necessary to meet deadlines.

Qualifications, education, and training

Creativity, artistic talent and drawing skills, the ability to see familiar
objects in new ways, and communication skills are necessary. An industrial designer must be able to design to meet the needs and tastes of
the public, not just to suit the designer's artistic ideas.

High school should include courses in art, mechanical drawing, and mathematics.

Courses in industrial design are offered by art schools, technical schools, and colleges and universities. Most large manufacturing firms require a bachelor's degree in industrial design.

Thirty-three colleges and art schools offer programs that are either accredited by the National Association of Schools of Art or recognized by the Industrial Designers Society of America. These programs take four or five years and lead to a bachelor's degree in industrial design or fine arts. Some schools also offer a master's degree in industrial design.

Some schools require the submission of samples of artistic ability before acceptance into their industrial design programs. After graduation, job applicants are expected to show a portfolio of their work to demonstrate their creativity and design ability.

Potential and advancement

There are about 12,000 industrial designers. This is a relatively small field with only limited growth expected in the foreseeable future. Job opportunities will be best for college graduates with degrees in industrial design.

Industrial designers may be promoted to supervisory positions with major responsibility for design of a specific product or group of products. Those with an established reputation sometimes start their own consulting firms.

Income

Beginners in this field earn from $10,000 to $14,000 a year. Experienced designers earn from $15,000 to $30,000, depending on talent and the size of firm.

Sources of information

Industrial Designers Society of America
1750 Old Meadow Road
McLean, VA 22101

INDUSTRIAL ENGINEER

The job

Industrial engineers are concerned with people and methods while other engineers may usually be concerned with a product or progress.

Industrial engineers determine the most efficient and effective way for a company to use the basic components of production—people, machines, and materials.

Industrial engineers develop management control systems for financial planning and cost analysis, design production planning and control systems, design time study and quality control programs, and survey possible plant locations for the best combination of raw materials, transportation, labor supply, and taxes.

About two thirds of all industrial engineers are employed by manufacturing industries, but, because their skills can be used in almost any type of company, industrial engineers work in many industries that don't employ other types of engineeers. They may work for insurance companies, banks, hospitals, retail organizations, and other large business firms as well as more traditional engineering employers such as construction companies, mining firms, and utility companies.

Related jobs are: Office Manager, Interior Designer/Decorator, Systems Analyst.

Places of employment and working conditions

Industrial engineers work in all parts of the country and are concentrated in industrialized and commercial areas.

This is a physically active engineering specialty involving daily visits to departments within the plants, offices, and grounds of the employer as well as travel to possible plant locations.

Qualifications, education, and training

The ability to think analytically, a capacity for detail, and the ability to work as part of a team are all necessary. Good communication skills are important.

Mathematics and the sciences must be emphasized in high school.

A bachelor's degree in engineering is the minimum requirement in this field. In a typical curriculum, the first two years are spent in the study of basic sciences such as physics and chemistry and mathematics, introductory engineering, and some liberal arts courses. The remaining years are usually devoted to specialized engineering courses. Engineering programs can last from four to six years. Those that require five or six years to complete may award a master's degree or may provide a cooperative plan of study plus practical work experience with a nearby industry.

Because of rapid changes in technology, many engineers continue their education throughout their careers. A graduate degree is necessary for most teaching and research positions and for many management jobs. Some persons obtain graduate degrees in business administration.

Engineering graduates usually work under the supervision of an experienced engineer or in a company training program until they become acquainted with the requirements of a particular company or industry.

All states require licensing of engineers whose work may affect life, health, or property or who offer their services to the public. Those who are licensed, about one third of all engineers, are called Registered Engineers. Requirements include graduation from an accredited engineering school, four years of experience, and a written examination.

Potential and advancement

There are about 200,000 industrial engineers. Job opportunities in this field are expected to increase substantially in the 1980s because of the increased complexity and expanding use of automated processes and increased recognition of the importance of scientific management and safety engineering in reducing costs and increasing productivity.

Income

Starting salaries in private industry average $16,800 with a bachelor's degree; $18,700 with a master's degree; and $24,000 or more with a Ph.D.

The federal government pays beginners $13,657 to $20,500 depending on degree and experience. Average salary for experienced engineers federally employed is about $27,700.

Experienced engineers average $30,500 in private industry; $15,000 to $21,000 for nine-month faculty positions in colleges and universities.

Additional sources of information

American Institute of Industrial Engineers, Inc.
25 Technology Park/Atlanta
Norcross, GA 30092

Engineers' Council for Professional Development
345 East 47th Street
New York, NY 10017

National Society of Professional Engineers
2029 K Street, NW
Washington, DC 20006

American Society for Engineering Education
One Dupont Circle, Suite 400
Washington, DC 20036

Society of Women Engineers
United Engineering Center
345 East 47th Street
New York, NY 10017

INSURANCE AGENT AND BROKER

The job

Insurance agents and brokers sell insurance policies to individuals and businesses to protect against financial losses and to provide for future financial needs. They sell one or more of the three basic types of insurance: life, property-liability (casualty), and health.

An *agent* may be either the employee of an insurance company or an independent representative of one or more insurance companies. A *broker* is not under contract to a specific insurance company or companies but places policies directly with whichever company can best serve the needs of a client. Both agents and brokers spend the largest part of their time discussing insurance needs with prospective customers and designing insurance programs to fill each customer's individual needs.

Life insurance agents and brokers (life underwriters) sell policies that provide payment to survivors (beneficiaries) when the policyholder dies. A life policy can also be designed to provide retirement income, educational funds for surviving children, or other benefits.

Casualty insurance agents and brokers sell policies that protect against financial losses from such things as fire, theft, and automobile accidents. They also sell commercial and industrial insurance such as workers' compensation, product liability, and medical malpractice.

Health insurance policies offer protection against the cost of hospital and medical care as well as loss of income due to illness or injury, and are sold by both life and casualty agents and brokers.

More and more agents and brokers are becoming multiline agents, offering both life and property-liability policies to their clients. Some agents and brokers also sell securities such as mutual funds and variable annuities or combine a real estate business with insurance selling. Successful insurance agents or brokers are highly self-motivated.

Anyone interested in this work as a career should be aware that many beginners leave the field because they are unable to establish a large enough clientele. For those who succeed, the financial rewards are usually very good.

Recognizing that the professional working woman represents a new market, the insurance industry has recently been designing insurance programs to meet her special needs. The need for women insurance agents and brokers to service these new clients has expanded, and some insurance companies are actively recruiting women for their sales forces. While some companies hire only college graduates, others are interested in women with experience in sales, business, and finance. At present there are about 40,000 women agents and brokers in the United States.

Related jobs are: Actuary, Claim Representative, Underwriter.

Places of employment and working conditions

Insurance agents and brokers are employed throughout the country, in all locations and communities, but the largest number work in or near large population centers.

Agents and brokers are free to schedule their own working hours but often work evenings and weekends for the convenience of their clients. In addition, hours devoted to paper work and continuing education often add up to much more than 40 hours a week.

Agents and brokers usually pay their own automobile and travel expenses. If they own and operate their own agency, they also pay clerical salaries, office rental, and operating expenses out of their own incomes.

Qualifications, education, and training

Agents and brokers should be enthusiastic, self-confident, and able to communicate effectively. They need initiative and sales ability to build a clientele and must be able to work without supervision.

Many insurance companies prefer a college degree (in almost any field), but will hire high school graduates with proven sales ability or other potential. Courses in accounting, economics, finance, business law, and insurance subjects are the most useful, whether the agent works for an insurance company of is self-employed.

New agents receive training at the agency where they will work or at the home office of the insurance company for which they work. Much of this training involves home study courses.

All states require agents and most brokers to be licensed. In most states, this takes the form of a written examination covering state insurance laws. Insurance companies often sponsor classes to prepare their new agents for the licensing exam, while other new agents study on their own. Some trade and correspondence schools offer courses for insurance agents.

Agents and brokers who wish to succeed in this field are constantly studying to increase their skills. They take college courses and attend educational programs sponsored by their own company or by insurance organizations. The Life Underwriter Training Council (LUTC) awards a diploma in life insurance marketing after successful completion of the council's two-year life program. The council also sponsors a program in health insurance. Experienced agents and brokers earn the Chartered Life Underwriter (CLU) designation by passing a series of examinations given by the American College of Bryn Mawr, Pennsylvania. Property-liability agents receive the Chartered Property Casualty Underwriter (CPCU) designation in the same way from the American Institute for Property and Liability underwriters.

Potential and advancement

There are approximately 465,000 full-time insurance agents and brokers with thousands more working part-time.

Employment of insurance agents and brokers is expected to grow through the next decade. Although sales volume should increase rapidly as a larger proportion of the population enters the period of peak earnings and family responsibilities, the employment of agents and brokers will not necessarily grow as rapidly as sales volume. This is due to the fact that more policies will be sold to groups and by multiline agents and because more of an agent's time-consuming paper work will be done by computer, releasing agents to spend more time in actual selling and client contact.

Promotion to positions such as sales manager in a local office or to management positions in a home office or agency is open to agents with exceptional sales ability and leadership. However, many agents who have a good client base prefer to remain in sales with some establishing their own independent agencies or brokerage firms.

Income

Insurance agents and brokers usually work on a commission basis. Beginners are often provided with a moderate salary until they complete their training and begin to build a clientele. In large companies, this amounts to about $900 a month for about six months.

There is no limit to an agent's earnings. Commissions on new policies and on renewals can amount to between $12,000 to $25,000 a year after only a few years of selling. Many established agents and brokers earn over $40,000 a year; some highly successful ones earn over $100,000 annually.

Additional sources of information

General occupational information about insurance agents and brokers is available from the home office of many insurance companies. Information on state licensing requirements may be obtained from the Department of Insurance at any state capital. Additional sources are:

American Council of Life Insurance
1850 K Street, NW
Washington, DC 20006

National Association of Insurance Agents, Inc.
85 John Street
New York, NY 10038

The National Association of Independent Insurers
Public Relations Department
2600 River Road
Des Plaines, IL 60018

National Association of Insurance Women
Public Relations Committee
1847 East 15th Street
Tulsa, OK 74104

INTERIOR DESIGNER/DECORATOR

The job

Interior designers, also called *interior decorators,* plan and supervise the design and arrangement of building interiors and furnishings. Some work on private residences; others specialize in large commercial and public buildings.

An interior designer considers the purpose of the area and the client's budget and taste. Sketches are prepared for the client's approval and changes are made as required. In some cases, plans and sketches must be prepared several times before a client is satisfied. Once the plans and the cost are approved, the designer shops for and buys furnishings and accessories; supervises the work of painters, carpet layers, and others; and makes sure furnishings are delivered and properly arranged.

Designers who specialize in nonresidential work such as entire office buildings, or public buildings such as libraries or hospitals, plan the complete layout of the interior, working with the architect. In some instances, they design the furnishings and arrange for their manufacture.

Most interior designers work for large design firms that provide design services to a number of clients. Others work for large department or furniture stores, furniture and textile manufacturers, and antique dealers. A few have permanent jobs with hotel and restaurant chains.

A few interior designers design stage sets for motion pictures and television or work for home furnishing magazines.

About half of all interior designers are women.

Places of employment and working conditions

Interior designers work throughout the country, usually in larger communities.

The workweek is usually long in this field, and hours are often irregular.

Qualifications, education, and training

Artistic talent, color sense, good taste, imagination, and the ability to work well with people are all necessary.

High school courses should include art and business skills. Part-time or summer jobs in a home furnishings department or store are helpful.

Formal training in interior design is necessary for all the better jobs with architectural firms, well-established design firms, department and furniture stores, and other major employers. Programs are available at professional schools of interior design (three-year programs); colleges and universities, which award a bachelor's degree; or in graduate programs leading to a master's degree or Ph.D. Courses in sales and business subjects are also valuable.

Regardless of education, beginners almost always go through a training period with the company that hires them. They may function as shoppers, stockroom assistants, salesworkers, assistant decorators, or junior designers. This trainee period lasts from one to five years.

After several years of experience as a designer, including supervisory experience, an interior designer who has had formal training may become a member of the American Society of Interior Design, which is recognized as a mark of achievement in this field.

Potential and advancement

About 37,000 people work as interior designers. Even though growth is expected in this field, its popularity means competition for just about all job openings. The field is also affected by ups and downs in the economy.

After considerable experience, designers may advance to supervisory positions. Some open their own businesses.

Income

Beginners may be paid anywhere from minimum wage to about $150 a week. Some also receive a small commission.

Experienced interior designers may work on commission, salary plus commission, or straight salary. Good decorators with an established reputation can earn over $50,000 a year. A few nationally known designers earn even more.

Additional sources of information

American Society of Interior Design
730 Fifth Avenue
New York, NY 10019

INTERNAL REVENUE AGENT

The job

Internal revenue agents examine and audit the financial records of individuals, businesses, and other organizations to determine their correct federal income tax liability.

In district offices throughout the country, agents audit income tax returns, handle investigations, and provide information and assistance to the public on questions concerning income taxes.

A rapidly expanding career field within the Internal Revenue Service is computerized information processing. Job openings for mathematicians, statisticians, computer programmers, systems analysts, economists, and other computer specialists are increasing steadily.

Places of employment and working conditions

Internal revenue agents work throughout the country as well as in Washington, D.C.

Agents usually work a normal 40-hour workweek with occasional overtime during peak work loads. Agents involved in auditing and investigative work may spend some time in travel.

Qualifications, education, and training

An aptitude for mathematics, ability to do detailed work accurately and to work independently, patience, tact, and the ability to get along with people are important for this job.

In high school, a college preparatory course with plenty of mathematics should be followed.

A college degree is required for all internal revenue agents. A degree in accounting or law or a liberal arts degree with some study of accounting and directly related subjects has been the traditional background for agents. Degrees in computer-related specialties are now also accepted.

Most new agents are hired by district offices through local college recruitment programs. Applicants must pass a civil service examination before being hired. (See job description for Civil Service Worker, Federal.)

Potential and advancement

There are about 13,000 internal revenue agents. Requirements have remained stable in recent years with increases in work load being handled with the aid of computers. The number of interested applicants and the available job openings have just about matched. This situation is expected to continue into the mid-1980s.

Opportunities for advancement are numerous in the Internal Revenue Service. Agents may be promoted to supervisory and management positions in district and regional offices and to top-level positions in Washington.

Income

Internal revenue personnel are paid according to the federal General Schedule (GS) salary scale.

Beginning salaries range from GS-5 to GS-11 ($11,243 to $20,611) depending on education and college grades. Within-grade increases and promotion are rapid, for the most part.

Among experienced agents, approximately half are GS-11 and GS-12 ($20,611 to $32,110), and one fourth are GS-13 to GS-15 ($29,375 to $40,832).

Additional sources of information

Internal Revenue Service District Office in your locality.

INTERPRETER

The job

Oral interpretation is needed whenever a difference in language creates a barrier between people of different cultures. Interpreters can be found escorting foreign visitors and businesspeople, interpreting highly technical speeches and discussions at international medical or scientific meetings, or appearing in a courtroom when the proceedings involve persons who do not speak or understand English.

There are two basic types of interpretation: simultaneous and consecutive. In simultaneous interpretation, the interpreter translates what is being said in one language as the speaker continues to speak in another. This requires both fluency and speed on the part of the interpreter and is made possible by the use of electronic equipment that allows the transmission of simultaneous speeches. Simultaneous interpretation is preferred for conferences and meetings. Conference interpreters often work in a glass-enclosed booth using earphones and a microphone. Those attending the conference can tune into their preferred language by turning a dial or pushing a button.

In consecutive interpretation, the speaker and the interpreter take turns speaking. In addition to having fluency in the language, a consecutive interpreter must also have a good memory and usually takes notes to give a full and accurate translation. This method is very time-consuming but is the usual method with person-to-person interpretation.

The United Nations employs about 90 full-time interpreters. Full-time staff interpreters are also employed by the Organization of American States, the International Monetary Fund, the Pan American Health Organization, and the World Bank. The U.S. Department of State and the U.S. Department of Justice are the major employers of full-time interpreters in the federal government.

Free-lance interpreters usually work on short-term contracts, although some assignments can be of longer duration. The greatest number of free-lance interpreters work under contract for the U.S. Department of State and the Agency of International Development, serving as escort interpreters for foreign visitors to the United States. The next largest group of free-lance interpreters works in the conference field.

A related job is: Translator.

Places of employment and working conditions

This is a relatively small job field with the largest concentration of interpreters in New York City and Washington, D.C.

The conditions under which interpreters work vary widely. Free-lance interpreters have little job security because of the fluctuations in demand for their service. Free-lance assignments can last from a few days for a typical conference to several weeks on some escort assignments. Although interpreters do not necessarily work long hours, they often work irregular hours, with escort interpreters often required to do a great deal of traveling.

Qualifications, education, and training

Anyone interested in becoming an interpreter should be an articulate speaker and have good hearing. This work requires quickness, accuracy, tact, and emotional stamina to deal with the tensions of the job. Interpreters must be dependable as to the honesty of their interpretations and have a sense of responsibility as to the confidentiality of their work.

A complete command of two languages or more is the usual requirement for an interpreter. Interpreters at the United Nations must know at least three of the six official United Nations languages: Arabic, Chinese, English, French, Russian, and Spanish.

An extensive and up-to-date working vocabulary and ease in making the transition from one language structure to another are necessary as well as the ability to instantly call to mind appropriate words or idioms of the language.

Many individuals may qualify on the basis of their own foreign backgrounds, and the experience of living abroad is also very important. Interpreters should be generally well informed and, in the case of conference interpretation, be well grounded in technical subjects such as medicine or scientific and industrial technology.

Interpreters who speak Portuguese, Japanese, and German are also widely in demand in the United States.

Although there is no standard requirement for entry into this profession, a university education generally is essential. In the United States, two schools offer special programs for interpreters. Foreign language proficiency is an entry requirement in both.

Applicants to Georgetown University School of Languages and Linguistics in Washington, D.C., must qualify on the basis of an entrance examination and previous studies at the university level; they usually hold a bachelor's degree and often a master's degree. The school awards a Certificate of Proficiency as a conference interpreter upon successful completion of a one- or two-year course of study. The certificate is recognized by the International Association of Conference Interpreters.

The Department of Translation and Interpretation at the Monterey Institute of Foreign Studies in Monterey, California, offers a two-year graduate program leading to a master's degree in Intercultural Communication and a graduate certificate in either translation, translation/ interpretation, or conference interpretation. School entrance requirements include a bachelor's degree, an aptitude test, fluency in English plus one other language if studying translation, or two other languages for the interpretation field. After two semesters of basic courses in translating and interpreting, applicants must pass a qualifying examination for entrance into the translation or interpretation programs.

Potential and advancement

There are about 175 full-time and 500 free-lance interpreters. Many others do some interpretation work in the course of their jobs. Secretaries with foreign-language abilities are in demand by companies with foreign subsidiaries or customers.

Only highly qualified applicants will find jobs in this field. There is stiff competition for the very limited number of job openings, and the number of openings is not expected to increase through the mid-1980s. Some openings will occur, however, to replace those who retire, die, or leave the field for other reasons. In the past, any increase in the demand for full-time interpreters has been slight and usually temporary and has been met by the existing pool of free-lance interpreters.

Income

Beginning salaries for full-time interpreters employed by interpreting organizations are over $17,000 year. In addition, these interpreting organizations often pay supplementary living and family allowances. The starting salary for conference interpreters at the United Nations is tax-free $16,300 a year; outstanding U.N. interpreters earn $40,000.

Junior interpreters for the U.S. Department of State earn about $20,000 with other federal agencies paying slightly less.

Free-lance interpreters are paid on a daily basis with conference interpreters earning $150 to $185 a day and free-lance escort interpreters receiving $50 to $100 a day. While on assignment, interpreters are usually paid for a seven-day week. They also receive transportation expenses and an allowance for meals, lodging, and other expenses.

Additional sources of information

The American Association of Language Specialists
1000 Connecticut Avenue, NW
Suite 9
Washington, DC 20036

Division of Interpretation and Translation
School of Languages and Linguistics
Georgetown University
Washington, DC 20057

Department of Translation and Interpretation
Monterey Institute of Foreign Studies
P.O. Box 1978
Monterey, CA 93940

Language Services Division
U.S. Department of State
Washington, DC 20520

Secretariat Recruitment Service
United Nations
New York, NY 10017

INVESTMENT MANAGER

The job

An investment manager's function is to manage a company's or an institution's investments. Investment decisions involve such things as what to buy in the way of securities, property for investment, or other items; or what and when to sell existing holdings for maximum return on investment.

Also called Financial Analysts and Securities Analysts, these investment specialists work for banks (where they are usually officers), insurance companies, brokerage firms, and pension plan investment firms and mutual funds. They may function as trustees for institutions or individuals with large holdings or for colleges that have endowment funds to manage. Some use their expertise as financial journalists analyzing the market for financial publications, newspapers, and magazines.

(For a detailed description of the work of people involved in this field see the job description for Market Analyst.)

Places of employment and working conditions

Investment managers work in all parts of the country but are concentrated in Boston, Chicago, New York, and San Francisco.

The work is very time-consuming, since investment specialists must read constantly—newspapers, annual reports, trade publications—to keep abreast of developments and changes in the market.

Qualifications, education, and training

Facility in mathematics; ability to digest, analyze, and interpret large amounts of material; an inquiring mind; and good communication skills are important in this field.

A college degree in economics, political science, business administration, finance, or marketing is preferred in the investment field. Engineering or law, especially if combined with graduate work in business administration, can also provide an excellent background. Training in mathematics, statistics, and computers is becoming increasingly important.

The mark of professionalism in this field is the Chartered Financial Analyst (CFA) degree, which is comparable to the Certified Public Accountant (CPA) for an accountant. About one fourth of all investment specialists have this designation. To earn it, the applicant must fulfill the membership requirements of one of the financial analysts societies and complete three examination programs. Five or more years of experience as a financial analyst are necessary before the third examination can be taken.

Potential and advancement

There are about 15,000 people engaged in investment management. Job opportunities will be good into the 1980s for those with the appropriate degrees and experience.

Since this is already a high-level position in most organizations, further advancement for an investment manager would usually take the form of moving to a larger institution or organization, if he or she has achieved a reputation for accurate analysis and wise management of investments.

Income

Investment managers who work in banking or for large institutions such as colleges earn up to $50,000 or more a year.

The range for all top-level analysts in this field is about $25,000 to $65,000. Some with excellent reputations earn considerably more.

Additional sources of information

The Institute of Chartered Financial Analysts
Monroe Hall
University of Virginia
Charlottesville, VA 22903

New York Stock Exchange
11 Wall Street
New York, NY 10005

Securities Industry Association
20 Broad Street
New York, NY 10005

Financial Analysts Federation
219 East 42nd Street
New York, NY 10017

J

JOCKEY

The job

Jockeys ride horses in races at major tracks and at small race tracks and racing meets throughout the country.

Most jockeys secure an agent to help them book rides with various owners and trainers, although some jockeys ride for a single employer under contract. Jockeys with an established reputation often have more offers than they can handle.

Four or five races a day is considered an average schedule for a jockey. This schedule keeps the jockey sharp and in good physical condition. The leading jockeys often ride eight or nine races a day, but it is not possible to maintain such a strenuous schedule over long periods.

There are only a few women jockeys, and they usually come up through the hunter-jumper ranks.

Places of employment and working conditions

Jockeys are employed throughout the country wherever racetracks and racing stables are located.

They must lead a highly disciplined life with constant attention to physical fitness and weight. Their workday often begins at 4:00 a.m., and they live out of a suitcase as they move from track to track for various races.

Jockeys pay their own living expenses when traveling and also provide their own racing clothes and equipment. Since even the most inexpensive racing saddle costs about $150, boots about $45, helmet $30, plus breeches, saddle girths, and rainy weather gear, a beginning jockey must be prepared for a few lean years until his reputation is established.

Qualifications, education, and training

A jockey must have strength, stamina, quick mental and physical reflexes, and good judgment. Weight is very important; a jockey should weigh between 100 and 103 pounds at the start of his career. A jockey should be normally lightweight, and not have to starve himself to maintain his weight, since dieting would affect his stamina.

It takes about two years to become a race rider. Although jockeys often begin their careers in their teens, today's jockeys find that a high school education is a great help in handling personal and financial affairs during their working years.

There are no schools or training courses for jockeys; each jockey must acquire the necessary skills and complete the apprenticeship requirements on his own.

Most aspiring jockeys have some knowledge of riding acquired either on a family farm, in the hunter-jumper classification, or through working around horses at a racetrack or breeding stable. This background should result in the rider's having acquired the basics of balance and developed "good hands" (the ability to control a horse). With this background, a rider could secure a position at a track as a free-lance exercise rider.

Less frequently, a would-be jockey has no background with horses and must find a small stable willing to teach him even the fundamentals of riding. Such a nonrider will usually spend some time as a "hot-walker" (walks a horse till it cools downs after strenuous activity) or a groom (cleans and cares for horses) before being allowed to ride. The beginner would then become an exercise rider, working first with older horses and then with younger and better horses.

It takes about a year of "riding works," as the daily morning drills of exercise and training are called, before a rider can apply for an apprentice jockey license. The rider must be at least 18 years old and must ride two races for the track stewards, exhibiting a knowledge of racing rules.

The apprentice may then choose to complete the apprenticeship as a licensed free-lance apprentice, whose certificate entitles him to ride for any trainer, or as a contract apprentice who rides for only one stable. Many apprentices prefer the certificate because it gives them an opportunity to ride the better horses and to complete the apprenticeship as soon as possible. Trainers, however, feel that a contract apprenticeship produces a better all-around horseman who knows all aspects of racing, training, and caring for horses.

Apprentice jockeys are known as "bugs," because of the asterisk (*) behind their name in the daily racing program. An apprentice must ride 35 winners to qualify as a journeyman—this could take from one to four years. During the first year, the apprentice is allowed varying weight allowances, which provide an inducement for trainers to use a beginner. After completion of 35 wins, the apprentice receives a journeyman's license.

Potential and advancement

There are approximately 2,200 qualified jockeys in the United States. This is a relatively small job opportunity field and competition is keen.

Income

Jockeys are paid a percentage of the winnings of the horses they ride. In the first few years as a race rider, this could mean low earnings until a jockey establishes a reputation.

Top jockeys earn additional income by contracting their services to major racing stables on a "first call" basis. This means that the jockey's services are reserved for a particular stable. Popular jockeys often have second- and third-call contracts with still other stables. Contract prices vary depending on the size of the stable, but a top jockey at a major track could be paid up to $25,000 a year for a first-call contract, plus $10,000 for a second-call contract, and $5,000 for a third, as well as 10 percent of their purses won and $25 to $50 per ride. If none of his contract stables needs his service in a particular race, the jockey is free to free-lance a mount.

Additional sources of information

Aspiring jockeys should visit local racetracks and talk to owners and trainers regarding possible job openings. The best time for this is early in the morning while the horses are being exercised and trained.

Jockeys' Guild
Room 1501
555 Fifth Avenue
New York, NY 10017

LABOR RELATIONS SPECIALIST

The job

The field of labor relations covers the relationship between the management of a company and the company's unionized employees. Since more and more government employees are becoming unionized, specialists in the field of labor relations are now employed in government agencies as well as in private industry.

The day-to-day administration of the provisions of a union contract is usually the responsibility of a company's personnel department or, in a large company, the industrial relations department. In a small or medium-sized company, the personnel manager might handle union matters as part of his or her responsibilities, but in a large company one or more labor relations specialists are employed. Their responsibilities include handling grievances, preparing for collective bargaining sessions, and participating in contract negotiations. In some companies, labor relations specialists are also involved in accident prevention and industrial safety programs.

A labor relations specialist must stay abreast of developments in labor law and in wages and benefits in local companies and within the industry and must provide constant liaison between the company and union officials. An effective labor relations specialist must be able to work with union representatives in an atmosphere of mutual respect and cooperation.

In companies, usually large ones, that have both union and non-union employees, labor relations and the personnel department are part of the industrial relations department functions.

Labor relations specialists employed by government agencies perform much the same duties as those employed in private industry.

Labor unions do not employ many professionally trained labor relations specialists. At the company and local level, elected union officials handle all union-management matters. At national and international union headquarters, however, research and education staffs usually include specialists with degrees in industrial and labor relations, economics, or law.

Related jobs are: Personnel Manager and Employment Counselor.

Places of employment and working conditions

Labor relations specialists work throughout the United States with the largest concentrations in heavily industrialized areas.

A 40-hour workweek is usual in this field, but longer hours may be necessary during contract negotiations or during periods of labor problems.

Qualifications, education, and training

The ability to see opposing viewpoints is important for a labor relations specialist. Integrity, a sense of fairness, and the ability to work with people of many educational levels and social backgrounds are necessary qualities. Communications skills are a major requirement.

High school courses should include social studies, English, and any courses or extracurricular activities available in public speaking and debating.

Most labor relations specialists begin their careers in personnel work and move into labor relations as they gain experience. (Educational requirements for personnel workers are listed under the Personnel Manager job description.) Those who enter the field of labor relations directly are usually graduates of master's degree programs in industrial or labor relations or have a law degree with course work in industrial relations. Courses in labor law, collective bargaining, labor economics and history, and industrial psychology should be included in either undergraduate or graduate study.

Potential and advancement

There are about 335,000 people working in the overlapping fields of personnel and labor relations. Substantial growth is expected in both with the most job opportunities in state and local government agencies. There will be competition for available job openings in labor relations, since this is a relatively small specialty. Those with graduate training or a law degree will have the best opportunities.

Advancement often takes the form of moving to a larger company. Others advance by moving from middle-level positions in large companies to top-level positions in smaller companies.

Labor relations specialists who gain substantial experience and establish a widely known reputation sometimes work as federal mediators. Their services are made available to companies or industries who have arrived at a stalemate in contract negotiations with a union.

Income

Beginning salaries in labor relations and personnel work range from $12,000 to $16,000. Experienced workers earn $16,000 to $26,500.

Federal mediators earn about $33,892 a year.

Additional sources of information

American Society for Personnel Administration
19 Church Street
Berea, OH 44017

Director of Personnel
National Labor Relations Board
1717 Pennsylvania Road, NW
Washington, DC 20570

LANDSCAPE ARCHITECT

The job

Landscape architects design the outdoor areas of commercial buildings and private homes, public parks and playgrounds, real estate developments, airports, shopping centers, hotels and resorts, and public housing. Their work not only beautifies these areas but helps them to function efficiently as well.

A landscape architect prepares detailed maps and plans showing all existing and planned features and, once the plans are approved, may accept bids from landscape contractors on the work to be done. In addition to planning the placement of trees, shrubs, and walkways, the landscape architect supervises any necessary grading, construction, and planting.

Most landscape architects are self-employed or work for architectural, landscape architectural, or engineering firms. State and local government agencies employ landscape architects for forest management; water storage; public housing, city planning, and urban renewal projects; highways, parks, and recreation areas. The federal government employs them in the Departments of Agriculture, Defense, and Interior. A few are employed by landscape contractors.

Beginners in this field are given simple drafting assignments, working their way up by preparing specifications and construction details and other aspects of project design. It is usually two or three years before they are allowed to handle a design through all stages of development.

Less than 5 percent of all landscape architects are women. Since this field requires a flair for art and design, talents that many women possess, it could prove to be a good job opportunity field for women who like to work out-of-doors.

Related jobs are: Environmentalist, Farmer, Floral Designer, Forester, Forestry Technician, Urban Planner.

Places of employment and working conditions

Landscape architects work throughout the United States, but most job opportunities exist in the large metropolitan areas of the East and West. The biggest growth in this job field in recent years is in the Southwest.

Salaried employees in this field usually work a 40-hour week; self-employed landscape architects often work much longer hours. Although a great many of an architect's hours are spent outdoors, a substantial number of hours are also spent indoors in planning and mapping activities.

Qualifications, education, and training

Creative ability, appreciation of nature, talent in art and design, and the ability to work in detail are important. Business ability is necessary for those who intend to open their own landscape architectural firms.

High school should include courses in biology, botany, art, mathematics, and mechanical drawing. Summer jobs for landscaping contractors or plant nurseries provide good experience.

About 40 colleges offer bachelor's degree programs in landscape architecture that are approved by the American Society of Landscape Architects. Sixty other schools offer programs or courses in this field. Bachelor-degree programs take four or five years to complete.

A license is required in most states for the independent practice of landscape architecture. Requirements include a degree from an accredited school of landscape architecture, two to four years of experience, and a passing grade on a uniform national licensing examination. In some states, six to eight years of apprenticeship training under an experienced landscape architect may sometimes be substituted for college training.

Potential and advancement

There are about 13,000 practicing professional landscape architects. The outlook is for rapid growth in this field through the 1980s, although any periods of downturn in the construction industry could cause temporary slow periods. City and regional planning programs, interest in environmental protection, and the growth of transportation systems and recreational areas will contribute to the demand for qualified landscape architects as will the general growth in population.

Landscape architects usually advance by moving to a larger firm, by becoming associates in their firm, or by opening their own businesses.

Income

Beginning landscape architects earn from $10,500 to $15,000 a year. The federal government pays $10,500 to $15,900 depending on education.

Experienced landscape architects earn between $15,000 and $30,000 a year with $24,456 the average for those employed by the federal government.

Earnings of self-employed landscape architects range from $10,000 to over $25,000.

Additional sources of information

American Society of Landscape Architects
1750 Old Meadow Road
McLean, VA 22101

U.S. Department of Agriculture
Forest Service
Washington, DC 20250

LAWYER

The job

The basic work of a lawyer involves interpreting the law and applying it to the needs of a particular case or client.

Lawyers, also called attorneys, who have a general practice handle a variety of legal matters—making wills, settling estates, preparing property deeds, and drawing up contracts. Others specialize in criminal, corporate, labor, tax, real estate, or international law.

About three fourths of all lawyers are in private practice, either alone or in a law firm. Business firms employ about 38,600 lawyers as salaried in-house counselors to handle company legal matters. The federal government employs about 29,000 lawyers in the Justice Department and other regulatory agencies; state and local governments employ even more. About 8,000 lawyers teach full- or part-time in law schools.

Many people with legal training do not practice law but instead use their legal knowledge as a background for careers in financial analysis, insurance claim adjusting, tax collection, or management consulting. Others work as parole officers or law enforcement officers. Many elected public officials also have a background in law.

About 9 percent of all lawyers are women. Enrollment of women in law schools has increased substantially in recent years because of government insistence on more equitable admission policies. In spite of the general overabundance of job applicants with law degrees, many business firms and government agencies are actively recruiting women law-school graduates to fulfill government-mandated affirmative action programs.

Places of employment and working conditions

Lawyers are needed in every community and by businesses and government agencies throughout the country.

Lawyers often work long hours and are under considerable pressure when a case is being tried. Those in private practice, however, can determine their own hours and case loads and are usually able to work past the usual retirement age.

Qualifications, education, and training

Assertiveness, an interest in people and ideas, the ability to inspire trust and confidence, and top-notch debating and writing skills are necessary for this field. A successful lawyer must be able to research and analyze a case and to think conceptually and logically.

High school courses which develop language and verbal skills are important. Typing, American history, civics and government, and any training in debating, public speaking, or acting will prove useful.

At least seven years of full-time study beyond high school are necessary to obtain a law degree. This study includes four years of college and three years of law school. About one fifth of all graduates attend law school on a part-time basis, taking four years or longer to complete the work.

Although there is no specific "prelaw" college program, the best undergraduate training is one that gives the student a broad educational background while developing the writing, speaking, and thinking skills necessary for a legal career. Majors in the social sciences, natural sciences, and humanities are suitable and should include courses in economics, philosophy, logic, history, and government. Good grades are very important.

Most law schools test an applicant's aptitude for the study of law by requiring the applicant to take the Law School Admission Test (LSAT). Competition for admission to law school is intense. At one point in the mid-1970s, the ratio of applicants to available openings was ten to one. Although this has slowed to some extent and is expected to slow still more in the early 1980s, stiff competition for entrance into law school will remain for the foreseeable future.

Students should attend a law school that is approved by the American Bar Association (ABA) or by an individual state. ABA approval indicates that the school meets the minimum standards of education necessary for practice in any state; state-approved law schools that lack ABA approval prepare graduates for practice in that particular state only. A few states recognize the study of law done entirely in a law office or a combination of law office and law school study. California will accept the study of law by correspondence course, if all other qualifications are met. Several states require the registration and approval of law students by the State Board of Examiners before they enter law school or during the early years of legal study.

The first part of law school is devoted to the study of fundamental courses such as constitutional law, contracts, property law, and judicial procedure. Specialized courses in such fields as tax, labor, or corporate law are also offered. The second part of law school consists of practical training through participation in school-sponsored legal aid activities, courtroom practice in the school's practice court under the supervision of experienced lawyers, and through writing on legal issues for the school's law journal.

Upon successful completion of law school, graduates usually receive the degree of *juris doctor* (J.D.) Those who intend to teach, do research, or specialize usually continue with advanced study.

All states require a lawyer to be admitted to the state bar before practicing law. Requirements include a written examination, at least three years of college, and graduation from an ABA- or state-approved law school. Some states also require the completion of clerkship under an experienced lawyer.

Some states drop the written examination requirements for graduates of their own law schools.

Potential and advancement

There are about 396,000 lawyers practicing in the United States. Although this field is expected to grow steadily, a rapid increase in the number of law school graduates in recent years has created keen competition for available jobs. This situation will probably continue. Graduates of prestigious law schools and those who rank high in their graduating classes will have the best chance of securing salaried positions with law firms, corporations, and government agencies and as law clerks (research assistants) for judges. Lawyers who wish to establish a new practice will find the best opportunities in small towns and in expanding suburban areas.

Lawyers advance from positions as law clerks to experienced lawyers through progressively more responsible work. Many establish their own practice. After years of experience, some lawyers become judges.

Income

Lawyers who establish their own practice usually earn little more than expenses during the first few years, but their income increases rapidly as the practice develops. Private practitioners who are partners in a law firm generally earn more than those who practice alone.

Lawyers starting in salaried positions earn from $10,000 a year with most starting salaries in the $15,000 to $23,000 range. Starting salaries with the federal government are $15,920 to $19,263.

Experienced lawyers working for corporations earn from $31,000 to $50,000 or more; the average is $30,400 for lawyers working for the federal government.

Additional sources of information

Information Services
The American Bar Association
1155 East 60th Street
Chicago, IL 60637

Association of American Law Schools
Suite 370, One Dupont Circle, NW
Washington, DC 20036

National Association of Women Lawyers
1155 East 60th Street
Chicago, IL 60637

LIBRARIAN

The job

Librarians select and organize books and other publications and materials and assist readers in their use. Their work is divided into two areas: Librarians in user services deal directly with the public helping them to find the information and materials they need; those in technical services order, classify, and catalog materials and do not usually deal with the public. A librarian in a small or medium-sized library does both types of work.

Librarians are usually classified by the type of library in which they work—public, school, college and university, or special library.

Public librarians work in community libraries and provide a full range of library services for the citizens of the community. Depending on the budget and size of the community, the library staff may include acquisition librarians who purchase books and other materials and help users find what they need, reference librarians who help with specific questions and suggest information sources, and extension or outreach librarians who staff bookmobiles. Children's librarians and adult services librarians may be in charge of services for those particular age groups.

School librarians in elementary and secondary schools instruct students in the use of school library facilities, work with teachers to provide materials that interest students and supplement their classroom work, sometimes participate in team-teaching activities, and develop audio-visual programs.

College and university librarians provide services to students, faculty members, and researchers. Some operate documentation centers that record, store, and retrieve specialized information for university research projects or work in a special field such as law, medicine, or music.

Special librarians work in libraries maintained by government agencies and by commercial and business firms. They build and arrange the organization's information resources and provide materials and services covering subjects of special interest or use to the organization. They may be called upon to conduct a literature search or compile a bibliography on a specific subject.

Information science specialists work in much the same way as special librarians, but they have a more extensive technical and scientific background and greater knowledge of new information-handling techniques. They condense complicated information into readable form and interpret and analyze data for highly specialized clientele. They develop classification systems, prepare coding and programming techniques for computer information storage and retrieval, and develop microfilm technology.

Elementary and secondary schools employ about two fifths of all librarians. Public libraries employ about one fifth as do colleges and universities. The rest work in special libraries. The federal government employs about 3,300 professional librarians.

Eighty-five percent of all librarians are women. Because many opportunities for part-time work exist in public libraries and because elementary and secondary school librarians work a nine-month year, this is a good job opportunity field for people with family responsibilities.

213

Places of employment and working conditions

Librarians work in communities of all sizes.

A typical workweek is 35 to 40 hours. In public libraries and in college and university libraries, this usually includes some evening and weekend work.

Qualifications, education, and training

Intellectual curiosity and an interest in helping others are necessary characteristics for a librarian. A knack for organization and a retentive memory are very important.

High school should include courses and activities that develop verbal and language skills in a broad college preparatory program.

A liberal arts degree with a major in the social sciences, the arts, or literature, including course work in library science and a reading knowledge of at least one foreign language, is required for entrance into a graduate program in library science. The one-year program leads to a master's degree (M.L.S.). Those who intend to work as special librarians or information science specialists usually earn a bachelor's degree in their specialty plus a master's or Ph.D. degree in library or information science.

Both undergraduate and graduate programs offer course work in such library specialties as data processing fundamentals and computer languages and the use and development of audio-visual materials. Librarians who intend to work as public school librarians must also complete teaching certification requirements in most states.

A Ph.D. degree is usually necessary for administrative positions in large public library systems and in college and university libraries.

Potential and advancement

There are about 128,000 professional librarians. Employment opportunities will be somewhat competitive in the foreseeable future in spite of expansion in this field. Public library systems will offer the most job opportunities; schools will offer the fewest because of declining enrollments. Those trained as information science specialists will be in demand because of the expanding use of computers to store and retrieve information. Job competition will be greatest in large eastern cities and on the West Coast.

Experienced librarians with graduate training can advance to administrative positions. Those who acquire specialized training can advance to special librarian positions or to specialized libraries in government agencies or businesses.

Income

Starting salaries average about $11,894 a year, $15,000 with the federal government.

Experienced librarians average about $21,900 with the federal government, less in other facilities.

Additional sources of information

American Library Association
50 East Huron Street
Chicago, IL 60611

Special Libraries Association
235 Park Avenue, South
New York, NY 10003

Office of Libraries and Learning Resources
Office of Education
U.S. Department of Health, Education, and Welfare
Washington, DC 20202

Secretariat
Federal Library Committee
Room 310, Library of Congress
Washington, DC 20540

American Society for Information Science
1140 Connecticut Avenue, NW
Washington, DC 20036

LIFE SCIENTIST

The job

From the smallest living cell to the largest animals and plants, life scientists study living organisms and their life processes. Life scientists usually work in one of three broad areas: agriculture, biology, or medicine.

About one third of all life scientists are involved in research and development—doing basic research or applying it in medicine, increasing agricultural yields, and improving the environment. Another one third hold management and administrative positions in zoos and botanical gardens and in programs dealing with the testing of foods and drugs. Some work in technical sales and service jobs for industrial firms or work as consultants to business and government.

Some life scientists call themselves *biologists,* but the usual method of classification is according to type of organism studied or the specific activity performed. *Botanists* deal with plants—studying, classifying, and developing cures for plant diseases. *Agronomists* work with food crops to increase yields, to control disease, pests, and weeds, and to prevent soil erosion. *Horticulturists* are concerned with orchard and garden plants such as fruit and nut trees, vegetables, and flowers.

Zoologists, who study animal life, have titles that reflect the group they study: *ornithologists* study birds, *entomologists* study insects, and *mammalogists* study mammals. *Animal husbandry specialists* are involved in breeding, feeding, and controlling disease in domestic animals. *Embryologists* study the development of animals from fertilized egg through the hatching process.

Microbiologists investigate the growth and characteristics of microscopic organisms such as bacteria, viruses, and molds. *Medical microbiologists* study the relationship between bacteria and disease and the effects of antibiotics on bacteria.

Pathologists study the effect of diseases, parasites, insects, or drugs on human cells and tissue. *Pharmacologists* test the effect of drugs, gases, poisons, and other substances on animals and use the results of their research to develop new or improved drugs and medicines.

Anatomists, ecologists, geneticists, and *nutritionists* are also life scientists. About one half of these life scientists are employed in colleges and universities usually in medical schools and state agricultural colleges. About one fourth of these professionals are employed by the federal government, almost all of them in the Department of Agriculture. The remainder are employed by private industry in drug, food-products, and agricultural-related industries.

About 20 percent of all life scientists are women, and approximately 40 percent of the Ph.D. degrees awarded in this field go to women.

Related jobs are: Biochemist, Environmentalist, Oceanographer, Soil Scientist, and Veterinarian.

Places of employment and working conditions

Life scientists work throughout the United States with the largest concentrations in metropolitan areas.

Most life scientists work in laboratories; some jobs, however, require outdoor work and strenuous physical labor. Working hours may be irregular in some specialties due to the nature of the research or activity under way.

Qualifications, education, and training

The ability to work independently and to function as part of a team is necessary for a career in the life sciences. Good communication skills are also necessary. Physical stamina is necessary in some of the specialty areas that require outdoor work.

High school courses should include as much science and mathematics as possible.

Almost all liberal arts programs include a biology major, and life science students should also include chemistry and physics courses. Some colleges offer bachelor's degrees in specific life sciences; many state universities offer programs in agricultural specialties. A bachelor's degree is adequate preparation for testing and inspection jobs and for advanced technician jobs in the medical field. With courses in education, it is also adequate background for high school teaching positions.

An advanced degree is required for most jobs in the life sciences. A master's degree is sufficient for some jobs in applied research and college teaching, but a Ph.D. is required for most teaching positions at the college level, for independent research, and for many administration jobs. A health science degree is necessary for some jobs in the medical field.

Requirements for advanced degrees usually include field work and laboratory research.

Potential and advancement

There are approximately 205,000 life scientists in the United States including 40,000 engaged in agricultural sciences and about 65,000 in medical fields. Job opportunities in the life sciences will increase, but some fields will be better than others: Medical and environmental research will grow, while teaching opportunities will not. Overall predictions estimate that there will be 66,000 more Ph.D.'s in the 1980s. Life science degrees are useful in other fields, however, such as health care and laboratory technology.

Advancement in this field depends on experience and is usually limited to those with advanced degrees.

Income

Life scientists earn relatively high salaries with earnings of all life scientists averaging above $20,000 a year.

In private industry, beginners with a bachelor's degree average between $11,500 and $12,400. Pharmacologists are the highest paid in private industry.

217

Life scientists who have an M.D. degree earn more than other life scientists but not as much as physicians in private practice.

The federal government starts beginners with a bachelor's degree at $10,507 or $13,014 depending on their academic record. Starting salaries for life scientists with a master's degree are about $13,014 or $15,920, depending on academic record or experience; those with a Ph.D. degree start at about $19,263 or $23,800.

Additional sources of information

American Institute of Biological Sciences
1401 Wilson Boulevard
Arlington, VA 22209

American Society for Horticultural Science
National Center for American Horticulture
Mt. Vernon, VA 22121

American Physiological Society
Education Office
9650 Rockville Pike
Bethesda, MD 20014

U.S. Civil Service Commission
Washington Area Office
1900 E Street, NW
Washington, DC 20415

LOBBYIST

The job

Lobbying is an effort by an interested person or organization to influence legislation. On one hand, lobbying provides information relative to the target legislation and lets the legislator know the feelings of a particular group of constituents. Lobbying may also have the negative reputation of applying pressure.

Lobbyists may take the form of individual citizens who write to congressmen or state legislators about a particular matter. Groups of citizens who band together in demonstrations, telephone campaigns, or other efforts to influence lawmakers and regulatory agencies are also lobbying.

At the professional level, there are full-time officials of powerful organizations and industries who are paid to present their employer's side of a controversial question to the appropriate congressman or committee. Their titles may signify legislative liaison or public relations duties, but their actual work is lobbying. There are some professional lobbyists who represent several clients simultaneously.

Some of the most effective lobbyists are former congressmen, state legislators, and other adminstrative officials who are no longer active politically but who know their way around state capitols or federal agencies.

The most active lobbying groups at all levels are those from business, labor, farming, education, churches, and citizens' groups.

Places of employment and working conditions

Lobbyists operate at all levels of government in all parts of the country.

Although some lobbyists are involved in "wining and dining" activities, a lot of hard work accompanies the more glamorous activities. Long hours are normal, and it is often necessary to work irregular hours to get to see important congressmen and state officials.

Qualifications, education, and training

Personal integrity, good judgment, persistence, resourcefulness, patience, tact, an ability to get along with people, good communication skills, and physical stamina are necessary.

There are no specific educational requirements for a lobbyist. Training or experience in a particular field of interest, which provides a thorough background, plus a knowledge of how the government works and which people can make a difference are what makes an effective lobbyist.

Potential and advancement

So long as there is legislation being considered, there will be lobbyists employed to influence the legislators. Active participation in a professional or political organization can provide opportunities for lobbying, and membership in nationally active groups can lead to federal-level lobbying.

Income

Earnings of lobbyists are difficult to establish. Many people are unpaid lobbyists who work for organizations or causes in which they have an interest. Others, although registered lobbyists, earn the bulk of their income in some other line of work. An example is a public relations director for a large organization who spends most of his time in that function but also represents his company's interest as a lobbyist on a particular piece of pending legislation.

Additional sources of information

People's Lobby
3456 West Olympic Blvd.
Los Angeles, CA 90019

Women's Lobby
201 Massachusetts Avenue, NE
Washington, DC 20002

MACHINIST

The job

Machinists are skilled metal workers who know the working properties of a variety of metals and use this knowledge to turn a block of metal into a precisely machined part. In addition to making metal parts for automobiles, machines, and other equipment, machinists also repair or make new parts for factory machinery.

Machinists work from blueprints or written specifications and use a variety of machine tools, precision instruments such as micrometers, and hand tools.

All factories employ machinists to handle repairs and maintenance on equipment and machinery. Others are employed in industries that manufacture large numbers of metal parts such as the auto industry. Independent machine shops of all sizes employ many machinists; the federal government employs many more in navy yards and other installations.

Machinists are usually union members with most of them belonging to either the International Association of Machinists and Aerospace Workers; the International Union, United Automobile Aerospace and Agricultural Implement Workers of America; the International Union of Electrical, Radio, and Machine Workers; the International Brotherhood of Electrical Workers; or the United Steelworkers of America.

A related job is: Tool-and-Die Maker.

Places of employment and working conditions

Machinists work in all parts of the United States but mainly in large industrial areas such as Boston, Chicago, New York, Philadelphia, San Francisco, and Houston.

Machinists work in well-lighted areas, but the work is often noisy and can be tedious and repetitive. They use grease and oil in the course of their work and often stand most of the day. Finger, hand, and eye injuries are possible from flying metal particles, and safety rules usually require the use of specially fitted eyeglasses, protective aprons, and short-sleeve shirts.

Qualifications, education, and training

Anyone who wants to be a machinist should be mechanically inclined and temperamentally suited to doing work that requires concentration, precision, and physical effort. A machinist must also be able to work independently.

High school or vocational courses should include mathematics, physics, and machine shop classes, if possible.

A four-year formal apprenticeship is the best training for an all-around machinist. Some companies offer shorter courses for machinists who will work on single-purpose machines; and some machinists do learn through on-the-job training. But those who complete a formal apprenticeship program usually have the best opportunities for advancement since they are capable of handling a wider variety of jobs.

A typical apprentice program consists of about 8,000 hours of shop training and about 570 hours of related classroom instruction in blueprint reading, mechanical drawing, and shop mathematics.

Some companies require experienced machinists to take additional courses in mathematics and electronics, at company expense, so that they qualify to service and operate numerically controlled (computerized) machine tools.

Potential and advancement

There are about 400,000 machinists and the field is expected to grow steadily. Population growth will increase the demand for machined goods such as automobiles, household appliances, and industrial products and will result in a growing need for machinists. The increased use of computer-controlled machining operations in some industries will mean higher productivity possibilities for each machinist, but job opportunities will continue to increase in this large occupation field.

Advancement in this field is to supervisory positions. With additional training, machinists can also become tool-and-die makers or instrument makers. Some experienced machinists open their own machine shops or take technical jobs in machine tooling and programming.

Income

Income is stable for machinists since they work indoors and usually have steady work all year long. Earnings in metropolitan areas range from $6.65 to $9.56 an hour, and machinists often have opportunities for overtime work.

Apprentices begin at about 65 percent of the rate paid to experienced machinists and receive periodic increases during their training.

Additional sources of information

International Association of Machinists & Aerospace Workers
1300 Connecticut Avenue, NW
Washington, DC 20036

International Union, United Automobile, Aerospace & Agricultural
  Implement Workers of America
Skilled Trades Department
8000 East Jefferson Avenue
Detroit, MI 48214

International Union of Electrical, Radio, & Machine Workers
1126 16th Street, NW
Washington, DC 20036

National Machine Tool Builders Association
7901 Westpark Drive
McLean, VA 22101

National Tool, Die & Precision Machining Association
9300 Livingston Road
Oxon Hill, MD 20022

MANAGEMENT CONSULTANT

The job

Management consultants help managers analyze the management and operating problems of an individual organization. They recommend solutions to problems concerning the objectives, policies, and functions of the organization. They may also help with implementation of any recommended programs.

About half of all management consultants work for general management consulting firms. The next largest group, about one fifth of the total, are *internal management consultants* who work for a single large corporation and provide management consulting services to various departments and divisions as needed. Another one fifth are university-affiliated consultants who spend varying amounts of time consulting in addition to their teaching duties.

A substantial number of management consultants are employed by public accounting firms where they provide management advisory services to the firms' clients. There are also a number of self-employed, solo management consultants.

Businesses and industries of all kinds use the services of management consultants as do government agencies, nonprofit organizations, and institutions such as hospitals.

Related jobs are: Systems Analyst, Operations Research Analyst, Industrial Engineer, and Office Manager.

Places of employment and working conditions

Management consultants are employed in all areas of the country. Some jobs may involve temporary overseas assignment, if multinational corporations are involved.

Management consultants work long hours. A 50-hour week is a short week; most consultants work even more hours. Travel plays a large part in the consultant's work; some estimates say 20 to 35 percent of a consultant's time is taken up in traveling to a client's location or between different locations of a client's organization.

Qualifications, education, and training

An analytical mind, good judgment, objectivity, tact, good communication skills, and the ability to work as part of a team are necessary.

High school should provide a solid college preparatory course with emphasis on mathematics, social sciences, and communication skills.

A college degree in engineering, business administration, accounting, or other related fields should be followed by graduate study in business administration or public administration.

A number of professional societies offer examinations leading to various certifications in this field. Some of them are Certified Management Consultant (CMC), Certified Management Accountant, Registered Professional Engineer, and Certified Data Processor.

Potential and advancement

There are between 50,000 and 65,000 people engaged in management consulting, and knowledgeable experts in this field are anticipating close to a 20 percent per year growth rate into the mid-1980s. Even if the growth rate is slower than anticipated, there will be plenty of job opportunities for qualified management consultants.

Management consultants can advance to positions as project directors and, with extensive experience, may become associates or partners in their firm. Some advance by going into business for themselves or take a high-level job with a large corporation.

Income

The income of management consultants varies so greatly that average figures are difficult to estimate. Basic information on income in the various specialty fields that supply management consultants— engineering, economics, operations research, public relations, hospital administration, industrial designing, personnel and labor relations, office management, systems analysis—is included under separate job descriptions elsewhere in this book.

Additional sources of information

Institute of Management Consultants, Inc.
347 Madison Avenue
New York, NY 10017

MANUFACTURER'S SALES REPRESENTATIVE

The job

Most manufacturing firms sell their products to businesses, other industrial firms, and retail outlets through their own sales representatives. Familiarly known as *sales reps* or *manufacturers' reps,* these sales workers are thoroughly familiar with their employer's product and often provide advice and technical expertise to the customers they service.

When the product sold is highly technical, such as computers or industrial equipment, a manufacturer usually employs engineers or other technically trained people for sales. These *sales engineers* or *technical sales workers* may design systems for the client, supervise installation of equipment, and provide training for the client's employees who will use the new equipment or material.

The largest employer of manufacturer's sales representatives is the food products industry. Other major employers are the printing and publishing, chemicals, drugs, fabricated metal products, electrical, and machinery industries.

Only about 10 percent of all sales reps are women. As more women acquire engineering degrees, this field will probably employ an increasing number of women with sales ability.

Related jobs are: Sales Manager, Engineer, and Wholesaler.

Places of employment and working conditions

Some sales reps work out of local or regional offices, which keeps them fairly close to home. Others cover large territories and do a great deal of traveling. Since they almost always work on commission, successful sales reps spend as much time as possible calling on customers during business hours and do any necessary traveling evenings and weekends.

Qualifications, education, and training

Selling skills, assertiveness, a pleasant personality, physical stamina, and the ability to get along with all kinds of people are necessary for this job.

A college preparatory course should be followed in high school. Part-time or summer job experience in selling is valuable experience.

A college degree is becoming increasingly important for those who wish to work as a manufacturer's sales representative. Manufacturers of nontechnical products often prefer a liberal arts, business administration, or marketing degree. Other employers have special educational requirements: *Pharmaceutical retailers* (drug sales workers) need training at a college of pharmacy; chemical manufacturers require a degree in chemistry; a computer manufacturer might hire only electronic engineers for its sales positions.

Regardless of the field, employers usually provide a training period of up to two years for new employees. Some training programs consist of classroom instruction plus on-the-job training in a branch office under the supervision of a field sales manager. In other programs, trainees are rotated through a number of jobs and departments to learn all phases of production, installation, and service of the employer's product before being assigned to a sales territory.

Potential and advancement

There are about 360,000 manufacturers' sales representatives, 15,000 of them functioning as sales engineers. The employment outlook for this field is good through the 1980s, as the demand for more and more technical products will increase the demand for technically trained sales workers. Employers are expected to be very selective, however, and those with solid educational backgrounds will get the choice jobs.

Experienced and hard-working people in this field can advance to branch manager and district manager positions and to executive-level positions such as sales manager. Many of the top-level corporate positions in industry are filled by people who started out in sales positions.

Income

Manufacturers' sales representatives may be paid in a number of ways—a salary (usually for trainees), salary plus commission, or straight commission. Many companies also provide bonuses based on sales performance.

Earnings for beginning sales reps range from $15,400 to about $24,000 a year. The highest starting salaries are paid by manufacturers of electrical and electronics equipment, construction materials and tools, food products, rubber goods, and scientific and precision instruments.

Experienced sales reps average between $19,200 and $38,500 a year; a few earn from $49,500 to $57,200.

Additional sources of information

Sales and Marketing Executives International
Career Education Division
380 Lexington Avenue
New York, NY 10017

Manufacturers' Agents National Association
P.O. Box 16878
Irvine, CA 92713

National Association of Wholesalers-Distributors
1725 K Street, NW
Washington, DC 20006

National Association of Sales Training Executives
1040 Woodcock Road
Orlando, FL 32803

MARKET ANALYST

The job

The decision to buy, hold, or sell securities is sometimes made through utilizing the knowledge of the individual buyer or seller, but most individuals consult their stockbroker for advice. The stockbroker, in turn, depends on the expertise of the research department of his or her firm to provide the necessary information. These experts are called market analysts or securities analysts.

In addition to being employed in brokerage houses, market analysts and securities analysts are also employed by investment banking firms, bank trust departments, insurance companies, pension and mutual funds, investment advisory firms, and institutions such as colleges that have endowment funds to manage. All these organizations expect the same thing: expert advice that will help them to invest wisely with the best return on their money.

Market analysts evaluate the market as a whole. They study information on changes in the gross national product, cost of living, personal income, rate of employment, construction starts, fiscal plans of the federal government, growth and inflation rates, balance of payments, market trends, and indexes of common stocks. They also monitor events that might produce a psychological reaction in the market: international crisis, political activity, or a tragedy large enough to cause the market to change direction. Market analysts also keep an eye on business and industry developments and actions of the Federal Reserve to loosen or tighten credit.

Securities analysts study and analyze individual companies or industries, relating knowledge of the current and future state of the economy to predict the future performance of the company of industry. Analysts may specialize in a specific area such as companies involved in energy production or the aircraft manufacturing industry. The analyst studies all available material on an individual company including annual reports and details of company management and sometimes travels to the company to take a closer look in person.

An investor who has an investment portfolio containing a number of different securities needs advice not only on the individual securities but also on the makeup of the entire portfolio. A *portfolio analyst* has the broad general knowledge to give advice on the market and its relationship to the objectives of the investor. The accumulation of a balanced portfolio can then be accomplished.

Those who deal in securities actually combine elements of all of these three areas within the scope of their work. But, in organizations that employ large numbers of researchers, the jobs are often separate.

Only about 5 percent of all analysts are women. As more women acquire degrees in mathematics-related fields, this situation should improve.

Related jobs are: Actuary, Economist, Insurance Agent and Broker, Investment Manager, Statistician, Securities Sales Worker, Stockbroker.

Places of employment and working conditions

Analysts work in all parts of the country but are concentrated in Boston, Chicago, New York, and San Francisco. Major brokerage houses have branch offices in about 800 cities.

Analysts find their work fascinating but time-consuming. They must read constantly—newspapers, annual reports, trade publications—to keep abreast of developments and changes in market. Their advancement depends on the reputation they achieve for accurate analysis and predictions. They are sometimes required to make decisions quickly on securities worth thousands, or even millions of dollars.

Qualifications, education, and training

The ability to interpret and analyze large amounts of material, an inquiring mind, and facility in mathematics are absolutely necessary. Good communication skills are important.

A high school background with plenty of mathematics and preparation for college are essential. Some type of selling experience is usually necessary.

A college degree is required by just about all employers. Economics, political science, or business administration are the preferred degrees. Engineering, law, finance, and marketing, especially when combined with graduate work in business administration, are also accepted. The growing use of computers in this field requires the addition to research staffs of those trained in mathematics and statistics.

The mark of professionalism among analysts is the Chartered Financial Analyst (CFA) degree, comparable to the CPA for an accountant. About one fourth of all analysts have this designation. To earn this degree, an analyst must fulfill the membership requirements of one of the financial analysts societies in the United States and complete three examination programs. Analysts must have five or more years of experience before taking the third examination.

Potential and advancement

There are about 15,000 analysts, over 3,000 of them CFAs. Job opportunities in this field will be good into the 1980s for those with appropriate degrees and some knowledge of computers.

In the securities field, research departments are considered the best springboard to advancement since analysts acquire in-depth knowledge of the economy and the market. Within research, the career path is usually junior analyst, analyst, sometimes a specialty field, then senior analyst. Advancement to management positions in branch offices is also possible.

Income

Junior analysts earn $14,000 to $18,000 a year; experienced analysts $17,000 to $35,000.

Analysts who acquire a reputation or who work in an investment banking firm or for an institution such as a college earn up to $50,000 or more.

Portfolio analysts earn $14,000 to $24,000 a year; department heads $45,000 to $65,000.

Median pay for analysts in New York is $34,000; in Boston $31,000; in Chicago $30,000.

Additional sources of information

The Institute of Chartered Financial Analysts
Monroe Hall
University of Virginia
Charlottesville, VA 22903

New York Stock Exchange
11 Wall Street
New York, NY 10005

Securities Industry Association
20 Broad Street
New York, NY 10005

Financial Analysts Federation
219 East 42nd Street
New York, NY 10017

MARKETING RESEARCHER

The job

Marketing researchers plan and design research projects, conduct interviews and other fact-gathering operations, and tabulate and analyze the resulting material.

The information a marketing researcher provides may help a company to decide on brand names, product and packaging design, company locations, and the type of advertising to use.

A marketing research director designs a research project after studying a company's sales records, its competitors, and the consumer market that uses the type of product or service the company offers. He or she then calls on members of the marketing research staff to implement the project.

A statistician will determine a sample group of consumers to be studied. A *senior analyst* or *project director* might design a questionnaire or a mail or telephone survey for field interviewers to use. *Coders and tabulators* synthesize the results, which are reviewed by a *research analyst* who studies the results and makes recommendations based on the findings.

Advertising researchers specialize in studying the effects of advertising. They pretest commercials, test-market new products, and analyze the appropriateness of the various media (radio, television, newspapers, magazines, or direct mail) for a particular product or advertiser. Beginners in this field start by coding and tabulating data. They move on to interviewing and writing reports and may move up to jobs as research assistants as they gain experience.

Many opportunities for part-time work exist in marketing research. Coding, tabulating, interviewing, and making telephone surveys are jobs for which research organizations often hire people who can work odd hours or during peak work loads. High school and college students and housewives will find this a good field for summer jobs or for weekend or evening work.

As in advertising, this is a field where men hold the top professional jobs and few women achieve management status.

Related jobs are: Advertising Account Executive, Advertising Manager, Advertising Worker, Mathematician, Statistician, Psychologist.

Places of employment and working conditions

Most market researchers are employed by manufacturers, advertising agencies, and market research firms. The largest corporations are in Chicago and New York City, but job opportunities exist in almost every large city.

The usual workweek is 40 hours, but those conducting interviews and surveys are likely to have evening and weekend work. Market researchers often work under pressure and may be called upon to work overtime to meet deadlines. Although this is basically an office job, travel is a necessary part of the work in the information-gathering stages. The travel may be local or far afield depending on the scope and design of the research project.

Qualifications, education, and training

Assertiveness, analyzing skills, and communication skills are very important.

High school courses should include English, mathematics, and public speaking. Summer or part-time jobs coding or taking surveys are good experience.

A college degree is required for just about all of the full-time jobs in marketing research. A bachelor's degree in liberal arts, business administration, marketing, economics, or mathematics is necessary for most trainee positions. Courses in English, marketing economics, statistics, psychology, sociology, and political science should be included. A knowledge of data processing is of increasing importance as the use of computers for sales forecasting, distribution, and cost analysis is growing.

Advanced degrees are becoming more and more important for jobs beyond the entry level and for promotion. Job applicants with a combination background—for example, a bachelor's degree in statistics and a master's degree in marketing or business administration—have a good chance of being hired at the management level right out of college. Industrial marketing firms prefer those with a bachelor's degree in a related field, such as engineering, plus a master's degree in a marketing-related field.

Potential and advancement

There are about 25,000 marketing researchers and thousands more who work part-time taking surveys and interviewing consumers. Job opportunities will be good in this field, as the growth in population and continued emphasis on advertising will result in more marketing jobs. Those with degrees in statistics or economics will be the most in demand.

Promotion is slower in this field than in most others requiring similar training; the pay scale for beginners, however, is better than that in many fields. Once a marketing research worker reaches the research assistant level, promotion is possible to junior analyst, then to senior analyst or project director. Top jobs, such as marketing research director, are few and require many years of experience plus good management skills.

Many experienced marketing researchers go into business for themselves doing independent marketing surveys or acting as marketing consultants.

Income

College graduates starting in a training program earn about $14,000; beginners with master's degree about $18,000.

Experienced research assistants earn from $11,500 to $13,500; those experienced in planning and analysis earn from $14,000 to $17,000; senior analysts earn $21,000 to $25,000, or more.

Top-level managers average $35,000 to $75,000 a year.

Additional sources of information

American Marketing Association
222 South Riverside Plaza
Chicago, IL 60606

Marketing Research Association
31 East 28th Street
New York, NY 10017

MATHEMATICIAN

The job

The work of mathematicians falls into two sometimes overlapping categories—applied and theoretical mathematics.

Theoretical or pure mathematicians develop new principles and seek new relationships between existing principles of mathematics. This basic knowledge is the foundation for much of the work in the second category, applied mathematics. In this area, mathematical theories are used to develop theories and techniques for solving practical problems in business, government, and the natural and social sciences. Mathematicians may work in statistics, actuarial jobs, computer programming, economics, or systems analysis.

Three fourths of all mathematicians, usually theoretical mathematicians, work in colleges where they teach or do research. Mathematicians are found in the private sector in the aerospace, communications, machinery, and electrical equipment industries. The Department of Defense and NASA employ most of those who work for the federal government.

Related jobs are: Economist, Marketing Researcher, Statistician.

Places of employment and working conditions

More than half of the mathematicians in this country are found in California, Illinois, Maryland, Massachusetts, New Jersey, and Pennsylvania. One fourth live in New York City, Washington, D.C., and Los Angeles/Long Beach, California—primarily because these are large industrial areas and have many colleges and universities.

Qualifications, education, and training

Mathematicians need good reasoning ability and persistence in solving problems. In applied mathematics especially, they should be able to communicate effectively with nonmathematicians in the discussion and solution of practical problems.

A prospective mathematician should take as many mathematics courses as possible while still in high school and should obtain a bachelor's degree that includes courses in analytical geometry, calculus, differential equations, probability and statistics, mathematics analysis, and modern algebra.

Most positions in research or in university teaching require an advanced degree, frequently a Ph.D. Private industry and the government also prefer those with advanced degrees.

For work in applied mathematics, a background in a specialty field such as engineering, economics, or statistics is also necessary. This can be accomplished by including a minor in one of these fields while in college. In modern industry, knowledge of computer programming also is essential since most complex problems are now solved with the aid of computers.

Over 400 colleges and universities offer a master's degree program in mathematics and about 150 also offer a Ph.D. program. Candidates for graduate degrees in mathematics concentrate on a specific field such as algebra, geometry, or mathematical analyses and conduct research in addition to taking advanced courses.

Potential and advancement

There are about 38,000 mathematicians in the United States. Employment opportunities for the coming decade are expected to be few with competition keen for the available jobs. Fewest opportunities will exist in theoretical areas.

Applied mathematicians will need to possess a strong mathematical background as well as practical knowledge in a specialty field to qualify for jobs in industry and government. They will be hired to work in operations research, computer systems programming, and market research. New graduates may also find employment as secondary school teachers, if they meet teaching certification requirements.

Many mathematicians advance by taking a lesser job, such as a research or teaching assistant, and continue their studies until they have attained the degree(s) necessary for the positions they really want.

Income

Salaries in private industry range from an average of $14,800 for a bachelor's degree to about $17,000 for a master's degree and $22,500 for a Ph.D. Salaries in government are comparable.

College and university teachers are paid at the same rate as other faculty members; salaries tend to be lower than in private industry or government.

Additional sources of information

American Mathematical Society
P.O. Box 6248
Providence, RI 02940

Mathematical Association of America
1225 Connecticut Avenue, NW
Washington, DC 20036

Society for Industrial and Applied Mathematics
33 South 17th Street
Philadelphia, PA 19103

Interagency Board of U.S. Civil Service Examiners
1900 E Street, NW
Washington, DC 20415

MECHANICAL ENGINEER

The job

The production, transmission, and use of power is the concern of mechanical engineers. They design and develop power-producing machines such as internal combustion engines and rocket engines and power-using machines such as refrigeration systems, printing presses, and steel rolling mills.

The specific work of mechanical engineers varies greatly from industry to industry because of the wide application possibilities of their skills and training; many specialties within the field have developed as a result. These include motor vehicles, energy conversion systems, heating, and machines for specialized industries, to name a few. Many mechanical engineers are involved in research and testing while others work mainly in production and maintenance. Some utilize their training as a background for technical sales.

About three fourths of all mechanical engineers are employed in manufacturing, mainly in the electrical equipment, transportation equipment, primary and fabricated metals, and machinery industries. Others work for engineering consulting firms, government agencies, and educational institutions. Mechanical engineers are the single largest group of engineers in the nuclear energy field.

Places of employment and working conditions

Mechanical engineers work in all parts of the country with the heaviest concentrations in industrialized areas.

Qualifications, education, and training

The ability to think analytically, a capacity for detail, and the ability to work as part of a team are all necessary. Good communication skills are important.

Mathematics and the sciences must be emphasized in high school.

A bachelor's degree in engineering is the minimum requirement in this field. In a typical curriculum, the first two years are spent in the study of basic sciences such as physics and chemistry and mathematics, introductory engineering, and some liberal arts courses. The remaining years are usually devoted to specialized engineering courses. Engineering programs can last from four to six years. Those that require five or six years to complete may award a master's degree or may provide a cooperative plan of study plus practical work experience in a nearby industry.

Because of rapid changes in technology, many engineers continue their education throughout their careers. A graduate degree is necessary for most teaching and research positions and for many management jobs. Some specialties such as nuclear engineering are taught only at the graduate level. Some persons obtain graduate degrees in business administration.

Engineering graduates usually work under the supervision of an experienced engineer or in a company training program until they become acquainted with the requirements of a particular company or industry.

All states require licensing of engineers whose work may affect life, health, or property or who offer their services to the public. Those who are licensed, about one third of all engineers, are called Registered Engineers. Requirements include graduation from an accredited engineering school, four years of experience, and a written examination.

Potential and advancement

There are about 200,000 mechanical engineers. An increase in the demand for mechanical engineers—as a result of growth in the industrial machinery and machine tools field and the push to develop alternate energy sources—means ample job opportunities in this field into the 1980s.

Income

Starting salaries in private industry average $16,800 with a bachelor's degree; $18,700 with a master's degree; and $24,000 or more with a Ph.D.

The federal government pays beginners $13,657 to $20,500 depending on degree and experience. Average salary for experienced engineers federally employed is about $27,700.

Experienced engineers average $30,500 in private industry; $15,000 to $21,000 for nine-month faculty positions in colleges and universities.

Additional sources of information

The American Society of Mechanical Engineers
345 East 47th Street
New York, NY 10017

Engineers' Council for Professional Development
345 East 47th Street
New York, NY 10017

National Society of Professional Engineers
2029 K Street, NW
Washington, DC 20006

American Society for Engineering Education
One Dupont Circle, Suite 400
Washington, DC 20036

Society of Women Engineers
United Engineering Center
345 East 47th Street
New York, NY 10017

MEDICAL LABORATORY TECHNOLOGIST

The job

Medical laboratory work often appeals to people who would like to work in the medical field but who are not necessarily interested in direct care of patients. Those who work in medical laboratories are involved in the analysis of blood, tissue samples, and body fluids. They use precision instruments, equipment, chemicals, and other materials to detect and diagnose diseases. In some instances, such as blood tests, they also gather the specimens to be analyzed.

The work of medical laboratory technologists is done under the direction of a pathologist (a physician who specializes in the causes and nature of disease) or other physician or scientist who specializes in clinical chemistry, microbiology, or other biological sciences.

Medical technologists, who have four years of training, usually perform a wide variety of tests in small laboratories; those in large laboratories usually specialize in a single area such as parisitology, blood banking, or hematology (study of blood cells). Some do research, develop laboratory techniques, or perform supervisory and administrative duties.

Medical laboratory technicians, who have two years of training, have much the same testing duties but do not have the in-depth knowledge of the technologists. Technicians may also specialize in a particular field but are not usually involved in administrative work.

Medical laboratory assistants have about one year of formal training. They assist the technologist and technicians in some routine tests and are generally responsible for the care and sterilization of laboratory equipment, including glassware and instruments, and do some record-keeping.

Most technologists, technicians, and laboratory assistants work in hospital laboratories. Others work in physicians' offices, independent laboratories, blood banks, public health agencies and clinics, pharmaceutical firms, and research institutions. The federal government employs them in the U.S. Public Health Service, the armed forces, and Veterans Administration.

This is an excellent field for women who now hold a majority of the jobs in this field at all levels.

Places of employment and working conditions

Work in this field is available in all areas of the country with the largest concentrations in the larger cities.

Medical laboratory personnel work a 40-hour week with night and weekend shifts if they are employed in a hospital. Laboratories are usually clean and well lighted and contain a variety of testing equipment and materials. Although unpleasant odors are sometimes present and the work involves the processing of specimens of many kinds of diseased tissue, few hazards exist because of careful attention to safety and sterilization procedures.

Qualifications, education, and training

A strong interest in science and the medical field is essential. Manual dexterity, good eyesight, and normal color vision are necessary along with attention to detail and accuracy and the ability to work under pressure and to take responsibility for one's own work.

High school students interested in this field should take courses in science and mathematics and should select a training program carefully.

Medical technologists must have a college degree and complete a specialized program in medical technology. This specialized training is offered by about 700 hospitals and schools in programs accredited by the American Medical Association. The programs are usually affiliated with a college or university. Some training programs require a bachelor's degree for entry; others require only three years of college and award a bachelor's degree at the completion of the training program. Those who wish to specialize must complete an additional 12 months of study with extensive lab work.

Advanced degrees in this field are offered by many universities and are a plus for anyone interested in teaching, research, or administration.

Technicians may receive training in two-year educational programs in junior colleges, in two-year courses at four-year colleges and universities, or in the armed forces. Some vocational and technical schools offer training programs for medical laboratory technicians, but not all are accredited by the AMA or the Accrediting Bureau of Medical Laboratory Schools.

Medical laboratory assistants usually receive on-the-job training. Some hospitals—and junior colleges and vocational schools in conjunction with a hospital—also conduct one-year training programs, some of which are accredited by the AMA. A high school diploma or equivalency diploma is necessary.

Medical technologists may be certified as Medical Technologist, MT (ASCP), by the Board of Registry of the American Society of Clinical Pathologists; Medical Technologist, MT, by the American Medical Technologists; or Registered Medical Technologist, RMT, by the International Society of Clinical Laboratory Technology. These same organizations also certify technicians. Medical laboratory assistants are certified by the American Society of Clinical Pathologists.

A few states require technologists and technicians to be licensed. This usually takes the form of a written examination.

Potential and advancement

There are about 240,000 persons employed as medical laboratory workers. Of these, approximately 40,000 are medical technologists. Medical laboratory technology is a good job opportunity field since, like the entire medical field, it is expected to grow steadily due to population growth and the increase in prepaid medical insurance programs. Job opportunities will probably be slightly better for technicians and assistants, because the increasing use of automated lab equipment will allow them to perform tests that previously required technologists. Technologists will be needed for supervisory and administrative positions, however, and will continue to be in demand in laboratories where their level of training is required by state regulations or employer preference.

Advancement depends on education and experience. Assistants can advance to the position of technician or technologist by completing the required education; technicians can advance to supervisory positions or complete the required education for technologists. Advancement to administrative positions is usually limited to technologists.

Income

Salaries in this field vary depending on employer and on geographic location; the highest salaries are paid in the larger cities and on the West Coast.

Newly graduated medical technologists start at about $12,400 a year; technicians at about $10,600; assistants at about $9,100.

The federal government pays technologists with a bachelor's degree a starting salary of $10,500, $13,000 with a superior academic record or a year of graduate study. The starting salary for technicians and laboratory assistants ranges from $6,600 to $10,500 depending on education and experience.

Additional sources of information

American Society of Clinical Pathologists
Board of Registry
P.O. Box 4872
Chicago, IL 60680

American Society for Medical Technology
5555 West Loop South
Bellaire, TX 77401

American Medical Technologists
710 Higgins Road
Park Ridge, IL 60068

Accrediting Bureau of Medical Laboratory Schools
Oak Manor Office
29089 U.S. 20 West
Elkhart, IN 46514

International Society for Clinical Laboratory Technology
805 Ambassador Building
411 North 7th Street
St. Louis, MO 63101

METALLURGICAL ENGINEER

The job

Metallurgical engineers develop methods to process and convert metals into usable forms. Other scientists who work in this field are called *metallurgists* or *materials scientists*, but the distinction between scientist and engineer in this field is so small as to be almost nonexistent.

There are three main branches of metallurgy—extractive or chemical, physical, and mechanical. *Extractive metallurgists* are engaged in the processes for extracting metals from ore, refining, and alloying. *Physical metallurgists* work with the nature, structure, and physical properties of metals and alloys to develop methods for converting them into final products. *Mechanical metallurgists* develop methods to work and shape metals. These include casting, forging, rolling, and drawing.

Over half of all metallurgical engineers are employed by the metalworking industries—iron, steel, and nonferrous metals—where they are responsible for specifying, controlling, and testing the quality of the metals during manufacture. Others work in industries that manufacture machinery, electrical equipment, aircraft and aircraft parts, and in mining.

The development of new, lightweight metals for use in communications equipment, computers, and spacecraft is a growing field for metallurgical engineers as are the processing and recycling of industrial waste and the processing of low-grade ores. Problems associated with the use of nuclear energy will also require the expertise of metallurgists and metallurgical engineers.

241

Places of employment and working conditions

The work settings of metallurgical engineers vary from the laboratory to smelting and mining locations to factory production lines. Some of these operations are located in remote areas.

Qualifications, education, and training

The ability to think analytically, a capacity for detail, and the ability to work as part of a team are all necessary. Good communication skills are important.

Mathematics and the sciences must be emphasized in high school.

A bachelor's degree in engineering is the minimum requirement in this field. In a typical curriculum, the first two years are spent in the study of basic sciences such as physics and chemistry and mathematics, introductory engineering, and some liberal arts courses. The remaining years are usually devoted to specialized engineering courses. Engineering programs can last from four to six years. Those requiring five or six years to complete may award a master's degree or may provide a cooperative plan of study plus practical work experience in a nearby industry.

Because of rapid changes in technology, many engineers continue their education throughout their careers. A graduate degree is necessary for most teaching and research positions and for many management jobs. Some specialties such as nuclear engineering are taught only at the graduate level. Some persons obtain graduate degrees in business administration.

Engineering graduates usually work under the supervision of an experienced engineer or in a company training program until they become acquainted with the requirements of a particular company or industry.

All states require licensing of engineers whose work may affect life, health, or property or who offer their services to the public. Those who are licensed, about one third of all engineers, are called Registered Engineers. Requirements include graduation from an accredited engineering school, four years of experience, and a written examination.

Potential and advancement

There are about 17,000 metallurgical engineers. Substantial growth is expected in this field, providing excellent employment prospects into the 1980s.

Income

Starting salaries in private industry average $16,800 with a bachelor's degree, $18,700 with a master's degree, and $24,000 or more with a Ph.D.

The federal government pays beginners $13,657 to $20,500 depending on degree and experience. Average salary for experienced engineers federally employed is about $27,700.

Experienced engineers average $30,500 in private industry; $15,000 to $21,000 for nine-month faculty positions in colleges and universities.

Additional sources of information

The Metallurgical Society of the American Institute of
  Mining, Metallurgical, and Petroleum Engineers
345 East 47th Street
New York, NY 10017

American Society for Metals
Metals Park, OH 44073

Engineers' Council for Professional Development
345 East 47th Street
New York, NY 10017

National Society of Professional Engineers
2029 K Street, NW
Washington, DC 20006

American Society for Engineering Education
One Dupont Circle, Suite 400
Washington, DC 20036

Society of Women Engineers
United Engineering Center
345 East 47th Street
New York, NY 10017

METEOROLOGIST

The job

The study of the atmosphere—its physical characteristics, motions, and processes—is the work of meteorologists. Although the best-known application of this study is in weather forecasting, meteorologists are also engaged in research and problem solving in the fields of air pollution, agriculture, and industrial operations.

Physical meteorologists study the chemical and electrical properties of the atmosphere as they affect the formation of clouds, rain, and snow. *Climatologists* analyze past data on wind, rainfall, and temperature to determine weather patterns for a given area; this work is important in designing buildings and in planning effective land use.

The largest single employer of civilian meteorologists is the National Oceanic and Atmospheric Administration (NOAA) which employs over 1,800 meteorologists at stations in all part of the United States and at some locations overseas.

About 3,000 meteorologists work for private industry including airlines, private weather consulting firms, manufacturers of meteorological instruments, radio and television stations, and the aerospace industry.

Colleges and universities employ about 1,300 meteorologists in teaching and research.

Only about 2 percent of all meteorologists are women, most of them employed by weather bureaus.

Related jobs are: Geologist, Geophysicist, Oceanographer.

Places of employment and working conditions

Meteorologists work in all areas of the United States but the largest concentrations are in California, Maryland, and the Washington, D.C. area.

Since they continue around the clock, seven days a week, jobs in weather stations entail night and weekend shifts. Some stations are at remote locations and may require the meteorologist to work alone.

Qualifications, education, and training

Curiosity, analytical thinking, and attention to detail are necessary qualities for a meteorologist.

High school should include as many science and mathematics courses as possible.

A bachelor's degree with a major in meteorology or a related field is acceptable for some jobs. Teaching positions, research, and many jobs in private industry require advanced degrees.

The armed forces provide training for meteorologists including advanced training for officers. NOAA also provides advanced training and sponsors cooperative education programs for college students that provide valuable experience.

Potential and advancement

There are about 5,600 civilian meteorologists and several thousand members of the armed forces who do forecasting and meteorological work. This is a relatively small job field, and not many degrees are awarded in meteorology. Job opportunities will be fair with the number of job openings just about equal to the number of qualified jobseekers.

Meteorologists with advanced degrees and experience can advance to supervisory and administrative positions.

Income

Airline meteorologists earn between $17,000 and $31,000 a year.

Average salary for federally employed meteorologists is about $27,600.

Additional sources of information

American Geophysical Union
1909 K Street, NW
Washington, DC 20006

Personnel Operations Branch, AD 41
National Oceanic and Atmospheric Administration
6001 Executive Blvd.
Rockville, MD 20852

American Meteorological Society
45 Beacon Street
Boston, MA 02108

MINING ENGINEER

The job

Mining engineers frequently specialize in a specific mineral such as coal or copper. They find, extract, and prepare minerals for manufacturing use.

Some mining engineers work with geologists and metallurgical engineers (see appropriate job descriptions) to locate and appraise new ore deposits. Others design and supervise construction of open-pit and underground mines including mine shafts and tunnels or design methods for transporting minerals to processing plants.

Mining engineers engaged in the day-to-day operations of a mine are responsible for mine safety, ventilation, water supply, power and communication, and equipment maintenance. Direction of mineral processing operations, which requires separating the usable ore from dirt, rocks, and other materials, is also usually the responsibility of a mining engineer.

Some mining engineers specialize in the design and development of new mining equipment. An increasing number work on the reclamation of mined land and on the air and water pollution problems related to mining.

Most mining engineers work in the mining industry. Others work for mining equipment manufacturers or as independent consultants. Federal and state agencies employ mining engineers on regulatory bodies and as inspectors.

Places of employment and working conditions

Most mining engineers work at the location of the mine, usually near small communities in rural areas.

The work can be hazardous since at least some time is often spent underground.

Qualifications, education, and training

The ability to think analytically, a capacity for detail, and the ability to work as part of a team are all necessary. Good communication skills are important.

Mathematics and the sciences must be emphasized in high school.

A bachelor's degree in engineering is the minimum requirement in this field. In a typical curriculum, the first two years are spent in the study of basic sciences such as physics and chemistry and mathematics, introductory engineering, and some liberal arts courses. The remaining years are usually devoted to specialized engineering courses. Engineering programs can last from four to six years. Those that require five or six years to complete may award a master's degree or may provide a cooperative plan of study plus practical work experience with a nearby industry.

Because of rapid changes in technology, many engineers continue their education throughout their careers. A graduate degree is necessary for most teaching and research positions and for many management jobs. Some persons obtain graduate degrees in business administration.

Engineering graduates usually work under the supervision of an experienced engineer or in a company training program until they become acquainted with the requirements of a particular company or industry.

All states require licensing of engineers whose work may affect life, health, or property or who offer their services to the public. Those who are licensed, about one third of all engineers, are called Registered

Engineers. Requirements include graduation from an accredited engineering school, four years of experience, and a written examination.

Potential and advancement

There are about 6,000 mining engineers. Substantial employment growth is expected in this field because of the energy situation, the increased demand for mine safety and advanced mining technology, and the development of oil shale deposits and recovery of metals from the sea.

Income

Starting salaries in private industry average $16,800 with a bachelor's degree; $18,700 with a master's degree; and $24,000 or more with a Ph.D.

The federal government pays beginners $13,657 to $20,500 depending on degree and experience. Average salary for experienced engineers federally employed is about $27,700.

Experienced engineers average $30,500 in private industry; $15,000 to $21,000 for nine-month faculty positions in colleges and universities.

Additional sources of information

The Society of Mining Engineers of the American Institute of
  Mining, Metallurgical, and Petroleum Engineers
540 Arapeen Drive
Research Park
Salt Lake City, UT 84108

Engineers' Council for Professional Development
345 East 47th Street
New York, NY 10017

National Society of Professional Engineers
2029 K Street, NW
Washington, DC 20006

American Society for Engineering Education
One Dupont Circle, Suite 400
Washington, DC 20036

MINISTER (PROTESTANT)

The job

Protestant ministers lead their congregations in worship services and administer the rites of baptism and Holy Communion. They perform marriages, conduct funerals, visit the sick, and counsel members of the congregation who seek guidance. Ministers are also usually involved in community activities.

The exact services provided by ministers differ among the different denominations. The greatest number of ministers are affiliated with the five largest denominations—Baptist, United Methodist, Lutheran, Presbyterian, and Episcopal. Some serve small congregations where they provide all services; ministers of large congregations usually have one or more assistants who share duties.

Many ministers serve as chaplains in the armed forces, hospitals, prisons, or colleges and universities. Others teach in seminaries.

Some denominations are now allowing women to enter the ministry in small numbers. Some denominations and some congregations continue to oppose this, so women interested in becoming ministers should seek the counsel of clergy in the denomination of their choice.

Places of employment and working conditions

Ministers work in communities of all sizes. Larger communities may support more than one congregation of a particular denomination. Working hours can be long and are often irregular. Some ministers handle more than one congregation, especially in rural areas, and may spend considerable time in travel.

Qualifications, education, and training

The most important quality for anyone considering the ministry as a calling is a deep religious faith. A minister must also be a model of moral and ethical conduct.

Educational requirements vary depending on denomination. Bible colleges, bible institutes, and liberal arts colleges all provide training acceptable to some denominations, but training in a theological seminary is necessary for others.

Potential and advancement

About 190,000 ministers serve 72 million Protestants in the United States. There has been a reduced demand for ministers in recent years, and new graduates of theological schools will face competition for existing positions. Most openings will occur to replace ministers who retire or die.

Income

Earnings vary widely with the average income for the five major denominations in the $13,600 range. This is somewhat higher than the average for all Protestant denominations.

Additional sources of information

Anyone interested in becoming a minister should seek the counsel of a minister within the denomination of his or her choice. Theological schools can provide information on admission requirements.

MODEL

The job

Models are used to demonstrate and sell a wide variety of goods and services. Models display clothes for local fashion shows as well as for high-fashion magazines; those models working in television commercials sell everything from toothpaste to home appliances; and photographers and artists often employ models in the course of their work. Models usually specialize in live or photographic work.

Photographic models are usually hired for an individual assignment. Most model clothes or cosmetics, but they are also used for a wide variety of other products as well. In addition to serving for still photography, models may also be used for television commercials, especially if they have some acting ability or training.

Live modeling contains a variety of specialty areas. *Fashion models* usually work before an audience, modeling the creations of a well-known designer at fashion shows. *Showroom* or *fitting models* work in the manufacturer's or distributor's display room where they model the employer's products for prospective retail buyers and work with designers during the fitting stages of new designs.

Informal models work in local department stores and custom shops, at manufacturers' trade shows and exhibits to demonstrate products, and for artists and art schools.

Most models work through a modeling agency to ensure a continuous flow of job assignments.

Places of employment and working conditions

Some modeling jobs are available in almost every community, but Chicago, Detroit, Los Angeles, and especially New York provide the largest number of modeling jobs. New York's garment district has hundreds of clothing manufacturers, designers and wholesalers who employ permanent models to display their products. These models must usually meet certain standard physical requirements because sample clothes must fit the model without alteration. For women this means a height of 5 feet 7 inches to 5 feet 9½ inches and a weight of 110 to 122 pounds. Male models must be 6 feet tall and wear a size-40 suit. Specialty lines, such as teen-age clothes or styles for mature women, may have other requirements.

Photographic models must be thinner than other models because the camera adds at least ten pounds to a model's appearance.

Qualifications, education and training

Distinctive and attractive physical appearance, good health, physical stamina, the ability to withstand the pace and pressures of the field, and competitiveness are all necessary for a successful model.

There are no educational requirements for a model, but any training in acting, dancing, art, or fashion design is valuable for a model.

There are modeling schools in many communities that provide instruction in such things as proper posture, hairstyling and makeup, and how to pose in front of a camera, but these schools do *not* provide job assignments. Some modeling agencies also provide some training.

Potential and advancement

There are only about 9,000 models employed on a fairly regular basis, and there are always many more applicants than jobs in this glamorous field. Because most assignments go to experienced models, aspiring models should get as much local experience as possible before trying for a job in the larger cities or agencies.

Modeling can be a stepping-stone to many other careers in the fashion field. Fashion magazines, cosmetic firms, and department stores often hire former models for a variety of positions. Some models become actors or actresses.

Income

A few top models earn as much as top business executives, but most earn considerably less.

Models employed full-time by manufacturers or wholesalers earn up to $50,000 a year, but those outside New York usually earn $12,000 to $14,000.

Models who register with an agency pay the agency a commission for each new assignment they receive. In New York, models with major agencies usually earn $75 to $100 an hour. This high hourly rate is not indicative of total earnings, however, because models spend a great deal of unpaid time auditioning for prospective clients.

Models in television commercials are paid $170 to $250 per job. They may also receive additional income (residuals) if the commercial is used more than once.

Additional sources of information

The Fashion Group
Nine Rockefeller Plaza
New York, NY 10020

Federation of Apparel Manufacturers
450 Seventh Avenue
New York, NY 10001

MUSEUM CURATOR

The job

A museum curator is in charge of a museum or a museum department. The curator is responsible for planning exhibits; acquisition of material within budgetary limitations; development, care, and classification of collections; and laboratory research and field studies including museum-sponsored expeditions.

There are about 5,000 museums of various sizes in the United States. They are maintained by the federal government, state and local governments, nonprofit corporations, colleges and universities, business groups and industries, and private individuals and societies.

Most curators are employed by historical museums. These museums may specialize in the artifacts and memorabilia of a particular period in history; a specific area, industry, or group of people; a single person, such as a president; a sport; or an item, such as toys. They vary in size from small local museums to large, world-renowned institutions.

The largest in individual size are the natural history museums. Their collections are the most widely diversified and research and field expeditions form a major part of their programs. They employ *anthropologists* (experts in the study of man and his domain through the ages), *botanists* (plant-life specialists), *geologists* (structure and materials of the earth), and *zoologists* (specialists in all phases of animal life). Natural history museums also do a great deal of publishing as a result of their research and field studies.

Many museum curators work for art museums, which collect and exhibit art objects of all kinds including paintings, prints, drawings, photographs, sculpture, ceramics, jewelry, textiles, woodwork and carvings. Some large art museums have schools of art and design.

Curators employed by outdoor museums often oversee complete towns or villages such as Williamsburg, Virginia, or zoological parks or arboretums. A uniquely American idea, the trailside museum, incorporates bird, botanical, or geological walks with animal life. The Petrified Forest in Arizona is such a museum.

In general, more women than men work in the museum field. As curators they are found in art and history museums, in children's museums, and in state and county museums. Many are scientists engaged in research activities.

A related job is: Historian.

Places of employment and working conditions

Curator positions exist throughout the United States, but most are in the major cities that have the most museums—Boston, Chicago, Los Angeles, New York, and Washington, D.C.

Working conditions vary greatly depending on size and type of museum and specialty of the curator. Field trips can mean exposure to extreme climates, primitive living conditions, and hostile native tribes.

Qualifications, education and training

Patience, a logical mind, creative imagination, physical stamina, administrative ability, the ability to work with people, and communication skills are necessary for a museum curator. A curator is also usually a specialist in a particular field, such as art, or in a specific discipline, such as anthropology.

In high school, a college preparatory course should be followed. If the student is already interested in a specific field of museum work, the appropriate courses such as art, history, or science should be emphasized. If possible, the study of one or more languages should begin in high school and continue in college. French, German, Spanish, Italian, Latin or Greek are recommended.

College courses should be related to the student's field of interest. A bachelor's degree in history, art history, fine arts, anthropology, or one of the natural sciences is the usual first step. Many colleges and universities offer some course work in museum studies; a few provide a minor in museology.

A master's degree, and in some cases a Ph.D., is necessary for most curator positions. About 20 universities offer a master's degree in museum work; three offer a Ph.D.

Many museums, colleges, and universities offer assistantships, fellowships, internships, apprenticeships, summer programs, and certification programs. These programs are usually part of an undergraduate or graduate program, but some are open to other experienced museum employees. Some, especially summer programs, are also open to high schools students.

Potential and advancement

There are about 30,000 people engaged in museum work throughout the United States. This is a very competitive job field, and thousands of new graduates apply each year for the few available openings. Those with a graduate degree and some part-time or summer experience have the best chance of securing a job.

It takes years of training and experience to achieve the level of curator. One of the drawbacks of this field is the slowness with which advancement occurs, especially in older established museums.

Income

This is a relatively low-paying field, considering the level of education required. Although a few major museums may pay higher salaries, the average earnings for those in museum work are lower than in other fields that require comparable training and experience.

Beginners, even with a master's degree, may start as low as $10,000 a year—the average is about $12,400.

Curators who are department heads average about $17,800 a year. Those who are museum directors average about $22,200.

Additional sources of information

American Association of State and Local History
1400 Eighth Avenue, South
Nashville, TN 37203

American Association of Museums
1055 Thomas Jefferson Street, NW
Washington, DC 20007

MUSICIAN

The job

Professional musicians play in symphony orchestras, dance bands, rock groups, and jazz combos and accompany individual performers, musical comedies, and opera performances. Others teach in music conservatories, and colleges and universities or give private lessons. Many musicians combine performing careers with teaching or with arranging and composing.

A few musicians specialize in library science for work in music libraries or study psychology for work in music therapy in hospitals. The armed forces also offer many career opportunities for musicians.

Musicians put in many hours of practice and rehearsal in addition to performing. Many find that they are unable to support themselves by music alone and can only pursue it as a part-time career.

Most women in this field are teachers. In recent years, the number of women in symphony orchestras has increased steadily; one quarter of the musicians in major orchestras are now women. Very few women work in dance bands or rock groups.

Places of employment and working conditions

Musicians work throughout the entire country, but the best opportunities are in large metropolitan areas and in the cities where entertainment and recording activities are concentrated—New York, Chicago, Los Angeles, Nashville, Miami Beach, and New Orleans.

Musicians normally work evenings and weekends and usually do a lot of traveling. The work is often unsteady, and performers do not usually work for one employer for any length of time.

Qualifications, education, and training

Necessary qualities for a professional musician, in addition to musical talent, are creative ability, poise and stage presence, self-discipline, and physical stamina.

Musicians usually start studying an instrument at an early age with private lessons. Those who perform popular music gain experience by performing in amateur programs, by forming small groups or bands, and by gradually obtaining work with better-known bands as they gain a reputation. Some expand their knowledge and understanding of music by taking some classical training.

Classical musicians study privately, in music conservatories, or in colleges and universities that have strong music programs. Auditions are usually required for entrance into these schools or for private lessons with the best teachers.

Music conservatories and colleges and universities offer bachelor-degree programs that include liberal arts courses in addition to musical training. Many schools also offer a bachelor-degree program in music education, which qualifies graduates for state certification in elementary and secondary teaching positions.

College teaching positions usually require advanced degrees except in the case of exceptional musicians.

Potential and advancement

About 127,000 musicians work as performers with many more employed as teachers. Competition for jobs in this field is always keen, especially for those jobs that offer stable employment. The best opportunities will be for skilled, experienced accompanists and for outstanding stringed-instrument players—two areas that are usually lacking in accomplished musicians.

Income

Music teachers earn salaries comparable to other faculty in the same school.

Earnings of musicians vary widely depending on geographic location and professional reputation. Most jobs are covered by union minimum wage scales.

Additional sources of information

American Federation of Musicians
1500 Broadway
New York, NY 10036

National Association of Schools of Music
11250 Roger Bacon Drive
Reston, VA 22090

Music Educators National Conference
1902 Association Drive
Reston, VA 22091

American Music Conference
150 East Huron
Chicago, IL 60611

N

NEWSPAPER REPORTER

The job

Newspaper reporters gather the latest news and write about it. They do research, interview people, attend public events, and do whatever else is necessary to give a complete report of a news event. When deadlines require it, reporters may phone in their information to be transcribed by a rewriter.

General assignment reporters handle all types of news stories; other reporters are assigned to a specialized "beat," such as police stations, the courts, or sports. Reporters with specialized backgrounds may be assigned to write about and analyze the news in such fields as medicine, politics, labor, or education.

On small newspapers, reporters often take their own photographs, do some layout or editorial work, solicit subscriptions and advertising, and perform some general office work.

Some reporters work for national news services where they are usually assigned to a large city or to a particular specialty. *Stringers* work part-time for one or more employers and are paid according to how much of their work is published.

Beginning reporters usually work for small daily or weekly newspapers where they function as general assignment reporters or copy editors. As they gain experience they cover more important news.

The percentage of women reporters is increasing rapidly. Once relegated to fashion, household hints, and cooking stories, women now cover politics, crime, and other subjects on an equal footing with their male counterparts. There are about 16,000 female reporters, and about half of all new journalism degrees are now awarded to women.

Related job is: Editor, Newspaper and Magazine.

Places of employment and working conditions

Newspaper reporters work in communities of all sizes. Although the majority of newspapers are in medium-sized towns, most reporters work in cities where each daily newspaper employs many reporters.

Reporters generally work a five-day, 35- to 40-hour week. On morning newspapers, the working hours are from late afternoon to midnight. Coverage of certain news events sometimes requires extended or irregular working hours, and a fast pace and constant deadline pressures are a part of every reporter's working life.

Qualifications, education, and training

Writing skills, curiosity, resourcefulness, an accurate memory, stamina, and the ability to work alone are essential for newspaper reporters.

High school should include as many English courses as possible and typing, social sciences, and experience on school publications, if possible. Summer or part-time jobs on local newspapers also provide valuable experience.

Most newspapers require a new reporter to have a bachelor's degree in either journalism or liberal arts; some require a master's degree. Small newspapers will usually accept less education if the applicant demonstrates exceptional ability or has at least junior college training in the basics of journalism.

Potential and advancement

Over 40,000 persons work as newspaper reporters on 1,762 daily newspapers and 7,579 weeklies. Journalism schools are turning out many more graduates than there are job openings in this field, and reporters face stiff competition for all job openings. Beginners will find the most opportunities on small papers; those who have some knowledge of photography or other aspects of newspaper work will have the best chance of being hired.

Reporters can advance to editorial or administrative positions or can move on to larger newspapers or press services. Some reporters become columnists, correspondents, editors, or top executives. Others turn to public relations, writing for magazines, or preparing news copy for radio and television.

Income

The average starting salary for reporters on daily newspapers is between $10,400 and $14,300.

Experienced reporters average $16,700—this figure includes a salary range from $13,000 paid by the smallest dailies to $31,120 paid by a few of the largest. Some top reporters earn even more.

Reporters working for national wire services earn $21,320 or more annually.

Additional sources of information

American Newspaper Publishers Association Foundation
P.O. Box 17407
Dulles International Airport
Washington, DC 20041

The Newspaper Fund, Inc.
Box 300
Princeton, NJ 08540

The Newspaper Guild
Research and Information Department
1125 15th Street, NW
Washington, DC

American Council on Education for Journalism
School of Journalism
University of Missouri
Columbia, MO 65201

NURSE, LICENSED PRACTICAL

The job

Licensed practical nurses (LPNs) provide much of the bedside care for patients in hospitals, nursing homes, and extended care facilities. They work under the direction of physicians and registered nurses and perform duties that require technical knowledge but not the professional education and training of a registered nurse. In some areas they are called licensed vocational nurses.

LPNs take and record temperatures and blood pressures, change dressings, administer certain prescribed medicines, bathe patients, care for newborn infants, and perform some special nursing procedures.

Those who work in private homes provide daily nursing care and sometimes prepare meals for the patient as well. LPNs employed in physicians' offices or clinics may perform some clerical chores and handle appointments.

Places of employment and working conditions

Licensed practical nurses work in all areas of the country, most of them in hospitals.

LPNs usually work a 40-hour week including weekend and shift work. They spend most of their working hours on their feet. LPNs on private duty in homes often work between eight and twelve hours a day.

Qualifications, education, and training

Anyone interested in working as a practical nurse should have a concern for the sick, be emotionally stable, and have physical stamina. The ability to follow orders and work under close supervision is also necessary.

A high school diploma is not always necessary for enrollment in a training program. One-year, state-approved programs are offered by trade, technical, and vocational schools; junior colleges; local hospitals; health agencies; and private institutions. Some army training programs are also state-approved.

Applicants for state licensing must complete a program in practical nursing that has been approved by the state board of nursing and must pass a written examination.

Potential and advancement

There are about 460,000 licensed practical nurses. The employment outlook for LPNs is very good through the next decade.

Advancement in this field is limited without formal education or additional training. Training programs in some hospitals help LPNs complete the educational requirements necessary to become registered nurses while they continue to work part-time.

Income

Starting salaries for LPNs working in hospitals average about $9,000 a year. Federal hospitals pay beginners about $8,366 a year.

Additional sources of information

National League for Nursing
10 Columbus Circle
New York, New York 10019

National Association for Practical Nurse Education and Service, Inc.
122 East 42nd Street, Suite 800
New York, NY 10017

National Federation of Licensed Practical Nurses, Inc.
250 West 57th Street
New York, New York 10019

Department of Medicine and Surgery
Veterans Administration
Washington, DC 20420

NURSE, REGISTERED

The job

Registered nurses (RNs) play a major role in health care. As part of a health care team, they administer medications and treatments as prescribed by a physician, provide skilled bedside nursing care for the sick and the injured, and work toward the prevention of illness and promotion of good health.

Most nurses are employed in hospitals where they usually work with a group of patients requiring similar care such as a postsurgery floor, the children's area (pediatrics), or the maternity section. Some specialize in operating room work.

Doctors, dentists, and oral surgeons employ about 50,000 nurses in their offices who perform routine laboratory and office work in addition to nursing duties. Industries employ about 20,000 nurses to assist with health examinations, treat minor injuries of employees, and arrange for further medical care if it is necessary. Industrial nurses may also do some recordkeeping and handle claims for medical insurance and workers' compensation.

Fifty-five thousand *community health nurses* work with patients in their homes, the schools, public health clinics, and in other community settings. Nurses also teach in nursing schools and conduct continuing education courses for registered and licensed practical nurses.

Private duty nurses are self-employed nurses who provide individual care in hospitals or homes for one patient at a time when the patient needs constant attention. This care may be required for just a short time or for extended periods.

Registered nurses who received special advanced training may become *nurse practitioners.* They are permitted to perform some services, such as physical examinations, that have traditionally been handled by physicians. Nurse practitioners are an important part of many neighborhood health center staffs.

The federal government employs nurses in Veterans Administration hospitals and clinics, in the U.S. Public Health Service and as commissioned officers in the armed forces.

Most nurses are women but young men are entering the field in increasing numbers in recent years.

Places of employment and working conditions

Nurses work in all areas of the country, in communities of all sizes.

Nurses are usually on their feet during most of their working day. Those who work in hospitals, nursing homes, or as private duty nurses must be prepared to work evenings and weekends and may have some shift work.

Qualifications, education, and training

Nurses need the ability to follow orders precisely, use good judgment in emergencies, and cope with human suffering and must have good physical and emotional stamina.

In high school, students should take a college preparatory program with an emphasis on science.

There are three types of training for registered nurses. Many hospitals offer three-year diploma programs in their own nursing schools that combine classroom instruction and clinical experience within the hospital. Four-year bachelor-degree programs are available at many colleges. Two-year associate-degree programs are offered by some junior and community colleges. These degree programs are combined with clinical practice in an affiliated hospital or health care facility.

A bachelor's degree is required for administrative or management positions in nursing; research, teaching, and clinical specializations usually require a master's degree.

Potential and advancement

There are about 960,000 registered nurses, one third of them working part-time. Future employment opportunities should be good with some competition for the more desirable, higher-paying jobs in large metropolitan areas. Nursing opportunities exist in every community; there are shortages of qualified nurses in many inner-city areas and in some southern states.

Experienced hospital nurses can advance to head nurse or assistant director or director of nursing services. Many supervisory and management positions require a bachelor's degree, however.

Income

Registered nurses working in hospitals average about $11,800 a year. Those employed in nursing homes earn slightly less.

Industrial nurses average about $14,300 a year. Nurses employed by the federal government average $16,800.

Additional sources of information

Coordinator, Undergraduate Programs
Department of Nursing Education
American Nurses' Association
2420 Pershing Road
Kansas City, MO 64108

Career Information Services
National League for Nursing
10 Columbus Circle
New York, NY 10019

Department of Medicine and Surgery
Veterans Administration
Washington, DC 20420

O

OCCUPATIONAL THERAPIST

The job

This fast-growing field offers personal satisfaction as well as financially rewarding job opportunities. Occupational therapists work with both the physically and emotionally disabled, helping some to return to normal functions and activities and others to make the fullest use of whatever talents they may have.

Occupational therapists plan and direct educational, vocational, and recreational activities; evaluate capabilities and skills; and plan individual therapy programs, often working as part of a medical team. Their clients are all ages and can range from a stroke victim relearning daily routines such as eating, dressing, and using a telephone to an accident victim learning to reuse impaired limbs before returning to work.

To restore mobility and dexterity to hands disabled by injury or disease, occupational therapists teach manual and creative skills through the use of crafts such as weaving, knitting, and leather working. They design games and activities especially for children or make special equipment or splints to aid the disabled patient.

Many part-time positions are available for occupational therapists; some occupational therapists work for more than one employer, traveling between job locations and clients.

In addition to hospital rehabilitation departments, other types of organizations that employ occupational therapists are rehabilitation centers and nursing homes, schools, mental health centers, schools and camps for handicapped children, state health departments and home care programs, Veterans Administration hospitals and clinics, psychiatric centers, and schools for learning and development disabilities.

About three quarters of all occupational therapists are women. Because there are many opportunities for part-time work, this is a good field for people with family responsibilities.

Related jobs are: Physical Therapist, Respiratory Therapist.

Places of employment and working conditions

Occupational therapists work throughout the country in communities of all sizes.

Conditions vary depending on the institution. Some occupational therapists work in large well-equipped quarters while others work with limited space and equipment.

Qualifications, education, and training

Maturity, patience, imagination, manual skills, and the ability to teach and instruct are important as is a sympathetic but objective attitude toward illness and disability.

Anyone considering this career field should have above-average grades (B or better) in high school science courses, especially biology and chemistry. Courses in health and social studies along with training in crafts are also important. Volunteer work or a summer job in a health care facility can provide valuable exposure to this field.

Professional certification or a degree is required to practice in this field.

Forty-nine colleges and universities offer bachelor's degrees in occupational therapy programs that are accredited by the American Medical Association. Some have two-year programs and will accept students who transfer from another discipline after two years of college. Competition for admission to these programs is stiff; those transferring into the program in their sophomore or junior year face even stiffer competition than those entering as freshmen.

Some schools offer a still shorter program leading to certification or to a master's degree in occupational therapy for students who already have a bachelor's degree in another field.

Occupational therapy students study physical, biological, and behavioral sciences as well as the application of occupational theory and skills. Students also spend from six to nine months working in hospitals or health agencies to gain clinical experience.

Graduates of accredited programs take the certification examination of the American Occupational Therapy Association to become a registered occupational therapist (OTR).

Potential and advancement

There are about 11,000 occupational therapists with approximately 40 percent employed in hospitals. Employment in this field is expected to grow substantially because the public is becoming more interested and more knowledgeable about programs for rehabilitating the disabled. Job opportunities will be excellent on the whole through the 1980s; however, as the increasing number of qualified graduates catches up to the number of available jobs, competition for job openings may develop in some geographic areas.

Advancement in this field is usually to supervisory or administrative positions. Advanced education is necessary for those wishing to teach, do research, or advance to top administration levels.

Income

Beginning therapists employed by hospitals average about $13,000 a year; experienced therapists earn up to $22,000. Those in administrative positions can earn up to $30,000 a year.

The Veterans Administration pays beginning therapists about $10,700 a year while the average yearly salary for occupational therapists employed by the Veterans Administration is approximately $17,100.

Additional sources of information

American Occupational Therapy Association
6000 Executive Blvd., Suite 200
Rockville, MD 20852

OCEANOGRAPHER

The job

Using the principles and techniques of natural science, mathematics, and engineering, oceanographers study the movements, physical properties, and plant and animal life of the oceans. They make observations, conduct experiments, and collect specimens at sea that are later analyzed in laboratories. Their work contributes to improving weather forecasting, locating fishing, locating petroleum and mineral resources, and improving national defense.

Most oceanographers specialize in one branch of the science. *Marine biologists* study plant and animal life in the ocean to determine the effects of pollution on marine life. Their work is also important in improving and controlling sport and commercial fishing. *Marine geologists* study underwater mountain ranges, rocks, and sediments of the oceans to locate regions where minerals, oil, and gas may be found. Other oceanographic specialists study the relationship between the sea and the atmosphere and the chemical composition of ocean water and sediments. Others with engineering or electronics training design and build instruments for oceanographic research, lay cables, and supervise underwater construction.

About one half of all oceanographers work for colleges and universities. In addition to holding teaching positions, they take part in research projects sponsored by universities at sea and in facilities along our coasts.

The United States Navy and the National Oceanic and Atmospheric Administration (NOAA) employ almost one fourth of all oceanographers. State fisheries employ a few. The remainder work for private industry.

There are very few women employed as oceanographers.

Related jobs are: Chemist, Geologist, Geophysicist, Life Scientist, Meteorologist.

Places of employment and working conditions

Most oceanographers work in the states that border the ocean; almost half of all oceanographers work in California, Maryland, and Virginia.

Oceanographers engaged in research that requires sea voyages are often away from home for long periods of time, and they may have to live and work in cramped quarters.

Qualifications, education, and training

Anyone interested in this career field should have curiosity and the patience necessary to collect data and do research.

High school should include as many science and mathematics courses as possible. Hobbies or summer jobs that involve boating or ocean fishing are helpful.

A bachelor's degree with a major in oceanography, chemistry, biology, earth or physical sciences, mathematics, or engineering is the first step for a would-be oceanographer and is sufficient for entry-level jobs such as research assistant.

Graduate training in oceanography or a basic science is required for most jobs in research and teaching and for all top-level positions; a Ph.D. is required for many. Graduate students usually spend part of their time at sea conducting experiments and learning the techniques of gathering oceanographic information.

Potential and advancement

There are about 2,700 people employed as oceanographers. This is a relatively small field, and there will be competition for any available job openings. Those who combine training in other scientific or engineering fields with oceanography will have the best chances for employment.

Oceanographers with advanced degrees and experience can advance to administrative or supervisory positions in research laboratories. They may also advance by becoming directors of surveys or research programs.

Income

Oceanographers employed by colleges and universities receive the same salaries as other faculty members. In addition, they may earn extra income from consulting, lecturing, and writing.

The average yearly salary for experienced oceanographers working for the federal government is about $25,900. The federal government pays beginners $10,507 to $13,014 with a bachelor's degree; $15,920 to $19,263 with a master's degree; $19,263 to $23,067 with a Ph.D.

Additional sources of information

American Society of Limnology and Oceanography
Great Lakes Research Division
University of Michigan
Ann Arbor, MI 48109

U.S. Civil Service Commission
Washington Area Office
1900 E Street, NW
Washington, DC 20415

International Oceanographic Foundation
3979 Rickenbacker Causeway
Virginia Key
Miami, FL 33149

OFFICE MANAGER

The job

The title office manager brings to mind the secretary or clerk who has worked her (or his) way up in the office hierarchy to the top supervisory position. While this position is accurate to some degree, the field also includes office management positions that are much more complex and far-reaching.

In a small or medium-sized company, an office manager would supervise the day-to-day work of a clerical staff that might include accounting functions such as billing, maintenance of personnel records, payroll, plus all other secretarial and clerical functions. The mail room, telephone switchboard, and duplicating and copier equipment would also be part of the office manager's responsibilities. The size and makeup of the office staff would vary depending on the company and its requirements.

In a large company, the office manager is responsible for a larger and much more complex office staff, often at multiple locations within the company buildings. With one of many possible titles—director of secretarial support systems, administrative manager, office administrator—a manager at this level is involved in systems analysis and electronic data processing as well as office systems, procedures, and operations.

A rapidly growing specialty within this field is management of a centralized word processing facility within a company in which trained specialists, specific procedures, and the latest in automatic equipment are combined to handle the clerical needs of a variety of departments. Such a *word processing manager* coordinates the word processing services with the needs of the user departments, is responsible for staff levels and training, budgets, and design and implementation of word processing systems.

The number of the clerical workers varies from organization to organization depending on the nature of the organization. The greatest concentrations of clerical workers and the managers necessary to oversee their work are in public administration, insurance, finance, and banking. Other large employers are the wholesale and retail fields and manufacturing firms.

Related jobs are: Accountant, Bank Worker, Civil Service Worker (Federal, Municipal, and State), Computer Programmer, Industrial Engineer, Personnel Manager, Secretary, Systems Analyst.

Places of employment and working conditions

Although the usual office workweek is 40 hours, office managers often put in extra hours. The responsibilities of planning and organization plus meetings with executives of user departments sometimes add many hours to the daily schedule.

The entire clerical staff may work under a great deal of pressure at times to meet deadlines and handle busy seasons.

Qualifications, education, and training

A successful office manager must have a talent for organization, an analytical mind, and the ability to work with detail. Creativity, resourcefulness, flexibility, self-assurance, tact, and the ability to get along with people are also necessary. Good communication skills and a background that includes clerical skills are solid assets.

A high school student looking forward to a career in office management should include business courses as well as those courses necessary to enter college or a good business school. Work experience in an office in a part-time or summer job is valuable preparation.

A college degree is usually necessary for a person to achieve the top levels in this field. Small businesses that require a degree often prefer a bachelor's degree in accounting, while large companies often prefer a degree in business administration. Some colleges offer a major or minor in office management.

Business schools, trade and technical schools, community colleges, and university extension programs also offer a variety of programs in this field, some leading to a degree. In addition to taking courses in office management, the student should include systems and procedures, data processing, accounting, and personnel management to acquire diversified business training. A number of two- and four-year degree programs offer electives in law or economics and other liberal arts courses to provide a well-rounded education.

Home study programs are also available for office management. The diploma awarded by such programs does not carry the prestige of a college degree, but many people find them convenient for supplementary study in specific areas of business management.

Large corporations often have training programs in office management, but these programs are usually open only to college graduates.

Regardless of educational background, people in this field continue to study throughout their careers. New development in office technology alone would require this. In addition to taking college courses, most office managers attend seminars and conferences sponsored by various professional societies as well as training sessions and workshops presented by office equipment manufacturers.

Potential and advancement

Qualified office managers will continue to be in demand into the 1980s. While there will continue to be a place for the skilled clerical worker who advances through the ranks, the growing complexity of the office communications and data processing functions of even small companies will require more comprehensive knowledge and training than is acquired by that route. The best job opportunities will be for those with a college degree and diversified business experience.

Office managers are already at the middle-management level. In companies where the office administration function is a major component of the firm's service, office managers can advance to top-level executive positions.

Income

Salaries of office managers vary widely depending on size of the company and its clerical staff, responsibilities of the manager, and complexity of its operation.

In a small office, the supervisor or manager averages $10,000 to $12,000, while the administrative manager in a large corporation may earn $27,000 or more. The average for office managers in medium-sized facilities is about $18,000 a year.

Additional sources of information

American Management Association
135 West 50th Street
New York, NY 10020

International Word Processing Association
Maryland Road
Willow Grove, PA 19090

Administrative Management Society
World Headquarters
Willow Grove, PA 19090

OFFICER, U.S. ARMED FORCES

The job

A career as an officer in the army, navy, marines, or Coast Guard may be achieved through four different methods: the Reserve Officers Training Corps (ROTC), the service academies, Officer Candidate School (OCS), or direct commissioning of physicians, dentists, and other professionals. (See job descriptions for Dentist, Hospital Administrator, Lawyer, Minister, Nurse, Optometrist, Osteopathic Physician, Rabbi, Veterinarian.)

Women are eligible for all of these career paths but at the present time are excluded from actual combat and jobs related to combat. In the army this includes the infantry and artillery; in the air force, flying.

Places of employment and working conditions

Members of the U.S. Armed Forces serve throughout the world. Although some effort is made to allow choice of location at the time of enlistment, assignments are not always to the location of choice.

Officers who receive their training at one of the service academies as well as officers who receive their training and college education through ROTC scholarships are obligated to serve on active duty for four to six years after receiving their commission. Other officers serve various lengths of time on active duty.

Qualifications, education, and training

Leadership qualities are important for anyone interested in a career as an officer. Applicants must be between 18 and 28 years of age (there are a few exceptions), be U.S. citizens, and be in good physical condition. The service academies require a rigorous physical examination and have specific height, weight, eyesight, color vision, and hearing requirements. The academies also require cadets to remain unmarried until after graduation.

Women applicants to any of the programs cannot have dependents under 18 years of age.

High school courses should include English, science, and mathematics. Extra curricular activities that develop leadership qualities are valuable.

Ninety percent of the officers in the armed forces are college graduates, and it is very difficult to achieve this status without some college education.

ROTC programs are offered at over 150 colleges and universities; some scholarships are available. Most are four-year programs but there are some two-year programs as well. The minimum age for ROTC programs is 14. Candidates must receive a passing grade on the Officers Qualifying Test at the end of the second year of college to continue the program. Information on ROTC programs may be obtained directly from participating colleges or from local recruiting offices of the various services.

Enlisted personnel in the various services may be appointed to Officer Candidate School through classification exams and interviews and grades received on specific aptitude tests and the Officer Candidate Test. Civilian applicants should apply at local recruiting offices where they may take the appropriate examinations. OCS training lasts from 9 to 39 weeks, depending on branch of service and previous military training.

Applicants for West Point, Annapolis, and the Air Force Academy must be appointed by their congressman. The Coast Guard Academy does *not* require applicants to be appointed; the Coast Guard recruits through an annual nationwide competition. The army, navy, and air force academies require the College Board Entrance Exam, while the

Coast Guard requires the Scholastic Aptitude Test (SAT) or the American College Testing Assessment (ACT). High school guidance counselors can usually provide up-to-date information on requirements at the service academies, or interested students may write to the academies directly.

The Army Nurse Program is open to applicants between the ages of 18 and 24. A four-year program leading to a commission includes two years of college and two years at Walter Reed Army Medical Center. A one- to two-year Army Student Nurse Program is also available at some hospital and university schools of nursing.

The Naval Air Reserve has an 18-month program for naval aviation cadets. Applicants must have completed two years of college and must receive a passing score on the Aviation Qualification Test and the Flight Aptitude Rating Test.

Potential and advancement

The need for qualified officers in all of the services will provide career opportunities for applicants with a wide range of skills, and promotion to higher rank is possible for everyone.

Income

Newly commissioned officers earn about $11,914. They have medical and dental benefits, 30 days' paid vacation, and receive extra allowances for some duties or assignments. They may retire after 20 years at half pay.

Additional sources of information

High school and college guidance counselors and local recruiting offices can provide information on careers in the armed forces. Information is also available from:

United States Military Academy
West Point, NY 10996

United States Naval Academy
Annapolis, MD 21402

U.S. Air Force Academy
Colorado Springs, CO 80901

Naval Reserve Center
Pensacola, FL 32509

U.S. Coast Guard Academy
New London, CT 06320

OPERATING ENGINEER

The job

Operating engineers, who are also called construction machinery operators, operate all kinds of construction equipment. They are usually classified by the type or capacity of the machines they operate.

Heavy equipment operators are highly skilled in the operation of complex machinery such as cranes. They must accurately judge distances and heights while operating the buttons, levers, and pedals that rotate the crane, raise and lower the boom and loadline, and open and close attachments such as steel-toothed buckets or clamps for lifting materials. At times, operators work without being able to see the pickup or delivery point, depending on hand or flag signals from another worker. When constructing new buildings, they work far above the ground.

The operation of medium-sized construction equipment requires fewer controls and is done at ground level. *Bulldozer operators,* for example, lift and lower the blade and move the bulldozer back and forth over the construction area. Trench excavators, paving machines, and other construction equipment are also in this category.

Lightweight equipment such as an air compressor is the simplest to operate. (An air compressor is a diesel engine that takes in air and forces it through a narrow hose. The resulting pressure is used to run special tools.) The operator makes sure the compressor has fuel and water, adjusts and maintains pressure levels, and makes minor repairs.

Operating engineers often work with helpers called *oilers* who keep the equipment properly lubricated and supplied with fuel.

About half of all operating engineers operate excavating, grading, and road machinery; about one fifth are bulldozer operators; about one fourth operate cranes, derricks, hoists, air compressors, trench-pipe layers and dredges.

Most operating engineers work for contractors in large-scale construction projects such as highways, dams, and airports. Others work for utility companies and business firms that do their own construction; state and local highway and public works departments; and in factories and mines using power-driven machinery, hoists, and cranes. Very few operating engineers are self-employed.

The International Union of Operating Engineers is the bargaining unit for many workers in this field.

Places of employment and working conditions

Most operating engineers work outdoors. They work steadily during the warm months but have slow periods in cold months or in bad weather. Operation of medium-sized equipment is physically tiring because of constant movement and the jolting and noise levels of the equipment. Those working on highway construction sometimes work in remote locations.

Qualifications, education and training

Operating engineers need physical stamina, mechanical ability, excellent eyesight and eye-hand coordination, and manual dexterity.

Driver education and automobile mechanics courses in high school are helpful, and experience in operating a tractor or other farm equipment can provide a good background for this work.

A number of private schools offer instruction in the operation of some types of construction equipment, but anyone considering such a school should check with local construction employers for their opinion of the training received by the school's graduates. Not all schools produce suitably trained people.

Most employers prefer to hire operating engineers who have completed a formal apprenticeship program, since they are more thoroughly trained and can operate a variety of equipment. Programs are usually sponsored and supervised by a joint union-management committee; the armed forces also provide apprenticeship programs. An apprenticeship consists of at least three years of on-the-job training plus 144 hours per year of related classroom instruction in hydraulics, engine operation and repair, cable splicing, welding, safety, and first aid.

Apprenticeship applicants usually need a high school or vocational school diploma, but not always. They must be at least 18 years old.

Apprentices start by working as oilers or helpers. They clean, grease, repair and start engines. Within the first year of apprenticeship, they usually begin to perform simple machine operations and progress to more complex operations, always under the supervision of an experienced operating engineer.

Potential and advancement

There are about 600,000 operating engineers; jobs should be plentiful over the long run for well-trained applicants. Ups and downs in the economy, however, can cause temporary slumps in this industry. Job openings are most plentiful in the spring and early summer in many areas.

Promotion opportunities in this industry are few, but a few operating engineers do advance to supervisory positions.

Income

Wage rates vary depending on the machine operated. Average union rates in metropolitan areas are $10.07 an hour for crane operators (heavy equipment); $9.55 for bulldozer operators (medium-sized equipment); and $8.65 for compressor operators (light equipment). Because of seasonal and bad-weather down periods, annual earnings do not reflect these high hourly rates.

Apprentices start at 70 percent of the hourly rate for experienced workers and receive periodic increases during their training.

Additional sources of information

Associated General Contractors of America, Inc.
1957 E Street NW
Washington, DC 20006

International Union of Operating Engineers
1125 17th Street, NW
Washington, DC 20036

OPERATIONS RESEARCH ANALYST

The job

An organization or system can usually be operated in several ways, but the best way is not necessarily the most obvious one. Operations research specialists use their knowledge of engineering, mathematics, and economics to decide on the most efficient way to use all available resources to achieve maximum results.

This relatively new field is concerned with the design and operation of man-machine systems. Using a number of scientific methods of analysis, operations research analysts decide on the best allocation of resources within an organization or system. These resources include such things as time, money, trained people, space and raw materials.

In another application of operations research techniques, analysts might apply appropriate theories and methods to two possible research projects that are competing for funding. Their analysis could produce information on which project would probably achieve the best results in the shortest time with the available money and other resources.

The applications of operations research are numerous. Originated during World War II to deal with the allocation and tactical employment of available equipment, men, and materials, operations research is now a standard and growing aspect of management in industry, marketing, capital development, financial planning, government, and exploration activities.

A number of people in this field are engaged in teaching and research.

Women as well as men find this an interesting and well-paid career field. As more women obtain degrees in engineering and economics, they will probably enter operations research in greater numbers.

Related jobs are: Industrial Engineer, Systems Analyst, Office Manager.

Places of employment and working conditions

While many operations research analysts work in an office setting, many others work in classrooms; out-of-doors; and in laboratories, factories, and hospitals. It is often an active field, with the analyst moving throughout a building or to several different locations to study the operation of a company or system.

Operations, education, and training

An analytical mind, resourcefulness, patience, good communication skills, and the ability to get along with people are necessary.

High school should include as much mathematics and science as possible.

A degree in engineering, mathematics, economics, or the physical sciences are all acceptable beginnings for this field, since there is no typical operations research program. Graduate study is, however, usually necessary, and a working knowledge of computers should be acquired during undergraduate or graduate education.

Over 50 universities offer graduate degrees in operations research.

Potential and advancement

The demand for competent operations research analysts far exceeds the supply. This trend is expected to continue into the 1980s, providing increasing job opportunities for those who pursue it as a primary career or as an adjunct to another area of specialization.

The potential for advancement in this field is excellent. Experienced analysts can advance to supervisory and management positions in all types of organizations. Because this field provides exposure to the full spectrum of operations within a company or organization, it is becoming recognized as a major training ground for senior management and executive positions.

Many experienced operations research analysts become management consultants, opening their own companies or working for an established management consulting firm.

Income

Entry-level salaries for applicants with a master's degree in operations research are in the $22,000 range.

Experienced operations research analysts within an organization earn from $19,000 to $60,000 a year. Government positions pay $16,000 to $43,000. Colleges and universities pay from $19,000 to $47,000 a year.

Analysts who work for management consulting firms earn $24,000 to $47,000 a year. Operations research managers earn up to $60,000.

Additional sources of information

Education Committee
Operations Research Society of America
428 East Preston Street
Baltimore, MD 21202

OPHTHALMOLOGIST

The job

Ophthalmologists are also called eye physicians-surgeons. They are qualified physicians and osteopathic physicians who have completed additional specialized training in the treatment of eye diseases and disorders. They treat a full range of eye problems including vision deficiencies, injuries, infections, and other disorders with medicines, therapy, corrective lenses, or surgery. Their job is distinct from that of optometrists and opticians who are not physicians and who treat only vision problems.

Most ophthalmologists are in private practice. Others are employed by hospitals and clinics, medical schools and research foundations, federal and state agencies, and the armed forces.

Related jobs are: Optometrist, Dispensing Optician, Physician, Osteopathic Physician.

Places of employment and working conditions

Ophthalmologists work in all areas of the country. Those who are osteopathic physicians are concentrated in the areas that have osteopathic hospital facilties—mainly in Florida, Michigan, Pennsylvania, New Jersey, Ohio, Texas, and Missouri. The workweek for ophthalmologists is from 35 to 50 hours. Those involved in general patient care are always on call for emergencies.

Qualifications, educations, and training

Information on the training and licensing requirements for physicians and osteopathic physicians is contained in the appropriate job description elsewhere in this book.

An additional three to five years of residency in an accredited ophthalmology program must be completed by doctors who wish to specialize in this field. Candidates for the specialty must then pass the certification examination of the American Board of Ophthalmology or the American Osteopathic Board of Ophthalmology.

Potential and adavancement

The demand for ophthalmologists will continue to grow as the population grows. Greater interest in eye care, the growing number of senior citizens, and the increase in health insurance plans will all add to the need for qualified practitioners of this medical specialty.

Income

Ophthalmologists who start a private practice face a few lean years until the practice is established. In addition, a sizable investment in specialized equipment is necessary. Earnings during this early period may barely meet expenses.

As a practice grows, earnings usually increase substantially. Average annual earnings for all ophthalmologists are in the $18,000 to $50,000 range with some earning even more. In general, ophthalmologists in private practice earn more than those in salaried positions.

Additional sources of information

Council on Medical Education
American Medical Association
535 North Dearborn Street
Chicago, IL 60610

American Osteopathic Association
212 East Ohio Street
Chicago, IL 60611

The Osteopathic College of Ophthalmology and Otorhinolaryngology
405 Grand Avenue
Dayton, OH 45405

OPTICIAN, DISPENSING

The job

Over 100 million people in the U.S. use some form of corrective lenses (eyeglasses or contact lenses). These corrective lenses are prepared and fitted by dispensing opticians who are also called ophthalmic dispensers. Working with the prescription received from an ophthalmologist (eye physician) or optometrist, the dispensing optician provides the customer with appropriate eyeglasses. He or she measures the customer's face, aids in the selection of the appropriate frames, directs the work of ophthalmic laboratory technicians who grind the lenses, and fits the completed eyeglasses.

In many states, dispensing opticians also fit contact lenses, which requires even more skill, care, and patience than the preparation and fitting of eyeglasses. Opticians measure the corneas of the customer's eyes and, following the ophthalmologist's or optometrist's prescription, prepares specifications for the contact lens manufacturer. The optician will instruct the customer on how to insert, remove, and care for the contact lenses and will provide follow-up attention during the first few weeks.

Some dispensing opticians specialize in the fitting of artificial eyes and cosmetic shells to cover blemished eyes. Some also do their own lens grinding.

Most dispensing opticians work for retail optical shops or other retail stores with optical departments. Ophthalmologists and optometrists who sell glasses directly to patients also employ dispensing opticians, as do hospitals and eye clinics. A number of dispensing opticians operate their own retail shops and sell other optical goods such as binoculars, magnifying glasses, and sunglasses.

Some dispensing opticians are members of unions, the largest being the International Union of Electrical, Radio and Machine Workers (AFL-CIO).

Places of employment and working conditions

Dispensing opticians are located throughout the United States with most employed in large cities and in the more populous states. Working conditions are usually quiet and clean with a workweek of five or six days. Dispensing opticians who own their own businesses usually work longer hours than those employed by retail shops or by opthalmologists and optometrists.

Qualifications, education, and training

The ability to do precision work is essential for anyone planning a career as a dispensing optician. Patience, tact, and the ability to deal with people are other valuable assets.

Applicants for entry jobs in this field need a high school diploma with courses in the basic sciences. High school courses in physics, algebra, geometry, and mechanical drawing are especially valuable.

Most opticians acquire their skills through on-the-job training. A small number of dipensing opticians learn their trade in the armed forces. In addition, large manufacturers of contact lenses offer nondegree courses in lens-fitting.

Fifteen schools offer a two-year full-time course in optical fabricating and dispensing which leads to an associate's degree. Students learn optical mathematics, optical physics, and the use of precision measuring instruments.

Apprenticeship programs lasting from three to four years are also available. In these programs, the students study optometric technical subjects and basic office management and sales and work directly with patients in the fitting of eyeglasses and contact lenses.

Dispensing opticians must be licensed in some states. Specific requirements vary from state to state but generally include minimum standards of education and training along with a written or practical examination.

Potential and advancement

About 14,500 persons work as dispensing opticians. Employment opportunities in this field are expected to increase steadily as the population increases. Increased health insurance coverage, medicare services, and state programs to provide eye care to low-income families—along with current fashion trends, which encourage sales of more than one pair of glasses to individual buyers will add to the demand for dispensing opticians.

Many dispensing opticians go into business for themselves. Others advance to positions in the management of retail optical stores or become sales representatives for wholesalers or manufacturers of eyeglasses or contact lenses.

Income

Hourly wage rates for dispensing opticians range from $5.75 to $9.25 an hour. Those who own their businesses usually earn much more.

Apprentices start at about 60 percent of the rate paid to experienced workers with periodic raises during the training period.

Additional sources of information

National Academy of Opticianry
514 Chestnut Street
Big Rapids, MI 49307

National Federation of Opticianry Schools
300 Jay Street
Brooklyn, NY 11201

International Union of Electrical, Radio and Machine Workers
1176 16th Street, NW
Washington, DC 20036

Opticians Association of America
1250 Connecticut Avenue, NW
Washington, DC 20036

OPTOMETRIST

The job

Approximately one half of the U.S. population wear corrective lenses (eyeglasses or contact lenses). Before obtaining lenses, people need an eye examination and a prescription to obtain the correct lenses for their particular eye problem. Optometrists (doctors of optometry) provide the bulk of this care.

In addition to handling vision problems, optometrists also check for disease. When evidence of disease is found, an optometrist refers the patient to the appropriate medical practitioner. Optometrists also check depth ad color perception and the ability to focus and coordinate the eyes. They may prescribe corrective eye exercises or other treatments that do not require drugs or surgery.

Some optometrists specialize in work with children or the aged, or work only with the partially sighted who must wear microscopic or telescopic lenses. Industrial eye safety programs also are an optimetric specialty. A few optometrists are engaged in teaching and research.

Although most optometrists are in private practice, many others are in partnerships or in group practice with other optometrists or with other physicians as part of a health care team. Some work in retail vision chain stores. Many combine private, group, or partnership practice with work in specialized hospitals and eye clinics.

About 500 optometrists serve as commissioned officers in the armed forces. Others are consultants to engineers specializing in safety or lighting; to educators in remedial reading; and to health advisory committees of federal, state, and local governments.

Only about 3 percent of all optometrists are women. This will probably change as more women realize the opportunities and advantages of this field. Family responsibilities can be very easily accommodated since most practitioners are in private practice and can work whatever days or hours are convenient. Women optometrists often work part time if they have children and return to a full schedule as their children enter school.

Places of employment and working conditions

Although over half of all optometrists work in California, Illinois, New York, Pennsylvania, and Ohio, opportunities exist in towns and cities of all sizes.

Most self-employed optometrists can set their own work schedule but often work longer than 40 hours a week. Because the work is not physically strenuous, optometrists can practice past the normal retirement age.

Qualifications, education, and training

Because most optometrists are self-employed, anyone planning on a career in this field needs business ability and self-discipline in addition to the ability to deal effectively with people.

High school preparation should emphasize science and business courses are also helpful.

The Doctor of Optometry degree is awarded after successful completion of at least six years of college. The two years of preoptometrical study should include English, mathematics, physics, chemistry, and biology or zoology. Some schools also require psychology, social studies, literature, philosophy, and foreign languages.

Admission to optometry schools is highly competitive. Because the number of qualified applicants exceeds the available places, applicants need superior grades in preoptometric courses to increase their chances of acceptance by one of the 13 schools and colleges of optometry approved by by the Council of Optometric Education of the American Optometric Association.

Optometrists who wish to advance in a specialized field of optometry may study for a master's or Ph.D degree in physiological optics, neurophysiology, public health administration, health information and communication, or health education. Career officers in the armed forces also have an opportunity to work toward advanced degrees and to do research.

Potential and advancement

There are about 19,700 practicing optometrists, most of them in private practice. Employment opportunities are expected to grow steadily into the 1980s. Increasing coverage of optometric services by health insurance, greater recognition of the importance of good vision, and the growing population—especially older people who are most likely to need eye glasses—should contribute to an increase in the demand for optometrists.

Income

Incomes for optometrists vary greatly depending on location, specialization, and factors such as private or group practice. New optometry graduates average $16,900; but those who begin their careers working in retail chain stores can earn much more.

Experienced optometrists average about $40,000 a year with those in associate or partnership practices earning substantially more than those in private practice. Optometrists working for the federal government average $19,500 a year.

Additional sources of information

American Optometric Association
7000 Chippewa Street
St. Louis, MO 63119

OSTEOPATHIC PHYSICIAN

The job

Webster defines osteopathy as "a system of medical practice based on the theory that diseases are due chiefly to a loss of structural integrity in the tissues and that this integrity can be restored by manipulation of the parts, supported by the use of medicines, surgery, proper diet, and other therapy."

Most osteopathic physicians are family doctors engaged in general practice. They see patients at the office or make house calls and treat patients in osteopathic and other private and public hospitals. About one quarter of all osteopathic physicians specialize in such fields as internal medicine, neurology, psychiatry, opthalmology, pediatrics, anesthesiology, physical medicine and rehabilitation, dermatology, obstetrics and gynecology, pathology, proctology, radiology, and surgery.

Most osteopathic physicians are in private practice, although a few hold salaried positions in private industry or government agencies. Others hold full-time positions with osteopathic hospitals and colleges where they are engaged in teaching, research, and writing.

Nine percent of all practicing osteopathic physicians are women.

Place of employment and working conditions

Most osteopathic physicians practice in states that have osteopathic hospital facilities; over half are in Florida, Michigan, Pennsylvania, New Jersey, Ohio, Texas, and Missouri. Most general practicioners are located in towns and cities having less than 50,000 people; specialists are usually located in larger cities.

Qualifications, education, and training

Anyone interested in becoming an osteopathic physician should have emotional stability, patience, tact, and an interest in and ability to deal effectively with people.

The education requirements for the Doctor of Osteopathy (D.O.) degree include a minimum of three years of college (although almost all applicants have a bachelor's degree) plus a three- to four-year professional program. The education and training of an osteopathic physician is very expensive due primarily to the length of time involved. Federal and private funds are available for loans, and federal scholarships are available to those who qualify and agree to a minimum of two years of service for the federal government after completion of training.

Undergraduate study must include courses in chemistry, physics, biology, and English, with high grades an important factor in acceptance into the professional programs. In addition to high grades, schools require a good score on the New Medical College Admissions Test, recommendations from premedical college counselors, and recommendation by an osteopathic physician acquainted with the applicant. One very important qualification is the applicant's desire to study osteopathy rather than some other field of medicine.

During the first half of the professional program, the student studies basic sciences such as anatomy, physiology, and pathology as well as the principles of osteopathy. The second half of the program consists primarily of clinical experience. After graduation, a 12-month internship is usally completed at one of the 79 osteopathic hospitals approved for internship or residency by the American Osteopathic Association. Those who intend to specialize must complete an additional two to five years of training.

All practicing osteopathic physicians must be licensed. State licensing requirements vary, but all states require graduation from an approved school of osteopathic medicine and a passing grade on a state board examination. Most states will accept the exam given by the National Board of Osteopathic Examiners as a substitute for the state examination. Most states also require internship at an approved hospital. A few states require an examination in the basic sciences in addition to the professional examination. All states except Alaska and Florida will grant a license without examination to a properly qualified osteopathic physician who is already licensed by another state.

Potential and advancement

There are about 15,000 practicing osteopathic physicians in the United States. Population growth, an increase in the number of persons covered by medical insurance, and the establishment of additional osteopathic hospitals will contribute to an increasing demand for osteopathic physicians. The greatest demand will continue to be in states where osteopathic medicine is well known and accepted as a method of treatment.

Opportunities for new practitioners are best in rural areas (many localities lack medical practitioners of any kind), small towns, and suburbs of large cities. The availability of osteopathic hospital facilities should be considered when one is selecting a location for practice.

Income

As is usually the case in any field where setting up an individual practice is the norm, earnings in the first few years are low. Income usually rises substantially once the practice becomes established and, in the case of osteopathic physicians, is very high in comparison with other professions. Geographic location and the income level of the community are also factors that affect the level of income. The average income of general practitioners is $32,500.

Additional sources of information

American Osteopathic Association
Department of Public Relations
212 East Ohio Street
Chicago, IL 60611

American Association of Colleges of Osteopathic Medicine
4720 Montgomery Lane
Washington, DC 20014

PAROLE OFFICER

The job

An offender who has completed a sentence in a prison or jail is usually assigned a parole officer upon release. The ex-offender is required to report to the parole officer at specific time intervals, and the parole officer, in turn, provides counseling and assistance during the transition from prison to community life.

The parole officer helps the ex-offender to find a job or secure job training; arranges for welfare or other public assistance for the family, if necessary; and provides positive support and a helping hand in any way possible to aid the parolee in his return to society. The parole officer's main concern is helping the parolee to go straight instead of returning to a life of crime.

Probation officers deal with juvenile delinquents and first offenders who are often released by the court, subject to proper supervision, instead of being sentenced to jail or prison. A probation officer may also be involved in the presentencing investigation of a defendant's family, background, education, and any problems contributing to the defendant's offense.

Parole and probation officers are usually employed by state or municipal governments. In the course of their work, they deal with teachers, chaplains, social workers, rehabilitation counselors, local employers, and community organizations. A number of parole and probation officers come from the ranks of police officers.

Perhaps the most important ingredient of the work of a probation officer is the rapport the officer is able to establish with the juvenile offender. The opportunity to discuss problems with an understanding adult can result in the juvenile being put back on the right track. At the same time, the probation officer must be objective enough not to be deceived by lies or false promises of better behavior.

Related jobs are: Police Officer (Municipal and State), Social Worker, Prison Warden, Rehabilitation Counselor.

Places of employment and working conditions

Emotional wear and tear is a factor in the work of parole and probation officers. The frustration of seeing a parolee or a juvenile return to a life of crime in spite of all the officer's efforts is part of every officer's experience.

In many jobs, the case load itself can be a hindrance to effective work. Instead of carrying the recommended 30 to 50 cases, many parole and probation officers must keep track of up to 100 assigned cases. This makes it virtually impossible to give each person the attention and help that is usually necessary.

Qualifications, education, and training

Personal characteristics of understanding, objectivity, good judgment, and patience are necessary. Good communication skills and the ability to motivate people are very important.

High school should include the social sciences, English, and history.

People who work in this field need training and experience in sociology, psychology, criminology, or law. Those who start out as police offiers usually acquire additional training in these fields through college courses. Requirements vary depending on employers, with some states and municipalities requiring a degree, sometimes in a specfic field.

Potential and advancement

Manpower shortages in all areas of law enforcement will increase even more as the population grows. The demand for qualified parole and probation officers will be especially great in large metropolitan areas.

Parole and probation officers are not usually promoted to other positions but they do advance in salary as they gain experience. Some officers advance by acquiring additional education that qualifies them for positions in other areas of law enforcement.

Income

Probation and parole officers earn between $8,000 and $16,000 a year.

Additional sources of information

American Correctional Association
4321 Hartwick Road
College Park, MD 20740

Association of Paroling Authorities
804 State Office Building
Indianapolis, IN 46204

PERSONNEL MANAGER

The job

Personel managers conduct and supervise the employment functions of a company. These include recruiting, hiring, and training employees;

developing wage and salary scales; administering benefit programs; complying with government labor regulations; and other responsibilities that affect the employees.

In a small company, a personnel manager performs all these functions, usually assisted by one or two workers who help with interviewing and perform clerical duties related to the personnel department. In a large company, the personnel manager supervises a staff of trained personnel workers that includes some or all of the following specialists.

A *personnel recruiter* searches for promising job applicants through advertisements and employment agencies. A recruiter may also travel to college campuses to talk to students who are about to graduate. *Employment interviewers* talk to job applicants, sometimes administer and interpret tests, and may make some final hiring decisions.

Job analysts collect and analyze detailed information on each job within a company to prepare a description of each position. These descriptions include the duties of a particular job and the skills and training necessary to perform the job. Position decriptions are used by *salary and wage administrators* when they develop or revise pay scales for a company. They also use information gathered in surveys of wages paid by other local employers or by other companies within the same industry. Wage and salary administrators also work within government regulations such as minimum wage laws.

Training specialists may supervise or conduct orientation sessions for new employees, prepare training materials and manuals, and handle in-house training programs for employees who wish to upgrade existing skills or gain promotion. In some companies, a training specialist may handle details concerning apprenticeship or management trainee programs.

An *employee benefits supervisor* provides information and counseling to employees regarding the various fringe benefits offered by a company. The supervisor is also in charge of the administration of these programs which may include health, life, and disability insurance and pension plans. Other employee services such as cafeterias, newsletters, and recreational facilities are also covered.

Some companies now employ a special personnel worker to handle all matters pertaining to the government's equal employment opportunity regulations and the company's affirmative action programs.

Personnel workers in federal, state, and local government agencies have the added duties of devising, administering, and scoring the competitive civil service examinations that are administered to all applicants for public employment. Others oversee compliance with state and federal labor laws, health and safety regulations, and equal employment opportunity programs.

Personnel specialists also work for private employment agencies, executive search organizations, and "office temporaries" agencies. A few work as self-employed management consultants, and others teach at the college and university level.

About 40 percent of all personnel workers are women.

Related jobs are: Employment Counselor and Labor Relations Specialist.

Job opportunities for personnel specialists and personnel managers exist throughout the country with the largest concentrations in highly industrialized areas.

Qualifications, education, and training

Integrity and fairmindedness are important qualifications for those interested in personnel work and because they are often called on to act as the liaison between the company and its employees in the day-to-day administration of company policies. Personnel workers must be able to work with people of many educational levels and must have excellent written and oral communications skills.

In high school, a college preparatory course should include emphasis on English and social studies.

Some personnel workers enter the field as clerical workers in a personnel office and gain experience and expertise in one or more specialty areas over a period of time. In some small and medium-sized companies, they may advance to personnel manager positions on the basis of experience alone, but most employers require a college education even for entry-level jobs in personnel.

People in personnel work come from a variety of college majors. Some employers prefer a well-rounded liberal arts background; others want a business administration degree. A few insist on a degree in personnel administration or in industrial or labor relations. Government agencies prefer applicants who have majored in personnel administration, political science, or public administration. Any courses in the social sciences, behavioral sciences, and economics are valuable.

Graduate study in industrial or labor relations is necessary for some top-level jobs in personnel work.

Potential and advancement

About 335,000 people are employed in the overlapping fields of personnel and labor relations. These fields are expected to grow steadily with the largest growth in the area of public personnel administration.

State and local government agencies will provide more job openings than federal agencies.

Personnel workers can advance to supervisory and management positions in most companies. Those in middle-management positions in large companies can also advance to positions such as director of industrial relations.

Income

Personnel workers earn starting salaries of about $12,000 in private industry; $10,000 to $15,300 in state and federal government agencies.

Experienced personnel specialists average about $22,600 in private industry; personnel managers about $23,600. Top personnel executives in large corporations earn considerably more.

In state government agencies, salaries of experienced personnel specialists vary widely—from a low of $11,100 to about $14,500. Those with supervisory responsibilities earn from $16,200 to $21,600; and state directors of personnel average from $31,000 to $36,000.

The federal government pays experienced personnel specialists from $21,400 to $33,800.

Additional sources of information

American Society for Personnel Administration
19 Church Street
Berea, OH 44017

American Society for Training and Development
P.O. Box 5307
Madison, WI 53705

International Personnel Management Association
1313 East 60th Street
Chicago, IL 60637

PETROLEUM ENGINEER

The job

Petroleum engineers are responsible for exploring and drilling for oil and gas and for efficient production. Some concentrate on reasearch and development into methods to increase the proportion of oil recovered from each oil reservoir.

Most petroleum engineers are employed by the major oil companies and by the hundreds of small, independent oil exploration and production companies. Drilling equipment manufacturers and suppliers also employ petroleum engineers. Engineering consulting firms and independent consulting engineers use their services, and federal and state agencies employ petroleum engineers on regulatory boards and as inspectors.

Banks and other financial institutions sometimes employ petroleum engineers to provide information on the economic value of oil and gas properties.

Place of employment and working conditions

About three fourths of all petroleum engineers work in California, Louisiana, Oklahoma, and Texas. Many work overseas for American companies and for foreign governments.

This can be dirty work and is sometimes dangerous. Assignments to offshore oil rigs or remote foreign locations can make family life difficult.

Qualifications, education, and training

The ability to think analytically, a capacity for detail, and the ability to work as part of a team are all necessary. Good communication skills are important.

Mathematics and the sciences must be emphasized in high school.

A bachelor's degree in engineering is the minimum requirement in this field. In a typical curriculum, the first two years are spent in the study of basic sciences such as physics and chemistry and mathematics, introductory engineering, and some liberal arts courses. The remaining years are usually devoted to specialized engineering courses. Engineering programs can last from four to six years. Those requiring five or six years to complete may award a master's degree or may provide a cooperative plan of study plus practical work experience with a nearby industry.

Because of rapid changes in technology, many engineers continue their education throughout their careers. A graduate degree is necessary for most teaching and research positions and for many management jobs.

Engineering graduates usually work under the supervision of an experienced engineer or in a company training program until they become acquainted with the requirements of a particular company or industry.

All states require licensing of engineers whose work may affect life, health, or property or who offer their services to the public. Those who are licensed, about one third of all engineers, are called Registered Engineers. Requirements include graduation from an accredited engineering school, four years of experience, and a written examination.

Potential and advancement

There are about 20,000 petroleum engineers, and substantial employment growth is expected in this field. Demand for increased domestic oil and gas resources means increased exploration and production, which will provide many job openings for petroleum engineers.

Income

Starting salaries in private industry average $16,800 with a bachelor's degree; $18,700 with a master's degree; and $24,000 or more with a Ph.D.

The federal government pays beginners $13,657 to $20,000 depending on degree and experience. Average salary for experienced engineers federally employed is about $27,700.

Experienced engineers average $30,500 in private industry; $15,000 to $21,000 for nine-month faculty positions in colleges and universities.

Additional sources of information

American Society for Engineering Education
One DuPont Circle, Suite 400
Washington, DC 20036

Engineers' Council for Professional Development
345 East 47th Street
New York, NY 10017

National Society of Professional Engineers
2029 K Street, NW
Washington, DC 20006

Society of Petroleum Engineers of AIME
6200 North Central Expressway
Dallas, TX 75206

Society of Women Engineers
United Engineering Center
345 East 47th Street
New York, NY 10017

PHARMACIST

The job

Pharmacists dispense drugs and medicines prescribed by physicians and dentists, advise on the use and proper dosage of prescription and nonprescription medicines, and work in research and marketing positions. Half of all pharmacists own their own businesses.

Over 90,000 pharmacists work in community pharmacies (drugstores). These range from one-man operations to large retail establishments employing a staff of pharmacists.

Hospitals and clinics employ pharmacists to dispense drugs and medication to patients, advise the medical staff on the selection and effects of drugs, buy medical supplies, and prepare sterile solutions. In some hospitals, they also teach nursing classes.

Pharmaceutical manufacturers employ pharmacists in research and development and in sales positions. Drug wholesalers also employ them as sales and technical representatives.

The federal government employs pharmacists in hospitals and clinics of the Veterans Administration and the U.S. Public Health Service; in the Department of Defense; the Food and Drug Administration; Department of Health, Education and Welfare; and in the Drug Enforcement Administration. State and local health agencies also employ pharmacists.

Many community and hospital pharmacists also do consulting work for nursing homes and other health facilities which do not employ a full-time pharmacist.

About 16 percent of all pharmacists are women; they work mainly in hospital pharmacies and research laboratories.

Places of employment and working conditions

Just about every community has a drugstore employing at least one pharmacist. Most job opportunities, however, are in larger cities and densely populated metropolitan areas.

Pharmacists average about a 44-hour workweek; those who also do consulting work average an additional 15 hours a week. Pharmacists in community pharmacies work longer hours—including evenings and weekends—than those employed by hospitals and other health care institutions, pharmaceutical manufacturers, and drug wholesalers.

Qualifications, education, and training

Prospective pharmacists need an interest in medicine and should have orderliness and accuracy, business ability, honesty, and integrity.

Biology and chemistry courses along with some business courses should be taken in high school.

At least five years of study beyond high school are necessary to earn a degree in pharmacy. A few colleges admit pharmacy students immediately following high school, but most require one or two years of prepharmacy college study in mathematics, basic sciences, humanities, and social sciences.

Seventy-two colleges of pharmacy are accredited by the American Council on Pharmaceutical Education. Most of these schools award a bachelor of science (B.S.) or a bachelor of pharmacy (B.Pharm.) degree upon completion of the required course of study. About one third of the schools also offer an advanced degree program leading to a doctor of pharmacy (Pharm.D.) degree. A few schools offer only the Pharm.D. degree.

A Pharm.D. degree, or a master's or Ph.D. degree in pharmacy or a related field, is usally required for research, teaching, and administrative positions.

Pharmacists are usually required to serve an internship under the supervision of a registered pharmacist before they can obtain a license to practice. All states require a license and an applicant must usually have: (1) graduated from an accredited pharmacy college, (2) passed a state board of examination, and (3) had a specified amount of practical experience or internship. Many pharmacists are licensed to practice in more than one state, and most states will grant a license without examination to a qualified pharmacist licensed by another state.

Potential and advancement

About 120,000 people work as pharmacists, over 75 percent of them in community drugstores. Job opportunities are expected to be good through the mid-1980s, but competition may eventually develop in this field because of the increasing number of degrees being awarded. Most job openings will occur in hospitals, nursing homes, and other health care facilities.

Many pharmacists in salaried positions advance by opening their own community pharmacies. Those employed by chain drugstores may advance to management positons or executive-level jobs within the company. Hospital pharmacists may advance to director of pharmacy service or to other administrative positions.

Pharmacists employed by the pharmaceutical industry have the widest latitude of advancement possibilities because they can advance in management, sales, research, quality control, advertising, production, or packaging. There will be fewer job opportunities, however, with manufacturers than in other areas of pharmacy.

Income

Starting salaries for pharmacists range from $17,000 to $20,000 a year.

Experienced pharmacists earn from $21,000 to $29,000. Store owners or managers and those who also do consulting work often earn considerably more.

Pharmacists who teach in pharmacy colleges earn from about $20,000 to $36,000 a year, within the following ranges: assistant and associate professors, $22,000 to $26,000; assistant and associate deans and full professors, $32,000 to $33,000; deans, about $42,000.

Additional sources of information

American Association of Colleges of Pharmacy
Office of Student Affairs
4630 Montgomery Avenue, Suite 201
Bethesda, MD 20014

American Pharmaceutical Association
2215 Constitution Avenue, NW
Washington, DC 20037

National Association of Chain Drug Stores
1911 Jefferson Highway
Arlington, VA 22202

American Council of Pharmaceutical Education
One East Wacker Drive
Chicago, IL 60601

PHOTOGRAPHER

The job

A photographer takes pictures as an artistic or commercial occupation. Some specialize in portrait photography; others work as photojournalists or industrial photographers. Photographers with knowledge in a special field may specialize in scientific, medical, or engineering photography. Artists who employ photography as an art form have undergone a surge in recent years.

Portrait photographers take pictures of individuals and groups in studios, at weddings, and at other types of gatherings. Many portrait photographers own their own studios and often begin their careers working part-time. These people should have firm business skills to succeed in their own businesses. They must also have a knack for getting people to relax.

Commercial photographers, many of whom work in advertising, photograph everything from livestock to buildings to manufactured articles. They must be familiar with many different photographic techniques.

Industrial photographers work in industry and handle everything from photographs for the company newspaper or stockholders' report to photographs of the company's products or manufacturing processes. Those who specialize in fields such as science or medicine may use special equipment and techniques such as infrared photography, X rays, or time-lapse photography.

Photojournalists are newspaper and magazine photographers who must have a "nose for news" in addition to photographic skills. Those who work for nationwide publications or prestigious newspapers are among the highest-paid photographers.

Other specialists include *educational photographers* who prepare slides, filmstrips, and movies for classroom use; *photomicrographers* who work with microscopes; and *photogrammetrists* who specialize in the use of aerial photographs for surveying.

Most photographers work in portrait or commerical studios. The next largest group works as photojournalists. Government agencies and industrial firms employ a significant number, and a few photographers teach in colleges and universities. About one third of all photographers are self-employed.

About 16 percent of all professional photographers are women.

Places of employment and working conditions

Photographers work in all areas of the United States.

Those employed in salaried jobs usually work a 35- to 40-hour, five-day week. Those in business for themselves work longer hours. Press photographers usually have to work some evening and weekend hours to cover news assignments. Free-lance, press, and commercial photographers do a great deal of traveling.

Qualifications, education, and training

Good eyesight and color vision, artistic ability, and manual dexterity are necessary for a photographer. Patience, accuracy, and an ability to work with detail are also important.

There are no formal educational requirements in this field, although a high school education does provide a good general background for a photographer. Many would-be photographers acquire their skills through two or three years of on-the-job training in a commercial studio. Technical training, however, is the best preparation and is usually necessary for industrial, medical, or scientific work.

Photographic training is available in colleges, universities, junior colleges, and art schools. The armed forces also train many photographers. Two-year training courses sometimes offer an associate degee in photography. Some colleges offer a bachelor's degree in photography, and a few offer a master's degree in specialized areas such as photojournalism. Art schools provide useful training in design and composition but do not usually offer technical training in photography.

A background in a particular science, medical, or engineering field is necessary for many specialty areas of photography. Some employers may require a bachelor's degree in a particular field in addition to photographic skills and experience. News photographers may be expected to have a background in journalism.

Potential and advancement

There are about 85,000 photographers, and the field is expected to grow slowly over the next decade. Job opportunities will be best in business and industry and in such fields as medicine where technical training and a specialty background are important. There will be competition for jobs as portrait or commercial photographers, since this is the largest job field and the one that requires the least training and education.

Advancement usually depends on experience. Some industrial and scientific photographers may be promoted to supervisory positions; magazine and news photographers may eventually become photography editors or heads of graphic arts departments. Self-employed photographers advance as they build a reputation and receive more lucrative assignments. Photographers in salaried positions may open their own studio or do free-lance work.

Income

Beginning news photographers earn between $200 and $275 a week; experienced ones earn from $250 to about $560 with the average about $320 a week.

Experienced photographers with the federal government earn $13,010 to $19,260 a year.

Self-employed and free-lance photographers usually earn more than salaried photographers in the same geographic area.

Additional sources of information

Professional Photographers of America, Inc.
1090 Executive Way
Oak Leaf Common
Des Plaines, IL 60018

Photographic Art and Science Foundation
111 Stratford Road
Des Plaines, IL 60016

PHOTOGRAPHIC LABORATORY TECHNICIAN

The job

The development of film, preparation of prints and slides, enlarging and retouching of photographs, and other film processing chores are performed by photographic laboratory technicians. They service both the amateur photographer (in labs that mass-process film) and the professional photographer in independent labs or for individual studios.

All-around *darkroom technicians* can perform all tasks necessary to develop and print film including enlarging and retouching. They can handle black-and-white negative, color negative, or color positive work. Since color work is more difficult than black-and-white, some highly skilled technicians specialize as *color technicians*.

Technicians who work in photography studios often function as assistants to the photographer setting up lights and cameras. Many future photographers begin this way, dividing their time between processing film and learning photography.

In some labs, technicians may be asisted by helpers or assistants who specialize in just one process such as developing or retouching. In large photo labs with automatic film-processing equipment, darkroom technicians supervise semiskilled workers who handle many individual tasks such as film numbering, chemical mixing, or slide mounting.

Places of employment and working conditions

Photographic laboratory technicians are employed in all parts of the country with most job opportunities in large cities.

Photographic laboratory technicians usually work a 40-hour week. In labs that process film for amateur photographers, the summer months and several weeks after the Christmas season require considerable amounts of overtime. Jobs in this field are not physically strenuous, but many of the semiskilled jobs are repetitious and fast-paced; some of the processes can cause eye fatigue.

Qualifications, education, and training

Good eyesight and color vision are necessary, as well as manual dexterity.

A high school diploma is not always necessary but can provide a good background. Chemistry and mathematics courses are valuable, and any courses, part-time jobs, or amateur photography and film processing work are helpful.

Most darkroom technicians acquire their skills through on-the-job training, which takes about three years. Others attend trade or technical schools or receive their training in the armed forces.

A few junior and community colleges offer a two-year course in photographic technology leading to an associate degree. College-level training is helpful in securing supervisory and management positions.

Potential and advancement

There are about 35,000 people employed in some phase of photographic laboratory work. This job field is expected to grow steadily in spite of the increasing use of automated processing equipment and self-processing cameras. Job opportunities for well-trained, all-around darkroom technicians will be best in business and industry and in independent labs that service photographers in specialty fields.

Income

Experienced darkroom technicians earn between $5.00 and $8.00 and hour. Semiskilled workers and helpers earn between $2.90 and $5.00.

Additional sources of information

Photo Marketing Association
603 Lansing Avenue
Jackson, MI 49202

Professional Photographers of America, Inc.
1090 Executive Way
Des Plaines, IL 60018

Photographic Art and Science Foundation
111 Stratford Road
Des Plaines, IL 60016

PHYSICAL THERAPIST

The job

At some point in their treatment, accident and stroke victims, crippled children, and disabled older persons are usually referred by their doctor to a physical therapist. The therapist will design and carry out a program of testing, exercise, massage, or other therapeutic treatment that will increase strength, restore the range of motion, relieve pain, and improve the condition of muscles and skin.

Physical therapists provide direct patient care and usually do their own evaluation of the patient's needs. The physical therapist works, however, in close cooperation with the physician and any other specialists involved in the care of the patient such as vocational therapists, psychologists, and social workers. In large hospitals and nursing homes, the physical therapist may carry out a program designed by the director or assistant director of the physical therapy department rather than develop the program himself. Some physical therapists specialize in one variety of patient such as children or the elderly or one type of condition such as arthritis, amputations, or paralysis.

Most physical therapists work in hospitals. Nursing homes employ a growing number and also use the services of self-employed therapists. Rehabilitation centers, schools for crippled children, public health agencies, physicians' offices, and the armed forces all employ physical therapists. Some therapists also work with patients in their own homes or provide instructions to the patient and the patient's family on how to continue therapy at home.

About three quarters of all licensed physical therapists are women. Because this field has so many opportunities for part-time practitioners, it appeals to people with family responsibilities.

Places of employment and working conditions

Physical therapists are employed throughout the country with the largest number working in cities with large hospitals or medical centers.

Since physical therapy, unlike many other medical procedures, does not have to be provided on a 24-hour basis, most therapists work a 40-hour week. In the case of self-employed and part-time therapists, some evening and weekend work may be required.

Qualifications, education, and training

Patience, tact, emotional stability, and the ability to work with people are important for anyone interested in this field. Manual dexterity and physical stamina are also important.

High school students considering this field should take courses in health, biology, social science, mathematics, and physical education. Part-time or volunteer work in the physical therapy department of a hospital can provide a close look at the work for anyone trying to decide on a career in physical therapy.

There are three types of programs for physical therapy training, depending on the previous academic qualifications of the applicant. (1) High school graduates may study at the college or university and earn a four-year bachelor's degree in physical therapy.

(2) Applicants who already hold a bachelor's degree in a related field, such as biology or physical education, can earn either a second bachelor's degree or a certificate in physical therapy by completing a special program, usually lasting twelve to sixteen months. They also have the option of working for a master's degree in physical therapy.

(3) There are master-degree programs that provide advanced training for those already in the field.

All training programs for physical therapists must be accredited by the American Physical Therapy Association and the American Medical Association.

Physical therapists must be licensed. A degree or certificate from an accredited program and a passing grade on a state board examination completes the requirements for obtaining a license.

Potential and advancement

There are about 25,000 licensed physical therapists. Employment in the field is expected to expand rapidly as the demand grows for more rehabilitative facilities for accident victims, the elderly, and crippled children. Opportunities for part-time work will also continue to grow.

As the number of new graduates in the field catches up with the number of job openings, job competition will probably develop in large population centers. Job opportunities will continue to be good in suburban and rural areas, however.

Advancement in this field depends on experience and advanced education especially for teaching, research and administration positions.

Income

Newly graduated physical therapists earn about $13,000 a year. Earnings of experienced therapists average about $16,000.

The Veterans Administration pays starting salaries of about $11,700; the average for experienced therapists is about $16,000. Some supervisors earn over $23,000.

Additional sources of information

American Physical Therapy Association
1156 15th Street, NW
Washington, DC 20005

PHYSICIAN

The job

Physicians diagnose diseases, treat illnesses and injuries, and are involved in research, rehabilitation, and preventive medicine.

Most physicians specialize in a particular field of medicine such as internal medicine, general surgery, psychiatry, or pediatrics. The fastest growing specialty is family practice, which emphasizes general medicine.

Nine out of every ten physicians are involved in direct patient care. This includes 94,000 who work as residents or full-time staff members in hospitals and about 215,000 who have office practices. About ten percent of all physicians hold full-time positions in research, teaching, or administration.

Most new physicians open their own offices or join associate or group practices. Those who enter the armed forces start with the rank of captain in the army or air force or lieutenant in the navy. Other federal positions are in the Veterans Administration; the U.S. Public Health Service; and the Department of Health and Human Services.

Only 7 percent of physicians are women. Medical school admission policies, which in the past have discriminated against women, are being changed by recent laws, but women still face difficulties in medical school because of the attitudes of male medical students and faculty as well as efforts to steer women away from some specialties such as surgery. Women now make up about 25 percent of the entering classes in medical schools, and, as more qualified women secure faculty positions in medical schools, attitudes and opportunities for women in medicine should improve. More positive attitudes by high school counselors could also encourage more women to enter this field.

Places of employment and working conditions

Just about every community has at least one physician.

The northeastern states have the highest ratios of physicians to population; the southern states have the lowest. Physicians tend to locate in urban areas close to hospital facilities and educational centers; rural areas are often underserved.

Many physicians have long and irregular working hours. Specialists work fewer hours than general practitioners. Physicians do have the option of curtailing their practices as they grow older, thus being able to work at a reduced pace past the normal retirement age.

Qualifications, education, and training

Anyone interested in this field must have a strong desire to serve the sick and injured. He or she must have emotional stability and the ability to make quick decisions in an emergency and be able to relate well to people. The study of medicine is long and expensive and requires a commitment to intense, vigorous training.

High school should include as much mathematics and science as possible, and grades should average "B" or above.

Most medical school applicants have a bachelor's degree, although medical schools will accept three years of premedical college study. Competition for entrance into medical school is fierce with almost three times as many applicants as there are openings. Premedical college grades of "B" or better are usually necessary along with a high grade on the New Medical College Admission Test. Other relevant factors are the applicant's character, personality, and leadership qualities; letters of recommendation from premedical instructors and others; and, in state-supported medical schools, area of residence.

It usually takes four years to complete medical school; students with outstanding ability sometimes complete it in three. A few schools have programs that allow completion of premedical and medical studies in a total of six years.

The first half of medical school is spent in classrooms and laboratories studying medical sciences. The remaining time is spent in clinical work under the supervision of experienced physicians. At completion of medical school, students are awarded a doctor of medicine (M.D.) degree.

After graduation, a one- to three-year hospital residency is usually completed. Those seeking certification in a specialty spend an additional two to four years in advanced residency training; this is followed by two or more years of practice in the specialty before the required specialty board examination is taken.

Physicians who intend to teach or do research must earn a master's or Ph.D. degree in a field such as biochemistry or microbiology.

All physicians must be licensed to practice medicine. Requirements usually include graduation from an accredited medical school, completion of a residency program, and a passing grade on a licensing examination—usually the National Board of Medical Examiners (NBME) test. Applicants who have not taken the NBME test must be sponsored by a state to sit for the Federal Licensure Examination (FLEX) that is accepted by all jurisdictions. Physicians licensed in one state can obtain a license in most other states without further examination.

Graduates of foreign medical schools must pass an examination given by the Educational Commission for Foreign Medical Graduates before they are allowed to serve a residency in the United States.

Potential and advancement

There are about 360,000 professionally active physicians in the United States. Employment opportunities should be very good through the 1980s. Anticipated increases in the number of medical graduates of existing and new U.S. medical schools, combined with foreign medical graduates, should improve the supply of physicians. This should also encourage more physicians to establish practices in areas that have traditionally lacked sufficient medical services such as rural and inner-city areas. An increase in the supply of new physicians will also mean a sufficient number of practitioners in some specialty fields by the mid-1980s. Primary care practitioners, such as family physicians, pediatricians, and internal medicine specialists, will continue to be in demand.

Income

Physicians have the highest average annual earnings of any occupational or professional group—about $65,400 a year.

New physicians setting up their own practice usually have a few very lean years in the beginning but, once a practice is established, earnings rise rapidly. Physicians in a private practice usually earn more than those in salaried positions, and specialists earn considerbly more than general practitioners.

Because practitioners in metropolitan areas have much better incomes than those in rural areas, some rural communities offer a guaranteed annual income to a physician who is willing to practice in their area.

Additional sources of information

Council on Medical Education
American Medical Association
535 North Dearborn Street
Chicago, IL 60610

Association of American Medical Colleges
Suite 200, One Dupont Circle, NW
Washington, DC 20036

American Medical Women's Association
1740 Broadway
New York, NY 10019

PHYSICIST

The job

Physicists develop theories that describe the fundamental forces and laws of nature. Most physicists work in research and development. Their work in recent years has contributed to progress in such fields as nuclear energy, electronics, communications, aerospace, and medical instrumentation.

Physicists usually specialize in one branch of the science—elementary particle physics; nuclear physics; atomic, electron, and molecular physics; physics of condensed matter; optics; acoustics, and plasma physics; or the physics of fluids.

About one half of all physicists teach or do research in colleges and universities. Private industry employs about one third of all physicists mainly in companies manufacturing chemicals, electrical equipment, aircraft, and missiles. About 8,000 physicists work for the federal government, most of them in the Departments of Defense and Commerce.

Only 4 percent of all physicists are women, but this may increase as more high school guidance counselors encourage girls who are good in science and mathematics to enter this field.

Places of employment and working conditions

Physicists are employed in all parts of the country with the heaviest concentrations in industrial areas and areas with large college enrollments. Over one fourth of all physicists work in the areas in and around New York City, Boston, Washington, D.C., and Los Angeles–Long Beach, California.

Qualifications, education, and training

An inquisitive mind, imagination, the ability to think in abstract terms, and mathematical ability are necessary for a physicist.

High school courses in science and mathematics are necessary.

A career in physics usually requires a Ph.D. A bachelor's degree in physics or mathematics is usually the first step followed by a master's degree. Some graduate students are able to work as research assistants while they study for a master's degree and may be hired as instructors while completing the Ph.D. requirements.

Potential and advancement

There are about 48,000 physicists. The number of graduate degrees awarded in physics has been declining since 1970, and this trend is expected to continue in the 1980s. Most job openings will occur to replace those who retire or leave the field. There will be some growth of job opportunities in the private sector, but job openings in colleges and universities will decline. Those with only a bachelor's degree in physics may become secondary school teachers if they fulfill state teacher certification requirements.

Physicists advance to more complex tasks as they gain experience and may move up to positions as project leaders or research directors; some advance to top management jobs. Physicists who develop new products often form their own companies.

Income

Physicists in manufacturing industries start at about $14,000 with a bachelor's degree; $17,400 with a master's; and $23,000 with a Ph.D.

Colleges and universities pay starting salaries of $12,900 with a master's and $13,900 with a Ph.D. Faculty physicists frequently supplement their income by doing consulting work and independent research projects.

Additional sources of information

American Institute of Physics
335 East 45th Street
New York, NY 10017

Interagency Board of U.S. Civil Service Examiners for Washington, D.C.
1900 E Street, NW
Washington, DC 20415

PLANT (NURSERY) MANAGER

The job

Plant nurseries grow and sell trees, flowers, shrubs, and other plants. They may be wholesale or retail operations, garden centers, or mail-order businesses. Nursery managers are in charge of these facilities.

Work as a nursery manager includes a variety of special tasks: plant propagation through seeds, cuttings, and root division; preparation of soil in outdoor growing areas; greenhouse management; weed, disease, and insect control; plant breeding; storage and packaging of plant; and business operations. In small nurseries and in many owner-operated ones, the nursery manager performs all these functions with the aid of a few laborers. In large wholesale, retail, and mail-order nurseries, the manager has a staff of trained assistants who handle specific areas or provide general assistance.

Nursery managers are also employed by other establishments that use large numbers of plants and trees requiring expert care and maintenance. These include parks and botanical gardens, large estates and institutions such as schools, industrial and commercial facilities with extensive outdoor areas, and planned residential areas such as senior citizen retirement communities or public housing.

State and federal government agencies employ nursery managers in agricultural extension services, inspection and law enforcement, and in developmental and administrative positions.

Some specially trained nursery specialists are called *plant scientists.* They do research on specific plants or groups of plants, especially food-producing plants to improve their yield or to find solutions to problems such as insect infestation. Plant scientists also develop new plants.

Related jobs are: Landscape Architect, Farmer, Range Manager, Biologist.

Qualifications, education, and training

Curiosity about and a love of growing things are a basic qualification for anyone in this field. Good health and average strength, manual dexterity, color perception and a sense of design, and patience are important. Business management skills and sales ability are also valuable.

High school courses in science, social studies, mathematics, mechanical drawing, and art are good preparation for this field. Summer jobs at plant nurseries or with landscape contractors provide valuable experience.

There are no specific educational requirements for nursery managers, and many of them acquire their skills through on-the-job training. Many employers, however, prefer some formal training. Two-year courses in this field are available at junior and community colleges, four-year colleges, and technical and vocational schools.

Professional nursery managers who are in charge of grounds keeping for large companies usually need at least a bachelor's degree; in some cases an advanced degree. Majors in the biological sciences, landscape architecture, urban planning, and environmental design are recommended.

Research work requires advanced study in a specialty field such as agronomy, entomology, chemistry, soil science, or biology.

Potential and advancement

This is a growing field of employment at all levels. Openings exist in small local nurseries, large retail and wholesale companies, and in basic research. In the future there is expected to be a greater demand for specialists in ornamental nursery stock, agricultural products, and insect and plant disease control.

For the most part, advancement in this field depends on ambition and experience. Many persons start as laborers and then work their way up through jobs as landscape helpers, grounds keepers, greenhouse workers, tree trimmers, or other positions. Supervisory and management positions are available to those who acquire a broad range of experience and knowledge. Many managers advance by opening their own nursery businesses.

Income

Earnings vary widely depending on the size and location of the business and whether the business is owned by the nursery manager.

Average salaries for experienced nursery managers range from $11,000 to $20,000 a year. Those skilled in landscaping or environmental horticulture and those involved in teaching or research earn from $18,000 to $38,000.

Those who work in landscape sales often work on a commission basis. Their earings range from $18,000 to $28,000.

Additional sources of information

American Association of Nurserymen, Inc.
230 Southern Building
15th and H Streets, NW
Washington, DC 20005

American Society of Consulting Arborists
12 Lakeview Avenue
Milltown, NJ 08850

Cooperative Extension Service
College of Agriculture and Home Economics
Ohio State University
2001 Fyffe Court
Cleveland, OH 43210

PLUMBER AND PIPEFITTER

The job

Plumbing and pipefitting are usually considered a single trade with workers specializing in one or the other. Plumbers install, repair, and maintain water, gas, and waste disposal systems in homes, schools, factories, and other buildings; pipefitters install high- and low-pressure pipes that carry hot water, steam, and other liquids and gases used in industrial processes.

Plumbers and pipefitters work from blueprints and use a variety of hand and power tools. They glue, solder, or weld pipe connections to prevent leaks and may have to drill holes in ceilings, floors or walls or hang steel supports from ceilings to position pipes properly.

Most plumbers and pipefitters work for contractors engaged in new construction. A substantial number of plumbers are self-employed or work for contractors who do repair, alteration, and remodeling work in homes and other buildings. Others are employed by government agencies and public utilities, do maintenance work in industrial and commercial buildings, or work in construction of ships and aircraft. Many pipefitters are employed as maintenance personnel in the petroleum, chemical, and food-processing industries.

There are very few women in this field—only about 0.8 percent of all plumbers are women.

Places of employment and working conditions

Plumbers and pipefitters work throughout the country in communities of all sizes. The largest concentrations are in heavily industrialized areas, especially those with petroleum, chemical, or food-processing plants.

Plumbers and pipefitters often work in cramped or uncomfortable positions and must stand for long periods of time. They are subject to cuts and burns and risk falls from ladders.

Many plumbers and pipefitters belong to the United Association of Journeymen and Apprentices of the Plumbing and Pipe Fitting

Industry of the United States and Canada. Those who are contractors usually belong to the National Association of Plumbing-Heating-Cooling Contractors.

Qualifications, education, and training

Mechanical aptitude and physical stamina are necessary for this job field.

A high school diploma is recommended but is not always required. Vocational or technical school training is usually preferred, and courses in chemistry, general mathematics, mechanical drawing, physics, and shop are useful.

Apprenticeship to experienced workers is considered the best way to learn all aspects of the trade. Apprenticeship programs are usually sponsored by local union-management committees. Applicants must be at least 16 years old and are usually given an aptitude test. Those accepted receive five years of on-the-job training and spend about 216 hours each year in related classroom instruction.

Some communities require plumbers and pipefitters to be licensed. This requires a passing grade on an examination covering knowledge of the trade and of local building and plumbing codes.

Potential and advancement

There are about 385,000 plumbers and pipefitters. Job opportunities in this field are expected to be very good through the 1980s. Work should also be steady because plumbing and pipefitting are less sensitive to the ups and downs in construction activity than most other building areas.

Plumbers and pipefitters can advance to supervisory positions. Many prefer to advance by going into business for themselves.

Income

Plumbers and pipefitters are among the highest paid in the building trades, since their work is affected less by bad weather and fluctuations in construction activity. Union wages in metropolitan areas average about $10.40 an hour.

Additional sources of information

National Association of Plumbing-Heating-Cooling Contractors
1016 205th Street, NW
Washington, DC 20036

National Automatic Sprinkler and Fire Control Association
P.O. Box 719
Mt. Kisco, NY 10549

United Association of Journeymen and Apprentices of the Plumbing
and Pipe Fitting Industry of the United States and Canada
901 Massachusetts Avenue, NW
Washington, DC 20001

National Association of Women in Construction
2800 West Lancaster Avenue
Fort Worth, TX 76107

PODIATRIST

The job

The diagnosis and treatment of diseases and deformities of the feet is
the special field of podistrists. They treat corns, bunions, calluses, in-
grown toenails, skin and nail diseases, deformed toes, and arch
disabilities. If a person's feet show symptoms of medical disorders that
affect other parts of the body (such as arthritis or diabetes), the
podiatrist will refer the patient to a medical doctor, while continuing to
treat the patient's foot problem.

In the course of diagnosis, podiatrists may take X rays and perform
blood tests or other pathological tests. They perform surgery; fit corrective devices; and prescribe drugs, physical therapy, and proper shoes.

Most podiatrists provide all types of foot care, but some specialize in
foot surgery, orthopedics (bone, muscle, and joint disorders), children's
foot ailments, or foot problems of the elderly.

Some podiatrists purchase established practices or spend their early
years in a salaried position while gaining experience and earning the
money to set up their own practices. Podiatrists in full-time salaried
positions usually work in hospitals, podiatric medical colleges, or for
other podiatrists. Public health departments and the Veterans Administration also employ both full- and part-time podiatrists, and some
serve as commissioned officers in the armed forces.

Six percent of all podiatrists are women. While this has traditionally
been a male field, interested women are beginning to realize that podiatry
is a well-paid profession with a good future. The opportunity to work with
the elderly and with children is also attractive to many women.

Places of employment and working conditions

Podiatrists work in all sections of the country but are usually found in
cities with large enough populations to support this specialty.

Most podiatrists are in private practice, work about 40 hours a week, and set their own schedules. They also spend some hours handling the administrative and paper work of their practice. This is not physically strenuous work, a fact that allows practitioners in private practice to work past normal retirement age.

Qualifications, education, and training

Anyone interested in a career as a podiatrist should have scientific aptitude, manual dexterity, and ability to work with people.

High school courses in mathematics and science are important preparation.

The degree of doctor of podiatric medicine (D.P.M.) is available after successful completion of at least three years of college and four years of a school of podiatric medicine. Competition for entry in these schools is strong and, although three years of college is the minimum requirement, most successful applicants have a bachelor's degree and an overall grade-point average of "B" or better. College study must include courses in English, chemistry, biology or zoology, physics, and mathematics. All schools of podiatric medicine also require applicants to take the New Medical College Admission Test.

The first two years in podiatry school are spent in classroom and laboratory study of anatomy, bacteriology, chemistry, pathology, physiology, pharmacology, and other basic sciences. In the final two years, students obtain clinical experience. Additional study and experience are necessary for practice in a specialty.

All podiatrists must be licensed. Requirements include graduation from an accredited college of podiatric medicine and written and oral state board proficiency examinations. Georgia, Michigan, New Jersey, and Rhode Island also require a one-year residency in a hospital or clinic. A majority of states grant licenses without examination to podiatrists licensed by another state.

Potential and advancement

There are about 7,500 practicing podiatrists, most of them located in large cities. Employment in this field is expected to grow, and opportunities for graduates to establish new practices or enter salaried positions should be good through the 1980s.

Increasing population, especially the growing number of older people who need foot care and who are covered by Medicare, will contribute to the demand for podiatrists.

Income

Most newly licensed podiatrists set up their own practices and, as in most new practices, earn a great deal less in the early years than they will after a few years in practice. Beginners can look forward to earning about $20,000 a year. The average yearly income of all podiatrists is about $42,000.

Additional sources of information

American Association of Colleges of Podiatric Medicine
20 Chevy Chase Circle, NW
Washington, DC 20015

American Podiatry Association
20 Chevy Chase Circle, NW
Washington, DC 20015

POLICE OFFICER, MUNICIPAL

The job

The duties of a police officer may include law enforcement, crowd and traffic control, criminal investigations, communications, and specialties such as handwriting and fingerprint identification or chemical and microscopic analysis. All police officers are trained in first aid.

In a small community, police officers perform a wide variety of duties, while in a large city they may be assigned to one type, such as patrol, traffic, canine patrol, accident prevention, or mounted and motorcycle patrols. Law enforcement is complex and each police force is tailored to meet the particular problems of its own community. A police force in small community with a relatively stable population may require only a dozen police officers; New York City has 30,000 and Chicago 13,000. A city of any size that has heavy traffic congestion will need more police assigned to accident prevention and traffic control; a city with high juvenile crime rate will use more officers in criminal investigation and youth aid services.

New police officers usually begin a patrol duty with an experienced officer to become thoroughly familiar with the city and its law enforcement requirements. This probationary period can last from a few months to three years in some communities.

All police officers report to police headquarters at regular intervals by radio or walkie-talkie or through police call boxes. They also prepare written reports about their activities and may be called upon to testify in court on cases they handle.

Detectives are plain-clothes police officers whose primary activity is to carry out investigative procedures. They are often assigned to a specific case, such as a murder investigation, or a particular type of case, such as illegal drugs. Detectives gather information and evidence to be used by police and prosecuting attorneys.

Only about 4 percent of the nation's municipal police officers are women; they are employed in about one third of the nation's law enforcement agencies, usually in large cities. Even after they are hired, women police officers face problems with traditional attitudes about women working in physically dangerous professions.

Places of employment and working conditions

Police officers work throughout the country in communities of all sizes.

The usual workweek of a police officer is 40 hours including shift work and weekend and evening hours. Payment for extra hours worked on some police forces takes the form of extra time off. Officers must often work outdoors in all kinds of weather and are subject to call at any time.

Police officers face the constant threat of injury or death in their work. The injury rate for police officers is higher than in many other occupations.

Qualifications, education, and training

A police officer should be honest, have a sense of responsibility and good judgment, and enjoy working with people and serving the public. Good health and physical stamina are also necessary.

High school courses should include English, American history, and civics and government. Physical education and sports are very helpful in developing stamina and agility.

Local civil service regulations govern the appointment of police officers in most communities. Candidates must be at least 21 years old, be United States citizens, meet certain height and weight standards, and pass a rigorous physical examination. Character traits and backgrounds are investigated, and a personality test is sometimes administered. Applicants are usually interviewed by a senior police officer and, in some police departments, by a psychiatrist or psychologist.

An applicant's eligibility for appointment depends on his or her peformance on a competitive examination. Applicants are listed according to their scores on the examination, and when a police department appoints new police officers, it hires the required number of recruits from the top of the list.

Most police departments require a high school education; a few cities require some college training. More and more police departments are encouraging their officers to continue their education and to study subjects such as sociology, psychology, law enforcement, criminal justice, and foreign languages. These courses are available in junior and community colleges as well as four-year colleges and universities.

New police officers go through a training period. In small communities, this may consist of working with experienced officers. Large cities have more formal training programs that last from several weeks to a few months. Officers receive classroom instruction in constitutional law and civil rights, state and local ordinances, accident investigation, patrol, and traffic control. They learn to use a gun, defend themselves from attack, administer first aid, and deal with emergencies.

Experienced police officers improve their performance, keep up-to-date, and prepare for advancement by taking various training courses given at police department academies and colleges. They study crowd-control techniques, civil defense, the latest legal developments that affect police work, and advances in law enforcement equipment.

In some large cities, high school graduates between the ages of 18 and 21 may be hired as police cadets or trainees. They function as paid civilian employees and do clerical work while they attend training classes. If they have all the necessary qualifications, they may be appointed to the police force at age 21.

Potential and advancement

There are about 500,000 full-time police officers working in communities throughout the United States. All police departments are funded by local governments and, since police protection is considered essential, law enforcement expenses usually have a high priority in municipal budges. As the population grows, the demand for police officers will also grow. Applicants with some college training in law enforcement will have the best job opportunities.

Advancement in police work depends on length of service, job performance, and written examinations. In some large departments, promotion may also allow a police officer to specialize in one type of police work, such as communications, traffic control, or working with juveniles.

Income

Entry-level salaries range from $9,000 to over $15,000 a year; the average is about $13,200. Police officers receive periodic increases until they reach the maximum pay rate for their rank. Average maximum is about $16,650.

Higher rank brings a higher salary and the same periodic increases until maximum. The average starting rate for sergeants ranges from $16,000 to $20,000; for lieutenants, about $18,300.

Police officers are usually covered by liberal plans that allow them to retire at age 55 at half pay. Most police departments furnish revolvers, nightsticks, handcuffs, and other equipment and provide an allowance for uniforms.

Additional sources of information

International Association of Chiefs of Police
11 Firstfield Road
Gaithersburg, MD 10760

International Association of Women Police
6655 North Avondale Avenue
Chicago, IL 60631

Information is also available from local police departments and civil service commissions.

POLICE OFFICER, STATE

The job

State police officers, sometimes called state troopers, patrol the highways throughout the United States. They enforce traffic laws, issue traffic tickets to motorists who violate those laws, provide information to travelers, handle traffic control and summon emergency equipment at the scene of an accident or other emergency, sometimes check the weight of commercial vehicles, and conduct driver examinations.

In several areas that do not have a local police force, state police officers may investigate crime. They also help city and county police forces to catch lawbreakers and control civil disturbances.

Some officers are assigned to training assignments in state police schools or to investigate specializations such as fingerprint classification or chemical and microscopic analysis of criminal evidence. A few have administrative duties.

There are very few women on state police forces, although the federal government, through affirmative action programs, is pressuring states to remedy this situation.

Places of employment and working conditions

State police officers are employed by every state except Hawaii. California has the largest force—over 5,000 officers; North Dakota has the smallest—less than 100.

A 40-hour workweek is usual although some states require more. Officers must work holiday, weekend, and night shifts and are outdoors in all kinds of weather. Their work is sometimes dangerous.

Qualifications, education, and training

Honesty, a sense of responsibility, and a desire to serve the public are important. Physical strength and agility are necessary, and height, weight, and eyesight standards must be met.

High school courses in English, government or civics, American history, and physics are helpful. Physical education and sports develop stamina and agility. Driver education courses or military police training are also valuable.

State civil service regulations govern the appointment of state police officers. Applicants must be U.S. citizens at least 21 years old and must usually have a high school education. Applicants must pass a competitive written examination, a rigorous physical examination, and a character and background investigation.

Recruits enter a formal training program that lasts for several months. They study state laws and jurisdictions, patrol, traffic control, and accident investigation. They learn to use firearms, defend themselves from attack, handle an automobile at high speeds, and give first aid.

State police recruits serve a probationary period ranging from six months to three years. After gaining some experience, some officers take advanced training in police science, administration, law enforcement, criminology, or psychology. Courses in these subjects are offered by junior colleges, four-year colleges and universities, and special police training institutions including the National Academy of the Federal Bureau of Investigation.

Some states hire high school graduates between the ages of 18 and 21 to serve as cadets. They study police work and perform nonenforcement duties such as clerical work. If they qualify, they may be appointed to the state police force when they reach 21.

Potential and advancement

There are about 48,000 state police officers. Job opportunities should be good although investigative specialties are being increasingly handled by civilian specialists.

Promotion depends on the amount of time spent in a rank and the individual's standing on competitive examinations.

Income

Beginning officers average about $13,200 a year. Salaries for experienced officers range from $15,000 to over $19,000.

Salaries are usually highest in the West and lowest in the South.

Additional sources of information

State civil service commissions or state police headquarters, usually located in each state capital, can provide information to anyone interested in a career as a state police officer.

PRIEST

The job

Roman Catholic priests provide spiritual guidance, perform and administer rites and sacraments, and oversee the education of Catholics in the United States.

There are two main classifications of priests. *Diocesan, or secular, priests* generally are assigned to a parish by the bishop of their diocese. They work as individuals to provide complete pastoral services for their congregations and are involved in the elementary and secondary schools of their parish and diocese.

Religious priests are part of a religious order such as the Jesuits or Franciscans. They perform specialized work such as teaching or missionary work, which is assigned to them by their superiors in the order. Those involved in education usually work at the high school, college, or university level.

Places of employment and working conditions

There are Catholic priests in nearly every city and town and in many rural areas. The largest concentrations are in metropolitan areas where large Catholic parishes and educational institutions are located. Catholic populations are concentrated in the northeast, the Great Lakes region, California, Louisiana, and Texas.

Working conditions for priests vary greatly. Those assigned to parishes usually work long and irregular hours. Priests are not permitted to marry and the absence of a family life is a hardship for some priests.

Qualifications, education, and training

As with all members of the clergy, whatever denomination, a deep religious commitment and a desire to serve others are the most important qualifications for a priest. He must also be a model of moral and ethical conduct.

For young men who decide early in life to become priests, high school seminaries provide a college preparatory program.

Preparation for the priesthood requires eight years of study beyond high school. Seminary colleges provide a liberal arts program stressing philosophy and religion, behavioral sciences, history, and the natural sciences. Four additional years are spent in the study of the rites and teachings of the Catholic Church and field work.

Potential and advancement

There are about 59,000 priests in the United States. The need for priests is expected to grow along with the growth in population, but the number of ordained priests has traditionally been insufficient to meet the needs of the Church and will probably continue to be insufficient.

Newly ordained diocesan priests usually start out as assistants to pastors of established parishes. As they gain experience, they may advance to posts in larger parishes or be assigned to parishes of their own. Some priests advance to administrative positions within the diocese.

Newly ordained religious priests begin work immediately in the specialty for which they are trained. They may advance to administrative positions within their religious order or in the institutions where they work.

Income

The salaries of diocesan priests vary from diocese to diocese and range from $2,000 to about $6,000 a year. Those assigned to a parish live in the parish rectory where all living expenses are paid by the parish and a car allowance is usually provided. Some dioceses also provide group insurance and retirement benefits.

Priests engaged in other than parish work are usually paid at least a partial salary by the institution that employs them. Housing is sometimes also provided.

Religious priests take a vow of poverty and are supported by their religious orders.

Additional sources of information

Young men interested in entering the priesthood should seek the guidance of their parish priest or contact the diocesan Director of Vocations.

PRINTING PRESS OPERATOR

The job

The preparation, care, and operation of printing presses are the responsibilities of printing press operators. In a small commercial shop an operator may run simple equipment and learn through on-the-job training; the operator on a giant newspaper or magazine press is a highly trained and experienced worker with several assistants.

The press operator sets up and adjusts the press, inserts type setups or plates and locks them into place, adjusts ink flow, and loads paper—by hand on a small press, with mechanical assistance on a large one. When printing is complete, the press operator, or an assistant, cleans the press and may oil it and make minor repairs.

Press operators are usually designated according to the type of press they operate: letterpress, gravure, or offset. Offset press operators are further designated as sheet-fed or web-press operators. (Web-fed presses use paper in giant rolls instead of single sheets.) Companies that switch from sheet-fed to web-fed presses must retrain their entire press crew, since the two types of presses are very different. Web-fed presses are very large, operate at faster speeds, and require greater physical effort, monitoring of more variables, and faster decisions than sheet-fed presses.

Over half of all printing press operators work for commercial printing shops and book and magazine publishers; a substantial number work for newspapers. The remainder work for businesses, manufacturers, and other organizations that have their own in-house printing facilities. This includes many federal, state, and local government agencies.

Although women are finding increasing job opportunities in many areas of the printing industry, very few are press operators. The best press operator opportunities for women are found in small nonunion commercial printing shops, where about 13 percent of the press operators are women.

Places of employment and working conditions

Printing press operators work throughout the country but employment is greatest in large cities.

Pressrooms are noisy and press operators are subject to the hazards that go with working around machinery. Many printing companies have two or three shifts, and press operators may be required to do a certain amount of shift work; press operators who work for morning newspapers almost always work night shifts. Press operators often stand for long periods, and some presses require lifting of heavy plates and paper.

Qualifications, education, and training

Mechanical aptitude is important for a press operator. Physical strength is needed for some jobs.

High school courses in chemistry and physics are helpful. Printing shop classes can provide valuable experience.

Some printing press operators acquire their skills through on-the-job training or a combination of training and vocational or technical school courses. Most operators, however, complete a formal apprenticeship program.

An apprenticeship lasts from two to five years depending on the press being learned. In addition to receiving on-the-job instruction, the apprentice must complete related classroom or correspondence course work.

There are usually long waiting lists for apprenticeship programs, and many people take unskilled jobs as helpers until they secure an appreticeship. A wait of two or three years is not uncommon.

Potential and advancement

There are about 145,000 printing press operators and apprentices, and there is usually competition for any available openings which occur. Best opportunities in the future will be for web-press operators.

Advancement usually takes the form of learning to operate a more complex press. In large shops, some press operators move up to supervisory positions.

Income

Many press operators especially in large cities are members of a printing union. Average minimum hourly rates for union printers in large cities are as follows. Newspaper press operators average $8.77 an hour; operators-in-charge, $9.32. Book and job cylinder press operators, average $8.70; assistants and feeders, $8.70.

Additional Sources of Information

International Printing and Graphic Communication Union
1730 Rhode Island Avenue, NW
Washington, DC 20036

Printing Industries of America, Inc.
1730 North Lynn Street
Arlington, VA 22209

Graphic Arts Technical Foundation
4615 Forbes Avenue
Pittsburgh, PA 15213

Graphic Arts International Union
1900 L Street, NW
Washington, DC 20036

PRISON WARDEN

The job

The operation of a correction institution is the responsibility of a warden. Depending on the size and complexity of the particular penal system, the warden may be responsible for the day-to-day operation of a single prison, a prison within a complex of several correctional facilities, or a group of smaller facilities at several locations. Alternative titles for this position are *correctional superintendent* and *correctional administrator*.

A warden is responsible for custody and medical care of the prisoners, security, rehabilitation programs, budgeting, liaison with law enforcement and parole personnel, personnel administration, public relations, and maintenance of the prison. The warden must work within the regulations established by the federal, state, or local government body for which he or she works.

Related jobs are: Parole Officer, Police Officer (Municipal and State), and Rehabilitation Counselor.

Places of employment and working conditions

Every state has a penal system, and federal prisons are located throughout the United States.

Although a warden usually works a normal workweek within his or her prison office and the prison, additional time must be devoted to meetings and community activities. Wardens are on call at all times for any problems or emergencies that arise and are occasionally exposed to volatile, potentially dangerous situations.

Qualifications, education, and training

A prison warden needs management and administrative abilities, good judgment, tact, decisiveness, and the ability to act quickly and calmly in an emergency. Good communication skills and the ability to work with people are also necessary.

Although there are no specific educational requirements for this job, experience and training in a number of fields are usually the background of those who become prison wardens. College courses or training programs in law enforcement, police science, corrections, social welfare, behavioral sciences, criminal justice, political science, police administration, sociology, law and society, and business administration are all helpful.

Training and experience as a police officer are often the first step for someone interested in this field.

Potential and advancement

Employment in this field is not expected to grow. Most job openings will be to replace those who retire or leave the field. The best opportunities will be for those with a college degree that includes some course work in corrections.

In large penal systems, wardens may advance by being assigned to large prisons or by promotion to administrative positions.

Income

Prison wardens earn from $15,000 to $25,000 a year.

Additional sources of information

Association of State Correctional Administrators
Department of Corrections
6385 N. Academy Blvd.
Colorado Springs, CO 80907

American Association of Wardens and Superintendents
Arizona State Prison
Box 629
Florence, AZ 85232

PRODUCER/DIRECTOR OF RADIO, TELEVISION, MOVIES, AND THEATER

The job

These two jobs are often combined in actual practice, but this job description will deal with them as separate positions.

The *producer* is the business head of a production. Anyone with a script and a bankroll can be a producer, it has been said, but the successful ones have much more than that. They have taste and discrimination and the ability to raise money from backers.

A producer must be able to estimate production and operating costs, obtain or provide financing, hire a staff and performers, arrange for rehearsal facilities, and handle all other production details. In the theater and movies, producers take an enormous financial risk; radio and television are more stable fields. On any project, the producer is *the* boss, since he or she controls the purse strings.

The *director* is the unifying force that brings together the diverse talents involved in a production. To some, the director is the most important element. A well-known director can attract top stars and backers to a production on the strength of his or her reputation. A good director is said to be part psychologist and part disciplinarian in his or her handling of the creative, temperamental, and strong-willed people that make up a production. He or she must have a working knowledge of costume, lighting, and design as well as acting. Most directors have at least some experience as actors themselves. The director's ability to bring out the best in the performers, plus his or her interpretation of the script as a whole, usually means the difference between success or failure for a production.

In television and radio, the director's duties are a little different. The selection and scheduling of programs are also part of the director's organizational and administrative duties because many programs come prepackaged and ready for airing.

In the theater, touring shows employ an *advance director*. Because many shows send only the stars and a few other principal players on tour, remaining roles in the cast are filled by local actors. The advance director arrives ahead of time to select and rehearse the local cast and have the production ready when the stars arrive. This is not a very creative type of directing, since all decisions have been made and the director must prepare the cast to duplicate the performances being given in other cities on the tour.

An important position in any production is that of *stage manager* (*floor manager* in radio and television), who is, in effect, the "executive in charge of operations." The stage manager sees that everyone gets on stage at the right moment, that lighting crews and stage hands operate on cue. The stage manager assigns dressing rooms, handles emergencies of all types, and is sometimes the understudy for one or more roles in a production. Many stage managers start out as actors and, although stage managing is a demanding specialty in its own right, go on to become directors or producers.

Women hold many of the positions as assistant directors and assistant producers, and are generally moving into some top positions, especially in television. There are many women stage managers.

Places of employment and working conditions

There are opportunities for producers and directors in large cities throughout the country, but most are concentrated in Boston, Chicago, Houston, Los Angeles, New York, Philadelphia, and San Francisco—the prime locations of the movie, television, and theater industries.

As with all aspects of the entertainment field, work is not steady. For a producer or a director, the pressures of putting together a new production are enormous. When the production is not a success, the financial and emotional costs can be staggering.

Qualifications, education, and training

A producer has to have business and administrative ability as well as a grasp of what the public wants in the way of entertainment. A director must have artistic talent and good judgment, emotional and physical stamina, a thorough knowledge of techniques and devices, patience, and assertiveness.

There are no educational requirements for either of these positions. In the case of the director, talent is the most important factor combined with experience gathered through years of practice. Many of today's directors, however, received their basic training at a top drama school or college. Many colleges offer programs in dramatic arts that include course work in directing, production, costume, and other related fields as well as radio and television courses. One big advantage of formal training is the opportunity it provides for an aspiring director to work in college productions.

Producers with an educational background that combines the arts and business administration skills have an advantage in the modern entertainment field.

Potential and advancement

Many opportunities exist in addition to the glamourous jobs at the top of the entertainment field. Community theaters, summer stock, touring shows, industrial shows, and commercial production companies all require producers and directors. Teaching positions are available in colleges, drama schools, and some secondary schools (many require teacher certification). The trend is toward a good solid educational background combined with experience.

All experience is valuable in this field; nothing is irrelevant. Getting a job in almost any capacity of performing or production is important for the beginner. From there, advancement comes through hard work, talent, and being noticed by the right people. A prop man can work up to stage manager, an experienced actor can branch out into directing. Whatever the job, advancement to better companies, bigger radio or television stations, and working with well-known stars are the marks of progress.

Income

Producers' earnings vary greatly depending, in movies and the theater, on the success of failure of individual productions. Television and radio are most stable and dependable fields. In general, successful producers earn from $60,000 to $100,000 a year. Some earn a great deal more.

Directors have sporadic earnings. If they are employed fairly constantly in good productions, their earnings can be $60,000 to $100,000 a year, since they sometimes receive a percentage of the box office receipts. Those in summer stock community theaters and touring shows have a wide range of earnings depending on size and caliber of the productions.

Radio and television provide full-time salaried positions for directors. Earnings depend on stations size with major networks paying the highest salaries.

Additional sources of information

American Educational Theater Association
1317 F Street, NW
Washington, DC 20004

American Theater Association
1029 Vermont Avenue, NW
Suite 402
Washington, DC 20005

PRODUCTION MANAGER, INDUSTRIAL

The job

Production managers coordinate the activities of production departments of manufacturing firms. They are part of "middle management," just below corporate, or top-level management, which sets long-range goals and policies.

Production managers carry out the plans of top management by planning and organizing the actual production of company products.

They work closely with industrial designers, purchasing managers, labor relations specialists, industrial traffic managers, and production supervisors. Their responsibilities include materials control (the flow of materials and parts into the plant), production control (efficient production processes), and quality control (testing of finished products).

Places of employment and working conditions

Production managers work throughout the country with the largest concentrations in heavily industrialized areas.

Hours for production managers are often long and irregular. In addition to their regular duties, they spend a great deal of time on paper work and meetings and are expected to be available at all times to handle problems and emergencies.

Qualifications, education, and training

Strong leadership qualities and communication skills are necessary as well as the ability to work well under pressure.

High school should include mathematics and science courses.

A college degree is necessary for almost all jobs at this level. In some small companies, a production supervisor (foreman) or technical worker may occasionally rise through the ranks to production manager, but they usually acquire some college training along the way.

Some companies will hire liberal arts graduates as production managers, but most employers prefer a bachelor's degree or advanced degree in engineering or business administration. A very effective combination is a bachelor's degree in engineering and a master's degree in business administration.

Some companies have management training programs for new graduates. As a trainee, the employee spends several years, usually in several different departments, gathering experience.

Potential and advancement

Production managers are always in demand in companies of all sizes. Best opportunities will be for college graduates who have accumulated experience in a variety of industrial production areas.

Since this is already a high management level, it takes outstanding performance to be promoted to the corporate level; only a very few get to be vice president of manufacturing. Most production managers advance by moving to a larger company where the responsibilities are greater and more complex.

Income

Salaries vary greatly from industry to industry and also depend on size of plant. Production managers in large plants earn as much as $60,000 a year and receive bonuses based on performance.

Additional sources of information

American Management Association
135 West 50th Street
New York, NY 10020

American Production and Inventory Control Society
2600 Virginia Avenue, NW
Washington, DC 20037

Industrial Management Society
570 Northwest Highway
Des Plaines, IL 60616

PROFESSIONAL ATHLETE

The job

One of the most difficult aspects for many players of the move from amateur or college sports to the world of professional sports is the change in attitude from sports as a game to sports as big business. The drive to get to the top and the constant pressure to stay there can prove disillusioning to some players.

Athletes who reach the professional teams usually developed their interest in sports at an early age. By the time they reach high school, they have usually already decided on a particular sport as their favorite or the one they are best at playing.

Professional teams recruit most of their players from among the top-notch college players. A few are hired from industrial and business leagues, the military, and from minor and semi-pro teams. On rare occasions, an exceptional player is hired right out of high school.

Women as professional athletes have appeared mostly in golf. Women also play professional tennis and basketball and are securing a limited number of positions as professional jockeys. Although there are some regional women's softball leagues, they have never developed into a money-making professional status.

Related job descriptions are: Athletic Coach, Golf/Tennis Professional, Jockey, Sports Official.

Places of employment and working conditions

In general, all professional athletes face the possibility of being traded or dropped, and older players are constantly pressured by talented newcomers. Injuries are always a danger, and, for the most part, the active playing years are limited to the early twenties through the mid-thirties. Only golfers play longer.

Travel is a constant necessity during the playing season with very little time off for personal life and family. Rigorous training schedules, the need to be in top physical form, and the strict training rules and curfews of some coaches are a hardship for some players.

In baseball, spring training starts in February or March. The playing schedule of one or two games a day with occasional travel days lasts until October.

Football players report to training camp in July for eight or nine weeks. Fourteen weekly games make up the playing season, and bowl games can extend the season into January.

Basketball training starts in September or October. Three or four games a week, for a total of 82 to 84 games make up the regular season with a possible 4 to 21 post-season games.

Professional hockey players train in September and play from October to May. Soccer season is traditionally from April through August, but an indoor season from January to March is becoming popular in the United States.

Golfers manage to play a major part of the year because they follow the sun.

Qualifications, education, and training

Competitiveness, top playing skills, physical stamina, strength, good eyesight and hearing, self-discipline, and the ability to work as part of a team are all necessary for a professional athlete. Quick reflexes, concentration, timing, and speed are also necessary in most sports.

High school athletic training is very important. Good coaching at this level develops basic skills and physical condition and introduces the player to the regimen of exercise, dieting, practice, and training that will be necessary throughout a professional career. Good coaching in high school also increases the player's chances for a college scholarship.

Although a college education is not required to play professionally, college does offer some unique advantages. College-level coaching refines and upgrades the skills developed in high school. There is greater emphasis on technique and application of skills. College games usually reach a wider audience including scouts from professional teams.

The biggest advantage of a college education is the opportunity to prepare for an alternative life-time career. Not every talented player reaches the professional teams, and even those who do have a limited playing career. Not everyone gets to be a coach or a celebrity who earns a life-time living as a result of sports fame.

Potential and advancement

Only a very few make it to the top professional teams. Baseball employs the largest number: approximately 3,000 professional baseball players including those in the minor leagues. Football employs about 1,000 in the major leagues; basketball about 400. There are 800 professional hockey players; and 90 percent of them are from Canada. About 300 professional golfers make up the only other substantial group of professional athletes. Professional tennis employs only a handful, and soccer, which gets most of its players from abroad where the game has been played for years, is just beginning to attract audiences at the professional level.

Other opportunities exist in local amateur, semi-pro, and industrial leagues. Talented college players may fill openings for coaching positions in small colleges or secondary schools, some of which require teaching certification.

Professional athletes may also move into coaching and management positions after their professional playing careers end.

Income

Well-publicized three- and five-year contracts of $1,000,000 or more, earned by a few superstars, are few and far between. However, many professional athletes are well paid.

Professional baseball players in the minor leagues sometimes earn as little as $1,500 for the season. In the major leagues, players earn from $30,000 to above 1 million; average is about $111,000.

In football, starting salaries range from $17,000 to $22,000. Experienced players earn up to $450,000. Play-off, championship, and Super Bowl game shares can add another $2,000 to $30,000 in a season.

Professional basketball players earn $35,000 to start. Average for all professional basketball players is $85,000, although several starters earn much more.

Average salary for National Hockey League players is about $100,000. Soccer players earn $10,000 to $200,000 for a five-month season.

Professional golfers who play the circuit don't earn much unless they are among the top players. Weekly expenses are high, and some golfers are sponsored by manufacturers or other organizations until they become established. Golf tournament prizes are divided among the top few places with the winner getting 20 percent, second place 11 percent, and so forth. Top golfers make up to $300,000 a year.

Many professional athletes earn additional income through endorsements and personal appearances. Many also have businesses that they operate during off-season months.

Additional sources of information

Association of Professional Ball Players of America
337 East San Antonio Drive
Suite 203
Long Beach, CA 90807

North American Soccer League Players Association
1300 Connecticut Avenue, NW
Washington, D.C. 20036

National Hockey League Players Association
65 Queen Street
Suite 1000
Toronto, Ontario, Canada M5H 2M5

National Football League
410 Park Avenue
New York, NY 10022

PSYCHIATRIST

The job

A psychiatrist is a medical doctor (physician) who specializes in the problems of mental illness. Because a psychiatrist is also a physician, he or she is licensed to use a wider variety of treatments—including drugs, hospitalization, somatic (shock) therapy—than others who provide treatment for the mentally ill.

Psychiatrists may specialize as to psychiatric technique and age or type of patients treated.

Most psychiatrists are *psychotherapists* who treat individual patients directly. They sometimes treat patients in groups or in a family group.

This is a technique of verbal therapy and may be supplemented with other treatments such as medication. Some psychiatrists are *psychoanalysts* who specialize in a technique of individual therapy based on the work of Sigmund Freud. Psychiatrists who practice this specialty must themselves undergo psychoanalysis in the course of their training. *Child psychiatrists* specialize in the treatment of children.

Some psychiatrists work exclusively in research, studying such things as the effect of drugs on the brain or the basic sciences of human behavior. Others teach at the college and university level. Research and teaching psychiatrists, however, usually combine their work with a certain amount of direct patient care.

In addition to private practice, psychiatrists work in clinics, general hospitals, and private and public psychiatric hospitals. The federal government employs a number of psychiatrists in the Veterans Administration and the United States Public Health Service.

Psychiatry is one of the two medical specialties (the other is pediatrics) that attract a high proportion of women. One out of every ten psychiatrists is a woman. The fact that there are many opportunities for part-time work in psychiatry makes it possible for people to continue their practices during the years when their family responsibilities make full-time practice difficult.

Related jobs are: Psychologist, Rehabilitation Counselor.

Places of employment and working conditions

Psychiatrists work in all parts of the country, almost always in large metropolitan areas or near universities and medical schools.

This field can be emotionally wearing on the psychiatrist. The shortage of psychiatrists and the increasing demand for psychiatric services means that many practioners are overworked and often cannot devote as much time as they would like to each individual patient.

The expense and time involved in securing an education for this field deters some people from pursuing psychiatry as a career.

Qualifications, education, and training

More than in any other field, the personality of the psychiatrist is very important. Emotional stability, patience, the ability to empathize with the patient, and a manner that encourages trust and confidence are absolutely necessary. The psychiatrist must be inquisitive, analytical, and flexible in the treatment of patients and must have great self-awareness of his or her own limitations and biases.

A high school student interested in this field should take a college preparatory course strong in science.

After high school, the training of a psychiatrist takes from 12 to 14 years. (Educational requirements for a physician are detailed under that job description.)

After receiving an M.D. degree and completing a one-year medical internship in a hospital approved by the American Medical Association (AMA), a prospective psychiatrist begins a three- to four-year psychiatric specialty program. This program must take place in a hospital approved for this purpose by both the AMA and the American Psychiatric Association.

Training is carried on during a residency program that requires study, research, and clinical practice under the supervision of staff psychiatrists. After completion of the program and two years of experience, a psychiatrist is eligible to take the psychiatry examination of the American Board of Neurology and Psychiatry. Successful applicants then receive a diploma from this specialty board and are considered to be fully qualified psychiatrists.

At this point, a psychiatrist who wishes to specialize in child psychiatry must complete an additional two years of training, usually in a children's psychiatric hospital or clinic. A diploma in child psychiatry is then awarded after successful completion of the required examination.

Psychiatrists must also fulfill state licensing requirements before starting the residency period. Information is listed under this section in the job description for Physician.

Potential and advancement

There are about 9,000 psychiatrists, not all of whom are involved in direct patient care. A conservative estimate of the number needed is 20,000. Since only about 600 new psychiatrists enter practice each year, the job opportunities are excellent.

Psychiatrists who teach in colleges and universities may advance through the various academic ranks up to full professors. Those employed in psychiatric hospitals may advance to administrative positions.

Income

During training, psychiatric residents receive a salary and are often provided with living quarters.

At a univeristy medical center, average salary for a first-year resident is about $8,500 with a $500 increase each year. Private psychiatric hospitals with approved training programs pay almost twice that amount. Salaries at state hospitals are about $11,000 a year with a $1,000 increase each year.

Some state hospitals as well as psychiatric units of Veterans Administration hospitals offer career programs. In these programs, the resident receives an even higher salary during his training if he contracts to stay on for at least two years after completion of training.

Psychiatrists in salaried positions in clinics, state psychiatric hospitals, and the Veterans Administration start at $16,500 to $22,000 a year. Experienced psychiatrists earn $20,000 to $43,000.

In teaching positions, psychiatrists hired as full-time instructors earn $12,000 to $14,000 with 5- to 10-percent increases each year. Assistant professors average $16,500 to $19,000; associate professors $19,500 to $25,000. Full professors earn $30,000 to $35,000.

Psychiatrists in private practice earn from $50 to $100 an hour. When they function as consultants for law enforcement agencies and courts, and clinics and hospitals, they receive $150 a day or more. Average annual earnings range from $60,000 to $100,000 or more.

Additional sources of information

American Psychiatric Association
1700 18th Street, NW
Washington, DC 20009

American Medical Association
535 North Dearborn Street
Chicago, IL 60610

PSYCHOLOGIST

The job

Psychologists study the behavior of individuals and groups to understand and explain their actions. Psychologists gather information through interviews and tests, by studying personal histories, and conducting controlled experiments.

Psychologists may specialize in a wide variety of areas. *Experimental psychologists* study behavior processes by working with human beings as well as rats, monkeys, and pigeons. Their research includes motivation, learning and retention, sensory and perceptual processes, and genetic and neurological factors in human behavior. *Developmental psychologists* study the patterns and causes of behavior change in different age groups. *Personality psychologists* study human nature, individual differences, and the ways in which these differences develop.

Social psychologists examine people's interactions with others and with the social environment. Their studies include group behavior, leadership, and dependency relationships. *Environmental psychologists* study the influence of environments on people; *physiological psychologists* study the relationship of behavior to the biological functions of the body.

Psychologists often combine several of these or other specialty areas in their work. They further specialize in the setting in which they apply their knowledge.

Clinical psychologists work in mental hospitals or clinics or maintain their own practices. They provide individual, family, and group psychotherapy programs. *Counseling psychologists* help people with problems of daily life—personal, social, educational, or vocational. *Educational psychologists* apply their expertise to problems in education; while *school psychologists* work with students and diagnose educational problems, help in adjustment to school, and solve learning and social problems.

Others work as industrial and organizational psychologists (personnel work), engineering psychologists (human-machine systems), and consumer psychologists (what motivates consumers).

About one half of all psychologists work in colleges and universities as teachers, researchers, administrators, or counselors. Most of the rest work in hospitals, clinics, rehabilitation centers, and other health facilities. The remainder work for federal, state, and local government agencies, correctional institutions, research firms, or in private practice.

About 41 percent of all psychologists are women. Modern developments in this field are adding to the opportunities for women on teams engaged in basic research into human behavior. The mental health and characteristics of women have traditionally been determined by men who have defined women in terms of what men see as their nature; the inclusion of women psychologists in research efforts is contributing to new awareness of the unique characteristics of women.

Related jobs are: Psychiatrist, Rehabilitation Counselor, School Guidance Counselor, Marriage Counselor, Social Worker..

Places of employment and working conditions

Psychologists work in communities of all sizes. The largest concentrations are in areas with large colleges and universities.

Working hours for psychologists are flexible in general. Clinical and counseling psychologists often work in the evening to accommodate the work and school schedules of their patients.

Qualifications, education, and training

Sensitivity to others and an interest in people are very important as are emotional stability, patience, and tact. Research requires an interest in detail, accuracy, and communication skills.

High school preparation should emphasize science and social science skills.

A bachelor's degree in psychology or a related field such as social work or education is only a first step because a Ph.D. is the minimum requirement for employment as a psychologist. Those with only a bachelor's degree will be limited to jobs as research or administrative assistants in mental health centers, vocational rehabilitation offices and correctional programs, government, or business. Some may work as secondary school teachers if they complete state certification requirements.

Stiff competition for admission into graduate psychology programs means that only the most highly qualified applicants are accepted. College grades of "B" or higher are necessary.

At least one year of graduate study is necessary to earn a master's degree in psychology. Those with a master's degree qualify to work under the supervision of a psychologist and collect and analyze data, administer and interpret some kinds of psychological tests. They may also qualify for certain counseling positions such as school psychologist.

Three to five years of additional graduate work are required to earn a Ph.D. in psychology. Clinical and counseling psychologists need still another year or more of internship or other supervised experience. Some programs also require competence in a foreign language.

A dissertation based on original research that contributes to psychological knowledge is required of Ph.D. candidates. Another degree in this field is the Psy.D. (doctor of psychology). Acquisition of this degree is based on practical work and examinations rather than a dissertation.

The American Board of Professional Psychology awards diplomas in clinical, counseling, industrial, and organizational psychology. Candidates must have a Ph.D. or Psy.D., have five years of experience, pass an examination, and provide professional endorsements.

State licensing and certification requirements vary but usually require a Ph.D. or Psy.D., two years of professional experience, and a written examination.

Potential and advancement

There are about 90,000 people working as psychologists. Employment in this field is expected to grow but even with growth, there will be competition for job openings; there are many more Ph.D.'s in psychology than jobs available. Those with degrees from prestigious universities and those willing to work in new and smaller institutions will have the best employment opportunities.

Traditional academic specialties such as experimental, physiological, and comparative psychology will provide fewer job opportunities than the areas of clinical, counseling, and industrial and organizational psychology.

Income

Starting salaries with a master's degree are about $13,200 a year; Ph.D.'s start at about $15,000 for a 9-month academic job and about $18,000 to $19,000 for 12-month jobs.

Median salaries for experienced psychologists with doctoral degrees are: in educational institutions, $22,300; in the federal government, $30,300; in state and local governments and in hospitals and clinics, $23,000; in nonprofit organizations, $24,600; and in business and industry, $33,800.

Additional sources of information

American Psychological Association
1200 17th Street, NW
Washington, DC 20036

Association for Women in Psychology
243 Russell Road
Princeton, NJ 08540

PUBLIC RELATIONS WORKER

The job

Building, maintaining, and promoting the reputation and image of an organization or a public figure constitute the work of public relations specialists. They use their skills in sales promotion, political campaigns, and many other fields.

A large corporation employs public relations workers to present the company in a favorable light to its various audiences—its customers, employees, stockholders, and the community where the company is located. A college or university uses its public relations staff to present an image that will attract students. A government agency explains its work to the public by means of public relations specialists.

Public relations workers also have the opposite duty—to keep their employers aware of the attitudes of their various publics. For example, a public relations specialist working for a manufacturing firm located in a city neighborhood might advise the company that nearby residents blame the company for parking and traffic problems in the area. Resulting company efforts to provide more employee parking facilities or to reschedule deliveries and shipments to off-peak traffic hours would then be well publicized to improve the relations between the company and its nearby "public."

In small businesses, one person may handle all public relations functions including writing press releases and speeches for company officials, placing information with various newspapers or radio stations, representing the employer at public functions, or arranging public appearances for the employer. On a large public relations staff, a *public relations manager* would be assisted by many different specialists, each handling a single phase of publicity. In some companies, public relations functions are combined with advertising or sales promotion work.

Many public relations specialists work for consulting firms that provide services for clients on a fee basis. Others work for nonprofit organizations, advertising agencies, and political candidates. Those who work for government agencies are often called *public information specialists.*

Over a quarter of all public relations workers are women most of whom are employed by department stores, hospitals, hotels, and restaurants.

Related jobs are: Advertising Account Executive, Advertising Manager, Advertising Worker, Newspaper Reporter.

Places of employment and working conditions

Public relations specialists are found in organizations of all kinds and in all areas of the country. Public relations consulting firms, however, are concentrated in large metropolitian areas. Over half are located in New York, Los Angeles, Chicago, and Washington, D.C.

The usual workweek in this field is 35 to 40 hours but attendance at meetings and community affairs can often mean overtime or evening hours. In some assignments, a public relations specialist may be on call at all times or may be required to travel for extended periods while accompanying a client such as a political candidate or other public figure.

Qualifications, education, and training

Self-confidence, enthusiasm, assertiveness, an outgoing personality, and imagination are necessary characteristics for success in public relations. The ability to motivate people, an understanding of human psychology, and outstanding communications skills are also necessary.

High school courses should emphasize English—especially writing skills. Any courses or extracurricular activities in public speaking or writing for school newspapers are valuable as are summer or part-time jobs for radio or television stations or newspapers.

A college degree in journalism, communications, or public relations is the usual preparation for this field. Some employers prefer a degree in a field related to the firm's business—science, engineering, or finance, for example—plus course work or experience in public relations or communications. Some firms especially seek out college graduates who have work experience in one of the news media, which is how many writers, editors, and newspaper reporters enter the public relations field.

The Public Relations Society of America accredits public relations specialists who have worked in the field for at least five years. Applicants for this professional designation must pass a comprehensive six-hour examination that includes four hours of written and two hours of oral examination.

Job applicants in this field at all levels of experience are expected to present a portfolio of public relations projects on which they have worked.

Potential and advancement

About 115,000 people work in public relations. Because this is a glamorous and popular field, competition for jobs is stiff. Over the long run, job opportunities are expected to increase substantially, but general economic conditions can cause temporary slow periods when companies delay expansion or cut public relations budgets. Job applicants with solid academic backgrounds plus some media experience will have the best job opportunities.

Advancement usually takes the form of handling more demanding and creative assignments or transferring to a larger company. Experienced public relations specialists often start their own consulting firms.

Income

Starting salaries range from $9,600 to $14,000 depending on education and experience.

Experienced public relations specialists earn the highest salaries in public relations consulting firms. Median annual salaries for various other employers and positions are: the federal government, $31,200; state government agencies, $24,000; local government, $22,700; educational organizations, $25,000.

Business firms pay public relations managers an average of $23,000 to $34,000 a year; top public relations executives between $32,000 and $54,000. Advertising agencies pay between $18,000 and $25,000 a year to public relations account executives.

Additional sources of information

Career Information
Public Relations Society of America, Inc.
845 Third Avenue
New York, NY 10022

PR Reporter
Dudley House
P.O. Box 600
Exeter, NH 03833

Service Department
Public Relations News
127 East 80th Street
New York, NY 10021

PURCHASING AGENT

The job

Purchasing agents buy the raw materials, products, and services a company needs for its operation. They coordinate their buying schedules with company production schedules so that company funds will not be tied up unnecessarily in materials ordered too soon or in too large a quantity.

In small companies, a *purchasing manager*, assisted by a few purchasing agents and expediters, handles all aspects of buying. Large companies employ many purchasing agents with each one specializing in one item or in a group of related items.

Beginners in this field function as junior purchasing agents, ordering standard and catalog items until they gain enough experience to handle more difficult assignments.

Over half of all purchasing agents work in manufacturing industries. Others are employed by government agencies, construction companies, hospitals, and schools.

About 18 percent of all purchasing agents are women.

Related jobs are: Retail Buyer, Traffic Manager, Production Manager.

Places of employment and working conditions

Purchasing agents work in all sections of the country but are concentrated in heavily industrialized areas.

They usually work a standard 40-hour workweek but may have longer hours during peak production periods if they work in a seasonal industry.

Qualifications, education, and training

A purchasing agent must be able to analyze numbers and technical data to make responsible buying decisions. The person must have a good memory for details and be able to work independently.

High school should include mathematics and science; business courses are also helpful.

Small companies sometimes promote clerical workers or technicians into purchasing jobs or hire graduates of two-year colleges. Most companies, however, require at least a bachelor's degree in liberal arts or business administration with course work in purchasing, accounting, economics, and statistics. Companies that produce complex products such as chemicals or machinery may prefer a degree in science or engineering with an advanced degree in business administration.

Regardless of their educational background, beginners usually undergo an initial training period to learn the company's operating and purchasing requirements and procedures. Successful purchasing agents keep up with developments in their field through participation in seminars offered by professional societies and by taking courses at local colleges and universities.

In private industry, the recognized mark of experience and professional competence is the designation Certified Purchasing Manager (CPM) conferred by the National Association of Purchasing Management, Inc. In government agencies, the designation is Certified Public Purchasing Officer (CPPO), which is conferred by the National Institute of Governmental Purchasing, Inc. Both have educational and experience standards and require a series of examinations.

Potential and advancement

There are about 190,000 purchasing agents; substantial growth in this field is expected. Job opportunities will be excellent in the future, especially for those with graduate degrees in business administration or a bachelor's degree in science, engineering, or business administration with some course work in purchasing. Graduates of two-year programs will find the best opportunities with small firms.

Purchasing agents can advance to purchasing manager and to executive positions such as director of purchasing or materials management. Some advance by moving to larger companies with more complex purchasing requirements.

Income

Beginning salaries approximate $12,900 a year.

Experienced purchasing agents average $16,200 to $23,900. Purchasing managers in private industry average about $29,500; top executives earn $50,000 or more.

Purchasing agents employed by the federal government average $22,239. In state governments, earnings range from $11,549 to $21,028; state purchasing directors average $23,293 to $29,780.

Additional sources of information

National Association of Purchasing Management, Inc.
11 Park Place
New York, NY 10007

National Institute of Governmental Purchasing, Inc.
1001 Connecticut Avenue, NW
Washington, DC 20036

R

RABBI

The job

Rabbis are the spiritual leaders of their congregations and teachers and interpreters of Jewish law and tradition. They conduct religious services, preside at weddings and funerals, and provide counseling. There are three main types of congregations—Orthodox, Conservative, and Reform. Customs and rituals may vary among them, but all congregations preserve the substance of Jewish religious worship.

Rabbis also serve as chaplains in the armed forces, work in the many Jewish social service agencies, and teach in colleges and universities.

Newly ordained rabbis usually begin as leaders of small congregations, assistants to experienced rabbis, or directors of Hillel Foundations on college campuses.

The Reform branch of the small Reconstructionist branch are the only forms of Judaism that train and ordain women as rabbis. Women rabbis almost always function as assistant rabbis, with very few serving as rabbi-in-charge. This will probably change as more women enter the field and as more congregations come to accept women as capable of handling the duties of rabbi.

Places of employment and working conditions

Rabbis serve Jewish congregations in communities throughout the country. Those states with large Jewish populations have the highest concentrations of rabbis—New York, California, Pennsylvania, New Jersey, Illinois, Massachusetts, Florida, Maryland, and Washington, D.C.

Depending on the size of the congregation and the number of assistants a rabbi has, his or her working hours can be very long and are often irregular.

Qualifications, education, and training

As do all clergy, rabbis must have a deep religious faith and a desire to serve people. Their ethical and moral conduct must be of the highest order.

Educational requirements vary depending on the branch of Judaism. College is required by most branches as a preparation before entering a seminary. The seminary training lasts from three to six years and includes the study of the Bible and Talmud, Jewish history, pastoral psychology, and public speaking.

Potential and advancement

There are about 4,000 rabbis serving the six million Jews in the U.S. Approximately 1,550 are Orthodox rabbis; 1,350 Conservative; and 1,200 Reform. The demand for rabbis has decreased in recent years, and existing openings usually occur only to replace rabbis who retire or die. Employment opportunities vary, however—Conservative rabbis have good job opportunities, Reform rabbis face some competition for available positions, and Orthodox rabbis encounter stiff competition.

Rabbis usually advance from positions as assistant rabbi to rabbi-in-charge, or move to a larger congregation.

Income

Average annual earnings for rabbis range from $15,000 to $35,000 with earnings for Orthodox rabbis lower than Reform or Conservative rabbis.

Earnings of more established rabbis in large congregations average about $35,000 with a few senior rabbis in large temples receiving up to $60,000 a year.

Additional sources of information

Anyone considering this vocation should discuss his or her plans with a practicing rabbi. Information is also available from the following:

The Jewish Theological Seminary of America (Conservative)
3080 Broadway
New York, NY 10027

The Rabbi Isaac Elchanan Theological Seminary (Orthodox)
Yeshiva University
2540 Amsterdam Avenue
New York, NY 10033

Hebrew Union College and Jewish Institute of Religion (Reform)
40 West 68th Street, New York, NY 10023; or 3101 Clifton Avenue, Cincinnati, OH 45220; or 3077 University Mall, Los Angeles, CA 90007

RADIO/TELEVISION ANNOUNCER

The job

The average commercial radio or television station employs from four to six announcers with large stations employing ten or more.

Radio announcers act as disc jockeys, present the news, do commercials, and present other types of material. They may work from prepared scripts or do ad-lib commentary. In small stations, they may also operate the control board, write commercial and news copy, and sell radio advertising time.

Television announcers and radio announcers at large radio stations usually specialize in a particular field such as sports or news. They use written scripts and may do their own research and writing in some instances.

Some announcers work on a free-lance basis selling their services for individual assignments to networks, advertising agencies, and independent producers.

The number of women in this field is increasing steadily, especially in television. About 25 percent of all announcers are women, and many more work behind the scenes in various production jobs.

Places of employment and working conditions

Radio announcers are employed throughout the country in radio stations of all sizes. Television announcers do not have such a wide distribution but are concentrated in large metropolitan areas where most television studios operate.

Announcers in large stations work a 40-hour week and receive overtime pay for any extra hours worked. In small stations, announcers often put in up to 12 hours a week in overtime. Since many stations operate 24 hours a day, seven days a week, all announcers do their share of evening, weekend, and holiday duty.

Qualifications, education, and training

A pleasant speaking voice, good command of the English language, a dramatic flair, and an interest in sports, music, and current events are necessary in this field.

High school courses should include writing, public speaking, and English. Extracurricular involvement in acting, sports, and music is helpful.

A college liberal arts background is excellent for a radio or television announcer. Some colleges and universities offer courses in the broadcasting field, and students may also gain valuable experience by working on the campus radio station.

A number of private broadcasting schools offer training in announcing, but these should be checked out with local broadcasters and Better Business Bureaus before enrolling.

Potential and advancement

There are about 26,000 announcers employed by radio and television broadcasting stations. The popularity of this field plus its relatively small size mean stiff competition for jobs. The best opportunities for beginners exist in small radio stations; television stations usually hire only experienced announcers.

Announcers usually work in several stations in the course of their careers. As they gain experience, announcers advance by moving to larger stations, to stations in larger cities, or to network jobs. Others advance by getting their own program or by developing a specialty such as sportscasting or news reporting.

Income

Salaries for beginning announcers in television range from $11,000 to $15,000 a year. Experienced announcers earn from $18,000 to about $200,000 depending on the size of the audience.

Salaries for radio announcers are generally lower than in television. Many well-known announcers in both radio and television earn much more.

Additional sources of information

National Association of Broadcasters
1771 N Street, NW
Washington, DC 20036

Corporation for Public Broadcasting
1111 16th Street, NW
Washington, DC 20036

RADIOLOGIC (X-RAY) TECHNOLOGIST

The job

In the medical field, X-ray pictures (radiographs) are taken by radiologic technologists who operate X-ray equipment. They usually work under the supervision of a radiologist—a physician who specializes in the use and interpretation of X rays.

There are three specialties within the field of radiologic technology; a radiologic technologist works in all three areas.

The most familiar specialty is the use of X-ray pictures to study and diagnose injury or disease to the human body. In this specialty, the technologist positions the patient and exposes and develops the film. During fluoroscopic examinations (watching the internal movements of the body organs on a screen or monitor), the technologist prepares solutions and assists the physician.

The second specialty area is nuclear medicine technology—the application of radioactive material to aid in the diagnosis and treatment of illness or injury. Working under the direct supervision of a radiologist, the technologist prepares solutions containing radioactive materials that will be absorbed by the patient's internal organs and show up on special cameras or scanners. These materials trace the course of a disease by showing the difference between healthy and diseased tissue.

Radiation therapy—the use of radiation-producing machines to provide therapeutic treatments—is the third specialty. Here, the technologist works under the direct supervision of a radiologist, applying the prescribed amount of radiation for a specified length of time.

During all these procedures, the technologist is responsible for the safety and comfort of the patient and must keep accurate and complete records of all treatments. Technologists also schedule appointments and file X rays and the radiologist's evaluations.

About three quarters of all radiological technologists work in hospitals. The remainder work in medical laboratories, physicians' and dentists' offices, federal and state health agencies, and public school systems.

Many women work in this field. School systems and physicians' offices provide some opportunities for part-time work, which makes the field attractive to people with family responsibilities.

Places of employment and working conditions

Radiologic technologists are found in all parts of the country in towns and cities of all sizes. The largest concentrations are in cities with large medical centers and hospitals.

Full-time technologists usually work a 40-hour week. Those employed in hospitals that provide 24-hour emergency coverage have some shift work or may be on call. There are potential radiation hazards in this field, but careful attention to safety procedures and the use of protective clothing and shielding devices provide protection.

Qualifications, education, and training

Anyone considering this career should be in good health, be emotionally stable, and be able to work with people who are injured or ill. The job also requires patience and attention to detail.

A high school diploma or its equivalent is required for acceptance into an X-ray technology program. Programs approved by the American Medical Association (AMA) are offered by many hospitals, medical schools affiliated with hospitals, colleges and universities, vocational and technical schools, and by the armed forces. The programs vary in length from two to four years; a bachelor's degree in radiologic technology is awarded after completion of the four-year course.

These training programs include courses in anatomy, physiology, nursing procedures, physics, radiation protection, film processing, medical terminology and ethics, radiographic positioning and exposure, and department administration.

Although registration with the American Registry of Radiologic Technologists is not required for work in this field, it is an asset in obtaining highly skilled and specialized positions. Registration requirements include completion of an approved program of medical X-ray technology and a written examination. The technologist may then use the title Registered Technologist (ARRT). Once registered, technologists may be certified in radiation therapy or nuclear medicine by completing an additional year of education.

Potential and advancement

There are about 80,000 radiological technologists at the present time. Employment in this field, as in all medical fields, is expected to expand rapidly; the number of graduates, however, is also expected to grow rapidly. If this trend continues, competition will develop for the choicest jobs, as the number of applicants catches up with the number of job openings.

In large X-ray departments, technologists can advance to supervisory positions or qualify as instructors in X-ray techniques. There is more opportunity for promotion for those having a bachelor's degree.

Income

Starting salaries in hospitals and medical centers average about $10,700 a year; the federal government pays about $9,000 to beginners. Experienced technologists average about $13,300.

Sick leave, vacations, insurance, and other benefits are usually the same as other employees in the same institution receive.

Additional sources of information

The American Society of Radiologic Technologists
500 North Michigan Avenue
Suite 836
Chicago, IL 60611

RANGE MANAGER

The job

Range managers are specialists in grazing management. They plan the optimum combination of animals, size of herds, and conservation of vegetation and soil for maximum production without destroying the ecology of an area. Their work also involves timber production, outdoor recreation, erosion control, and fire prevention.

Most range managers work for the federal government in the Forest Service, Soil Conservation Service, and the Bureau of Land Management. State governments employ range managers in fish and game agencies, land agencies, and extension services.

Private firms that employ range managers include coal and oil companies and large livestock ranches. United Nations agencies and foreign governments also employ American range managers.

Places of employment and working conditions

Most range managers work in the West and in Alaska.

Outdoor work is usual for range managers and locations are often remote. They sometimes spend long periods away from home.

Qualifications, education, and training

Good physical condition, love of the outdoors, and scientific interest are necessary. Communication skills are also important.

High school should include as many science courses as possible.

About 20 colleges and universities offer degree programs in range management or range science; others offer some course work in this field. A degree in a related field such as forestry or agronomy is accepted by some employers. Studies include biology; chemistry; physics; mathematics; plant, animal, and soil sciences; and ecology. Electives in economics, computer science, forestry, wildlife, recreation are desirable.

Graduate degrees in range management are usually necessary for teaching and research positions.

Graduate degrees in range management are usually necessary for teaching and research positions.

Potential and advancement

There are about 3,000 people working as range managers. Job opportunities should be good, even though this is a small field, since the demand for qualified range managers is expected to grow steadily.

Income

Starting salaries range from $10,507 to $19,263 depending on education and experience.

Experienced range managers earn about $20,000 a year.

Additional sources of information

Society for Range Management
2760 West 5th Avenue
Denver, CO 80204

Bureau of Land Management
Denver Service Center
Federal Center Building 50
Denver, CO 80255

REAL ESTATE AGENT/BROKER

The job

The sale and rental of residential and commercial properties are handled by real estate agents and brokers. If they belong to the National Board of Realtors, brokers are called Realtors, agents are Realtor-Associates. They also appraise, manage, or develop property. Some combine a real estate business with an insurance agency or law practice.

Real estate brokers employ *real estate salesworkers*, or *agents*, to show and sell properties. Most real estate businesses sell private homes and other residential property. Some specialize in commercial or industrial property or handle farms and undeveloped land.

Before a property can pass from the seller to the buyer, a title search must be made to prove that there is no doubt about the seller's right to sell the property. This "abstract of title" is performed by an *abstractor* or an abstract company. The abstract is a condensed history of the property which includes current ownership chain of title (ownership); description of the property; and, in chronological order, all transactions that affect the property. These include liens, mortgages, encumbrances, tax assessments, and other liabilities. Abstractors work for the real estate firms, title insurance companies, and abstracting companies or may be self-employed.

Agents obtain listings (properties to sell) by signing an agreement with the seller giving the agent and the real estate firm the right to represent the seller in disposing of the property. It is the agent's responsibility to locate a buyer by advertising and showing the property to interested people. If the buyer requests it, the real estate agent may help locate mortgage funds. In cases where the seller's asking price is higher than the buyer is willing to pay, the agent often acts as a negotiator to bring the sale to a successful conclusion. Agents also are present at closing when the property actually changes hands.

A successful real estate agent must be well versed in all local information relative to the type of real estate sold. An agent selling houses must know local tax and utility rates and the availability of schools, shopping facilities, and public transportation. A commercial or industrial property agent must be able to provide information on taxes, marketing facilities, local zoning regulations, the available labor market, and nearby railroad and highway facilities.

Most real estate salespeople are employed in relatively small businesses. Some large real estate firms employ several hundred agents in many branch offices, but five to ten persons is the usual number employed by a single real estate business. Many agents sell real estate on a part-time basis—in fact, there are about three times as many part-time agents as full-time.

Brokers are independent business owners who are responsible for all business matters relating to the firm's function. Some brokers operate a one-person firm, doing all the selling themselves.

About 41 percent of all licensed real estate salespeople are women. A related job is: Real Estate Appraiser.

Places of employment and working conditions

Real estate agents and brokers work throughout the country in communities of all sizes.

The working hours of real estate agents and brokers are irregular, and evening and weekend hours are the norm. These persons spend a great deal of time on the phone obtaining listings and are also responsible for the paper work on the sales they handle.

Qualifications, education, and training

A pleasant personality, neat appearance, and tact are necessary qualities for a successful real estate agent. Sales ability along with a good memory for names and faces are very important.

Some real estate brokers prefer to hire college graduates with a degree in real estate or business, but most will hire high school graduates with sales ability.

All states and the District of Columbia require agents and brokers to be licensed.

A college degree is not necessary to obtain a license, but most states require at least 30 hours of classroom instruction. Local colleges, adult education programs, and correspondence schools offer the courses necessary to obtain a license, and many prospective real estate agents hold down a full-time job while studying to be a real estate agent. Many brokers hire real estate students as office assistants or rent collectors while they are preparing for the state licensing exam, but others hire only those who have already obtained a license.

Some colleges and universities offer an associate's or bachelor's degree with a major in real estate; several offer advanced education courses to agents and brokers.

A prospective agent must be 18 years old, a high school graduate, and pass a written test on real estate transactions and state laws regarding the sale of real estate to complete the licensing requirements.

Candidates for a broker's license must complete 90 hours of formal training, have a specified amount (usually one to three years) of real estate selling experience, and pass a more comprehensive exam. Some states waive the experience requirements if the candidate has a bachelor's degree in real estate.

Potential and advancement

There are about 1.5 million licensed real estate agents and brokers in the United States; 450,000 are employed full-time. The employment outlook is good through the 1980s, and beginners will find it relatively easy to find a job. But anyone entering real estate should be aware that they cannot earn enough to be self-supporting when working on commission.

In large real estate firms, experienced agents can advance to sales manager or general manager. Experienced sales workers often obtain a broker's license and go into business for themselves. Others go into property management or appraising. Many successful agents prefer to continue selling because the financial awards are very good.

Income

When property is sold, the seller pays a percentage—usually from 5 percent to 10 percent—to the broker. The agent who sells the property receives part of that fee, usually about 50 percent, as a commission.

Earnings vary but agents average about $15,000 a year. Experienced agents and brokers earn $30,000 to $50,000 a year.

Some real estate brokers provide their sales workers with fringe benefits such as life and health insurance.

Additional sources of information

National Association of Realtors
430 North Michigan Avenue
Chicago, IL 60611

Women's Council of Realtors
c/o National Association of Realtors
430 North Michigan Avenue
Chicago, IL 60611

REAL ESTATE APPRAISER

The job

A real estate appraiser studies and evaluates information about a property and estimates its market value. A written appraisal is then prepared to document the findings and conclusions.

An appraisal is usally required whenever a property is sold, insured, or assessed for taxation. Mortgage lenders require an appraisal as do federal, state, and local governments when acquiring property for public use. Insurance companies require an appraisal when determining the proper amount of insurance on a property.

An appraiser must be familiar with public records and their location, be able to read blueprints and mechanical drawings, recognize good and bad construction materials, and be up-to-date on building zoning laws and government regulations. Appraisers usually specialize in one type of property such as farms, single-family dwellings, industrial sites, or apartment houses.

Appraisers often enter the field from other jobs in real estate sales or management, but more and more are entering the field directly. Those with a college education have the greatest chance of success. Beginners in appraisals usually start as appraisal assistants or trainees.

Opportunities for beginners exist in local county assessors' offices and in federal, state, and city departments. Local independent appraisers also offer part-time and full-time work to beginners and college students studying real estate appraisal.

The majority of appraisers are male but women are entering the field in increasing numbers each year.

A related job is: Real Estate Agent/Broker.

Places of employment and working conditions

Appraisers work in all areas of the country in towns and cities of all sizes wherever property is bought, insured, or taxed.

Much of an appraiser's time is spent away from the office inspecting properties and researching records. Independent appraisers set their own working hours but frequently work evenings and weekends to meet client deadlines. Appraisers who work in salaried positions usually have more regular working hours.

Appraisers spend varying amounts of time in travel if they evaluate property in other areas or in other countries. These appraisers are usually involved in appraising industrial and commercial property or property for investment.

Qualifications, education, and training

An appraiser must have the highest standards of personal integrity and honesty and should possess good communication skills, both written and oral. An appraiser also needs good health and stamina because this is a physically demanding job.

Many private firms, financial institutions, and government agencies will hire only appraisers who have a college degree. Many colleges and universities offer programs in real estate and in real estate appraising. Other relevant courses are economics, finance, business administration, architecture, law, and engineering. The American Institute of Real Estate Appraisers also offers courses throughout the United States at various times and locations.

Appraisers may obtain professional recognition by working toward the designations awarded by the institute. For specialists in residential property, the RM (Residential Member) designation can be earned by successfully completing an examination and demonstrating specific expertise and experience. The MAI (Member, Appraisal Institute) designation is awarded to those who can deal with any property type and requires a college degree or its equivalent.

Some states require appraisers to be licensed or to have a real estate broker's license.

Potential and advancement

The number of persons engaged in real estate appraising on a full- or part-time basis is estimated to be between 20,000 and 55,000. The number of designated professional appraisers, however, is substantially less.

Unlike most fields, real estate appraising remains good, regardless of the ups and downs of the economy. The need for competent appraisers is consistent, making this an excellent job opportunity field.

Advancement in this field depends on experience, personal ability, and effort.

Income

This is a particularly well-paid profession. Experienced appraisers make more money than accountants, architects, and some lawyers. Those holding the prestigious MAI designation earn between $45,000 and $75,000 annually.

Federal agencies pay beginners about $11,000 a year; experienced appraisers up to $28,000. Salaries in state agencies run from $13,000 to $23,000.

Additional sources of information

Contact your local Board of Realtor office or state real estate commission for specific requirements in your area. Information is also available from:

American Institute of Real Estate Appraisers
430 North Michigan Avenue
Chicago, IL 60611

National Association of Realtors
430 North Michigan Avenue
Chicago, IL 60611

REHABILITATION COUNSELOR

The job

Rehabilitation counselors work with mentally, physically, and emotionally disabled persons to help them become self-sufficient and productive. Many counselors specialize in one type of disability such as the mentally retarded, the mentally ill, or the blind.

In the course of designing an individual rehabilitation program, the counselor may consult doctors, teachers, and family members to determine the client's abilities and the exact nature of the handicap or disability. He or she will, of course, also work closely with the client. Many counselors discuss training and career options with the client, arrange specialized training and specific job-related training, and provide encouragement and emotional support.

An important part of a counselor's work is finding employers who will hire the disabled and the handicapped. Many counselors keep in touch with members of the local business community and try to convince them to provide jobs for the disabled. Once a person is placed in a job, the rehabilitation counselor keeps track of the daily progress of the employee and also confers with the employer about job performance and progress.

The amount of time spent with an individual client depends on the severity of the person's problems and the size of the counselor's case load. Counselors in private organizations can usually spend more time with their clients than those who work for state and local agencies. Less-experienced counselors, and counselors who work with the severely disabled usually handle the fewest cases at one time.

About three fourths of all rehabilitation counselors are employed by state or local rehabilitation agencies. Others work in hospitals or sheltered workshops or are employed by insurance companies and labor unions. The Veterans Administration employs about 350 psychologists who act as rehabilitation counselors.

About one third of all rehabilitation counselors are women. The fact that there are many opportunities for part-time work makes this a good career field for people with family responsibilities.

Related jobs are: Employment Counselor, Psychologist, and Social Worker.

Places of employment and working conditions

Rehabilitation counselors work throughout the country with the largest concentrations in metropolitan areas.

A 40-hour workweek is usual, but attendance at community meetings sometimes requires extra hours. A counselor's working hours are not all spent in the office but include trips to prospective employers, training agencies, and client's homes.

The work of a counselor can be emotionally exhausting and sometimes discouraging.

Qualifications, education, and training

Anyone considering this field should have emotional stability, the ability to accept responsibility and to work independently, and the ability to motivate and guide other people. Patience is also a necessary characteristic of a rehabilitation counselor because progress often comes slowly over a long period of time.

High school courses in the social sciences should be a part of a college preparatory course.

A bachelor's degree with a major in education, psychology, guidance, or sociology is the minimum requirement. This is sufficient for only a few entry-level jobs.

Advanced degrees in psychology, vocational counseling, or rehabilitation counseling are necessary for almost all jobs in this field.

Most rehabilitation counselors work for state and local government agencies and are required to pass the appropriate civil service examinations before appointment to a position. Many private organizations require counselors to be certified; this is achieved by passing the examinations administered by the Commission on Rehabilitation Counselor Certification.

Potential and advancement

There are about 19,000 rehabilitation counselors, 2,000 of them working part-time. Employment opportunities are expected to be very good, but, since most job openings are in state and local agencies, the employment picture will depend to a great extent on government funding for such services.

Experienced rehabilitation counselors can advance to supervisory and administrative jobs.

Income

Beginning salaries range from $11,500 to $15,774 a year in state and local agencies.

The Veterans Administration pays starting salaries of $13,014 to $19,263 with a master's degree; and $19,263 to $23,087 for advanced degrees and experience.

Additional sources of information

American Rehabilitation Counseling Association
1607 New Hampshire Avenue, NW
Washington, DC 20009

National Rehabilitation Counseling Association
1522 K Street, NW
Washington, DC 20005

Commission on Rehabilitation Counselor Certification
520 North Michigan Avenue
Chicago, IL 60611

RESPIRATORY THERAPIST

The job

Respiratory therapists provide treatment for patients with cardiores-piratory problems. Their role is important and the responsibilities are great.

These therapists' work includes giving relief to chronic asthma and emphysema sufferers; emergency care in cases of heart failure, stroke, drowning, and shock; and treatment of acute respiratory symptoms in cases of head injuries, poisoning, and drug abuse. They must respond swiftly and start treatment quickly because brain damage may occur if a patient stops breathing for three to five minutes, and lack of oxygen for more than nine minutes almost invariably results in death.

In addition to respiratory therapists, the field includes *respiratory technicians* and *respiratory assistants.*

Therapists and technicians perform essentially the same duties with therapists having greater responsibility for supervision and instruction.

Assistants have little contact with the patients; their duties are usually limited to cleaning, sterilizing, and storing the respiratory equipment used by therapists and technicians.

Respiratory therapists and technicians work as part of a health care team following doctors' instructions. They use special equipment and techniques—respirators, positive-pressure breathing machines, and cardiopulmonary resuscitation (CPR)—to treat patients. They are also responsible for keeping records of materials costs and charges to pa-tients and maintaining and making minor repairs to equipment. All respiratory therapy workers are trained to observe strict safety precau-tions in the use and testing of respiratory equipment to minimize the danger of fire.

Most respiratory therapists, technicians, and assistants work in hospitals in respiratory, anesthesiology, or pulmonary medicine departments. Others work for nursing homes, ambulance services, and oxygen equipment rental companies.

Places of employment and working conditions

Respiratory therapy workers are employed in hospitals throughout the country in communities of all sizes. The largest number of job opportunities exist in large metropolitan areas that support several hospitals or large medical centers.

Respiratory therapy workers usually work a 40-hour week, including night and weekend shifts.

Qualifications, education, and training

Anyone interested in entering this field should enjoy working with people and have a patient and understanding manner. The ability to follow instructions and work as a member of a team is important. Manual dexterity and some mechanical ability are necessary in the operation and maintenance of the sometimes complicated respiratory therapy equipment.

High school students interested in this field should take courses in health, biology, mathematics, physics, and bookkeeping.

Although some respiratory therapy workers, especially assistants, acquire their skills through on-the-job training, formal training in respiratory therapy is now the usual way of entering the field. There are about 200 institutions that offer programs approved by the Council on Medical Education of the American Medical Association. All these programs require a high school diploma. Courses vary from 18 months to 4 years and include both classroom and clinical work. Students study anatomy and physiology, chemistry, physics, microbiology, and mathematics. A bachelor's degree is awarded to those completing a four-year program, with an associate degree awarded for some of the shorter programs.

Approximately 5,000 respiratory therapists are Registered Respiratory Therapists (RRT). They obtain this designation by completing an AMA-approved therapist training program, gaining one year of experience following completion of the program, and passing the written and oral examination of the National Board for Respiratory Therapy (NBRT).

Respiratory technicians can receive certification as a Certified Respiratory Therapy Technician (CRTT) if they have completed an AMA-approved technician training program and have one year of experience. They must pass a single written NBRT examination. About 16,000 respiratory technicians are certified.

Potential and advancement

There are currently about 36,000 respiratory therapists, technicians, and assistants. The field, also called inhalation therapy, is growing rapidly. Growth of health care services in general and the expanding use of respiratory therapy and equipment by hospitals, ambulance services, and nursing homes make this a good job opportunity area, as more and more respiratory specialists are hired to release nurses and other personnel from respiratory therapy duties.

Advancement in this field depends on experience and additional education. Respiratory assistants can advance to the technician or therapist level by completing the required courses; technicians can advance by achieving certification or completing education and testing requirements for the therapist level.

Respiratory therapists can be promoted to assistant chief or chief therapist. With graduate study, they can qualify for teaching positions.

Income

Starting salary for respiratory therapists in hospitals and medical centers is about $11,400 a year; experienced therapists earn as high as $18,000 in some hospitals. Technicians and assistants earn less.

Starting salaries with the federal government are in the $8,400 range if the applicant has one year of AMA-approved training; $9,400 with two years of training.

Hospitals usually provide paid vacations, medical insurance, and sick days with some hospitals also providing uniforms and tuition assistance.

Additional sources of information

American Association for Respiratory Therapy
7411 Hines Place
Dallas, TX 75235

The National Board for Respiratory Therapy, Inc.
Suite 124
1900 West 47th Street
Shawnee Mission, KS 66205

Information about on-the-job training can be obtained from local hospitals.

RETAIL BUYER

The job

Every item carried in every store has been selected by a retail buyer. The owner of a small retail business functions as a retail buyer when ordering the store's merchandise; but large retail stores or chains of stores employ professionally trained buyers to make decisions and purchases involving thousands, and sometimes millions, of dollars. The difference between a retail buyer and a purchasing agent is in the ultimate use of what they buy. The buyer purchases goods for resale; the purchasing agent buys materials to be used by his or her firm.

This is an exciting, fast-paced, often nerve-wracking job. The buyer must order merchandise that will satisfy the store's customers, sell at a profit, and move on and off the store's shelves within a reasonable time. With clothing and a number of other items, this means seasonally. Buyers must be familiar with manufacturers and distributors, be aware of fashion trends and local customer preferences, and work within the budget allotted for a particular store or department. They must be able to stock the basics as well as take advantage of unexpected good buys or fad items.

Buyers work closely with sales workers to keep up with customer likes and dislikes, and they study and analyze past store sales records and market research reports. They must be aware of the merchandise and prices of competitors and keep track of economic conditions in the areas where their customers live.

Some buyers are assisted by junior buyers who handle routine chores such as verifying shipments. Junior buyers may also be involved in sales and often take part in store training programs.

Merchandise managers coordinate all the buying and selling activities of a large store or chain. The merchandise manager decides what merchandise to stock, devises the budget, and assigns different buyers to purchase certain items or lines of goods. Merchandise managers are also involved in sales promotion.

About 40 percent of all retail buyers are women.

Places of employment and working conditions

About half of all buyers and merchandise managers work for clothing and general department stores. Although buyers are found in all parts of the country, most job opportunities are in cities and large metropolitan areas such as New York, Chicago, and Dallas.

Buyers regulate their own working hours and often work more than 40 hours a week. Depending on the store's location and the type of merchandise being purchased, a buyer might travel as little as four or five days a month or might spend one third of his or her working time in travel. Some buying trips are glamorous—to Paris, for example, for a showing of ladies' fashions—while most are routine but fast-paced.

Qualifications, education, and training

If you are interested in this field, you must be able to stand the pace and the pressure. You must be a good planner and able to make decisions, have good leadership and communication skills, and be assertive.

In high school, distributive education programs are excellent training grounds for anyone interested in the retail field.

Many buyers have worked their way up the ladder from sales or stockroom positions. Others attend junior and four-year colleges that offer degree programs in marketing and purchasing. Many trade schools offer courses in fashion merchandising.

More and more employers are requiring college training, especially those who include buyers in their management of executive training programs. Most employers will accept applications from almost any field of college study and consider courses or experience in merchandising, fashion, sales, or business a plus.

The formal training programs in retail stores usually last from six to eight months and include classroom instruction combined with rotating assignments to various jobs and departments. The buyer trainee's first job will probably be as assistant or junior buyer. Depending on the size of the store and the growing abilities of the trainee, it takes about a year to achieve buyer status.

Potential and advancement

There are about 110,000 buyers and merchandise managers working for retail firms. Job opportunities in this field will grow slowly through the next decade with most openings occurring to replace those who leave the field.

This is a popular career field, and competition for available openings will be keen. College graduates with courses or experience in relevant areas will have the best chances of securing choice positions.

It takes years of experience as a buyer to advance to the positions of merchandise manager. A few experienced buyers and merchandise managers can also advance to top executive positions in store or chain management, but these positions are limited by the size and growth of the company.

Income

Salaries depend on the product line purchased, sales volume of the store, and seniority. Discount department stores, mass merchandising firms, and large department store chains offer the highest salaries. Buyers for these retail companies earn $27,500 a year; merchandise managers earn considerably more.

College graduates in training programs start in the $11,000 to $15,000 range.

Buyers often earn large bonuses for exceptional performance and are included in store incentive plans such as profit sharing and stock options. Some stores also compensate buyers for long working hours by providing extra-long vacations.

Additional sources of information

National Retail Merchants Association
100 West 31st Street
New York, NY 10001

United States Office of Education
Division of Vocational/Technical Education
Washington, DC 20202

National Association of Trade and Technical Schools
2021 L Street, NW
Washington, DC 20036

The Fashion Group, Inc.
9 Rockefeller Plaza
New York, NY 10020

RETAIL STORE MANAGER

The job

The manager of a retail store, whether the store is large or small, has one goal—to operate the store at a profit. To this end the manager applies years of accumulated training and experience.

Retailing is one of few remaining fields where talented and hard-working people can still advance all the way to the top regardless of education. Several career paths are possible including sales work, merchandise and fashion buying, advertising, accounting, and personnel relations. Those who reach the level of store manager usually have experience in several of these areas.

Four major tasks are involved in the operation of a retail store: merchandising (buying and selling), store operations (staffing, shipping, and receiving), accounting, and advertising. In a small store, the manager handles all of these. The manager of a large store might handle one or two of these areas personally and assign assistant managers to supervise the others. In some stores, the manager provides overall supervision and policy making while employing four or more division heads to oversee specific functions. In chain stores, centralized buying and accounting relieves the individual store managers of these two responsibilities.

Women have always been employed in the retail field in large numbers. They hold a substantial number of positions in middle management such as senior buyer and merchandise manager and are fairly well represented as store managers in even the largest stores.

Related jobs are: Retail Buyer, Purchasing Agent, Wholesaler, Advertising Manager, Personnel Manager.

Places of employment and working conditions

This is a highly competitive field, and the store manager is under constant pressure to increase the store's sales volume. Many managers work 50 or more hours a week.

Managers employed by chain stores may be required to move frequently, especially during their early years with the company.

Qualifications, education, and training

Good judgment, tact, administrative ability, a feeling for what the public wants to buy, good communication skills, and the ability to deal with all types of people are necessary for a store manager.

High school should include mathematics, English, and social sciences; Distributive Education Programs, where available, provide and excellent background. Part-time or summer jobs in retail stores are good experience.

Education requirements in this field vary greatly. Some large stores and many chain stores will accept high school graduates into the management training programs. Many larger employers require a college degree in liberal arts, marketing, accounting, or business administration. Top positions in some stores require a master's degree in business administration.

Potential and advancement

There are over 2,000,000 retail stores of all sizes in the United States, about 90 percent of them independently owned. Growth in retailing is expected to accompany the growth in population creating substantial job opportunities through the mid-1980s. Positions in large independent stores will be the most competitive, but entry-level jobs in retailing will be numerous.

Regardless of educational background and career path within retailing, advancement to the top positions requires years of experience and a record of success at each level. When the store-manager level is achieved, sales volume figures become the deciding factor in the manager's career. Increased sales can mean promotion to field manager or transfer to a more desirable store in a chain store operation or the opportunity to work for a larger independent store.

Income

Trainees earn between $11,000 and $15,000 a year.

Experienced store managers earn from $17,000 to $27,000 or more. Many also receive bonuses or participate in profit-sharing plans, based on store sales volume.

Additional sources of information

National Retail Merchants Association
100 West 31st Street
New York, NY 10001

Association of General Merchandise Chains
1625 Eye Street, NW
Washington, DC 20006

SAFETY ENGINEER

The job

The specific duties of safety engineers (also called occupational safety and health specialists) vary depending on where they work. In general, they are responsible for the safe operation of their employer's facilities and for the physical safety of the employees. They inspect, advise, and train.

In a large manufacturing plant, a safety engineer might develop a comprehensive safety program covering thousands of employees. This would include making a detailed analysis of each job, identifying potential hazards, investigating accidents to determine causes, designing and installing safety equipment, establishing safety training programs, and supervising employee safety committees.

In a trucking company, a safety engineer inspects heavy rigs such as trucks and trailers; checks out drivers for safe driving practices; and studies schedules, routes, loads, and speeds to determine their influence on accidents. In a mining company, a safety engineer inspects underground or open-pit areas for compliance with state and federal laws, designs protective equipment and safety devices and programs, and leads rescue activities in emergency situations.

Safety engineers are also concerned with product safety. They work with design engineers to develop products that meet safety standards and monitor manufacturing processes to ensure the safety of the finished product.

Other occupational safety and health specialists work as *fire protection engineers* who safeguard life and property from fire, explosion, and related hazards. Some specialists research the causes of fires and the flammability of different building materials. Others identify hazards and develop protective measures and training programs. They work for fire equipment manufacturers, insurance rating bureaus, and consulting firms. Some are specialists in sprinkler or fire-detection systems.

Industrial hygienists detect and remedy industrial problems that affect the health of workers. They monitor noise levels, dust, vapors, and radioactivity levels. Some work in laboratories and study the effects of various industrial substances on humans and on air and water. They work with government regulatory agencies, environmental groups, and labor organizations as well as plant management.

Loss control consultants and *occupational health consultants* work for property-liability insurance companies. The services they provide include inspecting the premises for safety violations and giving advice, desiging safety training programs, and designing plant health and medical programs. They also work with the insurance company's underwriters to assess risks and develop premium schedules.

Related jobs are: Claim Representative, Engineering and Science Technician, Environmentalist, Firefighter, Industrial Designer, Underwriter.

Places of employment and working conditions

Safety engineers and other occupational and health specialists work throughout the country with the largest concentrations in heavily industrialized areas.

These jobs are usually very active and often entail climbing and other strenuous activities in the course of inspections or emergency situations. A great deal of travel is involved for some workers, especially those who work as consultants for insurance companies.

Qualifications, education, and training

Safety engineers and other safety and health specialists must have good communications skills and be able to motivate people. They should get along well with people and be able to deal with them effectively at all levels—from company president to production line worker. They should be assertive and have good judgment. Good physical condition is important.

A college preparatory course should be taken in high school with emphasis on mathematics and science.

Graduates of two-year colleges are sometimes hired to work as technicians in this field, but most employers require at least a bachelor's degree in science or engineering. Some prefer a more specialized degree in a field such as industrial safety, safety management, or fire protection engineering or graduate work in industrial hygiene, safety engineering, or occupational safety and health engineering.

Technological advancements make continuing education a necessity in this field. Many insurance companies offer training seminars and correspondence courses; the Occupational Safety and Health Administration (OSHA) conducts courses in occupational injury investigation and radiological health hazards.

After having successfully completed examinations and the required years of experience, specialists in occupational health and safety may achieve certification from their respective professional societies. These designations include Certified Safety Professional; Certified Industrial Hygienist; and Member, Society of Fire Protection Engineers.

Potential and advancement

About 28,000 people work in this field. Employment of occupational safety and health specialists is expected to grow substantially because of changes in government regulations, the growth of unions, and rising insurance costs. Most job openings will occur in manufacturing and industrial firms.

In large companies, advancement to top level management is possible for experienced occupational safety and health specialists.

Income

Beginning salaries range from $13,000 to $17,000 a year. Experienced workers earn $24,000 to $30,000; corporate level executives earn $35,000 or more.

Additional sources of information

American Society of Safety Engineers
850 Busse Highway
Park Ridge, IL 60068

American Industrial Hygiene Association
66 South Miller road
Akron, OH 44313

Society of Fire Protection Engineers
60 Batterymarch Street
Boston, MA 02110

Division of Training and Manpower Development
National Institute for Occupational Safety and Health
Robert A. Taft Laboratories
4676 Columbia Parkway
Cincinnati, OH 45226

SALES MANAGER

The job

The title of sales manager means different things in different companies. In general, a sales manager is responsible for supervising a firm's sales staff.

Depending on a company's size and management structure and the level of responsibility of the sales manager, this could mean only the day-to-day coordination of the activities of sales workers, branch managers, and sales training programs; or it could mean a corporate-level position that entails setting company marketing policy and sales goals. The sales manager may be responsible for a staff of five salespeople or for a marketing department employing hundreds of people.

Because the product or service sold, as well as the size of the company's sales force, readers should refer to the separate job descriptions for sales positions that appear throughout this book.

See: Advertising Sales Person, Engineer, Import/Export Worker, Insurance Agent and Broker, Manufacturer's Sales Representative, Office Manager, Pharmacist, Purchasing Agent, Real Estate Agent/Broker, Retail Store Manager, Securities Sales Worker, Travel Agent, and Wholesaler.

SCHOOL ADMINISTRATOR

The job

School administrators have the responsibility of running the various schools and school systems in the United States. Their duties depend on whether they work at the state or local level, whether they work in a public or parochial school system or private school, and on their area of responsibility.

At the state level, a *superintendent of schools* or *director of education* oversees the functioning of the public school systems and state colleges with the state. The superintendent is responsible for setting and enforcing minimum standards for schools and teachers, administering teacher certification programs, and administering whatever state and federal funds are provided for education.

At the local level, a superintendent of schools is appointed by a local public school board or by a parochial school system to administer an individual school system. The system may consist of just a few schools or many schools. The superintendent hires and supervises all personnel; prepares the school budget; is responsible for physical maintenance of buildings and equipment; makes projections for future needs; and oversees curriculum and textbook decisions, purchasing, public transportation, and many other details. The superintendent's job is often a thankless one—the local school board and citizens, on one hand, trying to keep taxes down, and teachers trying to provide the best education possible for the students, on the other. It is the superintendent, working to appease both groups, who usually gets the blame for everything.

The superintendent is usually assisted by various other administrators who handle special areas. *Special-subject supervisors* coordinate the activities and curriculum of a specific subject area throughout all the schools in the system. The most common special areas are music, art, remedial reading, physical education, libraries, and business or technical education. *Special-education supervisors* plan and supervise the instruction of handicapped students and, in school systems that provide them, handle programs for gifted students as well.

A *curriculum director* evaluates the subjects and activities included in the curricula of the schools within the school system and makes recommendations to teachers and other administrators.

Within an individual school, the *principal* is responsible for the day-to-day operation of the school. The principal must operate within a budget, be both an educator and a business manager, develop and maintain a good working relationship with teachers and students, handle discipline, and oversee building maintenance.

In a private school, the principal is often called a *headmaster* or *head-mistress*. If the school also provides residence facilities for its students, the headmaster has additional responsibilities besides those of a school principal. Living quarters, food, laundry, and recreation facilities and "substitute parent" functions would then be part of the *headmaster's* duties as well.

Although the teaching profession employs more women than any other, the number of women in school administration has been declining since the 1920s. In 1928, 55 percent of all elementary school principals were women; today only 18 percent are women. Only about 2 percent of secondary school principals are women. A woman superintendent of schools is very rare. At the college level, less than 5 percent of all colleges and universities—including women's colleges—are headed by women.

Places of employment and working conditions

School administrators function under constant pressure, especially at the highest levels. Frustration is often part of the job, and administrators must face the fact that they are often resented by the very people they work to serve.

Hours for most administrators are long and irregular. Evening meetings and civil functions often push the total up to 50 or 60 hours or more a week.

Qualifications, education, and training

An interest in the development of children, the ability to get along with people, communication and business skills, patience, tact, and good judgment are all necessary.

The first step in this career field is a degree in teaching or education. (See the job descriptions for teachers elsewhere in this book for educational requirements at the elementary, secondary, and college levels.)

Graduate study in educational administration is necessary for most administrative positions. A master's degree is the minimum requirement; top-level positions in large schools or school systems usually require a Ph.D.

Potential and advancement

There are about 60,000 school administrators at the present time. As in all phases of education, there will be stiff competition for all jobs in this field through the mid-1980s. Those persons who combine the appropriate educational credentials with wide experience will have the best chance of securing the choice jobs at all levels.

Advancement in this field may be from teacher up through the ranks in a single school system or may take the form of moving to a larger school system. Administrators in middle-level positions in large systems often advance by securing top-level positions in small school systems or private schools.

Income

Earnings vary widely depending mainly on the size of the school system.

Public school superintendents earn $17,000 to $22,000 a year in a small rural system; up to $48,000 in metropolitan areas. In some very large school districts, superintendents earn $50,000 or more.

Salaries of principals range from $7,000 to $27,000. Principals and headmasters in private schools have comparable earings and are sometimes provided with living facilities.

Additional sources of information

American Association of School Administrators
1801 North Moore Street
Arlington, VA 22209

National Council of Administrative Women in Education
1815 Fort Myer Drive North
Arlington, VA 22209

National Education Association
1201 16th Street, NW
Washington, DC 20036

SCHOOL GUIDANCE COUNSELOR

The job

Although their services are used in a wide variety of ways, the main function of school guidance counselors is to assist individual students with their problems, whether the problems are educational, social, or personal. To accomplish this, the counselors work closely with the school staff, parents, and the community.

Most guidance counselors are employed in secondary schools where they assist students in making career choices and work with them in selecting courses and meeting college requirements. Counselors also test and assess a student's abilities. A counselor's involvement in social problems includes work with drug and alcohol abuse, criminal behavior, and pregnancy. A student's personal problems can also require that the counselor help the student find a job or obtain medical or psychiatric help. In some schools, guidance counselors also teach some classes or supervise extracurricular activities.

The number of counselors in elementary schools is growing. At this educational level, counselors concentrate on the early detection of learning and personality problems because treatment and counseling can be most effective if started at an early age.

Most guidance counselors work in school buildings. A typical workday might include individual counseling sessions, meetings with small groups, or large meetings with students, parents, and community groups. Counselors may also be required to meet with law enforcement officers or agencies, and with parents—sometimes in emotionally charged or unpleasant situations.

Places of employment and working conditions

Guidance counselors work in all areas of the United States in communities and schools of all sizes.

This is an active job, not always limited to an office atmosphere. There can be unpleasant and highly emotional confrontations from time to time, and a counselor must be careful not to become overinvolved in the lives and problems of the individual students.

373

About half of all guidance counselors are women.

Qualifications and training

A sincere desire to help young people is the most important characteristic for potential guidance counselors. The ability to work not only with students but with all members of the educational team is also essential. Guidance counselors should also have a thorough background in the study of human behavior.

Most guidance counselors come from the teaching profession, and most states require teacher certification as well as counseling certification for school counselors. College courses leading to teacher certification with additional courses in psychology and sociology are the best preparation.

One or two years of additional study are usually necessary to obtain the master's degree needed for counseling certification. Graduate courses usually include student appraisal, individual and group counseling, career information services, professional relations, ethics, statistics, and research. Depending on the state, from one to five years of teaching experience are also required.

Some states allow other types of education and experience and requirements have been changing rapidly in recent years. A prospective counselor should check with the appropriate state department of education before selecting a graduate program.

Potential and advancement

About 43,000 people work full time as guidance counselors. Since school enrollments are dropping in many areas, the outlook for school counseling jobs is not particularly good; if federal funding for career education should increase, however, prospects may improve.

School counselors may advance to supervisory positions or administrative posts in larger schools or school districts. With additional education and experience, they can become educational psychologists or college counselors, positions that require a Ph.D.

Income

School counselors usually earn more than classroom teachers in the same school. Salaries range from $11,000 to $30,500 with increases usually granted for additional education and experience. Some counselors supplement their income with work for government, private, or industrial counseling units.

Additional sources of information

American School Counselor Association
1607 New Hampshire Avenue, NW
Washington, DC 20009

SECRET SERVICE AGENT

The job

The United States Secret Service is part of the Department of the Treasury and employs special agents and uniformed officers.

Special agents have both protective and investigative responsibilities. Their primary responsibility is the protection of the president of the United States. They also protect the vice president, the president-elect and vice president-elect, a former president and his wife, the widow of a former president until her death or remarriage, minor children of a former president until age 16, major presidential and vice-presidential candidates, and visiting heads of foreign states or foreign governments.

Special agents also work to suppress counterfeiting of U.S. currency and securities and investigate and arrest people involved in forging and cashing government checks, bonds, and securities. All special agents must qualify for both protective and investigative assignments.

The Secret Service Uniformed Division employs *uniformed officers* to provide protection for the president and his immediate family while they are in residence at the White House. Previously called the White House Police, their duties have been expanded to include protection of the vice president and his immediate family, the White House and grounds, the official residence of the vice president in Washington, D.C., buildings in which presidential offices are located, and foreign diplomatic missions located in the metropolitan Washington, D.C. area or such other areas of U.S. territories and possessions as the president may direct.

Uniformed officers carry out their responsibilities through foot and vehicular patrols, fixed posts, and canine teams.

Treasury Security Force Officers are also a part of the Secret Service Uniformed Division. They are responsible for security at the Main Treasury Building and the Treasury Annex and for security of the office of the secretary of the Treasury. They have investigative and special arrest powers in connection with laws violated within the

Treasury Building including forgery and fraudulent negotiation or redemption of government checks, bonds, and securities.

Women are employed in all these categories.

Related jobs are: FBI Special Agent, CIA Worker.

Places of employment and working conditions

Special agents may be employed at Secret Service Headquarters in Washington, D.C., or at one of over 100 field offices and residential agencies throughout the United States. Uniformed officers and Treasury Security Force officers work in Washington, D.C.

Special agents must be willing to work wherever they are assigned and are subject to frequent reassignment. Because the protective responsibilities of the Secret Service go on around the clock, all agents and officers perform some shift work.

Qualifications, education, and training

Each of these three Secret Service jobs has separate physical and educational requirements. All, however, require a comprehensive background investigation and top-secret security clearance.

Applicants for *Special Agent* appointments must be less than 35 years of age at the time of entrance to duty; be in excellent physical condition and pass a rigorous medical examination; have weight in proportion to height; and distance vision, uncorrected, of 20/20 in one eye and no less than 20/30 in the other.

Applicants must have (1) a bachelor's degree in any major field of study, or (2) three years' experience of which at least two are in criminal investigation, or (3) a comparable combination of experience and education. A passing grade on the Treasury Enforcement Agent Examination, administered by area offices of the United States Civil Service Commission, is a prerequisite for consideration.

Only a limited number of the most-qualified applicants reach the interview stage. They are rated on personal appearance, bearing and manner, ability to speak logically and effectively, and ability to adapt easily to a variety of situations. Applicants who achieve appointment must be prepared to wait an extended period of time for a vacancy to occur; it is usually during this period that background investigations are completed.

Once active duty begins, special agents receive general investigative training at the Federal Law Enforcement Training Center in Brunswick, Georgia, and specialized training at Secret Service facilities in Washington, D.C. They study protective techniques, criminal law, investigative procedures and devices, document and handwriting examination and analysis, first aid, use of firearms, and arrest techniques. They also receive on-the-job training. Advanced in-service training programs continue throughout an agent's career.

Uniformed Officers must be U.S. citizens, have vision of at least 20/40 in each eye (correctable to 20/20), have weight in proportion to height, and pass a comprehensive physical examination. They must have a high school diploma or equivalent or one year of experience as a police officer in a city of over 500,000 population. Applicants must pass a written examination and an in-depth personal interview and have a valid driver's license.

Uniformed officers undergo a period of training at Secret Service facilities in Beltsville, Maryland, and Brunswick, Georgia. They study legal procedures in law enforcement, first aid, community relations, self-defense, and the use and care of firearms. Additional on-the-job training takes place after assignment.

Potential and advancement

The total employment of the Secret Service is about 3,500. From time to time the service may actively recruit for a specific job category, but, for the most part, job opportunities are limited. The extremely high public interest in this work means that only the most highly qualified applicants are considered for appointment. Even after acceptance, special agents must wait until a vacancy occurs before they begin active service.

Promotion depends on performance and the needs of the Secret Service.

Income

Special agents start at the GS–5 ($11,243 a year) or the GS–7 ($13,925) level. Full performance level for an experienced agent is GS–12 ($24,703). Agents are eligible for retirement at age 50 with 20 years of service.

Uniformed officers start at $16,000 a year. They receive uniforms and equipment and are eligible for retirement after 20 years.

Additional sources of information

The nearest area office of the United States Civil Service Commission can supply information on examination schedules.

United States Secret Service
Personnel Division
1800 G Street, NW
Washington, DC 20223

SECRETARY

The job

A secretary is the center of communication activities in a firm or department. The secretary transmits information from her employer to other members of the firm and to other organizations. Most secretaries type, take shorthand, deal with visitors, keep track of the employer's appointments, make travel arrangements, and, generally, relieve the employer of excess paper work.

Executive secretaries work for the top executives in a firm. Jobs at this level require top-notch skills and usually some college education. *Social secretaries* arrange social functions, answer personal correspondence, and keep the employer informed about all social activities. Public figures such as politicians, elected officials, celebrities, and others with a busy social life usually employ social secretaries.

Some secretaries have training in specialized areas. *Medical secretaries* study medical terminology to prepare case histories and medical reports. *Legal secretaries* are trained to do some legal research and to help prepare briefs; they are familiar with legal terminology and the format of legal papers. *Technical secretaries* assist engineers and scientists in drafting reports and research proposals. They are acquainted with scientific and mathematical terms and are trained in the use of the technical vocabulary and symbols used in these fields.

Stenographers take dictation and then transcribe their notes on a typewriter. They do not handle the wide range of duties that a secretary does, although in some offices stenographers handle routine chores such as filing, answering the phone, or operating office machines. Stenographers may also specialize in medical, legal, or technical work; some specialize in a foreign language. *Public stenographers* serve traveling business people or others who have only occasional need for stenographic services. They are usually located in large hotels and busy downtown areas of cities.

Shorthand reporters are specialized stenographers who record all statements made during a proceeding. They record the sessions of state legislatures, the Congress of the United States, meetings and conventions, and record out-of-court testimony for attorneys. Their transcription then becomes the official record of the proceeding. About half of all shorthand reporters work as *court reporters* who take down all statements made during legal proceedings in courts of law.

About 95 percent of all secretaries and stenographers are women. Men who work as secretaries are usually given a different title—and a higher rate of pay. There are many opportunities for part-time work in smaller companies.

Places of employment and working conditions

Secretaries and stenographers are employed throughout the country. About two thirds of them are employed by banks, insurance companies, real estate firms, and government.

Working conditions vary, but full-time secretaries and stenographers usually work a 37- to 40-hour week. Shorthand reporters may work irregular hours and may have to sit for long periods of time while recording an event.

Qualifications, education, and training

Secretaries and stenographers must be accurate and neat. They must display discretion and initiative and have a good command of spelling, grammar, punctuation, and vocabulary. Shorthand reporters must have good hearing and be able to concentrate amid distractions.

High school business courses are valuable and so are college preparatory courses because secretaries and stenographers should have a good general background. In either type of high school preparation, there should be as many English courses as possible.

Secretarial training as part of a college education or at a private business school is preferred by many employers. Training can vary from a few months for basic instruction in shorthand and typing to a year or two for some of the specialty areas such as medicine or law. Shorthand reporters usually complete a two-year program in a shorthand reporting school.

Well-trained and highly experienced secretaries may qualify for the designation Certified Professional Secretary (C.P.S.) by passing a series of examinations given by the National Secretaries Association. This is a mark of achievement in the secretarial field and is recognized as such by many employers.

Potential and advancement

There are about 3.5 million people employed in this field; about 100,000 of them are stenographers. One out of every five secretaries and one out of every six stenographers work part-time.

The demand for qualified secretaries will continue to grow. Stenographers will not be as much in demand in the future, as the increased use of dictation machines and word processing centers will reduce the need for them. Skilled shorthand reporters, however, will be in demand, and competition for entry-level jobs will increase as more people enter this field.

Opportunities for advancement depend on the acquisition of new or improved skills and on increasing knowledge of the employer's firm or field of business. Some private firms and government agencies have their own training facilities to help employees upgrade their skills.

Executive secretaries are sometimes promoted to management positions because of their extensive knowledge of their employer's operation.

Income

Secretaries average from $817 to $1,085 a month in urban areas. Stenographers average $819 to $918 a month. Shorthand reporters are the highest paid at about $17,000 a year.

Additional sources of information

National Secretaries Association
2440 Pershing Road, Suite G10
Kansas City, MO 64108

Association of Independent Colleges and Schools
1730 M Street, NW
Washington, DC 20036

National Shorthand Reporters Association
2361 South Jefferson Davis Highway
Arlington, VA 22202

SECURITIES SALES WORKER (STOCKBROKER)

The job

When investors buy or sell stocks, bonds, or shares in mutual funds, they use the services of securities sales workers. These workers are also called registered representatives, account executives, or customers' brokers.

The securities sales worker relays the customer's "buy" or "sell" orders to the floor of the appropriate securities exchange or to the firm's trading department and notifies the customer of the completed transaction and final price. They also provide related services such as financial counseling, the latest stock and bond quotations, and information on financial positions of corporations whose securities are being traded.

Securities sales workers can help a client accumulate a financial portfolio of securities, life insurance, and other investments geared either to long-term goals such as capital growth or income or to short-term goals. Some sales workers specialize in one type of customer such as institutional investors or in certain types of securities such as mutual funds.

Beginners in this field spend much of their time searching for new customers. As they establish a clientele, they spend more time servicing their existing customers and less in seeking new ones.

Securities sales workers are employed by brokerage firms, investment banks, and mutual fund firms. Most work for a few large firms that have offices in cities throughout the country.

Women hold about 12 percent of all securities sales jobs and about 7 percent of the management jobs in this field. Women have yet to achieve top-level positions in the largest firms.

Places of employment and working conditions

Securities sales workers are employed in cities throughout the United States, usually in the branch offices of a few large firms.

Sales workers usually work in bustling, sometimes noisy offices. Beginners usually put in long hours until they acquire a clientele, and sales workers occasionally meet with clients on evenings or weekends.

Many sales workers leave the field each year because they are unable to establish a large enough clientele.

Qualifications, education, and training

Selling skills and ambition are necessary for success as a securities sales worker. A sales worker should also be mature, well groomed, and able to motivate people. Many employers prefer to hire applicants who have had previous experience in sales or management positions.

A college education is preferred by the larger firms. A liberal arts background with training in economics, prelaw, business administration, or finance is particularly helpful.

Most employers provide training to new sales workers to help them meet state licensing and registration requirements. In firms that are members of major exchanges, the training program lasts at least four months. In small firms and mutual funds and insurance companies, training is shorter and less formal.

Almost all states require securities sales workers to be licensed. Licensing requirements usually include a written examination and the furnishing of a personal bond. Those who intend to sell insurance in addition to securities must be licensed for that also.

Sales workers must be registered as representatives of the firm for which they work. To qualify, they must pass the Securities and Exchange Commission's General Securities Examination or examinations prepared by the exchanges or the National Association of Securities Dealers, Inc. (NASD). Character investigations are also required.

Potential and advancement

There are about 90,000 full-time securities sales workers and an additional 100,000 who sell part time. The demand for securities sales workers fluctuates with the ups and downs of the economy, but, over the long run, job opportunities should be favorable. Well-rounded, mature people with successfull work experience in sales or management will be most in demand.

Income

Securities sales workers earn commissions on the transactions they handle for clients.

Beginners are usually paid a salary until they complete their training and achieve licensing and registration. Salaries range from about $900 to $1,200 a month or slightly higher in large securities firms.

Earnings of full-time experienced sales workers servicing individual investors average about $29,000 a year. Those servicing institutional investors average about $57,000.

Additional sources of information

New York Stock Exchange
11 Wall Street
New York, NY 10005

Securities Industry Association
20 Broad Street
New York, NY 10005

SINGER

The job

Professional singers are employed in every field of music. For every singing star of popular, classical, country and western, and musical comedy music, there are many more who work in choruses; who teach in churches, schools, and music conservatories; and who are employed by commercial advertising firms.

Employment opportunities exist in radio, movies, and television; on the concert stage, in opera and musical comedy productions; in nightclubs; in elementary and secondary schools; and in colleges and universities. Many opportunities exist for part-time work in churches.

Anyone considering this field should be aware that few singers are able to secure full-time employment except in teaching. The time necessary for rehearsing and performing leaves little time for other part-time work, and many singers are unable to support themselves with singing alone.

Professional singers usually belong to some branch of the Associated Actors and Artists of America.

Places of employment and working conditions

The most job opportunities for performers are in New York City, Los Angeles, Las Vegas, San Francisco, Dallas, and Chicago. Nashville, Tennessee, is one of the major centers of the recording industry and offers many opportunities for musicians of all types.

Singers engaged in a performing career work evenings and weekends and must usually travel a great deal. The work is not steady, and many careers are short because of changes in public taste.

Qualifications, education, and training

In addition to a good voice, a singer needs poise, physical stamina, an attractive appearance and stage presence, perseverance, and determination.

Those persons who wish to pursue a singing career should acquire a broad background in music including piano lessons (for music theory and composition) and dancing lessons, because singers are sometimes required to dance as well. Voice training should not begin until physical maturity is achieved, although young boys sometimes receive some training for church choirs before their voices change.

Singers who intend to perform classical music can take private voice lessons, enroll in a a music conservatory, or enroll in the music department of a college or university. Those who attend a conservatory or a college also receive training in such music-related subjects as foreign languages, dramatics, history, and literature. In four-year programs, the student receives a bachelor of arts or science (in music), a bachelor of music, or a bachelor of fine arts degree.

Singers who plan to teach music must also meet state teaching certification requirements, and those who expect to teach at the college level usually need a master's degree or a Ph.D.

In the field of popular music, voice training is an asset but is not always necessary. Many singers in this field start singing with groups or in amateur contests and go on to employment with better-known bands or groups as they gain experience and popularity.

Potential and advancement

There are about 23,000 people working as professional singers and singing teachers. This is a field where there will always be many more qualified applicants than there are job openings. Except for a handful of top stars in opera and popular music, the only full-time steady employment for singers will continue to be in teaching positions.

Income

Singing teachers are paid on the same scale as other faculty members in the institution in which they teach.

As part of a chorus, concert singers have a minimum daily rate of $35, or $45 to $50 a performance; in an opera chorus, the minimum daily rate is $40 or $45 per performance. Soloists receive at least $200 a performance.

In television, the minimum rate is between $165 and $175 for a one-hour show.

Additional sources of information

National Association of Schools of Music
11250 Roger Bacon Drive
Reston, VA 22090

Music Educators National Conference
1902 Association Drive
Reston, VA 22091

American Guild of Music Artists (concert stage and opera singers)
1841 Broadway
New York, NY 10023

American Federation of Television and Radio Artists (radio,
 television, and recording singers)
1350 Avenue of the Americas
New York, NY 10019

American Guild of Variety Artists (variety and nightclub singers)
1540 Broadway
New York, NY 10036

Actor's Equity Association (musical comedy and operetta singers)
1500 Broadway
New York, NY 10036

Screen Actors Guild
7750 Sunset Blvd.
Hollywood, CA 90046

SOCIAL WORKER

The job

Social workers strive to help individuals, families, groups, and communities to solve their problems. They also work to increase and improve the community resources available to people.

Depending on the nature of the problem and the time and resources available for solving it, social workers may choose one of three approaches or a combination of them— casework, group work, or community organization.

In casework, social workers interview individuals or families to identify problems. They help people understand and solve their problems by securing appropriate social resources such as financial aid, education, job training, or medical assistance.

In group work, social workers work with people in groups, helping them to understand one another. They plan and conduct activities for children, teenagers, adult, older persons, and other groups in community centers, hospitals, and nursing homes.

In community organization, social workers coordinate the work of political, civic, religious, and business group working to combat social problems. They help plan and develop health, housing, welfare, and recreation services.

About two thirds of all social workers provide direct social services and work for the public and voluntary agencies such as state and local departments of public assistance and community welfare and religious organizations. Others work for schools, hospitals, business, and industry. Some social workers are in private practice and provide counseling services on a fee basis.

About 61 percent of all social workers are women. In spite of this fact, the administrative jobs are usually held by men.

A related job is: Rehabilitation Counselor.

Places of employment and working conditions

Social workers are employed throughout the United States, usually in urban areas.

Most social workers have 5-day, 35- to 40-hour workweek. Evening and weekend work is sometimes necessary.

Qualifications, education, and training

A social worker must be sensitive, have concern for the needs of others, be objective and emotionally stable, and be willing to handle responsibility.

A college preparatory course in high school should provide as broad a background as possible. Volunteer work or a part-time or summer job in a community center, camp, or social welfare agency are good experience.

A bachelor's degree in social work (B.S.W.) or a major in sociology or psychology can prepare the student for some positions in this field, but the usual requirement is a master's degree in social work (M.S.W.). Those with only a bachelor's degree have limited promotion opportunities.

Applicants for graduate programs in social work will face competition for places in available programs. The M.S.W. degree is awarded after two years of specialized study and supervised field instruction. A graduate degree plus experience are necessary for supervisory and administrative positions; research work also requires training in social science research methods.

A Ph.D. is usually required for teaching and for top administrative positions.

The National Association of Social Workers grants certifications and the title A.C.S.W. (Academy of Certified Social Workers) to members who have a master's degree, have at least two years of job experience, and pass an A.C.S.W. examination.

Twenty states require the licensing or registration of social workers. Requirements usually include specified experience plus an examination. Social workers employed by federal, state, and local government agencies are usually required to pass a civil service test before appointment to a position.

Potential and advancement

There are about 330,000 social workers, many of them employed on a part-time basis. Job opportunities should continue to be good. An increasing number of degrees are being awarded in this field, however, and competition for the choice jobs may develop in some urban areas within the next few years. Job opportunities will continue to be plentiful in rural areas and small towns.

Advancement in this field depends on experience and advanced education.

Income

Beginning social workers with a bachelor's degree earn about $10,300 a year. Positions requiring a master's degree start at about $13,300. Experienced social workers average around $17,000.

Additional sources of information

National Association of Social Workers
1425 H Street, NW
Washington, DC 20005

Social Work Vocational Bureau
386 Park Avenue
New York, NY 10016

Council on Social Work Education
345 East 46th Street
New York, NY 10017

SOCIOLOGIST

The job

Sociologists study human social behavior by examining the groups that human beings form—families, tribes, and governments and social, religious, and political organizations. Some sociologists study the characteristics of social groups and institutions; others study the way individuals are affected by the groups to which they belong.

Most sociologists are college and university teachers. Others are engaged in research and writing. Those doing research collect information, prepare case studies, and conduct surveys and laboratory experiments. Many research sociologists may apply statistical and computer techniques in their research.

The federal government employs sociologists in the Departments of Health, Education, and Welfare; Defense; Agriculture; Interior; Commerce; Transportation; Housing and Urban Development; and the Veterans Administration and the Environmental Protection Agency.

Others work in private industry, social work, and public health.

There are very few women working as sociologists at the present but the trend is for more and more women to enter the field.

Places of employment and working conditions

Sociologists work throughout the country but are heavily concentrated in areas with large colleges and universities.

Qualifications, education and training

Study and research skills are necessary as well as communication skills.

In high school, a college preparatory course with a strong academic program is the best background.

A master's degree with a major in sociology is usually the minimum requirement in this field. A Ph.D. is required for professorship and tenure, for directors of major research projects, and for important administrative positions.

Those with only a bachelor's degree in sociology will be limited to jobs as interviewers, research or administrative assistants, or recreation workers. Some may secure social worker or counselor positions or teach in secondary schools.

Potential and advancement

There are about 19,000 sociologists. Job competition will be very stiff as thousands of Ph.D.'s with degrees in sociology are expected to compete for the limited number of job openings in the 1980s. Most job openings will occur to replace those who retire or leave the field.

Advancement in this field depends on experience.

Income

Beginning sociologists earn from $10,500 to $13,014 a year with a bachelor's degree; about $13,000 to $15,920 with a master's degree; and $19,263 with a Ph.D.

The average salary for all sociologists working for the federal government is about $25,000.

Additional sources of information

American Sociological Association
1722 N Street, NW
Washington, DC 20036

SOIL CONSERVATIONIST

The job

Soil conservationists provide technical advice to farmers, ranchers and others on soil and water conservation as well as land erosion.

Most soil conservationists are employed by the federal government in the Department of Agriculture's Soil Conservation Service or in the Department of Interior's Bureau of Indian Affairs. They act as advisors for Soil and Water Conservation Districts throughout the United States; or work in or near Indian Reservations, which are located mainly in the western states.

Other soil conservationists work for state and local governments, public utilities, lumber and paper companies with large holdings of forested lands, and lending institutions in rural areas.

Related jobs are Soil Scientist, Range Manager, Farmer.

Places of employment and working conditions

Soil conservationists work throughout the United States.

Most of their work is done outdoors.

Qualifications, education, and training

A soil conservationist should have good communication skills, an analytical mind, and a liking for outdoor work.

High school courses should include chemistry and biology.

Soil conservationists usually have a bachelor's degree with a major in soil conservation, agronomy (interaction of plants and soils), or related fields of natural resource sciences such as wildlife biology or forestry. Courses in agricultural engineering and cartography (mapmaking) are also helpful.

An advanced degree is usually necessary for college teaching and research positions.

Potential and advancement

There are about 7,500 soil conservationists. Although there will be steady growth of job opportunities in this field, the relatively small size of the field will mean competition for available openings.

Advancement is limited. Conservationists working at the county level can move up to state positions.

Income

Starting salaries with the federal government are $10,507 with a bachelor's degree; $13,014 with a master's degree. Experienced soil conservationists earn $19,263 to $32,442.

Additional sources of information

U.S. Civil Service Commission
Washington, DC 20415

Soil Conservation Service
Department of Agriculture
Washington, DC 20250

American Society of Agronomy
677 South Segoe Road
Madison, WI 53711

SOIL SCIENTIST

The job

Soil scientists study the physical, chemical, biological, and behavioral characteristics of soils. Their work is important to farmers, builders, fertilizer manufacturers, real estate appraisers, and lending institutions.

A large part of soil science has to do with categorizing soils according to a national classification system. Once the soils in an area have been classified, the soil scientist prepares a map that shows soil types throughout the area.

A builder who wants to erect a factory or an apartment building will consult a "soil-type" map to locate a spot with a secure base of firm soils. Farmers also consult soft-type maps. Some communities require a certified soil scientist to examine the soil and test the drainage capabilities of any building lot that will be used with a septic system.

Some soil scientists conduct research into the chemical and biological properties of soil to determine what crops grow best in which soils. They also test fertilizers and soils to determine ways to improve less productive soils. Soil scientists are also involved in pollution control programs and soil erosion prevention programs.

More than half of all soil scientists are employed by the Soil Conservation Service of the U.S. Department of Agriculture. Others are employed by the state agricultural experiment stations and agricultural colleges. Private institutions and industries that employ soil scientists include fertilizer companies, land appraisal firms, farm management agencies, and lending institutions such as banks and insurance companies.

Related jobs are: Soil Conservationist, Farmer, Range Manager.

Places of employment and working conditions

Soil scientists work in every state and in most counties of the United States.

They spend much of their time doing fieldwork in a particular area—usually a county. During bad weather they work indoors preparing maps and writing reports. Soil scientists involved in research usually work in greenhouses or small farm fields.

Qualifications, education, and training

An interest in science and agriculture is necessary as well as a liking for outdoor work. Writing skills are also important.

High school courses should include chemistry and biology.

A bachelor's degree with a major in soil science or a closely related field such as agriculture or agronomy (interaction of plants and soils) is necessary. Courses in chemistry and cartography (mapmaking) are also important.

An advanced degree is necessary for many of the better-paying research positions.

Some states require certification of soil scientists who inspect soil conditions prior to building or highway construction. Certification usually entails a written examination plus specified combinations of education and experience.

Potential and advancement

There are about 2,500 soil scientists. Job openings in this rather small field usually occur to replace those who leave the field or retire, although some limited growth will probably occur.

Soil scientists who have been trained in both fieldwork and laboratory research will have the best opportunities for advancement, especially if they have an advanced degree.

Income

Soil scientists with the federal government start at $10,507 with a bachelor's degree; $13,014 with a master's degree. Experienced soil scientists earn $19,263 to $32,442 a year.

Additional sources of information

U.S. Civil Service Commission
Washington, DC 20415

Soil Conservation Service
U.S. Department of Agriculture
Washington, DC 20205

American Society of Agronomy
677 South Segoe Road
Madison, WI 53711

SPEECH PATHOLOGIST AND AUDIOLOGIST

The job

Speech pathologists and audiologists evaluate speech and hearing disorders and provide treatment. Speech pathologists work with children and adults who have speech, language, and voice disorders because of hearing loss, brain injury, cleft palate, mental retardation, emotional problems, or foreign dialect. Audiologists assess and treat hearing problems. Speech and audiology are so interrelated that expertise in one field requires thorough knowledge of both.

Over half of all speech pathologists and audiologists work in public schools; colleges and universities employ large numbers in teaching and research. The remainder work in hospitals, clinics, government agencies, industry, and in private practice.

About three fourths of those who work in this field are women.

Places of employment and working conditions

Speech pathologists and audiologists are employed throughout the country with most of them located in urban areas.

People in this field often work more than 40 hours a week.

Qualifications, education, and training

Patience is an extremely important personal characteristic for anyone who wants to work in this field, since progress is usually very slow. The therapist must also be able to encourage and motivate the clients who are often frustrated by the inability to speak properly. Objectivity and the ability to take responsibility and work with detail are also necessary.

High school should include a strong science background.

A bachelor's degree with a major in speech and hearing or in a related field such as education or psychology is the usual preparation for graduate work.

Most jobs in this field require a master's degree, and some states also require teaching certification to work in the public schools. Graduate study includes supervised clinical training as well as advanced study.

There are many scholarships, fellowships, and teaching and training grants available in this field. The U.S. Department of Health, Education, and Welfare as well as many private organizations and foundations provide financial assistance to students and schools.

The American Speech and Hearing Association (ASHA) confers a Certificate of Clinical Competence (CCC) on those who have a master's degree or the equivalent, who complete a one-year internship, and who pass a written examination. Certification is usually necessary to advance professionally.

In 29 states, speech pathologists and audiologists must be licensed if they provide services outside of the schools. Information on licensing requirements is available from the state Department of Education.

Potential and advancement

There are over 38,000 speech pathologists and audiologists. The field is expected to grow as a result of population growth, the trend toward earlier recognition and treatment of hearing and language problems in children, recent laws requiring services for the handicapped, and the expanded coverage of Medicare and Medicaid programs. Any decreases in government-funded programs could change this employment picture.

If present trends continue, the increasing number of degrees being awarded in this field may cause some job competition in large metropolitan areas. Job opportunities will continue to be good in smaller cities and towns.

Those with only a bachelor's degree will find very limited job opportunities; advancement will be possible only for those with graduate degrees.

Income

Salaries for experienced speech pathologists and audiologists average about $24,300 with the federal government. Starting salaries about about $15,900 with a master's degree and $19,300 with a Ph.D.

Outside of government, salaries are higher in large metropolitan areas.

Additional sources of information

American Speech and Hearing Association
9030 Old Georgetown Road
Washington, DC 20014

SPORTS OFFICIAL

The job

All sports have rules and regulations, and *officials* are necessary to enforce the rules and make decisions on disputed matters.

Officials for professional sports are scouted and offered contracts in the same manner as players. Major league administrators check out officials in amateur, semi-pro, and minor professional leagues and offer promising persons a chance to work pre-season games. Successful officials are offered season contracts.

Many officials are former players or coaches and, as such, have a thorough knowledge of whatever sport they referee. Most officials are employed only part-time except for a few in the top professional leagues.

In baseball, major league games require four umpires with six used in a World Series game. In football, referees, field judges, back judges, and linesmen are needed. Basketball games usually have two referees, two scorers, and two timekeepers.

Hockey requires the most officials in each game—eight: a referee, two linesmen, two goal judges, game timekeeper, penalty timekeeper and the official scorekeeper. Each has specific areas of responsibility.

Places of employment and working conditions

Officials in major professional leagues usually travel just as much as the players and spend just as much time away from home. Officials in amateur and semi-pro leagues work many evenings and weekends during the season, even though they work close to home.

Qualifications, education, and training

In addition to complete knowledge of a sport and its rules, officials need poise, good judgment, physical stamina, integrity, assertiveness, and the ability to make decisions.

Many officials acquire experience during their college years by officiating at college games. Even experience officiating in such nonprofessional sports as swimming and track and field provides valuable training and experience in the basic qualities needed by all sports officials.

A few schools exist for the training of sports officials, mostly baseball umpires.

Potential and advancement

Jobs for sports officials are extremely limited, especially at the top. As an example, there are only 40 umpires in each of the two major baseball leagues. Opportunities for officiating in amateur, semi-pro, and minor leagues are only slightly more numerous.

Advancement is achieved by being hired by a bigger league. Once the major league level is reached, there is no further advancement.

Income

Many officials work for the simple enjoyment of the game, especially at the amateur level. In hockey, officials earn as much as $30,000 during the regular season's major league professional games as well as during the Stanley Cup playoffs.

In baseball, the umpires in the minor leagues earn $900 to $1,400 a month during the playing season. In the major leagues, the umpires are well paid, earning up to $70,000 in addition to per diem salary, travel allowances, and bonuses for championship and World Series games.

Basketball officials are not paid by the game but they receive travel allowances in the major leagues. They usually officiate at two or three games a week, and top officials earn up to $40,000 in a season.

Football officials in the major leagues receive $300 to $800 a game; $1,000 to $3,000 for a Super Bowl game.

Additional sources of information

National Association of Leagues, Umpires and Scorers
Box 1420
Wichita, KS 67201

American Football Coaches Association
Box 8705
Durham, NC 27707

International Association of Approved Basketball Officials
1620 Dual Highway East
Hagerstown, MD 21740

STATISTICIAN

The job

Statisticians gather and interpret numerical data and apply their knowledge of statistical methods to a particular subject area such as economics, human behavior, natural science, or engineering. They may predict population growth, develop quality-control tests for manufactured products, or help business managers and government officials make decisions and evaluate programs.

Statisticians often obtain information about a group of people or things by surveying a portion of the whole. They decide where to gather the data, determine the size and type of the sample group, and develop the survey questionnaire or reporting form. Statisticians who design experiments prepare mathematical models to test a particular theory. Those in analytical work interpret collected data and prepare tables, charts, and written reports on their findings. Mathematical statisticians use mathematical theory to design and improve statistical methods.

Most statisticians are employed in private industry: in manufacturing, public utilities, finance, and insurance companies. The federal government employs about one eighth of all statisticians, primarily in the Departments of Commerce; Education; Health and Human Services; Agriculture; and Defense. The remaining statisticians are employed by state and local government and colleges and universities.

About one third of all statisticians are women.

Related jobs are: Mathematician, Economist.

Places of employment and working conditions

Statisticians work in all parts of the country; most are in metropolitan areas, especially New York City, Washington, D.C., and the Los Angeles–Long Beach, California areas.

Qualifications, education, and training

Statisticians must have good reasoning ability, persistence, and the ability to apply basic principles to new types of problems.

High school courses in mathematics are important.

A bachelor's degree with a major in statistics or mathematics is the minimum requirement for this field. A bachelor's degree with a major in a related field such as economics or natural science with a minor in statistics is preferred for some jobs.

Teaching positions and many jobs require graduate work in mathematics or statistics, and courses in computer use and techniques are becoming increasingly important. Economics and business administration courses are also helpful.

Potential and advancement

There are about 24,000 statisticians, and the field is expected to grow substantially. Those who combine training in statistics with knowledge of a field of application will have the best job opportunities.

Opportunities for promotion in this field are best for those with advanced degrees. Experienced statisticians may advance to positions of greater technical responsibility and to supervisory positions.

Income

Statisticians have average annual salaries of about $26,000. Those employed by colleges and universities receive salaries comparable to other faculty members and often earn extra income from outside consulting, research, and writing.

Additional sources of information

American Statistical Association
806 15th Street, NW
Washington, DC 20005

Interagency Board of U.S. Civil Service Examiners for
  Washington, D.C.
1900 E Street, NW
Washington, DC 20414

Institute of Mathematical Statistics
1367 Laurel Street
San Carlos, CA 94070

STUDENT PERSONNEL WORKER

The job

The job of the student personnel worker is to develop and administer programs and services that fulfill the housing, social, cultural, recreational, and personal needs of students on the campuses of colleges and universities. At a major university, a large staff performs these functions; at a small two-year college, one person may be responsible for all student personnel services. The services are organized in a wide variety of ways under titles that may include some or all of the following jobs.

The *dean of students* may be a college vice president. The duties include advising the president on the changing needs of students, formulating new programs and policies for dealing with problems on the campus, dealing with student participation in decision making, and outlining course offerings. This job can involve the supervision of a large staff.

Admissions officers oversee the process of admitting new students. They process applications, travel as representatives of the college to recruit new students, and help in setting standards for admission. They work closely with financial aid officers and are sometimes connected with the registrar's office, where a *registrar* maintains the academic records of past and present students.

Financial aid officers must keep abreast of all sources of financial aid—grants, loans, scholarships, jobs, and teaching research fellowships. Working closely with the counseling and financial offices, these officers must determine who is eligible for aid and devise aid packages with the available funds.

Career planning and placement counselors assist students in making career decisions, work with representatives of employers who visit the campus for job recruiting, and assist students with the mechanics of job placement such as writing résumés and handling interviews.

Student activities personnel assist student-run organizations and handle the orientation of new students. *College union personnel* may be a separate staff dealing with the food service, maintenance, and finances of student-run facilities.

Student housing officers may live in dormitories and deal with personal counseling as well as dormitory management.

General counselors, usually psychologists, help students with personal problems and handle crisis situations. Some larger colleges also employ special *foreign student counselors.*

About one third of all college administration personnel are women.

Places of employment and working conditions

Work on college campuses usually involves a wide variety of settings. Workers may be found in offices where they counsel students or in larger facilities directing many workers. Employment is usually on a 12-month basis rather than an academic year. Work hours, usually more than 40 a week, tend to be irregular.

Qualifications, education, and training

Student personnel workers must be able to work well with a wide variety of people. They should have the emotional stability and patience to deal with sharply conflicting points of view and with unexpected and emergency situations.

Backgrounds vary widely in this field, but a college degree in one of the social sciences is good preparation. The potential student personnel worker should then take a master's degree in some area of student personnel work. For example, psychology provides a foundation for counseling and career planning and placement positions; data processing is an asset in admissions, records, and financial aid work; and a specialty in recreation would be helpful in student activities work.

A master's degree in clinical or counseling psychology is usually required for those engaged in counseling. A Ph.D. is necessary for the top student personnel positions and for most such positions at large universities.

Potential and advancement

About 57,000 people are presently employed in this field in virtually every college and university in the country. Job prospects are expected to be quite limited in the coming decade because budgets are being tightened in both public and private institutions. The increase in the number of two-year colleges should, however, result in a certain number of new positions in that academic area.

Advancement in the student personnel field is usually through increased experience and education but is limited for those without a master's degree. Entry-level positions available to those with a master's degree include residence hall director, financial aid counselor, admissions counselor, and assistant to a dean.

Income

Salaries vary greatly in this field depending on the size and location of the institution. Top administrators average from $28,000 to $46,000 annually in very large institutions. In small colleges and two-year institutions, salaries for starting workers may be very low.

In many schools, student personnel workers are entitled to insurance, sabbatical leaves, and other benefits on the same basis as the faculty.

Additional sources of information

The American Personnel and Guidance Association
1607 New Hampshire Avenue, NW
Washington, DC 20009

SURVEYOR

The job

Surveyors measure construction sites, establish official land boundaries, assist in setting land valuations, and collect information for maps and charts.

Most surveyors serve as leaders of surveying teams: they are in charge of the field party and responsible for the accuracy of its work. They record the information disclosed by the survey, verify the accuracy of the survey data, and prepare the sketches, maps, and reports.

A typical field party consists of the *Party Chief* and three to six assistants and helpers. *Instrument workers* adjust and operate surveying instruments and compile notes, sketches, and records of the data obtained from the instruments. *Chain workers* use steel tape or surveyor's chain to measure distances between surveying points; they usually work in pairs and may mark measured points with pointed stakes. *Rod workers* use a level rod, range pole, or other equipment to assist instrument workers in determining elevations, distances, and directions. They hold and move the range pole according to hand or voice signals from the instrument worker and remove underbrush from the survey line.

Surveyors often specialize in highway surveys; land surveys to establish boundaries (these also require the preparation of maps and legal descriptions for deeds and leases); or topographic surveys to determine elevations, depressions, and contours and the location of roads, rivers, and buildings. Other specialties are mining, pipeline, gravity, and magnetic surveying.

Photogrammetrists measure and interpret photographs to determine various characteristics of natural or man-made features of an area. They apply analytical processes and mathematical techniques to aerial, space, ground, and underwater photographs to prepare detailed maps of areas that are inaccessible or difficult to survey. Control surveys on the ground are then made to determine the accuracy of the maps derived from photogrammatic techniques.

Federal, state, and local government agencies employ about 30 percent of all surveyors. Those who work for state and local governments usually work for highway departments and urban planning and development agencies. Those who work for the federal government are in the U.S. Geological Survey, Bureau of Land Management, Army Corps of Engineers, and the Forest Service.

Many surveyors work for construction companies, engineering and architectural consulting firms, public utilities, and petroleum and natural gas companies. Others own or work for firms that conduct surveys for a fee.

Places of employment and working conditions

Surveyors work throughout the United States.

Surveying is outdoor work with surveyors often walking long distances or climbing hills carrying equipment and instruments. They usually work an eight-hour, five-day week, but may work much longer hours in summer months when conditions are more favorable for surveying.

Qualifications, education, and training

Surveyors should be in good physical condition. They need good eyesight, coordination, and hearing and must have the ability to visualize and understand objects, distances, sizes, and other abstract forms. They also need mathematical ability.

High school courses should include algebra, geometry, trigonometry, drafting, and mechanical drawing.

Surveyors acquire their skills through a combination of on-the-job training and courses in surveying. Technical institutes, vocational schools, and junior colleges offer one-, two-, and three-year programs in surveying. Many four-year colleges offer some surveying courses, and a few offer a bachelor's degree in surveying.

High school graduates without any training usually start as rod workers. If they complete a surveying course and gain experience, they may advance to chain worker, instrument worker, and finally to party chief. Beginners who have some training usually start as instrument workers and work up to party chief as they gain experience.

Photogrammetrists usually need a bachelor's degree in engineering or the physical sciences.

All states require licensing or registration of land surveyors who are responsible for locating and describing land boundaries. Registration requirements are very strict because, once registered, surveyors can be held legally responsible fo their work. Requirements usually include an examination and from three to eight years of surveying experience.

Potential and advancement

There are about 52,000 surveyors, 23,000 of them registered. In addition, 13,500 engineers are also registered to do land surveying. Job opportunities are expected to grow steadily in this field; extended periods of slow construction activity, however, could cause temporary slow periods.

Advancement in this field depends mainly on accumulating experience.

Income

Rod or chain workers with no training or experience start at about $7,422 a year; those with one year of education at $8,366. Instrument workers start at about $9,391.

Experienced surveyors earn from $11,000 to $20,400 a year.

Additional sources of information

American Congress on Surveying and Mapping
210 Little Falls Street
Falls Church, VA 22046

American Society of Photogrammetry
105 North Virginia Avenue
Falls Church, VA 22046

SYSTEMS ANALYST

The job

Systems analysts decide what new data need to be collected, the equipment needed to process the data, and the procedure to be followed in using the information within any given computer system. They use various techniques such as cost accounting, sampling, and mathematical model building to analyze a problem and devise a new system to solve it.

Once a system has been developed, the systems analyst prepares charts and diagrams that describe the system's operation in terms that the manager or customer who will use the system can understand. The analyst may also prepare a cost-benefit analysis of the newly developed system. If the system is accepted, the systems analyst then translates the logical requirements of the system into the capabilities of the particular computer machinery (hardware) in use and prepares specifications for programmers to follow. The systems analyst will also work with the programmers to "debug" (eliminate errors from) a new system.

Because the work is complex and varied, systems analysts specialize in either business or scientific and engineering applications. Some analysts improve systems already in use or adapt existing systems to handle additional types of data. Those involved in research, called *advanced systems designers,* devise new methods of analysis.

Most systems are employed by banks, insurance companies, large manufacturing firms, and data processing services. Others work for wholesale and retail businesses and government agencies.

In many industries, all systems analysts begin as computer programmers and are promoted to analyst positions only after gaining experience. In large data processing departments, they may start as junior systems analysts. Many persons enter this occupation after experience in accounting, economics, or business management (for business positions) or engineering (for scientific work).

Fifteen percent of all systems analysts are women, usually promoted from computer programmer positions.

Places of employment and working conditions

Job opportunities for systems analysts are mainly concentrated in the Midwest and the Northeast, although opportunities exist throughout the entire country.

Systems analysts usually work a normal 40-hour week with occasional evening or weekend work.

Qualifications, education, and training

Systems analysts must be able to think logically, to concentrate, and to handle abstract ideas. They must be able to communicate effectively with technical personnel such as programmers as well as with those who have no computer background.

High school should include as many mathematics courses as possible.

Because job requirements vary so greatly, there is no universally accepted way of preparing for a career as a systems analyst. A background in accounting, business administration, or economics is preferred by employers in business. Courses in computer concepts, systems analysis, and data retrieval techniques are good preparation for any systems analyst.

Many employers require a college degree in computer science, information science, or data processing. Scientifically oriented organizations often require graduate work as well in some combination of computer science and a science or engineering specialty.

Because technological advances in the computer field come so rapidly, systems analysts must continue their technical education throughout their careers. This training usually takes the form of one- and two- week courses offered by employers, computer manufacturers, and softwear (computer systems) vendors.

The Institute for Certification of Computer Professionals confers the designation of Certified in Data Processing (CDP) on systems analysts who have five years of experience and who successfully complete an examination.

Potential and advancement

There are about 160,000 systems analysts. This job field is expected to grow steadily because of the expanding use of computers. College graduates who have had courses in computer programming, systems analysis, and data processing will have the best opportunities, while those without a degree may face some competition for the available jobs that don't require a degree.

Systems analysts can advance to jobs as lead systems analysts or managers of systems analysis or data processing departments.

Income

Beginners in this field average about $200 a week in the federal government; $300 a week in private industry.

Experienced systems analysts earn from $370 to $420 a week and lead systems analysts from $450 to $460.

Systems analysts in the North and West usually earn more than those in the South. Data processing services and manufacturing firms pay higher salaries than insurance companies or educational institutions.

Additional sources of information

American Federation of Information Processing Societies
201 Summit Avenue
Montvale, NJ 07645

Association for Systems Management
24587 Bagley Road
Cleveland, OH 44138

The Institute for Certification of Computer Professionals
35 East Wacker Drive, Suite 2828
Chicago, IL 60601

T

TEACHER, COLLEGE AND UNIVERSITY

The job

The function of a teacher at the college or university level is to present in-depth analysis of or training in a particular subject.

Depending on the subject matter and grade level of the students, a teacher may conduct large lecture classes for basic courses, lead advanced seminars for only a few students, or work with students in laboratories. Many teachers at this level carry on research projects and act as consultants to business, industry, and government agencies. They are active in professional societies and write for publications in their field. Those who are *department heads* also have supervisory and administrative duties.

There are four academic ranks on college and university faculties: *instructor, assistant professor, associate professor,* and *full professor.* Beginners usually start as instructors. Education and experience govern advancement to higher rank. Many teachers are assisted by part-time assistant instructors, teaching fellows, teaching assistants, and laboratory assistants. These posts are often filled by graduate students working toward advanced degrees.

Seventy percent of all teachers at this level teach in public colleges and universities. About one fifth teach at two-year colleges.

Women hold about one third of the college and university teaching positions mainly in nursing, home economics, and library science. Less than 10 percent of them are in engineering, physical sciences, law, and agriculture. By the age of 35, 21 percent of male faculty members have achieved the rank of associate professor—as opposed to only 8 percent of female faculty members. Only 12 percent of the women reach full professorship; 31 percent of the men achieve this position.

Places of employment and working conditions

College and university teachers work throughout the United States, but over half of them are employed in California, Illinois, Massachusetts, Michigan, New York, Ohio, Pennsylvania, and Texas.

Undergraduate faculty members in four-year colleges and universities teach between 12 and 15 hours a week; faculty members in graduate programs teach about 10 hours. Additional time spent on preparation and other duties equals a weekly total of about 55 hours a week on school-related activities. In two-year colleges, faculty members spend more time in the classroom but work fewer total hours per week.

Qualifications, education, and training

A master's degree, which qualifies the teacher for instructor rank, is the minimum requirement for college and university teaching positions.

A year of study beyond the master's degree and a year or two of experience as an instructor are usually necessary for assistant professors. Associate professors frequently need a Ph.D. as well as three years or more of college teaching experience.

For a full professorship, a Ph.D. degree, extensive teaching experience at the college and university level, and published articles and books are usually required. Full professors may achieve tenure after a certain number of years, thus being assured of a teaching position for as long as they choose to remain at the school.

Potential and advancement

There are approximately 593,000 college and university teachers. Although demand for teachers at this level is expected to increase in the 1980s, the number of master's and Ph.D. degrees awarded is expected to far exceed the number of job openings. Stiff competition for all college teaching positions will be the norm.

Advancement usually depends on advanced study and college teaching experience. Outstanding academic, administrative, or professional work as well as research and publication in a subject area can hasten advancement.

Income

Salaries range from an average of $9,000 for instructors in two-year colleges to an average of $25,100 for full professors in four-year colleges—usually for a nine- or ten-month academic year.

Other sources of income include writing, speaking engagements, additional teaching and research projects, and consulting work.

At all levels of college and university teaching, women receive lower salaries than men for equal work. On the average, women earn $3,000 a year less than men in comparable positions.

College and university teachers enjoy certain benefits unique to their field such as free tuition for dependents, housing and travel allowances, and paid leaves of absense (sabbatical leave) every six or seven years.

Additional sources of information

Professional societies in the various subject fields will generally provide information on teaching requirements and employment opportunities in their particular field. Other sources of information are:

U.S. Department of Health, Education, and Welfare
Office of Education
Washington, DC 20202

American Council on Education
One Dupont Circle, NW
Washington, DC 20036

American Federation of Teachers
1012 14th Street, NW
Washington, DC 20005

American Association of University Professors
One Dupont Circle, NW
Washington, DC 20036

TEACHER, KINDERGARTEN AND ELEMENTARY SCHOOL

The job

School teachers at the kindergarten and elementary levels introduce children to the basic concepts of mathematics, language, science, and social studies. They aid children in the development of good study and work habits and help them acquire the skills necessary for further education. They evaluate each child and work with parents to provide whatever help a child may need to develop his or her full potential.

Kindergarten and elementary teachers are also concerned with the social development and health of their students. They work to resolve behavior or personality problems and are alert for health problems or illness. In these early school years, teachers try to give students as much individual attention as possible.

Most teachers at this level teach a single grade and cover all subjects including music, art, and physical education. Recent trends, however, are for specialization in one or two subjects; the teacher then teaches these subjects to several classes or grades. Team teaching, with several teachers sharing responsibility for a group of students, is also popular in some areas.

Teachers have duties outside of the classroom as well. They attend faculty meetings, supervise after-school activities such as glee clubs, and supervise lunch and playground activities.

Most kindergarten and elementary teachers work in public school systems; only 13 percent work in private and parochial schools. During summer, many teachers teach in summer school programs or work as camp counselors. Others use the time to secure additional education.

Elementary school teaching is the largest professional field for women; 85 percent of the jobs are held by women. Women with family responsibilities find this an ideal field. Not only do their working hours correspond to their children's school hours, but reentry into this field after a prolonged absence is relatively easy. A teaching career interrupted by a move to another area is also easily resumed as soon as state certification is received—if there are available job openings.

Male interest in this teaching level has been increasing in recent years.

Places of employment and working conditions

Elementary teachers work in every geographic area—in cities and towns of all sizes and in rural areas throughout the United States.

The workweek for elementary teachers is about 36½ hours, but time spent grading papers, preparing lessons, and attending meetings increases the hours to about 46 a week.

At this level, teachers must be active physically. They do a great deal of walking, kneeling, sitting on low stools, chairs, and on the floor. In the lowest grades, they help children with boots and heavy clothing.

Most elementary teachers work a nine-month school year with a three-month summer vacation. Some school districts, however, function year-round; they have eight-week sessions, one week off, and a three-week midwinter break. This type of schedule makes extra employment difficult.

Many states provide for "tenure" after a certain number of years in a position; this assures teachers of a job for as long as they choose to remain with the school system.

Qualifications, education, and training

An enthusiasm for young children is a prime requisite for a kindergarten or elementary school teacher. Dependability, good judgment, creativity, and patience are also necessary.

In high school, a broad college preparatory course should be followed.

A bachelor's degree in an approved teacher education program is required. This includes a liberal arts program, education courses, and student-teaching experience.

All states require public school teachers to be certified by the state department of education; some also require private and parochial teachers to be certified. State requirements vary and may include a health certificate, U.S. citizenship, an oath of allegiance, or supplementary graduate education—usually a master's degree or a fifth year of study.

Some school systems sometimes have additional local requirements.

Potential and advancement

There are about 1.4 million elementary school teachers. Competition for available job openings is keen in many locations because of overproduction of new teachers and the number of people re-entering the field. Re-entrants have the advantage of experience, but new graduates command lower salaries. There will be less competition for teaching positions in inner-city schools and rural areas.

A few teachers advance to supervisory or administrative positions within a school system, but for most elementary teachers advancement takes the form of pay raises or a move to a job in a school district that has a higher pay scale.

Income

Starting salaries range from about $10,000 to $12,000. Experienced elementary teachers average about $14,669 for a nine- or ten-month year.

Additional soures of information

Information on certification requirements for local school systems is available from individual state departments of education. Other sources are:

U.S. Department of Education
400 Maryland Avenue, SW
Washington, DC 20202

American Federation of Teachers
1012 14th Street, NW
Washington, DC 20005

National Education Association
1201 16th Street, NW
Washington, DC 20036

TEACHER, SECONDARY SCHOOL

The job

Teachers at this level, high school, instruct students in specific subject areas such as English, social studies, or mathematics. They usually

409

teach four or five different classes each day and may teach different areas of their specialty to different grades. For example, a mathematics teacher might teach algebra to two ninth-grade classes, geometry to one tenth-grade class, and have two classes of seniors studying trigonometry.

The teacher must prepare lesson plans and examinations for each class and try to meet the needs of individual students. This could mean arranging tutoring for slower students or providing extra work for fast learners. Secondary school teachers also take students on field trips, attend faculty meetings and workshops, and supervise extracurricular activities such as sports, school plays, and student clubs.

Some teachers, called vocational teachers, train junior and senior high school students in specific job skills such as carpentry, auto mechanics, or distributive education (retail, production, and marketing training). They work with the actual tools of the particular trade.

A little over half of all secondary school teachers teach in senior high schools; over 90 percent of all secondary school teachers teach in public school systems.

Women fill over half of the secondary school teaching positions. Most supervisory and administrative positions, however, are held by men.

Places of employment and working conditions

Secondary school teachers work in all parts of the country with job concentrations in the most populated areas.

The average workweek is about 37 hours but meetings, lesson preparation, and grading papers increase the working hours to about 48 per week. Most teachers work a nine-month school year with a three-month summer vacation. In school systems with a year-around schedule, teachers usually work eight weeks and have one week off with a longer midwinter break.

Many states provide "tenure" after a certain number of years in a position; this assures teachers of a job for as long as they choose to remain with the school system.

Qualifications, education, and training

Secondary school teachers should enjoy working with adolescents, be interested in a specific subject area, and have the ability to motivate people.

A broad high school background with preparation for college is necessary. Courses in the student's specific area of interest should be included.

A bachelor's degree from an approved secondary teaching education program, with course work in the specialty area, is the minimum requirement. Some states require a master's degree or a fifth year of education within a certain time period after beginning employment.

All states require certification, and requirements vary. Recommendations from college instructors, a health certificate, or U.S. citizenship may be required in addition to education and student-teaching practice. Local school sytems may have still more requirements.

Teachers who intend to work as nonacademic specialtists such as *guidance counselors, school psychologists,* and *reading specialists* need additional special education as well as separate certification in the specialty.

Potential and advancement

There are over one million secondary school teachers; supply greatly exceeds demand. The overproduction of new secondary teachers plus the number of people re-entering the field means stiff competition for almost all job openings in the 1980s. Certain fields, however, may be less competitive; they include mathematics, natural sciences, and physical sciences. Teachers of vocational subjects will have the best chances for employment.

A few secondary teachers advance to supervisory and administrative positions, but, for most, advancement takes the form of salary increases or transfer to a school system with higher pay scales.

Income

Beginning salaries average $11,000 with a bachelor's degree; $12,500 with a master's degree. Experienced teachers average $15,474 for a nine-or ten-month school year. Salaries are highest in the Northeast and West.

Additional sources of information

Information on certification for local school systems is available from individual state departments of education. Other sources are:

U.S. Department of Education
400 Maryland Avenue, SW
Washington, DC 20202

American Federation of Teachers
1012 14th Street, NW
Washington, DC 20005

National Education Association
1201 16th Street, NW
Washington, DC 20036

TECHNICAL WRITER

The job

Writers who specialize in preparing scientific and technical material are much in demand. Technical writers may write for the professional members of a special field, detailing new developments and the work of others in the same field. On other assignments, the writer may write for those outside the field—the general public, equipment users, company officers, and stockholders.

Technical writers also prepare operating manuals, catalogs, and instructional materials for manufacturers of scientific equipment. This material is used by company salespeople, technicians who install and maintain the equipment, and the persons who operate the equipment. Writing manuals and training aids for miltary equipment and weapons is a highly specialized segment of this field.

Research laboratories employ many technical writers who report on the results of research projects. Others write proposals—requests for money or facilities to do research, conduct a project, or develop a prototype of a new product.

Technical writers also write technical books, articles for popular and trade magazines and newspapers, and prepare advertising copy and press releases.

Technical writers are employed by firms in many industries with the largest numbers working for electronics, aviation, aerospace, weapons, chemical, pharmaceutical, and computer manufacturing industries. The energy, communiciations, and computer softwear fields are employing increasing numbers of technical writers.

The federal government employs many technical writers in the Departments of Interior; Agriculture; Health, Education, and Welfare; and the National Aeronautics and Space Administration (NASA). The largest federal employer of technical writers, however, is the Department of Defense.

Publishing houses employ substantial numbers of technical writers and *technical editors*. These companies publish business and trade publications and professional journals in engineering, medicine, physics, chemistry, and other sciences. Textbook publishers also employ technical writers and editors.

Many technical writers work as free-lancers, sometimes in addition to holding a full-time technical writing job.

Most people do not enter this field directly from college. They usually spend several years or longer working as technicians, scientists, engineers, research assistants, or teachers before turning to technical writing or editing.

Places of employment and working conditions

Technical writers are employed throughout the country with the largest concentrations in the Northeast, Texas, and California.

Working hours are usually about 40 hours a week, but meeting deadlines can mean added hours.

Qualifications, education, and training

In addition to having writing skills and scientific or technical knowledge, a technical writer should be logical, accurate, able to work alone or as part of a team, and have disciplined work habits.

High school courses should develop writing skills and must include science and mathematics.

Technical writers come from a variety of educational backgrounds. Some employers prefer a degree in English, journalism, or technical communications plus course work or experience in a specific scientific or technical subject. Others prefer a degree in an appropriate science or in engineering with a minor in journalism or technical communications.

Only ten colleges and universities offer a bachelor's degree in technical writing; four others offer an associate degree. Six schools offer a master's degree program and one a Ph.D. Many journalism, communications, and language and literature programs, however, include appropriate technical writing courses, some given in close cooperation with scientific and engineering departments of the college.

Many technical writing workshops and seminars, usually intensive one- and two-week courses, are also available at colleges and universities throughout the country.

Potential and advancement

There are about 22,000 technical writers, and the field is expanding. Job opportunities will be best for talented writers with education in a specific scientific or technical field. Opportunities for federal employment have been declining and will probably continue to do so.

Technical writers can move up to technical editor or to supervisory and management positions. Some advance by opening their own firms where they handle technical writing assignments plus industrial publicity and technical advertising.

Income

In general, earnings in this field are higher on the East Coast and in California than in other parts of the country.

Starting salaries average about $10,000 a year, although a degree in engineering, a science, or technical communications can command a starting salary of $19,000 or more.

Experienced technical writers average $20,000; those in supervisory positions earn $25,000 or more.

Federal salaries are slightly lower.

Additional sources of information

Society for Technical Communication, Inc.
Suite 421
1010 Vermont Avenue, NW
Washington, DC 20005

American Medical Writers Association
Suite 290
5272 River Road
Bethesda, MD 20016

TELEVISION AND RADIO SERVICE TECHNICIAN

The job

Skilled television and radio service technicians repair many electronic products in addition to radios and television sets. They repair stereo components, tape recorders, intercom and public address systems, closed-circuit television systems, and some medical electronic equipment.

About two thirds of the technicians in this field work in shops and stores that sell or service radios, television sets, and other electronic products. Some work for major manufacturers and service only the products of that manufacturer. About one quarter of all television and radio service technicians are self-employed.

Related jobs are: Appliance Repairer, Electrician, Computer Service Technician, Communications Technician, Business Machine Service Technician, Broadcasting Technician.

Places of employment and working conditions

Television and radio service technicians employed in local service shops or dealer service departments work between 40 and 48 hours a week.

Qualifications, education, and training

Work in this field requires mechanical ability; manual dexterity and good eye-hand coordination; normal hearing, good eyesight, and color vision; and the ability to work with people.

High school courses should include mathematics and physics. Vocational or technical school courses in electronics or hobbies such as amateur "ham" radio operation are also helpful.

About two years of technical training in electronics plus two to four years of on-the-job experience are usually necessary to become a fully qualified service technician. Training is available from a number of sources including correspondence and technical schools. The armed forces also offer training.

Some employers provide training through four-year apprenticeship programs. The apprentice works under the supervision of a fully qualified technician who is responsible for the apprentice's work. Such programs usually include home study courses or classroom instruction as well.

Many manufacturers, employers, and trade associations conduct training programs to keep service technicians up-to-date on new models or products. Manufacturers also provide service manuals and other technical material.

Some states require licensing of television and radio technicians, which usually entails a written examination.

Potential and advancement

There are about 114,000 service technicians in this field, and substantial growth in demand for technicians is expected as the population increases. This field is not very sensitive to ups and downs in the economy, so employment is usually steady.

Income

Typical earnings range from $4.50 to $8.75 an hour. Self-employed technicians earn considerably more.

Additional sources of information

National Alliance of Television and Electronic Service Associations
5908 S. Troy Street
Chicago, IL 60629

Electronics Industries Association
2001 Eye Street, NW
Washington, DC 20006

TOOL-AND-DIE MAKER

The job

The production of the tools, dies, and special guiding and holding devices used by machining workers to mass produce metal parts is the work of tool-and-die makers.

Toolmakers produce and repair jigs and fixtures (devices that hold metal while it is stamped, shaved, or drilled). They also make gauges and other measuring devices for use on machinery-making precision metal parts.

Diemakers construct and repair metal forms (called dies) for use on machinery that stamps out or forges metal parts. They also make metal molds for diecasting and for molding plastics.

Tool-and-die makers usually receive training in the full range of skills needed to perform either job. They are required to have a broader knowledge of machining operations, mathematics, and blueprint-reading than workers in related fields. They use a variety of hand and machining tools as well as precision measuring instruments.

Most tool-and-die makers work in plants that produce manufacturing, construction, and farm machinery. Others work in automobile, aircraft, and other transportation equipment industries; small tool-and-die shops; and in electrical machinery and fabricated metal industries.

Tool-and-die makers are usually union members with most of them belonging to the International Association of Machinists and Aerospace Workers; or the International Union, United Automobile, Aerospace, and Agricultural Implement Workers of America; or the International Union of Electrical, Radio, and Machine Workers; or the International Brotherhood of Electrical Workers; or the United Steelworkers of America.

A related job is: Machinist.

Places of employment and working conditions

Tool-and-die makers work throughout the United States, but job opportunities are best in large industrialized areas. About one fifth of all tool-and-die makers work in the Detroit/Flint, Chicago, and Los Angeles areas—the leading automobile, machinery, and aircraft manufacturing areas. Other cities with large numbers of tool-and-die makers are Buffalo, Cleveland, Dayton, Newark, and New York.

Working conditions are those of a factory and can be quite noisy. Tool-and-die makers come into direct contact with grease and oil in the course of their work and may be subject to injuries to hands and eyes caused by flying metal particles. These workers are usually required to wear special protective eyeglasses and to avoid loose clothing that could catch on machinery.

Qualifications, education, and training

Anyone interested in tool-and-die making should have mechanical ability, finger dexterity, and an aptitude for precision work.

High school or vocational school courses should include machine shop classes, mathematics, and physics, if possible.

Some tool-and-die makers learn their skills in vocational schools or through on-the-job training, but the best training is usually obtained in a formal four-year apprenticeship program. Some companies have separate apprenticeship programs for toolmaking and diemaking.

An apprenticeship program combines practical shop training in all phases of tool-and-die making with classroom instruction in mathematics, shop theory, mechanical drawing, tool designing, and blueprint reading. After completion of an apprenticeship, several years of additional experience are usually necessary to qualify for the more difficult tool-and-die projects.

Some experienced machinists become tool-and-die makers without completing a formal tool-and-die apprenticeship. After years of experience and some additional classroom training, skilled machinists and machine tool operators can develop the skills necessary to qualify them as tool-and-die makers.

Potential and advancement

There are about 180,000 tool-and-die makers, and job opportunities will increase somewhat into the 1980s. The use of electrical discharge machines and numerically controlled machines that require fewer special tools, jibs, and fixtures will reduce the need for tool-and-die makers in some industries.

Tool-and-die makers can advance to supervisory positions and, because of their broad knowledge, can change jobs within the machining occupations more easily than less-skilled workers. Some become tool designers; others open their own tool-and-die shops.

Income

Tool-and-die makers are among the highest paid in the machining field. Hourly wage rates vary from $7.19 to $10.53 an hour with the highest rates paid on the West Coast.

Apprentices start at about 65 percent of the rate paid to experienced tool-and-die makers and receive periodic raises during training.

Additional sources of information

International Association of Machinists & Aerospace Workers
1300 Connecticut Avenue, NW
Washington, DC 20036

International Union, United Automobile, Aerospace & Agricultural
   Implement Workers of America
Skilled Trades Department
8000 East Jefferson Avenue
Detroit, MI 48214

International Union of Electrical, Radio, & Machine Workers
1126 16th Street, NW
Washington, DC 20036

National Machine Tool Builders Association
7901 Westpark Drive
McLean, VA 22101

National Tool, Die & Precision Machining Association
9300 Livingston Road
Oxon Hill, MD 20022

TRAFFIC MANAGER, INDUSTRIAL

The job

The efficient movement of materials into and finished products out of an industrial firm is the responsibility of an industrial traffic manager.

In the course of their work, traffic managers analyze various transportation possibilities—rail, air, truck, or water—and select the method most suited to the company's needs. They select the carrier and the route; prepare necessary shipping documents; handle claims for lost or damaged shipments; consult company officials about purchasing, producing, and scheduling shipments; and sometimes appear before rate-making and government regulatory agencies to represent their company.

Because many aspects of transportation are subject to federal, state, and local government regulations, industrial traffic managers must be well versed in all such regulations and any other legal matters that affect the shipping operations of their company. They must also be informed about advances in transportation technology and the present and future prices and availability of fuels necessary for the company's transportation requirements. Traffic managers often make decisions on or advise top management about the advisability of purchasing versus contracting for railcars or trucking fleets.

Most traffic managers work for maufacturing firms. A substantial number are employed by wholesalers, large retail stores, and chain stores.

Places of employment and working conditions

Industrial traffic managers usually have standard working hours but may put in some extra time on paper work, meetings, or travel to hearings before state and federal regulatory bodies.

Qualifications, education, and training

The ability to work independently, to analyze technical and numerical data, and to present facts and figures in a logical and convincing manner are all necessary for a traffic manager.

The high school curriculum should include mathematics courses.

Although some traffic managers arrive at their positions through experience only, college training is becoming more and more important in this field. Traffic managers who argue cases before the Interstate Commerce Commission, for instance, must have at least two years of college education.

Some employers prefer to hire graduates of trade or technical schools or two-year college programs in traffic management. Other employers require a college degree with a major or course work in transportation, logistics, physical distribution, business administration, economics, statistics, marketing, computer science, or commercial law.

Potential and advancement

About 21,000 people work as industrial traffic managers. This relatively small field is expected to have steady growth into the mid-1980s with first consideration for job openings going to college graduates with a major in traffic management or transportation.

Industrial traffic workers can advance to supervisory positions and to assistant traffic manager and traffic manager positions. Experienced industrial traffic managers very often advance by moving to a larger company where job responsibilities are more complex.

Income

Beginners in traffic management start at about $13,000 a year.

Salaries of experienced industrial traffic managers vary widely depending on the size of the company. Top traffic executives in large companies earn up to $50,000 a year, sometimes more.

Additional sources of information

American Society of Traffic and Transportation, Inc.
545 West Jackson Blvd.
Chicago, IL 60606

Directory of Transportation Education
U.S. Department of Transportation
Washington, DC 20590

Directory of Transportation Education in U.S. Colleges
    and Universities
American Trucking Associations, Inc.
1616 P Street, NW
Washington, DC 20036

National Association of Trade and Technical Schools
2021 L Street, NW
Washington, DC 20036

TRANSLATOR

The job

Translators render the written material of one language into written material in another language. Their work differs from that of interpreters who provide *oral* translation.

Most translators work on a free-lance basis. Those employed full-time usually work for literary or technical publishers, banks, or large industrial firms with foreign subsidiaries and customers.

The largest single employer of translators is the U.S. Government Agencies such as the Joint Publications Research Service have in-house translation staffs, while other government agencies contract their translating requirements to commercial translating agencies, which in turn employ free-lancers.

A related job is: Interpreter

Places of employment and working conditions

Translators who work for private companies and banks are found in large metropolitan areas such as Chicago and San Francisco. The largest concentrations, however, are in the New York and Washington, D.C. areas where government and publishing industry requirements provide the most job opportunities.

Working conditions vary from an office setting to the free-lancer's own home. Occasionally, a rush assignment may mean long or irregular working hours, but in-house translators usually work a 37- to 40-hour week. Free-lance translators can set their own schedules. Many work only part-time—some through choice, but many because they cannot secure enough free-lance work to provide a steady income.

Qualifications, education, and training

Translators need a working knowledge of one or more foreign languages. A translator's own foreign background, time spent living abroad, or intensive study of a language at the college or university level provide sufficient preparation for many translating jobs.

In the United States, two schools offer special programs for translators. Foreign language proficiency is an entrance requirement for both. Georgetown University School of Language and Linguistics requires an entrance examination and previous study at the university level. Successful applicants usually hold a bachelor's degree and often a master's degree. A certificate of proficiency is awarded after completion of a one- to two-year course.

The Department of Translation and Interpretation at the Monterey Institute of Foreign Studies offers a two-year graduate program leading to a master's degree in Intercultural Communication and a graduate certificate in either translation or translation/interpretation.

Potential and advancement

The American Translators Association estimates there are between 15,000 and 23,000 translators in the United States. Exact numbers are difficult because those employed full-time, as well as those handling only an occasional assignment in conjunction with other work, are all classed as translators. Job opportunities in this field are limited, since any full-time in-house positions are usually filled from the existing pool of free-lancers.

Advancement in this field usually takes the form of better translating assignments because of experience and reputation. Some translators form their own commercial translating agencies and secure contract work for themselves and their in-house or free-lance staff.

421

Income

Earnings for free-lancers vary so greatly that reliable figures are just about impossible to estimate.

In-house translators earn in the $15,000 to $20,000 range depending on ability and experience. Owners of commercial translating agencies often have high annual earnings but work very hard to secure the contracts necessary to make their agencies function profitably.

Additional sources of information

American Translators Association
Attention: Alison Bertsche
P.O. Box 129
Croton-on-Hudson, NY 10520

American Literary Translators Association
P.O. Box 7939
Austin, TX 78712

Division of Interpretation and Translation
School of Languages and Linguistics
Georgetown University
Washington, DC 20057

Department of Translation and Interpretation
Monterey Institute of Foreign Studies
P.O. Box 1978
Monterey, CA 93940

TRAVEL AGENT

The job

Travel agents are specialists who make the best possible travel arrangments to fit the requirements and budgets of individuals or groups traveling anywhere in the world. A travel agent can provide a client with plane tickets and a hotel reservation or can plan a trip down to the last detail—guided tours, rental car, passports and visas, currency exchange rates.

Many services of a travel agency are provided free of charge to the customer with a service fee charged only for complicated travel and lodging arrangements.

Although personal travel experience is part of a successful agent's background, travel agents do not spend most of their time traveling and vacationing. They are usually found behind a desk talking to a customer or completing necessary paper work or on the phone making airline, ship, or hotel reservations. Agents also speak to social and special interest groups—often presenting slide or movie presentations of vacation tours—or meet with business executives to plan company-sponsored trips and business travel.

Some large companies whose employees do a great deal of traveling employ experienced travel agents in-house to make all the company's travel arrangements.

Places of employment and working conditions

Travel agents work throughout the country, but most job opportunities are in urban areas.

Qualifications, education, and training

A travel agent is basically a sales representative and, as such, should have patience and a pleasant personality, like to deal with the public, and be willing to work with the hard-to-please customer as well as the timid or inexperienced traveler.

Travel experience is another important qualification for a travel agent. This is an asset when applying for a job in this field but can also be acquired during the years of training. Being able to speak from personal experience, an agent can provide more comprehensive advice to clients.

Part-time or summer jobs as a receptionist or reservation clerk in a travel agency or experience as an airline ticket clerk can provide valuable experience.

Some agencies prefer to hire college graduates and courses in geography, foreign languages, or history are helpful. Accounting and business management are important to those who intend to open their own agencies.

Travel agents usually learn on the job. Home study courses are also available; an advanced course, leading to the designation of Certified Travel Counselor, is offered only to experienced travel agents. The course is offered by the Institute of Certified Travel Agents to foster professionalism in the travel industry. Licensing of travel agents by some states may be required in the near future.

Potential and advancement

There are about 15,000 travel agents working in over 6,000 independent agencies. Even though the travel industry is expected to expand rapidly, competition for job openings will be tight. The number of people seeking jobs in this attractive field far exceeds the number of openings.

Spending on travel is expected to increase significantly through the mid-1980s. Rising incomes and increased leisure time mean more people traveling more often than in the past. More efficient planes and the economics of group tour packages have brought even international travel within the budget of more Americans than ever. In addition, increased business travel, much of it international, and an increasing flow of foreign visitors to the United States will add to the demand for travel agents.

The travel industry, however, is sensitive to fluctuations in the economy. The price and availability of gasoline also have an effect on the travel industry because rapidly rising fuel costs could make a significant difference in the price of travel.

Since individual agencies employ anywhere from one to 40 travel agents, those in larger agencies can be promoted to supervisory or management positions. Some agents advance by opening their own agencies—about one fourth of all travel agents are self-employed.

Income

Salaries of travel agents range from $9,000 to $16,000; standard fringe benefits such as pension plans, insurance, and paid vacations are usually available. Additional benefits in the form of substantially reduced travel rates and an occasional free holiday offered by a hotel or resort help to make this an attractive field.

Earnings of self-employed travel agents depend mainly upon commissions from airlines and other carriers, tour operators, and hotels and resorts. Commissions for domestic travel arrangements range from 5 to 10 percent; cruises, 10 percent; hotels, sight-seeing tours, and car rentals, 10 percent; and international travel, 7 percent. Travel agents must receive conference approval before they can receive commissions, however. (Conferences are organizations of shiplines, rail lines or airlines—such as the International Air Transport Association.) To obtain conference approval, the travel agency must demonstrate that it is in operation, that it is financially sound, and that it employs at least one experienced travel agent who can arrange foreign and domestic travel as well as hotel and resort accommodations. Obtaining conference approval usually takes up to a year or more, which means that self-employed agents make very little money during their first year except for hotel and tour operation commissions. For this reason, the American Society of Travel Agents suggests a minimum of $20,000 in working capital or enough money to carry a new agency through a profitless first year.

Additional sources of information

American Society of Travel Agents
360 Lexington Avenue
New York, NY 10017

TRUCK DRIVER

The job

The movement of goods throughout the country is the work of truck drivers. Many truck drivers are *owner-operators* who own their own trucks and operate independently by leasing their services and trucks to individual companies.

Local truck drivers move goods from warehouses and terminals to factories, stores, and homes within an area. Their skills include the ability to maneuver a truck through narrow streets and alleys, into tight parking spaces, and up to loading platforms. The work and schedule of a local truck driver varies depending on the product transported. With some products, the driver starts out in the morning with a loaded truck, makes deliveries to a number of locations during the day, and returns at the end of the day. The driver who works for a lumber company, on the other hand, might return to the lumberyard after each large delivery, thus making several round trips each day.

Long-distance truck drivers, also called *over-the-road drivers,* move goods between cities and across the country. They are considered to be the top professional drivers and receive the highest wages of all drivers. These drivers work both day and night with many preferring the nightruns when highways and turnpikes are less crowded.

The "runs" of long-distance truck drivers can include a short "turn-around" where they deliver a loaded trailer to a nearby city, pick up another loaded trailer, and return it to home base—all within one day. Other runs take an entire day to complete, and the driver remains away overnight. On longer runs, the driver could be away for a week or longer.

On very long runs, many companies use two drivers. One sleeps in a berth behind the cab while the other drives. On these "sleeper" runs, the truck keeps moving day and night except for stops to eat or refuel. At the end of a trip, drivers complete reports on the trip and on the condition of the truck; these are required by the U.S. Department of Transportation.

Depending on the product transported, a truck driver may or may not be responsible for unloading the truck. In deliveries to a warehouse or loading dock at a store or factory, the customer is usually responsible for unloading the truck. In other deliveries, the driver, sometimes with a helper, does the unloading. Drivers hauling cargo that requires special handling always do their own unloading: a gasoline tank truck driver attaches the hoses and pumps the gasoline into the gas station storage tanks; a truck driver transporting new cars drives and positions the cars on the racks and removes them at the final destination.

Most local truck drivers and a few long-distance truck drivers have regularly assigned runs. Drivers with smaller companies are more likely to be assigned regular runs early in their employment. In large companies, drivers usually start on the "extra board" where they bid for runs on the basis of seniority.

A small percentage of truck drivers are women. Among the long-distance truck drivers, husband-and-wife teams of owner-operators are becoming more common. More-comfortable trucks that are easier to drive, as well as the independent work schedule and high rate of pay, are making this field more attractive to women.

Most long-distance drivers and some local drivers are members of the Teamsters, Chauffers, Warehousemen and Helpers of America (Ind.). Others who are union members usually belong to the unions that represent the plant employees of the companies for which they work.

Places of employment and working conditions

Every community needs local truck drivers who usually work for businesses that deliver their own products and goods. Most, however, work in and around large communities and manufacturing centers.

Those who specialize in transporting agricultural products or minerals may live in rural areas.

Working conditions are somewhat different for local and long-distance truck drivers. Both must be excellent drivers, but the local truck driver faces a daily schedule that involves the driving strain of heavy city traffic, while the long-distance driver must contend with the fatigue of sustained highway driving. Time spent away from home for long-distance truck runs is another drawback.

Local truck drivers often work 48 hours or more a week; night or early morning work is often necessary. The working hours and conditions of long-distance drivers are government regulated. They may not drive more than 60 hours in any seven-day period or drive more than ten hours without at least eight hours off. A workweek of 50 hours is common, and, on very long runs, long-distance drivers usually work very close to the 60-hour limit.

Qualifications, education, and training

Reliability, good judgment, and good driving skills are necessary, as are good health and vision.

A high school diploma is not necessary, but some trucking companies prefer it. Driver education courses and shop classes in automotive mechanics are helpful.

Truck drivers usually acquire their skills through experience. They may start as a helper or extra driver on smaller trucks, be given some company training on larger vehicles, and gradually work up to driving the largest trucks. Long-distance truck drivers usually do some local driving before handling long-distance assignments.

A few private and public technical and vocational schools offer truck-driving courses. These courses should be checked out with local trucking companies before enrolling, however, since not all of them offer acceptable training.

Truck drivers in most states must have a commercial, that is, a chauffeur's, driving license. This is usually obtained by passing a general physical examination, a written examination on driving regulations, and a driving test.

The U.S. Department of Transportation establishes minimum qualifications for long-distance truck drivers who are engaged in interstate commerce. The driver must be at least 21 years old; pass a physical examination; and must have good hearing, 20/40 vision with or without glasses, normal blood pressure, and normal use of arms and legs. Drivers must also pass a road test in the type of vehicle they will be driving and a written examination on the Motor Carrier Safety Regulations of the U.S. Department of Transportation.

In addition to these requirements, some trucking companies have height and weight limitations and may require a driver to be at least 25 years old. Employers usually require a clean driving record as well.

Potential and advancement

There are about 1.6 million local truck drivers and 468,000 long-distance truck drivers. Because earnings are high and no formal training is required, long-distance truck drivers usually face competition for job openings, even though the field is growing. Opportunities for local truck drivers will be very good, as a growing population means increased movement of goods within every area.

Local truck drivers can advance to long-distance driving and occasionally to positions in scheduling or dispatching. Long-distance truck drivers have limited opportunities for advancement. Some move to positions as safety supervisors or driver supervisors, but the lower starting pay and lack of independence usually do not appeal to them.

Income

Average union wage scales for local truck drivers are about $9.10 an hour for drivers and $8.18 for helpers. Local drivers usually have steady work.

The earnings of long-distance truck drivers vary depending on miles driven, hours worked, and type of truck. Earnings of drivers employed by large trucking companies average about $29,000 a year.

Additional sources of information

American Trucking Associations, Inc.
1616 P Street, NW
Washington, DC 20036

National Woman's Trucking Association
40 Pendleton Street
Charleston, SC 29403

UNDERWRITER

The job

Because insurance companies assume millions of dollars in risks by transferring the chance of loss from their policyholders to themselves, they employ underwriters to study and select the risks the company will insure. Underwriters analyze insurance applications, medical reports, actuarial studies, and other material. They must use personal judgment in making decisions that could cause their company to lose business to competitors (if they are too conservative) or to pay too many claims (if they are too liberal).

Most underwriters specialize in one of the three basic types of insurance: life, property-liability, or health. Property-liability underwriters also specialize by type of risk: fire, automobile, or workers' compensation, for example. Underwriters correspond with policyholders, insurance agents, and insurance office managers. They sometimes accompany salespeople as they call on customers and may attend meetings with union representatives or union members to explain the provisions of group policies.

Underwriters who specialize in commercial underwriting often evaluate a firm's entire operation before approving its application for insurance. The growing trend toward "package" underwriting of various types of risks under a single policy requires that the underwriter be familiar with several different lines of insurance, rather than be specialized in just one line.

Beginners work under the close supervision of an experienced underwriter. They progress from evaluating routine applications to handling those that are more complex and have greater face value.

Related jobs are: Actuary, Claim Representative, and Insurance Agent and Broker.

Places of employment and working conditions

Most underwriters are employed in the home offices of their companies, which are usually located in and around Boston, Chicago, Dallas, Hartford, New York City, Philadelphia, and San Francisco. Some are also employed in regional offices in other parts of the country.

Underwriting is basically a desk job. The average workweek is 37 hours with occasional overtime required.

Qualifications, education, and training

A career as an underwriter can be very satisfying to someone who likes to work with details and who enjoys relating and evaluating information. Underwriters must be able to make decisions and be able to communicate well. They must often be both imaginative and aggressive when searching out information from outside sources.

High school courses in mathematics are valuable.

Some small insurance companies will hire underwriter trainees without a college degree. Large insurance companies require a college degree, preferably in liberal arts or business administration.

As in all jobs in the insurance industry, great emphasis is placed on the completion of independent study programs throughout an employee's career. Salary increases and tuition costs are often provided by the company on completion of a course. The study programs are available through a number of insurance organizations and professional societies.

Potential and advancement

About 25,000 underwriters work for insurance companies at the present time. The field is expected to grow moderately.

Experienced underwriters can advance to senior or chief underwriter or to underwriting manager if they complete appropriate courses. Some are promoted to supervisory and senior management positions.

Income

Life insurance underwriters average between $14,000 and $18,700 a year depending on experience. Supervisors earn between $17,670 and $23,860.

Property and liability underwriters average between $14,800 and $17,300 a year depending on their specialty and experience. Supervisors average $19,700.

Most insurance companies have liberal employee benefits including life and health insurance and retirement pensions. Paid holidays are more numerous than in most other industries, and vacation policies are generous.

Additional sources of information

American Council of Life Insurance
1850 K Street, NW
Washington, DC 20006

Insurance Information Institute
110 William Street
New York, NY 10038

American Mutual Insurance Alliance
20 North Wacker Drive
Chicago, IL 60606

The National Association of Independent Insurers
Public Relations Department
2600 River Road
Des Plaines, IL 60018

URBAN PLANNER

The job

Urban planners develop plans and programs to provide for the future growth of a community, revitalize run-down areas of a community, and achieve more efficient uses of the community's land, social services, industry, and transportation.

Before preparing plans or programs, urban planners conduct detailed studies of local conditions and current population. After preparing a plan, they develop cost estimates and other relevant materials and aid in the presentation of the program before community officials, planning boards, and citizens' groups.

Most urban planners (also called city planners, community planners, or regional planners) work for city, county, or regional planning agencies. State and federal agencies employ urban planners in the fields of housing, transportation, and environmental protection. Large land developers also employ urban planners, and some teach in colleges and universities.

Many urban planners do consulting work, either part-time in addition to a regular job, or full-time for firms that provide planning services to private developers and government agencies.

About 10 percent of the urban planners working in the United States are women.

Related jobs are: Architect, Engineer, and Landscape Architect.

Places of employment and working conditions

Urban planners are employed throughout the United States in communities of all sizes.

A 40-hour workweek is usual for urban planners, but evening and weekend hours are often necessary for meetings and community activities.

Qualifications, education, and training

The ability to analyze relationships and to visualize plans and designs are necessary for urban planners. They should be able to work well with people and cooperate with those who may have different viewpoints.

High school students interested in this field should take social science and mathematics courses. Part-time or summer jobs in community government offices can be helpful.

Almost all jobs in this field require a master's degree in urban or regional planning, even for entry-level positions. Most graduate programs require two or three years to complete, but students with a bachelor's degree in architecture or engineering can sometimes complete the work in one year. Part-time or summer work in a planning office is usually a required part of the advanced degree program.

Urban planners seeking employment with federal, state, or local governments usually must pass civil service examinations before securing a position. (See the separate job descriptions in this book for Civil Service Worker, Federal; Civil Service Worker, Municipal and State.)

Potential and advancement

There are about 16,000 urban planners at work in the United States. This field is expected to grow steadily, but the extent of the growth will depend on the amount of money available for urban planning projects. Federal aid to state and local governments for slum clearance, smog and traffic control, and urban renewal programs should provide many job opportunities for urban and regional planners. Jobs in the environmental and social services fields will also be available to those with urban planning experience.

Experienced urban planners may be promoted to positions as planning directors where they recommend policy and have greater budget responsibilities. The usual method of advancement, however, is by transfer to a larger community where the problems are more complex and the responsibilities greater.

Income

Starting salaries for urban planners range from about $13,500 to $15,920 a year.

Experienced urban planners generally average about $20,500 a year. State planning directors earn from $26,000 to $32,000.

Experienced urban planners who work as part-time or full-time consultants earn fees that are based on the reputations they have achieved.

Additional sources of information

American Institute of Planners
1776 Massachusetts Avenue, NW
Washington, DC 20036

American Society of Planning Officials
1313 East 60th Street
Chicago, IL 60637

V

VETERINARIAN

The job

Doctors of Veterinary Medicine diagnose, treat, and control diseases and injuries of animals. They treat animals in hospitals and clinics and on farms and ranches. They perform surgery and prescribe and administer drugs and vaccines.

While most familiar to the general public are those veterinarians who treat small animals and pets exclusively (about one third of all veterinarians), others specialize in the health and breeding of cattle, horses, and other farm animals. Veterinarians are also employed by federal and state public health programs where they function as meat and poultry inspectors. Others teach at veterinary colleges; do research on animal foods, diseases, and drugs; or take part in medical research for the treatment of human diseases. Veterinarians are also employed by zoos, large animal farms, horse-racing stables, and drug manufacturers.

In the army, the air force, and the U.S. Public Health Service, veterinarians are commissioned officers. Other federally employed veterinarians work for the Department of Agriculture.

Only about 3 percent of all veterinarians are women. Since 1970, however, the number of women veterinarians has increased greatly as veterinary colleges have developed more equitable admission policies. Women should find this an excellent career field with many job opportunities, but they must be well prepared educationally to meet the stiff competition for the limited number of places available in veterinary schools.

Places of employment and working conditions

Veterinarians are located throughout the country—in rural areas, small towns, cities, and suburban areas.

Working hours are often long and irregular, and those who work primarily with farm animals must work outdoors in all kinds of weather. In the course of their work, all veterinarians are exposed to injury, disease, and infection.

Qualifications, education, and training

A veterinarian needs the ability to get along with animals and should have an interest in science. Physical stamina and a certain amount of strength are also necessary.

High school students interested in this field should emphasize science courses, especially biology. Summer jobs that involve the care of animals can provide valuable experience.

The veterinary degree program (D.V.M. or V.M.D.) requires a minimum of six years of college: at least two years of preveterinary study with emphasis on physical and biological sciences followed by a four-year professional degree program. A few veterinary colleges require three years of preveterinary study, and most applicants complete three to four years of college before entering the professional program.

There are only 21 accredited colleges of veterinary medicine, many of them state supported. Admission to all of these schools is highly competitive with many more qualified applicants than the schools can accept. Successful applicants need preveterinary college grades of "B" or better, especially in science courses; part-time work or summer job experience working with animals is a plus. State-supported colleges usually give preference to residents of the state and to applicants from nearby states or regional areas.

The course of study in veterinary colleges is rigorous. It consists of classroom work and practical experience in diagnosing and treating animal diseases, surgery, laboratory work in anatomy and biochemistry, and other scientific and medical studies. Veterinarians who intend to teach or do research usually go on to earn a master's degree in pathology, physiology, or bacteriology.

While a license is not required for federal employment, all other veterinarians must be licensed. Licensing requires a doctor of veterinary degree from an accredited college and written and oral state board of proficiency examinations. Some states will issue licenses without examination to veterinarians licensed by another state.

Potential and advancement

There are about 30,500 active veterinarians, most of them in private practice. Employment opportunities for veterinarians are excellent primarily because of growth in the population of "companion animals"—horses, dogs, and other pets—and an increase in veterinary research. The growing emphasis on scientific methods of breeding and raising livestock and poultry as well as an increase in public health and disease control programs will also contribute to the demand for veterinarians. It has been estimated that in the early 1980s there will be twice as many openings for veterinarians as there will be qualified veterinarians.

Income

The incomes of veterinarians in private practice vary greatly depending on type of practice, years of experience, and size and location of community. They usually have higher incomes, however, than veterinarians in salaried positions.

The average salary for veterinarians employed by the federal government is about $27,300 with beginners starting at about $18,000.

Additional sources of information

American Veterinary Medical Association
930 North Meacham Road
Schaumburg, IL 60196

Agricultural Research Service
U.S. Department of Agriculture
Hyattsville, MD 20782

Animal and Plant Health Inspection Service
Personnel Division
12th and Independence Avenue, SW
Washington, DC 20250

Women's Veterinarian Medical Association
c/o Dr. Bonnie V. Beaver
College of Veterinary Medicine
Texas A & M
College Station, TX 77843

WHOLESALER

The job

The wholesaler is a middle link in the distribution chain between the producer of goods and the retail store in which the goods are sold. Because no producer could possibly contact all the retail outlets or industries that use his or her products and no retail store manager has the time to contact all his or her suppliers individually, the wholesaler provides a valuable service to both segments of the marketplace.

The largest number of wholesalers are *merchant wholesalers* who buy merchandise outright, warehouse the merchandise until needed, and then sell to retail outlets. They employ salespeople to call on retail customers, extend credit to customers, and loan money to suppliers in the form of prepaid orders.

The second largest group in wholesaling is *manufacturer's agents.* These are independent businesspeople who contract with a manufacturer to sell a specific product or group of products, usually in a specific geographic area. A manufacturer's agent usually represents several manufacturers and sells to retail stores, local distributors, industrial concerns, and institutions. If the business is large enough, the agent may employ additional sales personnel. An industrial distributor is a wholesaler who handles one or more products of only one manufacturer.

Merchandise brokers may represent either the buyer or seller in a wholesale transaction. The broker, however, does not buy or take direct responsibility for the goods being sold but acts as the agent of either the buyer or seller. Merchandise brokers work mainly in a few fields—food and grocery specialties, fresh fruits and vegetables, piece goods, cotton, grain, livestock, and petroleum products.

Commission merchants usually deal in agricultural products. They take possession of but not title to the merchandise. They may store it, transport it, and condition it for market (inspect, weigh, grade) before finding a buyer. They charge a commission for their services as a part of the final selling price.

Auction companies are wholesalers who sell a client's product at a public auction. Most sales of this nature are in tobacco, fresh fruits and vegetables, livestock, floor coverings, furs and skins, jewelry, and furniture.

Related jobs are: Retail Buyer, Auctioneer, Retail Store Manager, Manufacturer's Representative, and Sales Manager.

Places of employment and working conditions

Fifty percent of all wholesalers, especially the largest and best known, are in large cities such as Chicago, Kansas City, Los Angeles, New York, and St. Louis. The remaining 50 percent are located throughout the United States, many of them in small cities and towns.

Wholesalers, especially those dealing in perishable or seasonal goods, run the risk of sudden financial loss. They must have a secure financial base to carry them over lean periods or unexpected losses.

Qualifications, education, and training

Good judgment, business and management skills, experience as a buyer or salesperson, and an ability to deal with people are all necessary.

There are no specific education requirements for this field. The largest wholesalers, however, usually require experience or training in business administration, sales and marketing, retailing, or a particular technical area such as electrical products or other industrial fields.

Potential and advancement

There are about 200,000 wholesalers in the United States, four fifths of them merchant wholesalers. The best job opportunities for beginners are with smaller wholesalers, while persons with appropriate college education can often start in management-level positions with large wholesalers.

Income

Income varies greatly depending on the size of the business. Small wholesalers earn from $11,000 to $50,000 a year; large ones up to $100,000.

Manufacturer's agents average $20,000 to $60,000 a year; a few earn over $100,000.

All earnings in this field are by commission.

Additional sources of information

National Association of Wholesaler-Distributors
1725 K Street, NW
Washington, DC 20006

Manufacturer's Agents' National Association
2021 Business Center Drive
P.O. Box 16878
Irvine, CA 92713

National-American Wholesale Grocers Association
51 Madison Avenue
New York, NY 10010

Index